GW01250387

'A truly alive company like Fisha[...]
the national grid of dreams.' —**Se**[...]

'Every time Fishamble has turne[...]
into a play, I think they are marvellous and I laugh
helplessly out loud. They aren't nearly so funny in print! I
am full of admiration and support for their energy and
magic.'
—**Maeve Binchy**

'For years now, Fishamble has tackled the dangerous
problem of new writing. They are to be greatly admired for
their courage and persistence. This publication of Fishamble
plays is an endorsement of their endeavour. I hope it will be
bought and read by many lovers of theatre.'
—**Jennifer Johnston**

'I am delighted to see the publication of this collection of
Fishamble plays from relatively new Irish writers. Pigsback/
Fishamble have consistently provided some of the most
interesting new work in the past few years, and this book is a
fine record of that achievement.' —**Dennis Kennedy,
Beckett Professor of Drama, Trinity College Dublin**

'This collection is full of the spirit of experiment and
excitement that we associate with Fishamble. The anthology
is a treasury full of riches for readers and audiences.'
—**Brendan Kennelly**

'To do new work in theatre deserves congratulations. To do
work of this quality, Fishamble deserves celebration.'
—**Frank McGuinness**

'Jim Culleton's work with new playwrights at Fishamble has
detonated a controlled explosion of fresh talent. Individ-
ually, the plays collected here are vigorous pieces of theatre.
Collectively, they form a fascinating encounter between a
range of new imaginations and the strange new realities of
1990s' Ireland.' —**Fintan O'Toole**

FISHAMBLE
PIGSBACK

first plays

Plays by
Deirdre Hines, Gavin Kostick
Joseph O'Connor, Mark O'Rowe
Pat Kinevane, Ian Kilroy

Edited by
Jim Culleton

**NEW
ISLAND**

FISHAMBLE/PIGSBACK: FIRST PLAYS
First published September 2002 by
New Island Books, 2 Brookside, Dundrum Road, Dublin 14, Ireland.
ISBN 1 902602 89 7

The publishers would like to thank Methuen Drama for their kind
permission to reproduce *Red Roses and Petrol* by Joseph O'Connor, and
Nick Hern Books for their kind permission to reproduce *From Both
Hips* by Mark O'Rowe. Cover and inside photographs reproduced with
kind permission of Colm Henry, Colm Hogan and Paul Gaster.
A CIP record of this book is available from the British Library.

New Island Books receives financial assistance from The Arts Council
(An Chomhairle Ealaíon), Dublin, Ireland.

Printed in Spain by Estudios Gráficos Zure
Cover design: Sin É Design
Cover image: Colm Henry, from *The Nun s Wood* by Pat Kinevane,
featuring Fiona Condon and Emily Nagle

Contents

For everyone involved
– onstage, backstage and as audience members –
in Fishamble / Pigsback Productions

Fishamble – the company formerly known as Pigsback

Pigsback was formed in 1988 and – between 1990 and 1996 – it produced ten new plays by Irish writers, presented five Dublin Theatre Festival premieres, embarked on four national tours, won a number of prestigious awards and transferred to the Abbey and Britain (London's Tricycle, Edinburgh's Traverse and Glasgow's Tron and Mayfest). The company produced many new plays by first-time and emerging playwrights, including Marina Carr (*This Love Thing*), Deirdre Hines (*Howling Moons, Silent Sons*), Gavin Kostick (*The Ash Fire*, *Jack Ketch s Gallows Jig*, *The Flesh Addict*), Joe O'Connor (*Red Roses and Petrol*), Colin Teevan (*Buffalo Bill Has Gone to Alaska*) and Michael West (*Don Juan, The Tender Trap, Sardines*). This anthology contains the three award-winning, completely original plays by first-time writers which were given full-scale productions between 1991 and 1995. During this time, the Executive of the company was Kathy Downes, Paul Hickey (Company Manager) and Jim Culleton (Artistic Director). At the start of 1997 – to mark the departure of Kathy and Paul – Pigsback was renamed Fishamble.

Fishamble – a company history

The name is inspired by Dublin's Fishamble Street, particularly its Playhouse which, in 1784, became the first Irish theatre to pursue a policy of producing solely new Irish work. Jim Culleton remained as Artistic Director with Maureen Kennelly as General Manager and the company continued its passionate commitment to discovering, commissioning and producing new plays by first-time and established playwrights. Maureen was succeeded by Jo Mangan in 1999 and, in 2001, Gavin Kostick and Cerstin Gundlach joined the company as Literary Officer and Marketing & Development Officer, respectively.

From 1997 to 2001, Fishamble has commissioned and produced twelve new plays by established and emerging writers, toured extensively throughout Ireland, transferred to Britain (London's Tricycle and Glasgow's Tron), won a number of prestigious awards, developed several international collaborations and produced a festival of new work to mark the new millennium. The productions include first professionally produced plays by Mark O'Rowe (*From Both Hips*), Pat

Kinevane (*The Nun s Wood*) and Ian Kilroy (*The Carnival King*), as well as subsequent plays from Deirdre Hines (*Dreamframe*), Pat Kinevane (*The Plains of Enna*), Gavin Kostick (*Doom Raider*) and Joe O'Connor (*True Believers*), and new plays by Dermot Bolger (*Consenting Adults*), Maeve Binchy/Jim Culleton (*Wired to the Moon*), Jennifer Johnston (*Moonlight and Music*), Nicholas Kelly (*The Great Jubilee*) and Gina Moxley (*Tea Set*).

Fishamble – the future

At the time of going to print, Fishamble is about to produce two further first plays: *Still* by Rosalind Haslett and *The Buddhist of Castleknock* by Jim O'Hanlon. Plays are also under commission from Michael Collins, Pat Kinevane and Gavin Kostick. New work for the future is continuing to be developed through Fishamble's Playwright Development Initiative which includes a programme of courses, seminars, competitions and play readings, as well as a season of short work by new and emerging playwrights.

Fishamble is funded by the Arts Council and Dublin City Council. It relies on the generous support of these funding bodies, as well as its audiences and sponsors, to survive. Further information on the company is at www.fishamble.com

The Company

Fishamble Theatre Company
Shamrock Chambers
1-2 Eustace Street
Dublin 2
T: +353 1 6704018; F: +353 1 6704019
Email: info@fishamble.com; Website: www.fishamble.com

Artistic Director: Jim Culleton
General Manager: Jo Mangan
Literary Officer: Gavin Kostick
Marketing & Development Officer: Cerstin Gundlach
Board of Directors: Eoin Kennelly, Maureen Kennelly, Siobhan Maguire, Ken Monaghan, Andrew Parkes, Christine Poulter.

Fishamble is supported by

Introduction

This anthology is intended as a record and celebration of plays by new writers produced by Fishamble – and under the company's original name Pigsback – between 1991 and 2001.

First plays by first-time writers are a particularly exciting and nerve-racking experience for all involved. The courage of writers to share their stories – especially when they have never written a play before – is immense. The actors, audiences and all the creative, technical and administrative staff involved need an adventurous spirit to engage with something as thrilling as a new play by a new writer! The six playwrights represented here have created a selection of first plays that are innovative, original and diverse. The imaginations involved are so unique and powerful that the process of bringing each one to life in its first production was immensely exhilarating and rewarding.

Deirdre Hines' first play *Howling Moons, Silent Sons* contains a devastating honesty and unflinching anger at its core. Her insight into a young woman's traumatic upbringing in Derry is startling and she tells her story with an engaging mixture of intimate confession, haunting memories and street chants. Cathy Leeney wrote of it being 'poised masterfully between the everyday sing-song of growing up and setting out, and what one character calls "the borders of wishing and dreaming." The Northern brickscape is thick with the unspoken, but felt, power of the father, but the silence of Daddy's daylight street is finally crushed by the damaged Siubhan. In the dark night/sunlight split world of *Howling Moons, Silent Sons*, love is the boat that can carry her away, even if it is love lost, but remembered.'

The Ash Fire by Gavin Kostick is about a family which had fled Poland in 1935, heading for New York, but mistakenly jumped ship off the coast of Cork and ended up being the only Jewish family living on the northside of Dublin at that time! This first play is a powerful, heartwarming and immensely moving family drama. In her programme note for the original production, Ronit Lentin wrote 'The story of Ireland's Jewry has been told many times ... however, the story of Ireland's Jewish women has not been fully told yet, nor has the story of those of Ireland's Jewish men who, by marrying out, deem their children out of the faith, ending the line. *The Ash Fire* is the story of one, not very usual, Irish Jewish family (most Dublin Jews live in the southside, the Katzmeirs chose Cabra; the majority of Ireland's Jewish community arrived in the 1880s, the Katzmeirs in the 1930s). It is the story of uprooted people trying to make a life in a foreign land – the archetypal Jewish story since the beginning of time. But it is also an attempt to look at the "Jewish question" and tell the story of Ireland's Jews through women's experiences.'

Joe O'Connor's first play is incisive, hilarious and cruelly truthful. *Red Roses and* Petrol is a contemporary play about the Doyle family returning home for a funeral. Joe captures the relationships in a dysfunctional Dublin family with brutal honesty and overwhelming compassion as he explores the characters' attempts to come to terms with their recent bereavement, family secrets and wildly different memories of their shared past. Colm Tóibín has commented: 'This is Joseph O'Connor's version of *Hamlet*, where the young prince returning from abroad has no difficulty putting an antic disposition on, where his father's ghost shines out from the television, where Rosencrantz and Guildenstern appear in various guises all around him. It is also a dramatic exploration of that bottomless well of rich images and powerful emotions – the Irish family. It is written with sharpness and wit and a great moral seriousness as our young prince is forced to witness the web of sex, lies and videotape which seek to ensnare him.'

Mark O'Rowe's *From Both Hips* is an urban, comic thriller. It is both hilarious and disturbing, using comedy that is often near-fanatical to explore issues of violation and betrayal. He creates a dark threat of violence under a veneer of comic invention as he weaves an ingeniously structured plot that keeps audiences on the edge of their seats. In the programme note from the original production, Gerard Stembridge talks about Mark's writing which 'can seem like harmless, unimportant people saying and doing amusing quirky unimportant things. He is happy to creep up on his audience like this because the effect will be all the greater when we begin to feel the play; realise that seeping from all this pleasant nonsense is a sense of the real and important dangers in the foolishness, prejudice and vanity of people.'

Pat Kinevane's ability, as an actor, to create characters and dramatic situations of excellence, is a talent he displays just as powerfully as a writer in his first play. *The Nun s Wood* is set in Pat's native Cobh in the hot summer of 1974. Passions run high as a group of young people pick spuds and sunbathe in a convent wood that harbours a shocking secret. It is a fascinating synthesis of adolescent frustrations and classical mythology. In his programme note from the original production, Frank McGuinness wrote 'Pat Kinevane invites us to walk in The Nun's Wood, and it is a mythical location. Myths tell the most appalling stories. They concentrate the terrors of our dreams and repeat the worst of our fears. Myths need to be dramatised with detachment. That gives them the scope for comedy, and Kinevane exploits his comic energy to its fullest in this play. But the comic light is always shadowed by darker realities … There are many levels to take stock of and, in *The Nun s Wood*, Kinevane masterfully handles each and every one of those levels. It is a fearless, ambitious play.'

The Carnival King by Ian Kilroy is an intriguing mixture of farce, tragedy and folk drama that combines to create a wonderfully incisive, grotesque and macabre first play. Declan Kiberd, in his programme note for the original production, states 'Ian Kilroy's play combines the modes of carnival with those of the old Renaissance tragedies, in which revenge was often pursued as a kind of "wild justice." The method has real poignancy in a land where the "law" was often despised as an unjust imposition by a hated power and where native "custom" was seen as the superior alternative … His play seems to suggest that only in theatre itself may some resemblance of justice be found, as well as the very real dangers which attend all acts of imitation.'

This anthology contains photographs and credits from the original productions because the success of those first productions is inseparable from the energy and commitment shown by the extremely dedicated theatre artists and practitioners involved.

The nature of theatre is live, immediate and transitory. After a production ends, the play only lives on in the memories of those who shared the experience onstage, backstage and in the audience. Now, with this publication by New Island, comes the chance to give them further life in new productions that can explore and engage with their creative energy well into the future.

Jim Culleton
Artistic Director
Fishamble

Foreword

1988 was the year of the real millennium. Compared to it, the year 2000 was a minor sideshow relating to the historically unprovable date of the birth of Christ. No such doubt existed however in the minds of Dublin's City Fathers in relation to the birth of Ireland's capital. In 988 the Vikings – bored of battering the living daylights out of lice-infected Celts in local metropolises like Finglas and Crumlin – had reclaimed the muddy swamplands at the mouth of the Liffey and started the city of Dublin.

Having spent the next thousand years vainly trying to finish the job, the City Fathers were determined that we should celebrate, with culture central to our festivities. A host of worthy and well-funded initiatives were unleashed upon the capital. Some were of genuinely lasting effect, although my favourite was the millennium milk bottle, resplendent with coloured city crest, which was delivered to every household to be passed down through future generations as a family heirloom.

Ironically, however, no initiative from that year was to have a more lasting impact on the cultural life of Ireland than that shown by the small group of young people under the banner of Pigsback Theatre Company – led by Jim Culleton, Kathy Downes and Paul Hickey and, for an early but crucial stage, Fergus D Linehan and Martin Munrow – who began to stage drama in the tiny space of Players Theatre in Trinity College during the summer of 1988. Within two years they were no longer content to stage other people's plays. Moving to the old Project Arts Centre, they unleashed *Don Juan* – the first of Michael West's riotous adaptations of European classics – upon the unsuspecting Irish public. Inventive, boisterous, shot through with sharp and intelligent wit and played with an energy that made the Project's hard seats no place to be for anyone with a dodgy pacemaker, West's adaptations for Pigsback – most especially *The Tender Trap* – remain fresh in the mind for anyone lucky enough to see them.

By 1991, the company was ready to announce themselves forcefully as instigators of original and biting new Irish drama with Deirdre Hines' highly distinctive and mould-breaking *Howling Moons, Silent Sons*. This marked the launch not only of a deeply original playwright in Hines, but of a policy of nurturing and developing new writing talent, the fruits of which are evident in this remarkable volume of debut plays.

The old Project Arts Centre (with buckets suspended from the ceiling to collect rainwater – which some patrons actually mistook for an artistic installation) became a remarkable cradle of acting and writing talent at that time. I still vividly recall the wondrous experience of seeing Gavin Kostick's *The Ash Fire* for the first time, where the European–Jewish emigrant experience took root within the new housing estates of Cabra. It was a period play about the future. Its juxtapositioning of generational experiences provided a foretaste of life for a generation of immigrants growing up here today who are caught between the experiences of their parents and their own lives on the not entirely welcoming streets of Ireland.

I remember the same theatre packed night after night for *Red Roses and Petrol*, Joseph O'Connor's fine debut play which dissected the tensions, guilts and loyalties of Irish family life in a way that was both laceratingly painful and richly comic. It was becoming apparent that not only were Pigsback adept at nurturing new talent, but that in Jim Culleton they had a special director whom both actors and writers would happily wade through the blood of disemboweled critics to work with.

Red Roses and Petrol gave Fishamble an increased profile outside Ireland with successful runs in London and Scotland – their profile within Ireland having already been confirmed by the presence of the President of Ireland, Mary Robinson, at the first night of *This Love Thing*, by the then virtually unknown Marina Carr. And the change of the name to Fishamble signified their focus on unearthing and encouraging new Irish talent.

Mark O'Rowe's *From Both Hips* heralded the arrival of a dramatist intent on using language in a way that I had never previously encountered on an Irish stage. Underneath the play's humour there lurked an edge of menace that seemed poised to pounce if you relaxed for a moment. His mastery of plot and inherent street-wise command of language were further evidence that somebody special had arrived.

I already knew of Pat Kinevane as a highly powerful actor. Indeed, any Americans visitors unfortunate enough to be in the front row of The Gate Theatre – and therefore only feet away from his brooding, violent and maddened glare – during John B Keane's rarely performed *Sharon s Grave*, probably spent a fortune in therapy recovering from the experience. But *The Nun s Wood* was a revelation to me, a stunning evocation of the cusp world of adolescence with its haunting discoveries, possibilities, uncertainties and doubts. It was an intelligent, dark and beguiling piece of story-telling that deserved its enormous success.

Not least among the pleasures which a theatre-goer like myself looks forward to with each new Fishamble production is the lack of any agenda beyond sheer originality. It is a company happy to be led by the imagination of its playwrights and in Ian Kilroy's *The Carnival King* it once again unearthed an original and inventive voice, rich with resonances from earlier forms of drama made new by the author's tight and intelligent writing. It made for exhilarating theatre. Once again another playwright had been launched, another challenging and distinctive voice added to the tapestry which Fishamble has been weaving for the Irish public since those summer afternoons in 1988 when people came together to turn their dream into reality in the tiny cluttered space of the Players Theatre.

Outside, Dublin may have been celebrating its millennium with some concrete cultural plan. But original art can never be conjured by a committee. It comes from the creative energy of like-minded dreamers who are willing to share a vision and embark on a journey into the unknown, unafraid of failure. This book charts the vision of Jim Culleton and his colleagues, past and present. As theatre-goers, our sense of pleasure is doubled by the fact that it does not commemorate a completed journey; it is merely a brief glance back as Fishamble sail on into the future, preparing to introduce new voices to us while also granting new playwrights the terrifying and exhilarating experience of seeing the ghosts inside their head suddenly become flesh. Long may the voyage last.

Dermot Bolger
Dublin, June 2002

Playwrights' Note

The authors of the following plays wish to express their collective appreciation of Jim Culleton's support and commitment in commissioning, developing and directing these first works for the stage.

Howling Moons, Silent Sons

A Play in Two Acts

Deirdre Hines

Howling Moons, Silent Sons was first presented by Pigsback Theatre Company in Project Arts Centre on 7 October 1991 as part of the Dublin Theatre Festival. It subsequently transferred to the National Theatre's Peacock Stage. The production had the following cast and production team:

Tramp-Lady Caroline Gray
Siubhan Doherty Clodagh O'Donoghue
Mammy Doherty Geraldine Plunkett
Daddy Doherty Brendan Ellis
Nora Janice McAdam
Cathleen Kathy Downes
Kell Paul Hickey
Cormac Peter Ballance

Director Jim Culleton
Set Designers Fiona Leech and Fiona Whelan
Costume Designer Lynne Maguire
Lighting Designers Peter Dorney (Project) & Tony Wakefield
    (Peacock)
Production Manager Trevor Dawson
Stage Director Suzanne O'Halloran
Stage Manager John Kells (Peacock)
Administrator Kate Hyland
Original ballad by Raphael Rosenstock
Dublin Theatre Festival Director Tony O'Dalaigh

Howling Moons, Silent Sons won the Stewart Parker Trust Award for Best First Play in 1991.

Photo (l-r): Caroline Gray, Geraldine Plunkett and Clodagh O'Donoghue as Tramp-Lady, Mammy and Siubhan © Colm Henry

Dramatis Personae

Siubhan Doherty, a young woman

Mammy Doherty, her mother

Daddy Doherty, her father

Nora

Cathleen

Cormac } Siubhan's Gang

Kell

Tramp-Lady

The action takes place in an imaginary town somewhere in Northern Ireland.

Time: past and present

ACT ONE

Stage-Left lightens to show the front of No.15 O Donnell Estate, Westside, in an imaginary town somewhere in Northern Ireland.

Two dustbins in front of the house. Two chairs also.

Dilapidated aspect – empty bottles, beer cans, bits of the Doherty property. A ramshackle fence with peeling paint. A wreath is visible in a downstairs window.

In front of the Doherty house, on the street, a rope-swing dangles from a street-lamp. At the top of this street-lamp, a piece of wire is stretched beyond the house.

*As **Tramp-Lady** sings a song, **Siubhan** comes out of the house.*

The whirring of a helicopter can be heard above the roof-tops .

Lights rise.

Time: the present, July.

***Siubhan** (a young woman in her teens) comes out with a bag of rubbish, slamming the door behind her. She goes over to the bin and tries to cram the bag into an already full bin. She is wearing a high-heeled pair of shoes, but eventually has to take them off and stand on the rubbish to make the bag fit. Nearly falls off in her anxious surveyal of the area for onlookers. Gets down off dustbin and puts lid on quickly. Sits down on lid, dusting off her feet and puts shoes back on.*

*Door opens again and **Daddy Doherty**, on his way to work (overalls) stamps out past her, shoving another bag of rubbish at her. **Siubhan** grabs bag. They stare at each other in mutual hostility for a few moments. **Daddy Doherty** laughs a harsh, derisive laugh and stomps resolutely away.*

Daddy: Have a good day, Siubhan!

Siubhan: *(Shouts after him)* Go to hell! Not that they'd want you there either.

She kicks her shoes off viciously and starts squashing this new bag in. Once again she has to stand on rubbish to push the bag down. Anxiously surveys area for peeking windows. A wolf-whistle from across the street, followed by several others.

Siubhan *jumps off the dustbin, falling on the ground.*

Siubhan: *(Shouts)* Don't yiz have anything else to do? Morning after bloody morning … *(She is leaning against a bin, dusting off her feet and putting on her shoes. Another wolf-whistle from across the street. Quieter)* Jesus, to be somewhere else, anywhere else.

Mammy Doherty *comes out and moves chair to where she will receive the most sun.*

Mammy: Put the lid on that there bin, Siubhan. I don't want the place smelling.

Siubhan *bangs lid on bin.*

Mammy: If only all the days were as heavenly as this. Do you mind them summers we used to head down to Bundoran one week and Buncrana the next. Them were the days. *(Siubhan mimes 'Them were the days)* And the boys spending all the money in the amusements… the wee pets.

Siubhan: I wasn't allowed in the amusements.

Mammy: And your Daddy used to build you the most massive sandcastles …

Siubhan: The best thing was it was away from here.

Mammy: *(Ignoring her)* And your Daddy used to bring you and the boys swimming.

Siubhan: Paddling. We went paddling because he was afraid of the water.

Mammy: And the weather was pure heavenly then too.

Siubhan: No it wasn't.

Mammy: Yes it was … Oh and your Daddy always came first in them donkey races. *(Siubhan laughs)* Them were great days.

Siubhan: And two weeks from now, these will be the great days, when me and Siubhan used to sit out the front.

Mammy: I doubt this sun is going to your head, Siubhan pet!

Siubhan: Mammy, all I remember is running up and down the beach in the pouring rain looking for him and finding him night after night sprawled out on some bench, dead to the world from the drink, and you screaming at me because you didn't want him catching his death ... some holidays, and Óisín and Seán off gallivanting as usual.

Mammy: Stop girning and put the lid on that there dustbin.

Siubhan: *(Slamming lid on bin)* Well, it's true.

Mammy: Why were you always rarin' to get down there then?

Siubhan: I kept thinking it would change.

Pause.

Mammy: Look at the cut of Cassie Flynn out cleaning them windows again. Bless her wits, twenty-five years of scrubbing them windows every morning and every evening.

Siubhan: She has nothing else to do.

Mammy: It's a miracle that poor man ever got a wean and that's the truth.

Siubhan: Mammy!

Mammy: Tight as a duck's arse.

Siubhan: Not that it's anyone's business.

Mammy: The likes of her deserve what they get. Ask your Daddy if you don't believe me.

Siubhan: There's nothing wrong with Cassie. Eoghan Flynn is just a bad bastard.

Mammy: There's nothing he wouldn't do for the cause.

Siubhan: Nothing he wouldn't do for his own pocket, more like.

Mammy: If there hadn't been men the like of him, we'd be nowhere, Siubhan, remember that.

Siubhan: Well, if this is somewhere, I'll move to nowhere in the morning.

Mammy: And that daughter of hers off footing it with anyone but her own.

Siubhan: The woman's over thirty!

Mammy: I don't care if she's over sixty! Some women in that family. A disgrace – and your Daddy will never break breath with her again.

Siubhan: Big loss!

Mammy: He's a noble man, your Daddy. Everyone says so.

Siubhan: Aye! Everyone short of the money for a pint!

Mammy: I can hold my head with pride when I go down the street, which is more than can be said of poor Eoghan Flynn.

Siubhan: *(Pulls out an old moth-eaten shirt from the bag)* Mammy, you wouldn't give this thing to your worst enemy.

Mammy: That's a good shirt. Plenty of wear in it yet.

Siubhan: It's full of holes.

Mammy: Besides, beggars can't be choosers.

Siubhan finds a pair of platform shoes.

Siubhan: Would you look at these! *(Tries them on for the laugh)* Jesus. Mammy, they're wicked.

Mammy: I'll have you know they used to be my best shoes.

Siubhan: Wait till Nora sees these!

Mammy: That one! What does she know about anything?

Siubhan: Nora's the best.

Mammy: You'll learn.

Siubhan: Aye sure!

Mammy: Not that it'll take you longer than most.

Siubhan: At least the tinkers can leave a place when they want to. It must be great.

Mammy: Your head's a marley, Siubhan. Moving from place to place. Living in the country one minute, a town the next. With nowhere to call their own.

Siubhan: With nowhere and everywhere to call their own. They're the ones who're free.

Mammy: What's got you so interested in the tinkers all of a sudden? *(Pause)* Don't you ever bring one home, Madam. Your Daddy'd have a fit.

Siubhan: Mammy, you've a one track mind.

Mammy: It mightn't be as easy for you to find someone half as noble as your Daddy, but don't worry, someone will come along.

Siubhan: I think I'll pass. And if I don't it'll not be anyone from this street.

Pause.

Mammy: You know your Daddy thinks, maybe, you ought to go out a bit more, clear the puss on your face a bit … you see, you're the only girl and we can't help worrying about you. After all, a daughter's a daughter—

Siubhan: And a son's a son.

Mammy: Don't bring the boys into this, Siubhan.

Siubhan: Except they're not your sons, they're your sister's.

Mammy: When my sister died, God rest her, I brought those boys into my home. They were like my own, your own too.

Siubhan: But by the time you find out it's the boys you have to watch, one of them's dead, killed by his own—

Mammy: What harm was he doing … joyriding. Poor Óisín.

Siubhan: And the other's rotting in a human warehouse up in Belfast, and the shame of it, because it's not for the cause, and then you just shut up because I'm not the problem and I'm sick and tired of it all.

Mammy: If your Daddy—

Siubhan: I don't care. You're lucky I'm still here and you can't even see it.

Mammy: Funny sort of luck. *(Pause)* We have our way and there's others have theirs, and that's the way it should be.

Siubhan: Our way! Our way! There's only ever been one way in this house and that's his way.

Mammy: Well leave then. If you don't like it, leave. You're lucky your Daddy doesn't force you to go like everyone else's.

Siubhan: Don't worry, I will!

Mammy: And I'll tell you something else, Siubhan Doherty, the good die young. Remember that.

*Wolf-whistles from across the street. **Siubhan** sticks up her fingers on both hands and **Mammy** storms into the house, banging the door after her. **Mammy** opens door again immediately.*

Mammy: You know this, Siubhan Doherty, if Jesus came down from the cross, you still wouldn't be satisfied!

*Bangs door again. **Siubhan** goes to rope-swing and starts swinging.*

Tramp-Lady: *(Stage-Right)* Come with me to my old dell.

Siubhan: Would you like to play a game?
          Try and guess the boy's name.
          It started with K,
          It ended with L,
          Come with me to my old dell.

Stage-Right resembles den, partially built second floor of a house in the building site of an estate.

Halloween Night / Oíche Shamhna / Feast of the Moon.

Tramp-Lady *(Younger rather than older) makes a cushioned seat for herself by gathering a few newspapers. Pulls off her black laced boots.*

Tramp-Lady: Ahh! The Relief of Derry! *(Sighing with pleasure, she pulls sodden newspapers and plastic bags from boots)* Hurry along now! Don't let on you see ... Don't let on you see me! That's the trick! Let on it's nothing to do with you. That's it. That's right! Things to do, people to see, no time to help. On you go. Up the hill and down again. Sin mar a bhfuil. Nothing else for it but to rush on ... mind you don't trip. *(To distract herself, she takes out a bag of large shells and names each one as she lovingly handles them and places them around her)* Béaltrá ... Inisalla ... Leitirmel ... Trá na mBuailte ... Trá na mBuailte ... Fadó ó shin, that one. Long time ago. Noisy seagulls, watching me watching them watching boat on green ice sea. Maybe where it all began! Ara! Maybe not. *(Sudden)* I'm looking for to bury a ghost! One ghost? Maybe more than one. I'll know when I know. You will too. Slippery things ghosts. Seaweed too. Easy to bury something when you can see it. When you can say what it is. I knew a woman once ... or was it a man ... waited all their lives, these people for the ghosts of forgotten promises. A long time ago, fadó ó shin ... long time ago, this was chosen for me on Creachoileán Báite. Who by? Well, if we knew that! Fadó ó shin, a wee girl, girseach beag, a wee boy, garsún beag. There's the clue!

Croons.

> Dance to your Daddy, my bonnie lassie,
> Dance to your Daddy, my bonnie laddie,
> Dance to your Daddy, to your Mammy sing,
>
> You'll get a fishy on a little dishy,
> You'll get a fishy, when the boat comes home.

She exits crooning, forgetting shells.

Siubhan, **Nora** and **Cathleen** *come rushing in, panting and out of breath. They are wearing witch-costumes, rough and ready-made. Really, paper cardboard witches hats. Carrying paper bags filled with nuts. They are ten years old. They tramp on shells.*

Nora: If my lungs aren't busted, it's a miracle.

Siubhan: Miracle, my arse! No such thing.

Cathleen: Is bloody so. My Daddy said—

Siubhan: *(Derisively)* Daddy's wee girl
Had a wee curl
Right in the middle of her forehead ...

Nora joins in.

And when she was good
She was very, very good
And when she was bad

Nora: She was wicked.

Siubhan: She was Cathleen.

Cathleen: I don't care. Do you think I care? I'm starved, come on, put out everything we've gotten.

Nora: I've got the most stuff, so I'm not sharing! So there.

Siubhan: Piss off then, Nora!

Cathleen: Yeah! Piss off then Nora!

Siubhan: Shut up, Cathleen! If you don't share, you're not in our gang then. Your choice.

Nora: I was only joking. I'll share. I'll share.

*They start to pool their spoils, **Siubhan** dividing them up.*

Cathleen: Hoi, you've got too much, Siubhan Doherty!

Siubhan: No, I have not. You're a real wean, Cathleen!

Nora: Yeah Cathleen!

Cathleen: I hate the both of yous.

Siubhan and Nora laugh unconcernedly.

Cathleen: *(By way of making up)* Let's play the saucer game!

Siubhan: We don't have any saucers, stupid!

Nora: We don't need them, stupid yourself!

Siubhan: Well smarty, what'll we use then?

Nora: Bits of wood ... those over there.

Cathleen: Great!

Nora and Cathleen spread out the four pieces of wood on the floor.

Nora: Right, now we need a ring, a cross, water and a wee bit of earth. I have a ring. How about you, Siubhan, have you a cross?

Siubhan: No—

Cathleen: I have.

Siubhan: Here's a wee bit of sand. It'll do for the earth.

Cathleen: And water's a cinch.

Siubhan: This is for babies.

Cathleen: Who asked you to play, anyway?

Siubhan: Alright, I won't.

Nora: Shut up, you two! Everything's ready! Okay, Cathleen, close your eyes. And whatever you do, don't cheat or you'll die in your sleep!

Siubhan: Oh yeah!

Nora: *(Ignoring her)* If you choose earth, you or someone belonging to you will die! Choose water and you or someone belonging to you will go across the water; the ring, and you or someone belonging to you will marry. And last, if you choose the cross, you and you alone will become a nun.

They all laugh at this.

Siubhan: For God's sakes ...

Nora: Ssshhh! Now, turn around and keep your eyes closed! And don't cheat!

Cathleen: I'm not going to bloody cheat!

Nora switches the order of the pieces of wood.

Nora: Okay. Now you can turn around again.

She guides her over to the pieces of wood.

Nora: Right! Quick, go on, choose.

Siubhan: Babies!

Cathleen: Sssh! I'm contrating.

Siubhan: ConCENtrating!

Cathleen: How can I choose if you two keep making noise?

Siubhan: Bloody hell!!

Nora: Sssh! Sssh!

Silence. **Cathleen** *chooses the earth.*

Cathleen: Shit!

Nora: God! Poor Cathleen!

Siubhan: Jesus, it's only a stupid game. You don't believe it, do you?

Cathleen: Well, if you're so brave, why don't you play?

Siubhan: Because I'm not a baby.

Nora: Come on, quick, it's my turn.

Cathleen *does the honours.* **Nora** *chooses the ring.*

Nora: Brilliant! Married within the year.

Cathleen: You have all the luck.

Nora: *(Airily)* It's not luck. It's fate.

Siubhan: It's shit.

Two Boys aged ten come running in. The Girls gather in a defensive group.

Kell: Who the hell do yous think yous are? This is our den.

Siubhan: Says who?

Cathleen: Says us!

Nora: Shut up, Cathleen!

Cormac: Get out, or we'll make yous sorry!

Siubhan: And we're scared and all!

Nora: Are you two wee lads brothers?

Kell: This is our den.

Cathleen: There are three of us!

Nora: Shut the fuck up, will you!

Cormac: Nice girls don't swear.

Siubhan: Nice boys don't breathe. Get it.

Siubhan, Nora and Cathleen all shout at the same time.

Girls: Up the Westside! Up the Westside! Up the Westside!

Kell and Cormac also shout at the same time.

Boys: Up the Eastside! Up the Eastside!

Siubhan: Up the Westside! That's it then! This den's west of the river and that means it belongs to us!

Kell: My Granny lives down here—

Siubhan: Up here.

Kell: *(Ignoring her)* So that's one reason why it's ours, and the other is we're big lads and we'll beat yous up if yous all don't piss off!

Cormac: Kell! We can't.

Kell: Why not?

Cormac: They're only wee girls.

Kell: Shut up, Cormac!

Nora: You'd better listen to the wee boy, Kell.

Cathleen: Yeah, Kell!

Kell lifts his fist.

Siubhan: What are you doing up here if you're from the Eastside?

Kell: We're running a message for this fella, if you want to know. And he'll be here soon so's that'll scare you.

Siubhan: Pathetic. I'll tell you, if you swallow a ring you can stay.

Cathleen: No way!

Siubhan: Shut up, or I'll brain you!

Kell: I'm ten, not two! … If you think I'm swallowing some pissin' ring! Bloody Tagues!

Silence.

Siubhan: Church or Chapel, wee boy?

Kell: Church and Chapel, wee girl!

Cathleen: They're mad, they—

Siubhan: Look Cathleen, for the last time, shut up, if you don't want me to kill you!

Nora: *(To Cormac)* What about you?

Cormac: Same as him.

Siubhan: Don't listen to them! They're pissing about the place.

Kell: Oh yeah! Well, we're not!

Cormac: Mixed marriages!

Kell: It's not our fault!

Cormac: Who gives a shit?

Kell: We'll not fight yous if you like.

Cormac: Yeah, you can join our gang.

Siubhan and Nora look at each other and laugh.

Kell: Brits in, Brits out …

Nora: Shake them all about …

Siubhan: You do the hokey-pokey and you turn around …

Cormac: And that's what it's all about.

Cathleen doesn t join in and when the others join in a circle, she stays outside of it.

Siubhan, **Kell**, **Cormac** and **Nora:** Oooh hokey-pokey, Oooh hokey-pokey, Oooh hokey, hokey-pokey. Fuck the Pope, Fuck the Queen, and that's what it's all about.

They fall on the floor laughing.

Lights fade and come up Stage-Left again. **Tramp-Lady** *enters as children leave.* *She is singing:*

> Buy a baby bunting
> Daddy's gone a hunting
> Gone to fetch a rabbit skin
> To wrap the baby bunting in.

Siubhan: *(Stage-Left)* It started with K. It ended with L …

Sound of helicopters overhead. **Daddy** *enters with football. Looks at* **Siubhan** *asleep in the sun.* **Siubhan** *suddenly aware that someone is there.*

Siubhan: *(Groggy)* What? Oh, it's you.

Daddy: There's a back yard for that sort of thing.

Siubhan: And a dark night for your type of thing.

Daddy: Ever the smart answer, Siubhan.

Siubhan: You're standing in the way of the sun … your shadow! Anyway the sun isn't around the back.

Daddy: Can't you find something else to do. As lazy as sin!

Siubhan: It's my day off!

Daddy: Your Mammy's too soft by far.

Siubhan: Someone'd need to be.

Daddy: All you do is sleep.

Siubhan: All you do is talk.

Daddy: Listen to herself. Siubhan, you know the price of everything and the value of nothing!

Siubhan: Why aren't you at work?

Daddy: Your Daddy's not the sort of man not to come home when there's a problem.

Siubhan: What problem?

Daddy: Your Mammy thinks there's a problem.

Siubhan: She rang you at work?

Daddy: She did.

Siubhan: She didn't need to.

Daddy: But she did. *(Pause)* When are you going then?

Siubhan: It's my own business.

Daddy: Running away won't solve anything.

Siubhan: This heat's making me dizzy!

Daddy: Did you hear what I said?

Siubhan: Aye sure!

Daddy: And what'd your Mammy do without you?

Siubhan: Without my keep you mean!

Daddy: Now that she's all alone—

Siubhan: She has you.

Daddy: She needs you. *(Throws ball)*

Siubhan: Aye sure!

Daddy: Where are you planning on going?

Siubhan: I haven't gone yet.

Daddy: You'll not go anywhere I won't find you.

Pause.

Siubhan: I get the message.

Daddy: Good. *(Pause)* Then we can forget about it. Right!

Pause.

Siubhan: Right!

Daddy: You should find yourself a footballer, Siubhan. It'd make something of you. Supporting a team. You need a cause—

Siubhan: No thanks!

Daddy: The thing is Siubhan, you think you're above the rest of us. But the truth of the matter is that no one can remain on the sidelines for ever! I could hold my head up, maybe then—

Siubhan: I wouldn't run after no one.

Daddy: Well, you'd better start! For no one'd run after you! You don't take after your father in that regard!

Siubhan: For God's sake!

Daddy is kicking the football around. Dribbling it from foot to foot and generally showing off.

Siubhan: Stop making a show of yourself!

Daddy: Stop girning! *(Passes ball to Siubhan)* Let's see how good you are. *(Siubhan hesitates and then joins in. She tries to keep the ball from Daddy. Daddy sets up the dustbins as goalposts)* They're the goalposts. Stop! Wait! Siubhan, these are the goals. Stop a minute! *(Siubhan tries to keep the ball from Daddy. She dribbles it along the fence. Daddy wins ball and scores a goal)* And Daddy Doherty scores a hat-trick as the Westside team beats Queens Club of the First Division, in the Ulster Cup Second Round replay …

Siubhan sits down exhausted, laughing.

Siubhan: It's too hot to play!

Daddy: Get up and exercise yourself.

Siubhan: I can't.

Mammy looking out of window.

Mammy: *(Shouts out)* You're not going to let an old man beat you, are you? Get up! Come on, Siubhan Doherty! There's life in you yet!

Siubhan: I can't.

Mammy: And put them bins back when you're finished. *(Shuts window)*

Voices of kids on street: Give us back our ball! Give us back our ball!

Daddy: *(Shouts)* Come and get it, then!

Siubhan: Give it back to them!

Wolf-whistles from across the street. **Siubhan** *kicks it back to them.*

Daddy: Why'd you go and do that?

Siubhan: It's their ball!

Daddy: It's our land!

Siubhan: They're only kids.

Daddy: And you'd know all about that, I suppose!

Siubhan: You'll not appreciate what you have until it's taken away from you!

Daddy: Are you telling me I'd miss you?

Siubhan: You would.

Daddy: Aye sure! *(Pause)* And you'd miss me, I suppose.

Siubhan: I might—

Daddy: No one to fight with. You'd miss that.

Voices offstage/from street: Charlie! Right! Over here! On the head!

Siubhan: It's never quiet here, did you ever notice?

Daddy: There'll be peace enough in the grave! *(Football from street knocks Daddy. He punctures ball and kicks it back)* That'll learn ye, you snotty-faced whelps!

Siubhan: And you'd know all about that ...

Daddy: Watch it you! Go and put them bins back in their proper place.

Sneers and laughs from street.

Siubhan: I don't want to.

Daddy: So?

Siubhan: So, I don't want to.

Daddy: So what?

Siubhan: So what your bloody self!

Daddy: I'll so what you whenever I feel like so whatting you. Get it.

Siubhan: Aye sure!

Daddy: Shift then.

Siubhan: I'm only—

Daddy: Look, Siubhan, move! *(Pause)* Well?

Siubhan: Well what?

Daddy: Are you going to move or not?

Siubhan: What's the big deal? Why do you get so thick when people don't do what you say immediately? If you even asked nicely—

Daddy: Your Daddy doesn't have to ask, Siubhan. *(Pause)* Don't you know that by now? *(Pause)* If you're not going to move the bins, get into the house then …

Siubhan: Okay! Okay! *(Siubhan moves bins)* You're such a big shot, aren't you? You and your cronies parading up and down the street. Spending my keep on drink. *(Pause)* So what the fuck is it then? What's your problem?

Enter Nora.

Nora: Bonjour Siubhan! Comment ça va?

Daddy: *(Laughing, walks past them into the house)* My problem? *(Pause)* It's not me who has the problems.

Nora: Full of the joys of Summer, that man! Daddy Doherty – the Westside's Big Man strikes again—

Siubhan: Jesus, I could—

Nora: Leave it, Siubhan. He's not worth it.

Siubhan: I know … anyway, you're mad to have come back, I wouldn't have. How was it?

Nora: I've never seen so many weird people in all my life, all loo-la. Your Daddy would have fitted in well. And the hotel we were staying in was more like a geriatric ward than any hotel. You should have seen it, all these old, old-age pensioners from England on some 'Golden Oldies Get the Mouldies out of the Country Social Security Scheme'.

Nora sings.

> Hit me with your walking stick,
> Hit me, Hit me, Hit me quick,
> Hit me with your walking stick.

Siubhan: Shut up! He'll think you're singing about him!

Nora: As for the food. Yeuch. Frogs' legs! Like eating snots! Puke! And worse, long-legged lovelies leching after Cormac. It'll be Alaska next year, after that!

Siubhan: You're mad, Nora.

Nora: Did you get my postcard?

Siubhan: It arrived!

Nora: Did Daddy Doherty have a freak?

Siubhan: More or less.

Nora: Brilliant! Serve him right, the miserable old git!

Siubhan: Aye right! *(Pause)* One of these days it'll be me telling you stories.

Nora: If that's the case, you'd better get a move on, or else you'll be here till your teeth fall out.

Siubhan: Away and jump!

Nora: Get yourself a rich man then, and it'll be sooner than both of us think.

Siubhan: So that's why you stay with Cormac, 'cause of all his money!

Nora: The Pope's nose I do! Are you daft? It's the oul' fella has all the money, not Cormac. I could wait all my life for a lick of it.

Siubhan: Nora—

Nora: I'm only saying! Cormac doesn't part easy with what he has anyway.

Siubhan: So why do you stay with him?

Nora: Back to the start … I guess I'm used to him.

Siubhan: That's it. You're used to him! Nothing but that—

Nora: And he's used to me. So it's hunky-dory—

Siubhan: You're as great a liar as the clock of Strabane! You're mad about him! Go on, admit it.

Nora: Aye sure! Whatever you say!

Nora has gone out onto the street and is swinging round the pole.

Siubhan: What are you at?

Nora: Siubhan, wait till you hear this. How does the Pope travel?

Siubhan: God …

Nora: In a holy-copter.

Siubhan: Hah! Hah! Thud!

Nora: What's that?

Siubhan: Me laughing my head off!

*Nora is singing as she swings round and round. **Siubhan** pushes her on the swing and joins in.*

Nora: The Salvation Army's free from sin

Girls: Dooda, Dooda …

Nora: All went to heaven in a corned beef tin …

Girls: Dooda, Dooda, Day.

Nora: The corned beef tin was made of brass …

Girls: Dooda, Dooda …

Nora: They all fell off and skinned their ass.

Both collapse onto the street laughing.

Sound of helicopters receding into the distance.

Siubhan: There go your holy-copters. (*Pause*) If Cormac could see you now.

Nora: If his oul' fella could!

Siubhan: Maybe he can …

Girls: Dooda, Dooda, Do.

Nora: Aye sure!

Siubhan: Them ones probably have telescopes. To keep an eye on the likes of you and me.

Nora: Talk about me. You're the one whose head's a marley!

Siubhan: I'm sure!

Nora: Jesus, Cassie Flynn's out cleaning them windows again. That woman'll die with a cloth in her hand. Some people never change.

Siubhan: Some people do.

Nora: Not around here, they don't. How could you when you can't even pick your nose without someone telling you the colour of the hankie you used.

Siubhan: You know how to ruin a day off, don't you?

Nora: And how is the factory?

Siubhan: Going under, but that's no surprise.

Pause.

Nora: What will you do?

Siubhan: Get you married off to Cormac and live off the interest!

Nora: You'll be waiting!

Siubhan: Why? Wouldn't you help a friend in need?

Nora: As if you'd take help from anyone!

Siubhan: It's like this smarty! I'd do anything to get away from wee lads who spend their tea-breaks throwing darts in pigs' eyes!

Nora: Yeuch! That's sick.

Siubhan: And the lucky winner gets to go into the girls' bogs and throw a bag of the used ones over the doors.

Nora: I don't believe you! You mean they land all over you when you're having a piss. Yeuch! I feel sick! That's worse than ever I heard.

Siubhan: Well, if you think that's bad, wait till—

Nora: Shut up!

Siubhan: No, it's funny! Wait till you hear!

Nora: Jesus, I don't believe it! God, of all places! Help!

Siubhan: Nora, will you shut your mouth and listen. What's wrong with you? You look as though you've seen a ghost.

Nora: How long would it take us to do a runner?

Siubhan: Stop pissin' about!

Nora: Oh Jesus! Siubhan. Look across the street!

Siubhan: What. Where? I can't see anything! If this is another of your jokes …

Nora: Look across the street. Can you see her?

Siubhan: See who?

Nora: Would you look?

Siubhan stands up and Nora grabs her and rushes her across the street.

Siubhan: I knew this was another of your jokes!

Nora: I don't believe I just did that! Well, did you see her?

Siubhan: See you, Nora, you're really pissin' me off!

Nora: *(Grabs **Siubhan** and points)* Now!

Siubhan: I don't believe it.

Both scream.

Nora: It's not like her to slum it!

Siubhan: Piss off! *(Pause)* It's not though, is it?

Nora: She was a right wee bitch, wasn't she?

Siubhan: Don't I know!

Nora: Do you want to go over?

Siubhan: Do I want balls?

They are standing in doorway.

Nora: How many weans can you count?

Siubhan: I'm sure they're all hers and all!

Nora: I can see four! It's the likes of her has them ones calling us rabbits.

Siubhan: Who'd have thought it?

Nora: She's the same as us, isn't she?

Siubhan: They can't all be hers!

Nora: I'd die if she saw us, wouldn't you?

Siubhan: She'd be shamed rotten!

Nora: Your arse! She'd love it! I heard she's rolling in it!

Siubhan: So what about it. She still looks a sight.

Girls: Daddy's wee girl
Had a wee curl
Right in the middle of her forehead.
And when she was good
She was very, very good.
And when she was bad
She was *(**Nora** roars)* Cathleen!

Siubhan: Jesus, she heard … she's coming over!

Lights dim on Stage-Left and come up again on Stage-Right.

Cormac *sitting on tyres with torch.* **Tramp-Lady** *standing near him. She muttering, he counting.*

Cormac: And 65p and 30p that's 85p ... is it? No. That's 95p. 95p and 55 pence that's ... that's £1.50. Right, that's £1.50 from Duck Doogan ... 82p from Skitterarse Reilly and the git still owes 52p which'd make ... 52 plus 82. That's £1.34 ... and £1.50 and £1.34. That's £2 something, near enough £3 as makes no difference. And then Spud and Tot, they're owing 65 and 65 and 80 ... and ...

Tramp-Lady: One, two, sniff some glue,
Three, four, kick down the door,
Five, six, pick up bricks
Seven, Eight, throw them straight,
Nine, ten, away run the men—

Cormac: You're a geg, missus! What'd you know anyway? And Gacka Moran 15 pence—

Tramp-Lady: Don't count your chickens before they're hatched, Cormac. Bad luck.

Cormac: My Da says you make your own luck. That's how he made all his money. So.

Tramp-Lady: Is that what you're doing? Making your own luck!

Cormac: Mind your own business!

Tramp-Lady: You're a bad egg, do you know that?

Cormac: And what are you! *(Mutters under his breath)* Tinker's get!

Tramp-Lady: And what would your wee friends think if they knew where Mr Big Shot Cormac was getting his money from?

Cormac: Piss off, will you!

Tramp-Lady: I've known your sort all my life. Nice as pie people living in nice as pie houses and rotten to the core on the inside ...

Cormac: *(Mimics)* 'I've known your sort' … Pathetic! What would you know about a house?

Tramp-Lady: Your sort is committed to money, and that's all I need to know, money for themselves—

Cormac: Look you! I don't even get pocket money you know! So there! All the rest of them do—

Tramp-Lady: And that's why—

Cormac: One of these days I'll be a millionaire and there's your bloody for whys! *(Tramp-Lady exits to other room. Cormac, as if quoting from somewhere)* 'You have to get on nowadays.'

Enter Kell.

Kell: What's all the racket?

Cormac: Your one. She's deaf! You have to shout!

Kell: Where is everyone?

Cormac: Don't know. What time is it?

Kell: Time you had your own watch.

Cormac: Wise up!

Kell: Wise up yourself!

Cormac: *(Scratching his name on the wall with a penknife)* This stupid blade's blunt as hell!

Kell: And so is its owner!

Cormac: Act your age, not your shoe size! 12 going on one, pathetic!

Kell: Missing Nora are we?

Cormac: Jealous are you!

Enter Tramp-Lady.

Kell: Missus!

Tramp-Lady: Howya Kell *(Hitting Cormac with her bag)* I'm not deaf.

As she leaves, **Cormac** *hums the theme tune from 'The Twilight Zone'.*

Kell: See you!

Tramp-Lady: See you!

Cormac: *(Looking in bags)* Ever wonder what's in these ...

Kell: Nosey git! *(Joins him anyway)*

Kell *and* **Cormac** *pull out an old mirror. They put it against the wall.*

Kell: Mirror, mirror, on the wall. Who's the fairest of them all?

Cormac: Give me a break!

Kell: So tell us about Nora ...

Cormac: Tell us about Siubhan first!

Kell: Nothing to tell!

Cormac: Nora's a geg! She learnt how to snog in the girls' loos!

Kell: What!

Cormac: Get this! They practised on each other's necks ...

Kell: Siubhan didn't!

Cormac: Aye sure! And who did you think Nora practised with?

Kell: Cathleen!

Cormac: Excuse me! Siubhan can do no wrong ... I forgot. In love are you!

Kell: Listen, it's you who's ...

Enter **Siubhan** *and* **Nora.**

Cathleen: Hey, wait on me.

Cormac *lights a cigarette.* **Kell** *flicks through a magazine.*

Siubhan: Yes Kell!

Nora: Cormac …

They are all slouched around the den.

Nora: *(Sitting on **Cormac's** back)* What did the snail say on the tortoise's back? *(No one answers her)* Come on, at least try and pretend you're interested.

Cormac: What?

Nora: Wheeeeeeee!

Kell: Hilarious.

Nora: Piss off!

Siubhan: *(Sings).*

> Yum Yum
> Chewing gum
> Stick it up your old man's bum.
> When it's brown
> Take it down
> Yum Yum
> Chewing gum.

Kell: Yeuch! You dirty bitch!

Siubhan: Shut up!

Cathleen: This club's boring.

Cormac: You're boring.

Siubhan: Sssh! Listen! *(Sound of bin lids being banged on road)* Jesus! That's the fourth they've lifted tonight already.

Cathleen: Maybe we should go home.

Nora: Scaredy Cat!

Cathleen: No, I'm not. My Daddy said—

Siubhan: Will you shut your mouth about your Daddy. We're sick and tired about you and your Daddy.

Cathleen: He'll be worrying.

Kell: Rubbish!

Cathleen: How do you know?

Nora: Run away off home to Daddy then.

Cathleen: I was only saying.

Siubhan: What a wean!

Cathleen: No I'm not! I'm 13. You're the wean. You're only a 12!

Nora: Pathetic! Let's go out on the road and see what's going on!

Cathleen: I'm not going.

Nora: No one's asking you!

Cathleen: I should have been home an hour ago.

Nora: Go then! Jesus, do some people give me a sore head.

Cathleen: Leave me alone!

Nora: You coming Cormac?

Cormac: Yeah, okay.

Nora and Cormac exit.

Kell: Maybe they lifted your Daddy, Cathleen!

Cathleen: Shut up!

Kell: He might be dead or dying right at this very minute …

Cathleen: I hate you, Kell! I hate all of you. And this is a stupid gang and you're stray in the head, Siubhan Doherty. Everyone says so!

Siubhan: Oh yeah!

Cathleen: Yeah! You're just jealous, because everyone knows how much trouble you are at home and at school. You're stupid! Everyone says so!

Kell: Piss off, Cathleen! Piss off home, you fat bitch.

Cathleen: If I was your Daddy, I'd lock you up. You're queer in the head.

Kell: Get out, Cathleen, and don't come back.

Cathleen: I'm going. And don't worry, I wouldn't want to be in your stupid old gang anyway.

*Siubhan grabs a bag and circles **Cathleen**.*

Siubhan:

> Suffocation
> A game we all can play,
> First you take a plastic bag,
> Then you put it on your head.
> Go to bed
> Wake up dead.

Kell: Jesus Christ, Siubhan! Don't!

Cathleen: Daddy! Daddy! Daddy! Help me!

Siubhan: *(Mimics)* Daddy! Daddy! Daddy! Help me! Daddies don't like fat little girls, Cathleen. You'd better run away off home, and tell them about mad Siubhan Doherty. But you'd better watch out because I might follow you home and when you're fast asleep in bed, I'll put a plastic bag on your head and you'll wake up dead.

Cathleen: *(Crying)* I hate you! *(Screams)* You're mad! You really are! *(Running away)* Wait till I tell my Daddy on you. You're gonna be in trouble, Siubhan Doherty. I'll tell my Daddy on you. I will.

Siubhan: Get out!

Cathleen leaves.

Kell: You shouldn't have done that. You really scared her.

Siubhan: So!

Kell: She's not that bad.

Siubhan: Well, run away after her then and walk her home.

Kell: I didn't mean to—

Siubhan: Yeah! That's what everyone says. They didn't mean to.

Kell: Well, I didn't.

Siubhan: I'm not crazy, you know.

Kell: I know you're not.

Siubhan: Everyone keeps telling me I'm evil and I'm not. I'm not …

Kell: Even if you were, I'd still love you.

Siubhan: What?

Pause.

Kell: Even if you were I'd still … I'd still be mad about you!

Siubhan: Stop taking the piss!

Kell: I'm not. Stop hiding!

Siubhan incredulous as Kell grabs her and gives her a kiss. Lights dim to blackout. They come up again on Stage-Left.

Nora: Quick! Act normal! Sit on the bins!

Siubhan: Jesus!

They sit on bins. Enter Cathleen with baby in arms.

Cathleen: Siubhan Doherty! And Nora! I don't believe it! It's been years!

Nora: Jesus! Cathleen! How's about you!

Siubhan: After all this time …

Nora: Imagine.

Cathleen: Imagine is right! How's life treating you?

Siubhan: Great!

Nora: Fine!

Cathleen: That's great!

Siubhan: Yeah!

Nora: Yeah!

Cathleen: It all seems so long ago, doesn't it! And you're still both here. Imagine. You haven't changed a bit, either of you.

Nora: Neither have you. Has she, Siubhan?

Siubhan: I suppose …

Mammy has come out to see what all the noise is about.

Mammy: *(Delighted)* Cathleen love! Is it you?

Cathleen: It is.

Mammy: It's lovely to see you. And would you look, a wee babby!

Cathleen: A boy, it's a boy. John, after his Daddy.

Mammy: Haven't you done well for yourself! How long are you married now, pet?

Cathleen: Two years this Christmas.

Mammy: Two years this Christmas! Did you hear that, Siubhan? Two years this Christmas. Isn't it grand for you?

Cathleen: Tell me that when this one has me up all night.

Mammy: But sure it's the best time of your life when they're all wee. I mind when Siubhan was that age.

Siubhan: Mammy!

Mammy: Will you come in and have a cup of tea?

Siubhan: Mammy, I'm sure she has lots to do!

Mammy: Siubhan!

Cathleen: Any word of your big day, Siubhan?

Mammy: That one! I doubt I'll ever be rid of her.

Nora: Do you mind Cormac?

Cathleen: You're not still—

Mammy: Them pair! We've given up hoping.

Cathleen: Is he still as money-mad as ever? *(Sound of child crying in distance)* I'll have to go. That's probably one of mine.

Mammy: One of yours?

Cathleen: I mind two others ... the money, you know.

Mammy: Well sure, aren't you great! Isn't she just great. Siubhan?

Siubhan: Just great.

Cathleen: I'm sure I'll see you all again.

Mammy: Call in any time, love. You're always welcome, isn't she Siubhan?

Siubhan: Any time.

Nora: Bye, Cathleen.

Cathleen: Bye now. God bless!

Cathleen leaves.

Mammy: What a lovely girl. A credit to her family. *(Girls stick their fingers in their mouths, puking in disgust)* Pity you two couldn't take a leaf from her book.

Mammy goes inside.

Siubhan: I'll never hear the end of this for weeks now.

Nora: She looked awful, didn't she?

Siubhan: I kind of wish I'd been a bit nicer to her now.

Nora: What the hell for?

Siubhan: I don't know. I just—

Nora: Just nothing! You hated her. We all did.

Siubhan: I don't know. She got me into enough trouble, but I was just jealous, that's all.

Nora: Forget her!

Siubhan: I thought you said she was rich?

Nora: Yeah, so!

Siubhan: Well she doesn't look it!

Nora: Forget her! Anyway, she never knew how to dress. Christ, she never had a pair of Bay City Roller socks!

Siubhan: Still—

Nora: Still nothing. Wait till you hear my new joke!

Siubhan: Och Nora.

Nora: Why do blondes wear shoulder pads? Come on! Guess!

Siubhan: I can't. I don't know. Tell me.

Nora: So they can go *(Nods her head from one side to another, tittering, and sings)* If I was a rich man …

Siubhan: Nora, for God's sake, don't you ever think of anything else?

Nora: Yes, you bitch, I make up jokes.

Siubhan: Trust me to open my big mouth!

Nora: What relation is a doorstep to a doormat?

Siubhan: Nora, when are you going to realise, I don't care—

Nora: Step-farther! Typical, if a Doherty laughed their faces would probably crack open.

Siubhan: Piss off!

Nora: When I'm making millions on the television as 'Nora the Sexy Comedienne', you'll be sorry you didn't laugh!

Siubhan: In your dreams, woman!

Nora: How about this one then? Your Daddy reminds me of the sea.

Siubhan: Why so?

Nora: It's not because he's wild, restless and romantic. It's because he makes me sick.

*Nora laughs as **Siubhan** shakes her head and giggles quietly pretending to disapprove.*

***Daddy Doherty** comes out of the house with a can of beer in his hand.*

Nora: The Doherty Family started
When Daddy Doherty farted,
Then they all came out retarded,
That's the Doherty Family.

*Nora and **Siubhan** both in stitches.*

Daddy: You miserable bainirseach, get off my land!

Siubhan: Daddy, please! The whole street can hear …

Nora: What odds, Siubhan. Ignore him!

Daddy: I said get off my land. I'll not be ignored, you miserable seal-cow.

Siubhan: *(Looking at the beer can)* No one could make him hear sense now.

Nora: As carnaptious as a bag of weasels. Sure he never changes.

Siubhan: Daddy …

Daddy: What do you seal-cows know about the life of a man? At least Nora found herself a bit of a man, which is more than you'll ever do, Siubhan.

Siubhan: Do you think I care?

Daddy: It's a good clout I should have given you long ago. Mind there's others would have, but I'm an unusual man, too soft by far. The things I put up with … I said get off my land.

*Nora grabs **Siubhan** and they leave.*

Nora: Some land!

Daddy: Bad scran to the both of yous!

He drinks the beer, the proud surveyor of all he thinks he owns and commands.

Daddy: *(Shouts after them)* I've lived and worked in half the towns of Ireland, which is more than either of you will ever amount to, I can tell you that. I'm a travelling man ...

Nora: *(As Daddy rants)*

> Doherty Sausages
> Doherty Sausages
> Make you fart
> Doherty Sausages
> Doherty Sausages
> Bad for your heart. Ahh, piss off!

Daddy: *(Swilling his beer and extemporising to the world. Throws away his beer can)* Two cuts and a lift, that's the way the cutter works and the ... and then the lifter handing out two sods at a time and the spreader landing them in neat rows on either side of the bank. *(He has been miming the actions)* And that feeling you get out on the bogs, a special kind of loneliness. *(Swilling more beer)* You don't get it climbing mountains, you're moving too damned quickly. Swish ... swish plonk ... swish ... swish plonk ... plodding on and on in the same little patch of bog, changing about, an hour lifting and an hour throwing, a rest on the spade, a smoke, a drink ... and at the end of the day when it's almost dark but still sort of light you look back at your work spread out across the bog ... and that's some goddamned sight. It looks ten times its real size. And that's when you know something, it's hard to explain, but you feel ... you feel ... and after the sods have been turned in ten days time you still haven't lost that feeling ... and seven days from that the whole thing's rickled ... and seven days from that it's clamped ... and seven days from that it's stacked. And the feeling, that wonderful feeling's still there ... production, that's what it is ... or something like that. Here they wouldn't give you the air to breathe, nothing to see at the end of the week. I like that wind, it'll bring rain. (**Daddy** *sees* **Siubhan** *and laughs at her*) And where'd you go Siubhan? Your type never leave.

She stands staring at him as lights dim on Stage-Left and come up on Stage-Right. Lights on stage resemble moonlight.

Tramp-Lady: I knew an Irish girl, she sang me an Irish song.

Kell is walking around, picking up pieces of junk. Appears very engrossed.

Tramp-Lady: What are you doing?

Kell: Don't know yet!

Tramp-Lady: Stop lying.

Kell: Stop annoying me! It's a surprise, if you must know!

Tramp-Lady: Who for?

Kell: Sssshh!

Kell is building what appears to be a pretend boat: a big piece of wood for the base, a sweeping brush for the mast, an old steering wheel as well.

Tramp-Lady: *(Singing as Kell works)*

> Bobby Shafto's gone to sea
> Silver buckles on his knee
> He'll come back and marry me
> Bonny Bobby Shafto …

Kell: And does he?

Tramp-Lady: Waited all her life for the ghost of a forgotten promise … Paper hearts in paper boats along a paper stream. *(Croons)*

> Row, row, row the boat
> Gently down the stream,
> Merrily, merrily, merrily, merrily,
> That's the life for me.

Kell: How come it takes you so long to say something?

Tramp-Lady: More haste, less speed!

Kell: Ssshh! Is that Siubhan? Shit, I'm not ready. What do you think? Is it stupid? Quick!

*Sound of **Siubhan** on stairs.*

Siubhan: How's about you, Kell!

Kell: *(Putting his hand over her eyes)* If you were—

Siubhan: Rich, what would you do? Kell, we're not kids anymore! I'm sick of you asking me that!

Kell: So?

Siubhan: So. You're not wise in the head, that's so!

Kell: Say it again!

Siubhan: If I was rich, I'd build a boat and sail away …

Kell: For a year and a day …

Siubhan: *(Sighing and warming to the subject)* For a year and a day, far far away on the back of a wave …

Kell: With a song and a wave …

Siubhan: Up to the moon and far far beyond.

Kell lets her see. She goes over to the boat.

Tramp-Lady: The borders of wishing and dreaming.

Siubhan: *(Sitting down in boat)* On an ocean of milk …

Kell: *(Unfolding the flag, his T-shirt)* In a sky of silk …

Siubhan: *(Laughing)* To a magic land …

Kell: Hand in hand …

Siubhan: You'd be lucky!

Kell: For a year and a day …

Siubhan: What'd we eat?

Kell: Whoever we'd meet! Dragons and monsters and creeps from the deep.

Siubhan: And where'd we sleep?

Kell: Wherever we wanted.

Siubhan: So why come back?

Kell: Then, we won't!

Siubhan: But, maybe they'd catch us ...

Kell: But the boat can fly!

Siubhan: If only ...

Tramp-Lady: If 'ifs' and 'ans' were pots and pans there'd be no need for tinkers ...

Kell: Who asked you?

Tramp-Lady: I could come too!

Kell: As the ... maid!

Siubhan: Aye sure!

Kell: Why not?

Siubhan: Who'd row the boat?

Kell: You would!

Siubhan: Away on your bike!

Tramp-Lady: The mice would—

Siubhan: Yeuch!

Tramp-Lady: In the lands of bygones all the animals speak—

Kell: No one's asking you!

Tramp-Lady: And they wear clothes—

Siubhan: Ssshhh! Kell! What kind of clothes?

Kell: Trousers and shirts. What do you think?

Tramp-Lady: And dresses of cobweb weave ...

Siubhan: *(Repeats)* And dresses of cobweb weave.

Tramp-Lady: And feather hats.

Kell: And bullet-proof boots.

Siubhan: Stop pissin' about, Kell!

Kell: I'm not ...

Siubhan: Go on ...

Tramp-Lady: And everyone has wings and can do spells!

Kell: Everyone?

Tramp-Lady: Yes ... and once, a long long time ago an evil monster came to the land and cast a wicked spell. And the boys had forgotten their spells, so the girls had to fight the monster and save the lands—

Kell: That's shit! It's always the boys who fight the dragon, and another thing, they save the princess!

Siubhan: Well, this is a different story, Kell! The girls saved the whole lot of them!

Kell: No, but you can't change the story. That's not what you said last week!

Siubhan: *(Ignoring him)* And then what happened?

Tramp-Lady: And then after a long, long time the ghost of the monster came back ...

Kell: There's no such thing as ghosts!

Siubhan: Yeah!

Tramp-Lady: How do you know? Have you seen one?

Kell: No! But that's thick!

Siubhan: I don't know!

Kell: But there isn't!

Siubhan: I'm not scared of ghosts, anyway!

Kell: Neither am I!

Tramp-Lady: I am!

Kell: Would you shut up!

Siubhan: Leave her alone, Kell!

Kell: Why don't you go and play with your shells?

Tramp-Lady: I can't find them.

She exits.

Kell: She's mad.

Siubhan: No, she's not. Anyway, I think you're heart-scared of her!

Kell: I'm sure!

Siubhan: And you're heart-scared of ghosts!

Kell: I am not!

Siubhan: Yes, you are!

Kell: Are you saying I'm a liar?

Siubhan: I'm telling you, you're heart-scared of ghosts, that's all!

Kell: No, it's not!

Siubhan: What?

Kell: It's the same thing as calling me a liar! It's not 'that's all ...'

Silence.

Siubhan: Okay! I'm sorry then!

Kell: Well, maybe I am then. But just a wee bit!

Siubhan: Why? Sure they wouldn't harm you!

Kell: I seen one once!

Siubhan: I don't believe you!

Kell: Don't then!

Siubhan: Where'd you see it then?

Kell: At the bottom of my bed!

Siubhan: That was your Guardian Angel, you daft git!

Kell: Whatever the hell that is, it wasn't that. I'm telling you I seen a ghost!

Siubhan: Stop pissin' about!

Kell: Stop calling me a liar!

Siubhan: Did you really, Kell?

Kell: I did!

Siubhan: Well, go on then. Tell me!

Kell: Why should I!

Siubhan: Go on … ah Kell go on!

Kell: You'd better not laugh!

Siubhan: I won't, I promise!

Kell: Give us a kiss, first!

Siubhan: Tell me the story, first.

Kell: *(Laughing)* Okay … but I'll kill you if you laugh!

Siubhan: I won't!

Kell: I bet you won't believe me!

Siubhan: I will … I promise! Get on with it!

Kell: It's kind of mad. I was sitting in my bed, it was late … I couldn't sleep. I can't remember why. Probably it was cold. Something like that! And I felt a cold shiver round my neck. I wasn't scared or anything … not then. And that's when I saw her … the ghost like … a wee girl just sitting there, holding out her hand. But like I knew who she was. I just knew …

Siubhan: Who?

Kell: Even though I knew, I wasn't scared of her. I should have been. I only saw her the once. Just the once. The problem was the next day I went and opened my big mouth to the oul doll— I'll never let on to her about anything again. She said I was a liar, but I knew I wasn't. I knew it was my wee … I knew. I just knew it was her …

Siubhan: For God's sake, who was she?

Kell: The oul doll never forgave me. She thought she should have come to visit her. As if I wanted to torture her. She just came to let me know she was clean stone mad about her brother, that's all. It was nobody's fault. She came to visit, that's all. The only thing is she hasn't been back since ... or maybe ... I don't know ...

Siubhan: You had a sister ...

Kell: She'd grown up a bit. She was just a babby when she ... you know ... when she ... like it's not as if I ever knew her or anything ... but I know she came back to tell me she wasn't blaming me like ... not like the oul doll ... the oul doll, she'd prefer her ... she was just a babby ... but ... anyway, I'm glad she's happy - it's like I'm scared I'll see her again and the oul doll'll find out and they'll send me away. But ... like ... you're not laughing.

Siubhan: Why should I be?

Kell: Do you believe me?

Siubhan: Yes.

Kell: But you're dying to laugh, all the same.

Siubhan: No I'm not.

Kell: She was clean stone mad about me and she went and died on me.

Siubhan: You've got me, you daft thing ... and nobody's parents like them ... I think.

Kell: So that's the story. Do I get my kiss?

Siubhan: You might ...

Kell: *(Lifting her)* And then again, you might not ... You're a bad article, Siubhan Doherty.

Siubhan: If you were rich, what'd you do?

Kell: I'd want my kiss ...

Siubhan: Kell!

Kell: I'd build a boat and sail away ...

Siubhan: For a year and a day ...

Kell: On an ocean of milk ...

Siubhan: In a sky of silk ...

Kell: *(They go into the cabin)* To a magic land …

Siubhan: Hey!

Kell: Hand in hand …

Tramp-Lady: *(Singing)*

> Row, row, row the boat
> Gently down the stream
> Merrily, merrily, merrily, merrily

Siubhan: That's the life for us.

Lights fade to blackout.

End of Act One.

ACT TWO

Stage-Left lightens to show the front of No 15, O Donnell Estate, Westside, in an imaginary town somewhere in the North.

Two dustbins in front of the house.

The wreath is missing from the upstairs window.

Not yet dawn. Road still swathed with the yellow rays of the street-lights.

On the street, a rope-swing dangles from a street-lamp.

*Enter **Daddy Doherty** singing:*

Daddy:

> We're going to build a house ... boo!
> A public house ... hurrah!
> Only one bar ... boo!
> Forty yards long ... hurrah!

***Daddy Doherty** starts at his fence, painting etc.*

> No barmen ... .boo!
> Only barmaids ... hurrah!
> No glasses ... boo!
> Only buckets ... hurrah!

Continues to drink as he works.

> We won't sell beer ... boo!
> We'll give it away ... hurrah!

Mammy: Are you lost your senses? You'll wake the whole street.

Daddy: Not but that your tongue'll do the job first.

Mammy: Can you not leave that old fence alone? What are you at anyway?

Daddy: The three fortunes of the unlucky man are sharp-tongued daughters, long visits from his neighbours and—

Mammy: Sssh! She'll hear—

Daddy: and bad fences!

Mammy: Bad fences. They should put you and your fences away!

Daddy: Aye sure! Pick away until there's nothing left.

Mammy: What was there ever there to begin with?

Daddy: Hey!

Mammy: It's only an old heap of a thing! Like yourself!

Daddy: Look who's talking.

Pause. They start painting.

Mammy: If you built it high enough, we wouldn't know we had neighbours.

Daddy: What about them! There's no better sight than ourselves.

Mammy: Aye sure!

Daddy: Sure I'm sure.

Daddy *is painting the inside of the fence.*

Mammy *kneels down on street to paint the outside of fence.*

Daddy: What are you at?

Mammy: There's never on old slipper, but there's an old stocking to match.

Daddy: Watch who you're calling old—

Mammy: I never said you were old.

Daddy: The paint! You're wasting it—

Mammy: Let them say what they want, but they'll not say I was mean.

Daddy: Let them go to hell and paint their own fences. You should have stayed in your bed.

Mammy: I couldn't sleep.

Daddy: *(Sings)*

> Wee Willy lost his marley,
> Wee Willy lost his marley,
> Wee Willy lost his marley,
> Down by the Linfield Rd.
> Sure he shoved it down the grating.

He whistles.

Mammy: That's that bucket.

Daddy: If the boys were home, they'd see the money to be had—

Mammy: Where's the rest of it?

Daddy: There is none.

Mammy: I can't leave it half done.

Daddy: Even in a bit of ground.

Mammy: Daddy!

Daddy: There is no more!

Mammy: No more?

Daddy: When the new stock comes in we could buy more—

Mammy: So when's that.

Daddy: Next month, or so!

Mammy: Next month!

Daddy: That's it.

Mammy: Why didn't you tell me?

Daddy: I tried to.

Mammy: You did not.

Daddy: I did.

Mammy: They'll all be laughing now.

Daddy: They will.

Mammy: It's not funny, you! *(Silence)* What about them! There's no better sight than ourselves.

Daddy: Aye sure!

Mammy and **Daddy**:

> Yourself and myself *(Mammy)*
> Myself and yourself *(Daddy)*

Pause.

Mammy: Just ourselves … If only …

Street lamps dimming. **Daddy** *gets ladder.*

Mammy: What are you at now? Keeping up with you is a full-time job. That old thing, you'd swear it was gold the way you go on. You wouldn't even give the lend of it to your own mother.

Daddy: Why didn't she buy her own? Too proud. Thought she was too good to need a shovel, never mind a ladder. There's money in ladders. The boys understood. Mad to climb them they were, do you mind, when they were wee—

Mammy: I do not—

Daddy: They had your heart broke, climbing things … up on the roof shouting down the chimney—

Mammy: They're all nice when they're wee. Do you mind how Siubhan used to run away from school? Wee pet!

Daddy: *(Interrupting)* Look here till you see!

Mammy: What now?

Daddy: Get up here!

Mammy: I'm not climbing that thing!

Daddy: You'll miss the whole show then.

Mammy: Let you take the blame if I fall!

Mammy climbs ladder and peers into distance.

Mammy: There's nothing to see.

Daddy: Look!

Mammy: Your head's a marley! There's no one to see!

Mammy goes to climb down.

Daddy: *(Grabs her)* Wait! You'll get a chook of it in a minute ... Your one there ... coming over the hill, dressed in lace ... The May Queen, and her page carrying her train ... Now do you see?

Mammy: *(Melting)* You're teasing—

Daddy: Sssh! The show's starting ... there now! There she goes swinging round and round the street-lamp. And all the crowds gathered ... the faithful. And I'd be there, begging you to go round again ...

Mammy: And I thought you'd forgotten.

Daddy: Aye sure! *(Mimicking)* 'I might, but you'll have to pay me another penny.'

Mammy: Not that you ever did! Stingy then too!

Daddy: Bad-tempered then too! Some things stay the same! *(Mimicking)* 'Don't bother then, you old buggers'—

Mammy: Dressed in those lace curtains ...

Daddy: Like a princess!

Mammy: And all the wee girls, jealous as hell! I had my pick of the boys then too!

Daddy: You got the best there was!

Mammy: Sure I did!

Silence. **Mammy** *shivers and goes into the house.* **Daddy** *stays on the ladder and stares into the distance.*

Daddy: *(Sings)*

> Our wee queen can tumble her pole,
> Our wee queen can tumble her pole,
> Our wee queen can tumble her pole,
> Tumble ... her ... pole ...

The following morning. July 12th.

Sound of Music.

> Up comes the man with a shovel in his hand
> And he says boys we'll go no further
> For we'll get a great big rope
> And we'll hang the bloody Pope
> On the twelfth of July in the morning.

Siubhan *enters, standing at door with a bag of rubbish in her hand.*

Ladder still standing.

She goes over to the bins and bangs bag into already full bin. She is standing on rubbish to make the bag fit.

Wolf-whistles. She sticks up her fingers on both her hands.

Mammy *brings out chair.*

Mammy: Where do you think you're going?

Siubhan: Out!

Mammy: Not the day you're not.

Siubhan: Why not?

Mammy: Your Daddy said, that's why.

Siubhan: I never get no peace.

Mammy: We can all say that!

Siubhan *ignores her.* **Mammy** *puts clothes on ladder.*

Mammy: See us, Siubhan Doherty, we're worse than the tinkers!

Siubhan: *(Sarcastic)* Well, we have each other!

Mammy: Just ourselves …

Siubhan: Do you think they'll come today?

Mammy: *(Concentrating putting out washing)* Who?

Siubhan: Bill and Ben the Dustbin Men! Who else?

Mammy: Don't let your Daddy hear you talk like that!

Siubhan: Some heroes … bloody binmen!

Mammy: I'm fed up waiting on them too!

They laugh. **Mammy** *decides to hang the clothes on the rungs of the ladder. Leans it against the wall. Door opens again and* **Daddy Doherty** *comes out, not wearing overalls.*

Daddy: Keep yous both inside today! Jesus, my good ladder!

Mammy: I have nothing else. The sun isn't around the back. I'll never get it dried unless—

Daddy: You couldn't watch yous. *(Grabs some clothes from ladder and throws them on the ground)* You'll destroy the wood!

Mammy: Look at my good washing!

Siubhan: She has nothing else!

Mammy: It's alright. I'll put them … somewhere *(To Daddy although he ignores her)* And who's the one demands a clean shirt everyday?

Daddy *inspecting fence, paintwork and repairs.*

Daddy: That's a great job!

Siubhan: Sure it's hardly standing.

Daddy: Shows what you know! That's not the fault of the workmanship, Siubhan! That's the ground. Bad ground!

Siubhan: Right sure. *(Laughs)* Still, it brightens the place up a bit. Gives the neighbours something to talk about!

Daddy: What would the likes of them know about works of art?

Siubhan: Jesus—

Daddy: If the boys were here, they'd back me up. They'd know!

Siubhan: The kids on the road have been taking the piss out of the half-painted front all morning!

Daddy: That was your Mammy!

Siubhan: So it's her fault—

Daddy: Well, it's not mine!

Siubhan: It never is!

Daddy: See you, Siubhan. Anything and everything that could be you'd find a fault in it.

Siubhan: Put them on them window sills, Mammy.

Daddy: No!

Siubhan: Why? Don't tell me there's money and pride in them too—

Daddy: Don't talk to me about pride, Siubhan! You couldn't even spell the word—

Mammy: I'll spread them on the fence, then—

Daddy: My good fence—

Siubhan: Look Daddy ... she has to put them somewhere. They'll be dried in no time round here with the sun. What'll you wear if she doesn't get them dried?

Daddy: That's not my concern.

Pause.

Siubhan: I'm away!

Mammy: Siubhan, please!

Siubhan: Right! Right! I'll not go then!

Daddy: That damned song! Who do they think they are?

Siubhan: Them damned binmen! Who do they think they are?

Daddy: Go to hell, Siubhan!

Mammy: She's only saying they smell the place, Daddy!

Daddy: I've had complaints from the whole road about her and her carry-on ... her and that Nora.

Mammy: What complaints?

Daddy: She'd better watch her step, that's all.

Mammy: You can't believe everything you hear, Daddy!

Siubhan: That's never stopped him before—

Daddy: Expect a crowd of us for a feed tonight!

Mammy: How many?

Daddy: Just make enough to feed a crowd! Jesus!

Siubhan: Bastard!

Mammy: You'd better get a move on, Daddy! You'll be late for wherever you're going to.

Daddy stands threateningly in front of **Siubhan**.

Daddy: Why don't you say you're sorry *(Softly)* Siubhan …

Siubhan: What for?

Mammy: Daddy, she's not a child—

Daddy: I know that! *(Quietly)*

Siubhan: One day … you … you'll get what's coming to you—

Mammy: Come on inside, Siubhan and we'll have a cup of tea!

Siubhan: I don't want no cup of tea—

Mammy: I know … I know … Come on inside and you'll feel better—

Siubhan: It's not as if the whole street doesn't know what he's like. Mammy—

Mammy: Siubhan, he misses the boys …

Mammy starts putting the clothes on the fence.

Mammy: There now! We'll get our washing dry at least!

Siubhan: Typical … of course … I never learn. *(To her retreating back)* Why did you always let him get away with everything? It's as much your fault—

Mammy: It's easy to blame me, isn't it?

Siubhan: It's easy to cop out.

Mammy: Things aren't that simple ...

Siubhan: Aren't they?

Mammy: Your Daddy hasn't had it easy, Siubhan, and sometimes it comes out in him.

Siubhan: How many more excuses, Mammy? How many more?

Mammy: Don't take so much to heart, Siubhan. From when you were a wean you always took too much to heart.

Siubhan: Just tell me why!

Mammy: Laugh, and the world laughs with you. Cry, and you cry alone.

Siubhan: That's sick!

Mammy: That's life, Siubhan! You should take a leaf out of ... Cathleen's book. She's a happy wee thing. Happily married—

Siubhan: Is that where you'd like to see me? Happily *married?*

Mammy: If it'd clear the puss on your face, I would!

Siubhan: I don't want to talk about Cathleen. I'll never get married, Mammy.

Mammy: That's just because you had a fight with your Daddy ... it'll pass. Everything does, Siubhan—

Siubhan: I wish—

Mammy: Don't you know that it's far out for the cat to kiss the beetle?

Siubhan: What does that mean?

Mammy: It means you can't change the way things are.

Siubhan: Mammy, I'm not talking about a United Ireland! Christ!

Mammy: Neither am I. I'm talking about a United Home! You see, men are like beetles! They have their way, noses to the ground, running along in one direction, storming through any obstacle in their path. And women, they're the cats and they walk alone and all places are alike to them. Now do you see?

Siubhan: No.

Mammy: My own Mammy used to say that to me when I used to feel as if the whole world was against me ... I used to fight with my Daddy too—

Siubhan: Sure you did!

Mammy: I did!

Tramp-Lady is standing at the gate.

Mammy: Away off with you. We don't want your like hanging around.

Siubhan: Mammy!

Mammy: I have a bag of old clothes. You can have that.

Tramp-Lady: Whatever you have ... thanks.

Siubhan: Will you take a drop of tea?

Mammy: Siubhan! Their sort know only how to steal—

Tramp-Lady: I'm no thief, missus!

Siubhan: No one's saying you are. Milk and a wee bit of sugar?

Mammy: Are you lost your senses, Siubhan?

Siubhan: And a sandwich?

Mammy: Your Daddy'll kill you, Siubhan.

Tramp-Lady: Whatever you have, thanks.

Siubhan: Right then!

Silence.

Tramp-Lady: Would you like your palm read, missus?

Mammy: I would not ... I don't believe in all that oul' stuff.

Siubhan: I would. I believe in it.

Mammy: I thought you were making tea. I knew I'd have to make it. Siubhan, you keep an eye on things ... Siubhan! You can't trust a stranger, Siubhan.

Siubhan: Sorry ... she's ... afraid he'll come back. I think it's the people you know you can't trust. Do you?

Tramp-Lady: *(Looking at palm)* Well, well, well ... I do ...

Siubhan and Tramp-Lady walk to Stage-Right as lights dim.

Siubhan walking around impatiently.

Tramp-Lady: A watched kettle never boils.

Siubhan: Where is he?

Tramp-Lady: He'll be here.

Siubhan: He'd better.

Tramp-Lady: He will.

Siubhan grabs a hat, poses in front of an old mirror.

Siubhan: Mirror, mirror, on the wall
      Who is the loveliest of them all?

Tramp-Lady: Stop worrying ...

Siubhan pacing again.

Siubhan: You didn't tell no one, did you?

Tramp-Lady: No, I didn't. This time next week all this will be—

Siubhan: A memory.

Tramp-Lady: Just think of where you're going. Forget everything else ...

Siubhan takes poster off wall.

Tramp-Lady hums the air of a heady gavotte/waltz. Siubhan dances with the poster. A whirling dervish, wearing hat.

Siubhan: Far, far away for ever and ever.

Cormac standing at door.

*Tramp-Lady quickly covers **Siubhan's** hold-all with one of her layers. **Siubhan** staggers to a stop. Dizzy.*

Siubhan: What are you doing here?

Cormac: Where's Kell?

Siubhan: I don't know!

Cormac: Stop lying!

Siubhan: Stop bullying!

Cormac: Kell wasn't going to meet you here then … later on—

Siubhan: Nosey was hung! No, he wasn't. And the less time he spends with you the better!

Cormac: Piss off! Why don't you put him in a pram while you're at it!

Siubhan: If I were you Cormac, I'd mess someone else up. Bye missus!

Tramp-Lady: Bye Siubhan!

Siubhan leaves. Tramp-Lady continues humming.

Cormac: Shut up!

Tramp-Lady: Who are you running away from this time?

Cormac: Piss off! *(Silence)* I think she was lying! *(Sings James Bond music)* Vodka Martini, slightly shaken, not stirred! I reckon he'll be here soon enough.

Tramp-Lady: *(Sarcastic)* Whatever you say, Cormac!

Cormac: I've tried everywhere else! *(Cormac has picked up hat and is walking around wearing it. Catches sight of himself in mirror)* 'Well, this is another fine mess you've got me into' – but I'm not a kid anymore. It's me or— *(Enter Kell carrying a small bag and flowers.)* What about you Kell?

Kell: Jesus Cormac! How's about you?

Cormac: Expecting Siubhan were you?

Kell: Is Siubhan here?

Cormac: She just left. *(Kell goes to leave)* Hey! Where do you think you're going? I've scoured this city looking for you … *(Grabs him)* She can wait for just one night.

Kell: Mind the jacket.

Cormac: Come on Kell. Give me a break!

Kell: Cormac, look, some other time!

Cormac: Damn you Kell! I thought you were—

Kell: You only ever appear when you have a problem—

Cormac: You're always with her!

Kell: So!

Cormac: So … come on … for old times' sakes!

Kell: I'll meet you tomorrow!

Cormac: Tomorrow's too late.

Kell: Look—

Tramp-Lady: Kell … Tomorrow's always too late—

Cormac: Keep out of this! Just this once, Kell. Please!

Kell: Since when did you ever say please.

Silence.

Cormac: I'm in a wee spot of bother, Kell. And as I thought I could rely on you. I thought, you'd give me a hand. Help me out like—

Kell: No!

Cormac: Do you mind that lake we used to go to?

Kell: No!

Cormac: And you used to sail paper boats. Before we met the girls—

Kell: So …

Cormac: It's all a question of timing, do you see? If you could just meet some people for me, I'll be along later, you'd be buying me some time. I'll slip you something. Don't tell me Siubhan doesn't like the odd thing—

Kell: You're one jammy pig, Cormac. Spending time with you, in the pub, whatever, is one thing, but getting tangled up in your games ... No ... Piss off!

Cormac: I reckon Siubhan got the weaker man.

Kell: Fuck off! And leave her out of this! I have my own problems.

Cormac: She's a problem, all right.

Kell: You're a problem. Your head's a marley!

Cormac: Do you think I don't know you and Siubhan have something planned? *(Pause)* A wee holiday, is it?

Kell: What are you? My mother?

Cormac: You'll need the cash! *(Pause)* I'm asking you! Not anyone else. Doesn't that mean anything any more? I should be telling you to go to hell—

Kell: And why's that?

Cormac: Siubhan this, Siubhan that—

Kell: Don't tell me you're jealous!

Cormac: Piss off! But I'll tell you one thing, Kell, who else did you have before you met her? No one, that's who! The thing is you've forgotten the good laugh we used to have. And I reckon you'll forget her too in time—

Tramp-Lady: Kell! Be careful! He's a green eyed monster!

Cormac: Would you listen to the doll that's talking!

Kell: *(Laughs)* And what's that when it's at home?

Tramp-Lady: Plain and simple jealousy! He's driven by it! And it'll destroy all around him!

Kell: Aye sure he's not that bad! We go back a long way.

Tramp-Lady: And will you go on?

Cormac: I don't know!

Kell: Piss off, Cormac! What's that supposed to mean?

Cormac: She still spends all her time with Nora, doesn't she?

Kell: So?

Cormac: So!

Kell: You're still my best friend, and all that—

Cormac: And all that! The way I heard it, she was!

Kell: Piss off! You are, not her!

Cormac: Is it a deal then?

Kell: The lake?

Cormac: No, you daft get! The moon! And one more thing, you can't tell anyone, not even Siubhan!

Kell: Right! Right! I'll do it! I can see Siubhan tomorrow!

Tramp-Lady: Tomorrow's always too late—

Kell: Shut up you!

Cormac: And keep out of it. It's a deal then!

Kell: Right!

Cormac: I knew you wouldn't let me down! We go back too far, farther than her anyway! Tell us, don't you ever feel … like … do you ever look at anyone else?

Kell: Why? Do you?

Cormac: What do you think?

Kell: Nora'd kill you if she ever found out!

Cormac: Well she won't, will she!

Kell: *(Pause)* I miss not knowing things, no surprises. I know me and Siubhan … well it's her and me always … a bit boring … do you know what I'm trying to say?

Cormac: Always her and you! You're mad!

Kell: Sometimes, I wish I'd never met her!

Siubhan standing at the door.

Siubhan: Do you now?

Kell: Shit!

Cormac: Siubhan please! This is private!

Siubhan: Go to hell, Cormac!

Kell: Siubhan, look! Let me explain!

Siubhan: I suppose he's dragged you into another one of his schemes!

Cormac: *(Defensive and nervous)* It's not as if he'd be doing it for nothing, Siubhan. Not that I'm saying we're doing anything!

Siubhan: Get out, Cormac!

Cormac: Who do you think you are, telling me to get out! Get out, yourself!

Kell: Get out, Cormac!

Cormac: Typical! You promised!

Kell: I'll meet you later. I want to talk to Siubhan!

Siubhan: Forget it! I'll go! Forget the whole thing, you two-faced bastard!

Kell: Cormac! Get out!

Cormac: Right! *(As he goes out the door)* I'll wait for you downstairs …

Cormac leaves.

Silence.

Kell: Siubhan, will you just listen … let me explain!

Siubhan: I wish I'd never met her!

Kell: And I wish I'd met you when I was a bit older and richer! When we leave, well ... we're leaving a lot—

Siubhan: I don't care about bloody money! Is that why you're going off somewhere with him tonight?

Kell: One last favour. Siubhan, we used to be best friends. If it wasn't for him, we'd never have met.

Siubhan: So?

Kell: I don't trust him either. *You* ... I trust you!

Siubhan: I don't want anything to go wrong, Kell!

Kell: Nothing will! I promise!

Cormac: *(shouts from below)* Will you two get a move on!

Siubhan: But you couldn't say no to his money!

Kell: We'll need it for when we leave!

Siubhan: We?

Kell: Yes we!

Siubhan: Are you sure of that?

Kell: Yes, Siubhan, I am. Aren't you? *(Pause)* I'm sorry about what I said!

Siubhan: I won't forget, Kell!

Kell: I know that. I didn't mean it to come out like that. Cormac's a—

Siubhan: I know—

Kell: When we leave, we can begin all over. Forget about Cormac, about—

Siubhan: Begin all over?

Kell: Look back and laugh even!

Siubhan: The thing is ...

Kell gives her the flowers, she reads card. They embrace.

Siubhan: Me too!

Lights dim to blackout and come up again to show the front of the Doherty property.

Siubhan: *(To Tramp-Lady)* You might as well hang around for a while!

Mammy: I'm sure the woman has a mind of her own, Siubhan.

Siubhan: It's just that—

Mammy: Just nothing, if your Daddy was here—

Siubhan: *(To Tramp-Lady)* He'd have run you off this property from the word go. A brave man, my Daddy.

Mammy: Siubhan!

Tramp-Lady: I'll be going just as soon as I've put back on these boots.

Siubhan: No! Don't go—

Mammy: Stop telling people what to do, Siubhan!

Siubhan: Look at what's talking!

Tramp-Lady: It must be good to have a place you can call your own.

Mammy: Well, I suppose it is—

Siubhan: You must be joking, on this rotten road! You'd hate it, everyone watching everyone else watching them!

Mammy: That's Siubhan for you. Never a bad word to say about anyone, have you Siubhan?

Tramp-Lady: I've seen worse.

Siubhan: Worse houses or worse people?

Mammy: Siubhan! You're lucky you don't have a daughter, missus!

Tramp-Lady: I did have once … she was drowned.

Mammy: I'm sorry—

Siubhan: You and your big mouth!

Tramp-Lady: I've spent years trying to ... you know—

Mammy: I know ... believe me, I know. Would you like some more tea?

Tramp-Lady: I would.

Siubhan: I'll do it. You two just sit here and chat.

Mammy: Weans. Who'd have them?

Tramp-Lady: Who'd lose them?

Mammy: I know. She fights a lot with her Daddy. She has my heart broke.

Tramp-Lady: She tells me she's leaving. Fancies a life on the road. I told her it's hard.

Mammy: In her dreams she's leaving! I'll leave her!

Tramp-Lady: In her heart she's already gone.

Mammy: It's hard everywhere. I keep telling Siubhan you've got to have a sense of humour.

Tramp-Lady: She seems grand to me.

Siubhan comes out.

Siubhan: It'll take a wee while.

Tramp-Lady: Ah, I'll be going then.

Mammy: *(Grabbing one of black rubbish bags from side of house)* Here, take these.

Tramp-Lady: Thanks missus.

Mammy: We'll see you again, no doubt.

Tramp-Lady: Some other time.

Mammy: Right.

Tramp-Lady: *(To Siubhan)* Good luck!

Siubhan: Thanks.

Tramp-Lady leaves.

Mammy: What was all that about?

Siubhan: *(Airily)* Beats me.

Mammy: *(Hesitantly)* Looks like I owe you an apology. I liked her!

Siubhan: So do I …

*Enter **Cathleen**.*

Cathleen: Mrs Doherty, Siubhan, how's about you?

Mammy: *(Delighted)* Cathleen! How are you, love?

Cathleen: Siubhan, I just called round to tell you how sorry I am … about Kell. I just found out—

Siubhan: Right! Okay! Cathleen, thanks—

Mammy: It's over a year now though, Cathleen. The young get over things—

Siubhan: Shut up, will you!

Mammy: Siubhan Doherty! Have some manners.

Cathleen: No, it's Okay. I'm sure I'd be the same. I'm very sorry, Siubhan.

***Siubhan** leaves.*

Mammy: Siubhan! Where are you going?

Siubhan: To see Nora.

Mammy: Your Daddy said to stay in the day.

Siubhan: So? I don't care.

Cathleen: She's not over it yet, God love her.

Mammy: *(Furious)* Well she was just fine a minute ago.

Cathleen: You can't please some people.

***Cathleen** leaves.*

Mammy: Oh Cathleen, I'm sorry, I didn't mean to. *(Silence)* Ach, what's the use?

***Mammy** turns the clothes drying on the fence. Picks up rubbish.*

Mammy: There's a wee mountain road that branches off from Creeslough, Siubhan, and runs right up into the mountains. It's not that much of a road, rough and narrow and uneven, they say that's the way of the roads that lead to heaven. And sure as I'm standing here, Siubhan, this road leads to the most ... heavenly spot in Ulster. It's Colmcille's own country, Siubhan, where he was born and reared and wandered as a boy. It's your Daddy's own country too. There's a magnificent castle and black woods and whin and bracken and furze and two lines of mountains and if you climb to the top at night with the man you love ... and look down in the little lakes of Gartan and Kebben and Cailleach with the reflection of the moon in the waters ... and he was loving and he made me feel loved for myself ... and I had never seen anything like that night ... never felt. And your Daddy's as mad about you as he is about the boys. And through the woods the road runs up to a chapel and your Daddy and I were married there, and it all lingered in my mind and, Siubhan, it does so still.

Siubhan is standing at the gate.

Stage-Left dims to blackout and lights come up again on Stage-Right.

Kerosene lighting.

Pause.

Kell: I'd still love you!

Siubhan: What?

Kell: Even if you were, I'd still ... I'd still be mad about you!

Siubhan: Stop taking the piss!

Kell: I'm not ... Och, stop hiding!

Siubhan incredulous as Kell grabs her and gives her a kiss. She walks away. Silence.

Siubhan: Why did the skeleton go to the party on its own?

Kell: Because it had *no-body* to go with.

Siubhan: How'd you know that?

Kell: Everyone knows that.

Siubhan: Nora must have told you!

Kell: No, she didn't.

Siubhan: Yes, she did.

Kell: No, she didn't. Get off my back.

Siubhan: Okay! Sorry!

Kell: Sorry!

Pause.

Siubhan: Do you have a nickname?

Kell: Why, do you?

Siubhan: Maybe.

Kell: Go on, what is it?

Siubhan: I didn't say I did and I didn't say I didn't, did I? *(Laughs)*

Kell: Very funny ... go on, please tell me.

Siubhan: Only if you promise never to tell anyone ever ever.

Kell: I promise. I promise.

Siubhan: Swear on your Ma's grave!

Kell: I swear!

Siubhan: *(Pause)* Saggy Arse ...

Kell bursts out laughing.

Siubhan: You promised you wouldn't laugh.

Kell: No, I didn't.

Siubhan: It's not true, is it?

Kell: Hmmmmm!

Siubhan: Kell!

Kell: Well!

Siubhan: Kell!

Kell: Of course it's not bloody true. You're not that bad, a bit skinny, but not that bad!

Siubhan: I don't give a shit anyway. Nora says she was born for kissing.

Kell: *(Laughing)* Did she?

Siubhan: Maybe. *(Laughing)*

Kell: You're a bad bitch, Siubhan Doherty.

Siubhan: A bitch is a dog, a dog is nature and nature is beautiful.

Kell: Very funny. I'm going to Belfast for the summer.

Siubhan: On your own?

Kell: Yeah. To stay with my auntie, my Da's sister. She's kind of English too.

Siubhan: Do you want to go?

Kell: I don't know. I have to … she's very swanky. Speaks like the Queen. *(Siubhan sniggers)* She does too and there's these humungous iron gates leading up to the house.

Siubhan: Jesus! It sounds like a prison.

Kell: Don't be stupid. Sometimes it's like a prison, I guess, but then most of the time I can do what I want and there's loads of food. Are you going anywhere?

Siubhan: Bundoran for a week and later on Buncrana for another week. Caravan parks—

Kell: Camping! Wow, I've always wanted to go camping but I'll never be let. I bet it's class.

Siubhan: We go every year.

Kell: Yeah, I go to Belfast every year.

Siubhan: I'd swap places with you any day.

Kell: I was just going to say the same thing.

Siubhan: Kell, if you were a girl what would you like to be like … or, I mean, who would you like to be?

Kell: You ask the weirdest questions.

Siubhan: Go on, tell me.

Kell: I don't know … The Queen.

Siubhan: Piss off!

Kell: I'd make a great queen, don't you think? *(He gives the royal wave.* **Siubhan** *doesn t laugh)* Alright. If I was a girl, I'd be you.

Siubhan: No! Don't say that! Don't ever say that!

Kell: Why not? You wanted me to, didn't you?

Siubhan: No, I didn't! *(Pause)* If I was a boy and I could choose what girl I'd like to be like, I'd be the very, very last person I'd choose.

Kell: Why?

Siubhan: Anyway, it's a stupid question.

Kell: No, it's not!

Siubhan: Yes, it is!

Kell: No, it's not!

Siubhan: It could never happen anyway.

Kell: Yes it could—

Siubhan: Your head's a marley—

Kell: Oh yeah! Have you never heard them talking on the telly about sex-changes?

Siubhan: Talking about what!

Kell: It's all the fashion! I'm telling you! Everyone's doing it!

Siubhan: You mean men are becoming women and women are becoming men?

Kell: Yes, stupid.

Siubhan: What stations do they show these programmes on?

Kell: I don't know. Channel Four or BBC2, I think.

Siubhan: We only get RTE1 and 2. My Daddy won't allow any British Channels.

Kell: What an idiot!

Siubhan: He says I'm the wickedest person on earth.

Kell: Why for?

Siubhan: *(Pause)* You see, I hate porridge and I'm always trying to get Seán and Óisín to eat mine without Daddy seeing. Then last night when I was in my bed he came into my room and asked me why I hadn't all my blankets pulled up. You see, I wasn't cold. I didn't mean to make him angry, but Mammy says I always make everyone angry. You see how mad I made Cathleen. That's how I make everyone. *(Pause)* Anyway, I pulled all the blankets up over me and then he said he was going to … kill himself, because he c-c-couldn't … shit … he couldn't stand the shame of having a daughter like me. And it's all my fault, Seán says, because I never do anything right. And I'm really stupid and hopeless at school but I didn't used to be and anyway—

Kell: *(Gently)* What did he do then?

Siubhan: What?

Kell: Did he, you know … kill himself?

Siubhan from now on is very much lost in her own world and whether or not she is physically close to Kell, we do not get the impression that she is talking to him.

Siubhan: You see, when I was wee I was always sucking my thumb. And it's a really disgusting habit, but I was able to stop and then I didn't get into as much trouble. Right! You see …

Kell: *(Unsure)* Right …

Siubhan: Then Mammy was sick for ages and Daddy was very angry all the time, specially with me. I kept burning the potatoes all the time and he said I was a dirty bitch. I can't cook very well, you see. So Mammy tried to get up and do the cooking but it was no good, because Daddy said I was spoiled and something would have to be done. So I didn't go to school any more and I did my best, but I was still useless and everyone was getting more and more angry, because I was stupid, and I was cooking worse and worse—

Kell: Jesus Christ, what a fucker!

Siubhan: No! No one understands. It was all my fault. It's all my fault because Daddy said I was as thick as a brick, and Óisín and Seán laughed and I started crying and Daddy hit them then, because Daddy said he's the only one who's allowed to make me cry. And now they hate me, because they say I get all the attention and I do, you see ... you see Daddy says I'm bad deliberately and if I don't stop he'll have to really really punish me, harder than before. And Mammy's fed up with all of it, and she doesn't sit me on her knee anymore because she's cross, very very cross with me. She's ... she says I make Daddy wild and I'll have to stop if I know what's good for me. And Daddy says Mammy doesn't love me any more because I'm awful evil, but that nothing will ever, ever beat him so he'll always have to tell me what to do, and I don't eat sweets anymore because Daddy says that Daddies don't like fat little girls, and Daddies don't like fat Mammies and when Daddy asked Mammy to put me on a diet Mammy was crying and when I asked Daddy why, he said it was because Mammy got fat when I was born and it was all my fault, and so you see ... I'm pretending every day is Lent ...

Kell: Your Da's queer in the head.

Siubhan: You're not listening ... I'm trying to say something and you're not listening.

Kell: I am.

Siubhan: I'd better go home now. Does your Daddy say the same things as my Daddy?

Pause.

Kell: No.

Siubhan: Would you die for your Daddy?

Kell: No.

Siubhan: Not even if the soldiers were going to kill him?

Kell: They don't do that, Siubhan.

Siubhan: Yes, they do. Does your Daddy sing to you?

Kell: No.

Siubhan: *(Sings)*

> Dance for your Daddy
> My bonnie lassie
> Dance for your Daddy
> For your Mammy sing
> You'll get a little fishy
> On a little dishy
> When the boat comes in.

What's wrong, Kell?

Kell: Does your Daddy kiss you?

Siubhan: Why?

Kell: I won't tell anyone.

Siubhan: *(Slightly delirious from laughing and crying)* Cross your heart and hope to die.

Kell: Cross my heart and hope to die.

Siubhan: On your Mammy's grave!

Kell: On my Mammy's grave. *(Pause)* When you're in trouble does he kiss you a lot?

Siubhan: *(Pause)* Yes. *(Silence)* Daddy says that's what girls are for.

Kell: I'm mad about you, Siubhan. I love you. I really think I love you.

Siubhan: That's what Daddy says. He calls me his Baby, his hot Baby … and sometimes it can hurt everywhere—

Kell: I know he's your Daddy, Siubhan, but he's a bad bad man.

Siubhan: No, Kell. *(Laughs)* I'm bad. Daddy says—

Kell: But you know that's not true, Siubhan. Don't you Siubhan? Don't you Siubhan? *(Silence)* When I grow up will you marry me? We can live in a big house, far away from here … I'll never tell you you're bad. I'll be good to you. Where are you going?

Siubhan: Daddy says I'm too old to be running wild.

Kell: To hell with your Daddy … I'm sorry Siubhan. Come back. You'll be here tomorrow, won't you?

Siubhan: *(nods)* Don't be silly, Kell!

Kell: I'll kill your Daddy if he hurts you one more time. *(Siubhan runs off)* Fuck! Siubhan! Please! Siubhan! Wait …

Kell runs after her.

Lights dim to blackout and come up again Stage-Left to show the front of the Doherty property.

Two dustbins in front of the house, etc.

*The moonlight casts a shimmering glow, a surreal feeling onto the bastion of **Daddy Doherty**'s power.*

The front door is hanging open and chairs are scattered around the garden.

***Nora** sings 'I'm too sexy for this street*. ***Nora** comes running out carrying a bag of rubbish. She parades around laughing and giggling, slightly tipsy. She goes over to the bin and puts the rubbish in, repeating the procedure of standing on the rubbish. Perched in the bin, she waves across the street.*

***Siubhan** is perched at the top of **Daddy Doherty**'s ladder. Waves.*

Nora: How's about you, Madge?

Siubhan: Madge McGinley, the best cow's lug in the street.

Nora: *(Mimicking)* Did you know this, Daddy Doherty, when I was in my bed last night minding my own business, I saw—

Siubhan: I happened to hear—

Nora: I happened to get out of my bed to close the window—

Siubhan: To spy on my neighbours!

Nora: Funny how you always forget to close your window, Madge …

They laugh.

Nora: The whole road'll be out in a minute!

Siubhan: Who cares?

Nora: When are they coming back?

Siubhan: Don't know, don't care. Why, do you want to go?

Nora: Well, it's just that Cormac—

Siubhan: I thought you told him you were visiting me tonight?

Nora: I did, but he thought you'd be at my place, what with … the way your—

Siubhan: Daddy is and all!

Nora: Yeah! And he'll probably ring and think we're out …

Siubhan: On the tear!

Nora: Aye, well maybe!

Siubhan: And so? He doesn't own you!

Nora: I know! It's just that …

Siubhan: You miss him?

Nora: I'm sure!

Siubhan: Why doesn't he make a decent woman of you then, if your whereabouts is so important to him?

Nora: *(Getting out of dustbin)* Siubhan, it's not that! I wouldn't know how to start all over again.

Siubhan: I don't know why you just don't forget about him, Nora—

Nora: Maybe he'll come looking for me—

Siubhan: Cormac? Slumming it? You must be joking!

Nora: Stranger things have happened!

Siubhan: Have another drink, Nora!

Nora: Maybe I should get back!

Siubhan: Nora? For the love of God, would you forget about him for one night … I've had to forget about Kell …

Nora: I blame myself, I should have thought to say … I blame myself …

Siubhan: So do we all, doesn't mean we should though, doesn't mean we are to blame.

Nora: All the same—

Siubhan: Who cares. Forget about him … I've forgotten about Kell.

Silence.

Nora: Yeah, Kell! God, why do all the decent ones have to go and get themselves killed?

Siubhan: I don't know, Nora. The good die young!

Nora: Doesn't say much for us then, does it?

Siubhan: *(Wryly)* Don't tell me you blame yourself for that too!

Nora: It … well, you know, it was a good funeral. You still love him, don't you? You'll never forget him, Siubhan!

Siubhan: Well, a person … he … you … I have to, if you see what I mean—

Nora: What's done is done, Siubhan—

Siubhan: Nora, I'm trying to say something and you're not listening—

Nora: Siubhan—

Siubhan: Nora, do you think I'd lie?

Nora: Depends?

Siubhan: You see ... Kell—

Nora: And there will be someone else, Siubhan! One day.

Siubhan: You're as bad as Mammy—

Nora: I know, it's sick, isn't it! We all end up like our Mammies—

Siubhan: Shut up ... for a minute. Do you mind them roses he gave me that time?

Nora: He wasn't stingy, I'll say that for him ... not like Penny-Pinching Cormac—

Siubhan: We were going to go to America that next week ... supposed to be going—

Nora: And you never told me! Bitch!

Siubhan: Cormac knew!

Nora: He would have told me—

Siubhan: Cormac knew we were going away—

Nora: So are you saying you're still wanting to go?

Siubhan: And of course Daddy Doherty had a great laugh, when I was left on my own—

Nora: Needless to say.

Silence.

Siubhan: After the funeral, I took the bus to Bundoran. I didn't intend coming back. I brought the roses. I had put them in a box ... Jesus, the things you do to trap a memory. When I got to the beach at Rossnowlagh it was about midnight, and I wasn't sure why I was there ... so I threw the petals out across the water as far as I could throw ... way out far ... so part of us arrived in America, and maybe the best part ... you know, the dream part ... you know what I mean? I'd never go now ... to America. It wouldn't be the same.

Nora: It's only been a year, Siubhan. It'll take time but you'll meet someone else. Sure you were always the one with the guts—

Siubhan: Aye sure! All mouth. Then I slept on the beach and watched the sun come up ... the petals were gone, you know ... they were on their way ... and you know that gave me the strength to come back ... and then last night, I ... I buried the special wreath I kept ... God knows why ...

Nora: Jesus!

Cormac is standing at the gate.

Siubhan: Cormac?

Nora: Cormac!

Cormac: Where have you been all night? I've looked everywhere—

Siubhan: Where do you think she was, Cormac? Didn't she tell you she was coming here?

Cormac: No, she did not!

Nora: Yes, I did!

Siubhan: You've a right cheek, Cormac, turning up here uninvited. You didn't even come to Kell's funeral ... but that's typical of you.

Cormac: *(To Nora)* Are you coming?

Nora: Siubhan—

Cormac: He wouldn't have wanted me to ... I was his best friend—

Siubhan: *(Slaps him)* I was his best friend! Not you! You wee shit!

Nora: Siubhan, please!

Cormac: I never did understand what he saw in you, anyway, Siubhan Doherty!

Siubhan: And what's that supposed to mean?

Nora: Cormac, stop it! Leave her alone!

Cormac: Well, alone is all the place she'll end up—

Siubhan: You couldn't stand it, could you, Cormac! Me and Kell, and you figuring nowhere. You tried to split us up and now you're trying to split me and Nora up—

Cormac: She's too good for the likes of you—

Nora: Cormac, will you shut your mouth!

Siubhan: What really happened that night, Cormac?

Nora: Siubhan, stop it! Why do you want to hurt yourself like this?

Cormac: Kell was a fool, Siubhan, in more ways than one!

Siubhan: Why? Because he didn't do everything you said ... and then the one last favour! Is that what happened, Cormac? Did you sell him out to save your own hide?

Cormac: Dream on, you stupid bitch!

Nora: Cormac, shut your mouth now or you'll never see me again—

Cormac: Aye, Nora, sure!

Nora: Yes, Cormac!

Mammy and Daddy Doherty standing at the fence.

Nora: And ... Daddy Doherty!

Daddy: Clear to hell out of here now!

Mammy: Daddy, please!

Daddy: Shut your mouth! And you, you drunken cow, in the house!

Siubhan: Watch me, I'm shaking.

Nora: Don't you think Siubhan's a bit old to be hit now, Mr Doherty?

Mammy: I think you youngsters should run off home now.

Siubhan: Let Nora alone, Mammy!

Mammy: I told you to look after the place, Siubhan! How often does your Daddy bring me out? Well, Siubhan! Couldn't you have done as you were told, just the once?

Cormac: Come on, Nora. Let's hit the road!

Nora: You go. I'm not leaving Siubhan.

Lights come up on Stage-Right to show partially built second floor of a house in a building site of an estate.

The moonlight casts a shimmering glow, a surreal feeling, onto the bastion of **Daddy Doherty** *s property, his power, on Stage-Left.*

Stage-Right is the bastion of the Children and Dream, as it were.

Kell *enters. He stands in the entrance, then sits down.*

He talks to **Siubhan** *as if she were there. This is the past.*

Siubhan *answers him in the present.*

Simultaneous action and dialogue from the characters increasing the alienation of the characters from one another, except **Siubhan** *and the dead* **Kell** *in the end.*

Daddy *is trying to repair the rung on his ladder.*

Cormac *is trying to talk sense to* **Nora.**

Mammy *is trying to placate* **Daddy.**

The **Tramp-Lady** *is seated on the street, on the rope-swing, pulling old clothes from a black plastic bag.*

Kell: Next week Siubhan, we'll sail away—

Siubhan: For a year and a day!

Daddy: I'll year and a day you—

Mammy: Siubhan, please—

Nora: Go home Cormac please—

Cormac: Come with me.

Siubhan: I know something'll happen—

Kell: To stop us going? Your head's a marley. What could possibly happen?

Mammy: Daddy, leave that till the morning … Siubhan, get in the house—

Siubhan: This is our life!

Kell: Our life!

Nora: Siubhan?

Daddy: This is my house.

Mammy: This is your Daddy's house.

Siubhan: And their house isn't my life any longer! We're leaving and—

Kell: And we won't be back—

Daddy: No one's going anywhere until I give the say so.

Mammy: Cormac, will you please take Nora home.

Nora: I'll go when Siubhan tells me to go.

Kell: They'll be sorry when you go—

Siubhan: No!

Mammy: Siubhan!

Kell: They miss the boys—

Siubhan: The boys, the bloody boys—

Daddy: I hope for your sake that you'll do as you're told! Understand!

Siubhan: No more: do this, do that!

Kell: Get here, get there—

Mammy: She's drunk … you're drunk, Siubhan—

Nora: Back off Doherty!

Cormac: Stop interfering, Nora …

*Nora stands in front of him shielding **Siubhan**.*

***Cormac** stands beside **Nora** in front of **Daddy Doherty**.*

***Mammy** walking everywhere.*

Daddy: I thought I told you to leave!

Nora: You watch your step then!

Cormac: You're not the only one with pull around here, you know!

Mammy: Haven't yous your own homes to go to?

Siubhan: Some homes!

Kell: Our own will be different, I promise you.

Siubhan: Have you ever been sea-sick?

Mammy: Siubhan, what are you blathering on about now?

Kell: Once … it's not that bad!

Mammy decides to take control.

Mammy: Now look, Nora, there's nothing going to happen to Siubhan … I promise you. We've all had a bit too much to drink—

Nora: Well, if it's alright with you, Mrs Doherty, I'll stay till he's calmed down—

Mammy: Look Nora! No one interferes with my family! Go home!

Siubhan: What a joke! Don't you mean outsiders, Mammy? No one interferes with your family! His family is what we are. His pieces of trash! Who let him go right ahead, who suffered the most, Mammy? Him? Or Óisín? Or Seán? Or you? Or … me?

Mammy: Don't be silly, Siubhan!

Cormac: This is none of our business, Nora. For the last time, we're going!

*Cormac goes to leave. **Nora** watches him leave.*

Nora: Coward!

Mammy: You should go with him!

Nora: No one tells me what to do!

Daddy: Clear off my land, you miserable seal-cows!

Mammy: Daddy! Stop shouting!

Tramp-Lady: *(Pulling out more clothes)* All they give me is rubbish!

Mammy: I'm sorry you're so upset … Siubhan … I'm sorry—

Daddy: What is there to be sorry about for her?

Mammy: Daddy!

Daddy: It's her should be sorry-

Siubhan: I never thought I'd have anyone who'd care about what I thought!

Daddy: Why should anyone?

Kell: Neither did I!

Siubhan: I'd love to see Cormac's face, when he finds out we're gone for good.

Nora: So would I, Siubhan when he realises I'm not going to follow him home—

Siubhan: Do you think Nora'll—

Kell: Be mad? No, I doubt it. She wants to see you happy—

Daddy: Get in the house, Siubhan! Do you think it matters what you think? Eh? Ehhh? Get in the house and get to your bed!

Mammy: Do as your Daddy says, Siubhan!

Siubhan: My bed! That's a laugh!

Mammy: The man's the head of the house! That's the way it is, Siubhan.

Daddy: He who pays says, Siubhan—

Siubhan: I pay—

Daddy: Aye sure!

Siubhan: That's right! I pay … I've paid my price, you bastard!

Mammy: That's the way it is—

Siubhan: No Mammy! That's the way you let it be, not the way it is. How can he ever do anything decent for his wife, when he never never did anything decent with his own daughter? Did you hear me? God damn you. Listen to me! When he never did anything decent with his own daughter!

Nora: Siubhan … Oh God … I'm sorry!

Mammy: Stop making things up, Siubhan.

Nora: Siubhan doesn't lie, Mrs Doherty!

Daddy: This is ridiculous—

Mammy: This is none of your business Nora. Now go home before I call the police—

Daddy: No one'll call the police. Everyone is going inside! *(Gentler)* Come on, Siubhan! You don't take after me as regards holding your drink, anyway!

Siubhan: I've never seen you scared before—

Mammy: Nora, go home!

Siubhan kicks down a portion of Daddy s fence.

Siubhan: You miserable … good for nothing … there, there's your damn fence in bits—

Daddy hits Siubhan across the fence.

Daddy pushes her aside and goes to kneel beside the fence.

Mammy rushes to his side.

Daddy stands up.

Daddy: Get inside, Siubhan!

Siubhan: No! No more excuses ... fine! Your bloody house! Your rules! Your brothel! Your torture chamber!

Mammy is crying.

Mammy: Siubhan, how could you do this to me?

Siubhan: How could he do it to me?

Daddy: She's making it up!

Mammy: Siubhan, tell me you're making it up—

Siubhan: No!

Mammy: Siubhan, please!

Siubhan: Don't tell me you didn't know—

Mammy: I—

Daddy: Don't tell me you believe her?

Mammy: I ... I—

Daddy: Understand this, you little slut ... *(Goes to hit her, but Nora pushes him back)*

Nora: Leave her alone.

Mammy gets up to go.

Mammy: I don't believe this is ... I can't ...

Mammy sits down on the doorstep.

Kell: You tried very hard, Siubhan—

Siubhan: So did you, Kell!

Kell: It's nearly over—

Siubhan: Soon it'll all be a memory—

Kell: You might never forget, Siubhan ... but I'll always be with you.

Siubhan: You always will, Kell ... and I'm going to leave all of this and all of them—

Kell: The two of us—

Siubhan: Hand in hand—

Kell: With a song and a wave—

Siubhan: Up to the moon, and far far beyond—

Tramp-Lady: The borders of wishing and dreaming—

Kell: On an ocean of milk.

Daddy: You're mad … mad as a coot … talking to yourself all the time.

Nora: Look at yourself!

Siubhan: Don't bother … I'm leaving … I wouldn't mind, if it wasn't for Mammy—

Daddy: Leave then … I won't have you upsetting your Mammy much more—

Mammy: Please … someone, please …

Nora: You can stay with me, Siubhan!

Siubhan: I think there is such things as ghosts, Kell!

Nora: It'll get better … I promise. You've got more guts than the rest of us, and I'll help you.

Siubhan: They'll blame—

Nora: What would they know!

Siubhan: They'll deny—

Nora: People always do. Forget about them … as … as much as you can …

Siubhan: Right!

Nora: After you …

Siubhan: After you …

Nora: *(Siubhan knocks over the dustbin as she leaves)* Doctor, Doctor, I keep thinking I'm a dustbin—

Mammy: I love you, Siubhan!

Siubhan: Nora, don't talk rubbish …

Siubhan and *Nora* laugh and *Daddy* peeks from behind a
curtained window.

Lights dim on rope-swing.

Lights come up.

Mammy is sitting at the front door. *Daddy* comes out with a bag of
rubbish. He offers it to *Mammy*. She doesn t take it. *Daddy* goes
over to the dustbin and crams the bag into the bin by standing on
the rubbish. He goes inside. Lights dim to blackout.

The End.

When I began to write this play, it seemed to me that the predominant centre-stage relationships in the history of Irish theatre were between fathers and sons, men and history, and culture as it related to the dominant rituals. Breaking the silence of the absent centre-stage figures was essential to me if there were to appear female characters who might evolve from being extensions of the cipher into holistic characters in their own right.

In writing *Howling Moons, Silent Sons,* I was attempting to demythologise some of the more prevalent myths in the society and on the stage. The location of the play encompassed the private domesticity as opposed to the bar – the No-place of the Tramp-Lady, the private den of the children, the cramped housing conditions of the residents on the Westside. The play attempts to look at the inseparable connection between how we treat children and what we as adults think of ourselves, to look at female friendship – the notion of History – debunking it as a linear phenomenon. Time for Siubhan is a set of relationships. The present is the past and the future is the past. Her flashbacks and attempts to empower herself are hampered by all the old myths and rituals. In order to creatively self-actualise, she needs to forge a new set of belief systems.

I look back fondly on the long train journeys from Pontoon to Dublin, armed with new pages of script throughout the year between the staged reading and the final production. That first entry into the collaborative world between playwright, actor, director, stage manager, lighting person, etc., forged the way I have always tried to work since.

As regards rights of participation, abuse and neglect, freedom of expression, thought, conscience, religion, association and privacy, adoption and health services, any complacency about children's rights is totally misplaced. The courts imprison children; there are increasing numbers of homeless children, and the traveller child is the recipient of all the inequities that society can offer. If we say that culture is a set of stories, then it is imperative that the stories of women move centre-stage and not be left languishing off-stage.

Deirdre Hines

The Ash Fire

A Play in Two Acts

Gavin Kostick

The Ash Fire was first presented by Pigsback Theatre Company at Project Arts Centre on 5 October 1992 as part of the Dublin Theatre Festival. It then returned to Project and toured to the Tricycle Theatre (London), Foyle Arts Centre, Riverside Theatre, Everyman Palace, Belltable Arts Centre, Garter Lane Arts Centre, Hawkswell Theatre, Garage Theatre, Old Museum Arts Centre, Mayfest (Glasgow), Traverse Theatre (Edinburgh) and Taibhearc Theatre from January to May 1993. The production had the following cast and production team:

Cissy Katzmeir Kathy Downes
Nat Katzmeir Peter Hanly
Cait O'Shaughnessy Clodagh O'Donoghue
Rube Katzmeir Paul Hickey
Abe Katzmeir Paul Meade
Doris Hughes Karen Ardiff

Director Jim Culleton
Set Designers Fiona Leech and Fiona Whelan
Costume Designer Léonore McDonagh
Lighting Designer Paul Keogan
Choreographer Gráinne McArdle
Production Manager Susie Shiel
Stage Manager Eadaoín Keenan
Administrator/PR Janice McAdam
Dublin Theatre Festival Director Tony O'Dalaigh

The Ash Fire won the BBC/Stewart Parker Trust Award for Best First Play in 1992. The production was nominated for an EMA award.

Photo (l-r): Paul Meade, Peter Hanly and Paul Hickey as Abe, Nat and Rube © Colm Henry

Dramatis Personae

Nat, **Abe**, and **Rube** are three Polish–Jewish brothers, in their twenties or perhaps early thirties (they themselves would not possess birth certificates). What do they look like? Essentially, they look like each other. The director should not be too quick to search for actors that look 'Jewish' to play the parts. The search for an archetypal 'Jewish' look is, in any case, a fool's errand. It is more important that the audience can believe that these three men are all stamped by the look of their father. In relation to each other, **Abe** would be the tallest and most handsome, **Nat's** physique would be the more sinewy, particularly in his hands, and **Rube's** essentially pleasant features and frame should be off-set by a nervous clumsiness, and a self-conscious aura of embarrassment – at least when he is in company.

   Cissy, wife of **Nat**, is a straight-backed matriarch in the making. She does not need to be tall, but her carriage is proud and certain. **Nat** married 'up' when he married her, and though she slots into the traditional family position of wife and mother, this in no way implies a meek subservience. **Cait**, the girl from downstairs, is an Irish teenager, whose face suggests a lively nature, somewhat damaged already by years of poverty and the essential dishonesty of her father. Last is **Doris,** the political activist and 'problem' character of the play. She, and the incident in which she first appears, are in fact taken from newspaper reports of the day. There we see a pale, rather moon-faced young woman, whose severity of hair and clothes seem to contract around a figure of great beauty.

ACT ONE

A medium-sized, new-looking room on the upper floor of a two-storey house. It has a lino floor and darkish walls. The entrance to the flat is at the front, Stage-Right. We can see the stairs leading down to the front door of the house. At Stage-Left there are two sinks with a draining board in between them. They have no taps. Between the sinks and the back wall there is access to a small cooking area, where there is also a fire. The window to the street is at the front. There is an exit to another room at the back of Stage-Left.

Scene One

*At the moment the room is full of tea chests and covered furniture. **Cissy** and **Nat** are in the process of unpacking, and we can perhaps make out the shapes of a dresser, a tin bath and an easy chair. An old-fashioned crib is in plain view. **Cissy** is singing. **Nat** is hovering by the window. It is September.*

Cissy: It's as if you'd never learned to write.

Nat: Write? I did write.

Cissy: A letter of three sentences.

Nat: What was there to say? They said they would arrive the first Monday after Rosh Hoshanna, I told them the address.

Cissy: So I'm getting things ready, stop fretting.

Nat: Who's fretting? It is you who are hurling yourself around. Upsetting Padraig.

Cissy: Are you upset Padraig? Are you fast asleep? Are you dreaming Padraig?

Nat: They'll be delighted to have their own rooms.

Cissy: I'm delighted they'll be delighted. Now get the other end of this.

Nat: They were in with Hyam during his illness. It is not an easy thing to share with a sick man.

Cissy: They'll be happy here.

Nat: He could never have lasted to America. I don't know how Abe supported them.

Cissy: Nat, I think your precious delivery boys have made a mistake.

Nat: What do you mean?

Cissy: With us Nat, we've got an extra tea chest.

Nat: How do you mean?

Cissy: I mean there's one more than there ought to be. How do you think I mean?

Nat: You oversaw the packing. How did it go?

Cissy: Bedding and clothes, your tool box and work, my crockery and cutlery. This is silly, what box is that?

Nat: The dresser.

Cissy: How do you mean the dresser?

Nat: *(Reveals bits of wood)* The dresser see. We decided to put it in a box.

Cissy: *(Faintly)* How did you fit it in?

Nat: Oh the bits that wouldn't fit I broke up, look. It was all dowels, panel pins and not enough glue. We can use it for firewood. That's all it was worth.

Cissy: You've broken up our dresser. If that's the dresser, *(Turning to covered piece of furniture)* what's?—

Nat: Aha. *(Reveals much finer dresser)* A moving-in present Mrs Katzmeir, that's what.

Cissy: Oh Nat. You said you were taboganning.

Nat: *(Dismissively)* Toboganning! I was busy getting the necessaries ready.

Cissy: How did you sprain your wrist then?

Nat: I still had a little free time. You'll have to allow for this carving being done left handed.

Cissy: I'd be surprised if there is a difference.

Nat: *(Excitedly)* Do you see?

Cissy: *(Dutifully)* It is beautiful.

Nat: Look, this is in three panels, one for each day Jonah was in the belly of the fish. The same number of days we were on the boat. And this design is repeated forty times, for Moses led our people through the wilderness for forty years, and it took forty days for us to come from Lublin to Dublin.

Cissy: *(Amused by her husband s enthusiasm)* Forty days?

Nat: If you add on six days for … for no good reason.

Cissy: That is oak isn't it?

Nat: It is, very good Mrs Katzmeir.

Cissy is dreaming.

Nat: *(Gently)* I didn't drop it deliberately.

Cissy: You held on to Yzaak's tool box.

Nat: Well, one was more important than the other.

Cissy: It was my only possession.

Nat: That you'll never see again. *(Pause)* Unless, my bride, you stop dreaming and open this drawer.

Cissy opens drawer.

Cissy: My dowry box! How did you … ? It's beautiful. It's like new. It is new. It's identical. *(Opens it)* If only it could have …

Nat: You married a cabinet-maker, not a magician.

Cissy: This is magic enough for me. The inscription.

Nat: I modernised it a little.

Cissy: *(Reading)* 'To my wife Cissy and my son … ', Nat, do you think you should have?

Nat: I had already done it before the name was changed. Then I hurt my wrist and couldn't alter it again.

Cissy: It's not such a good idea.

Nat: Why not? It's unspoken. Something to remind us of the way we could have been. It's a fitting tribute, and one day when Padraig is a man, God be willing, it will be a good story to tell him.

Cissy: As you say.

Cait enters, carrying milk.

Cait: I hope that'll be enough to last.

Cissy: *(Slightly stiffly)* I'm sure it will be.

Cissy puts milk down, then goes over to sing a lullaby to Padraig.

Nat: How is your Da?

Cait: He's got a fever to distract him from his hip. It doesn't matter, he won't be out of bed for weeks anyway.

Nat: Think of reasons for him to want to get better. A man is only sick so long as he has given up on fate. *(Pause)* This is none of my business …

Cissy: True.

Nat: *(Ignoring her)* But, are you … Have his sickness benefits run out?

Cait: Two weeks ago.

Nat: And you could use some money?

Cait: Yes. But your rent is plenty. We can't put you under the hammer the second you move in.

Nat: I should hope not, but you do need some more income.

Cait: Everything that isn't pawned is on HP, we have the worst credit on the street.

Nat: I wasn't thinking of a loan. I was thinking of a job. A favour for a favour. Would you be interested in being employed by us?

Cait: Me?

Nat: As a *(Searches for right phrase)* domestic help. We are going to be expanding, here and down at the shop. I could pay you three pence an hour, maybe six hours a week.

Cait: That's far too much, anyway, I couldn't.

Nat: If you won't do it, I'll have to get in someone else. I need a cleaner.

Cait: *(Firmly)* Tuppence an hour. No more than a shilling a week. And thank you. What needs doing, Mrs Katzmeir?

Cissy: *(Distracted with putting objects in box).* Hmm?

Cait: *(In mock Cork accent)* At your service Ma'am. *(Curtsies)*

Nat: You will need the help.

Cissy: You can't be our maid. I am quite capable *(Sees **Nat's** face, realises there is more to it, takes out kitchen utensils).* You'll have to learn what goes where. We have to be very particular about this.

Nat: *(At window)* Here they are! We are not unpacked. Cait, please go and show them up.

Cait gives a little curtsey – she is still play-acting a maid. Then goes out. Cissy and Nat get themselves ready to receive. Nat licks his fingers and wets down the front of his hair neatly.

Nat: I will tell them to treat you as a mother.

Cissy: *(With irony)* I'll put my black shawl on. *(Looking him over)* You look very prosperous.

Nat: We shall sit here.

Cissy: I'll stay out of the way. I hope all goes well.

*Cait returns with **Rube** and **Abe**. They have a tin trunk each. They are wearing large crumpled coats and hats, which they tip politely.*

*Nat and Cissy say 'Shalom to each, and **Rube** and **Abe** respond 'Shalom .*

Abe: The old mezuzah on the door gave you away.

[Stage note: A mezuzah is a rectangular block of wood, about the size of the edge of a box of matches, which is put on the outer doors of Jewish houses at a slightly off-vertical angle.]

Their eyes are shining and they are almost laughing with pleasure.

Nat: What a thing, what a thing. To see my brothers again. Sit down, sit down. You must be exhausted. I have a special treat for you.

*Nat looks around, **Cissy** is making tea. **Cait** has gone to help.*

Abe: What a crossing. Koussevitsky's samovar, you hung on to it.

Cissy: Would you like some tea, boys?

Abe: Yes please.

Rube: Yes.

Cait passes cups around.

Abe: Thank you.

Nat: This is Miss Caitlin O'Shaughnessy, she is our downstairs neighbour, who is also our landlord.

Cait: Also your domestic.

Nat: These are my brothers, Abe and Rube, fresh from London. You were saying about the crossing.

Abe: The Leinster.

Rube: We posted ourselves.

Abe: We came on the mail ship.

Rube: I found a lovely sack to sleep on.

Abe: I brought the letters we'd meant to send.

Rube: Which contained half a cured ham. So I stink of pig. Sorry.

Nat: *(Proud of his house s amenities)* Don't worry. You can have a bath. Would you care to rest? We have a spare bed in the other room.

Rube: Later, thank you. These are lovely rooms.

Cissy: Thank you.

Nat: When we first came to Dublin we were put up by the Goldsterns in Portobello. They kept us for three years but our family was becoming too large.

Abe: Oy, Cissy. We should have asked, did you ...? I see a crib.

Nat: Boys, I am a father.

Abe: Congatulations.

Rube: Yes, congratulations.

Hugs are exchanged. They look in the crib.

Abe: Congratulations Cissy.

Cissy: A boy.

Abe: You really should have told us. Hyam would have loved to have heard.

Nat: You know me and writing. I thought, Hyam will know *(With religious emphasis)* all things soon enough. A little surprise for him in the New World.

Abe: And how old is he?

Nat: Six weeks old.

Rube: You called him Yzaak then?

Nat: No, no.

Cissy: We called him Padraig.

Abe: Padraig?

Rube: But you promised to call him after Cissy's uncle—

Nat: No, no. We changed his name to Padraig.

Cissy: After the great Irish nationalist Padraig Pearse.

Abe: An Irish Nationalist already. You do settle down quickly.

Nat: We have to look forward. Pearse was a man who died for the creation of his country. It seemed a suitable choice.

Rube: Oh Cissy, he's ...

Cissy: Sick, that's what he is. Don't worry, that's my job. You must settle down and have a milk cookie and talk.

Nat: Ah, yes. Boys, I have been thinking what is to be done for the best, Abe. I know what we were like in the old country, but a decision was made that neither of us wished for, and now here we are in a country none of us had heard of. When I came here I had nothing but this box, which was Cissy's uncle's box, and now I will pass it on to you. You can be my apprentice, and when you have mastered the trade, my partner. There is a kind of good fate in this.

Abe: This is too kind.

Nat: Not at all. *(Dante s dedication)* 'The better craftsman'. I've been reading. We'll be able to corner the market. Brother cabinet-makers.

Abe: I am going to say something difficult.

Nat: We could start this afternoon. You can come down to the shop with me.

Abe: I am too old to become an apprentice.

Nat: What else have you qualifications for? It has not been your fault, but you need a career now.

Abe: But not necessarily as a cabinet maker.

Nat: Why not as a cabinet maker? It was good enough for your grandfather and his father.

Abe: But this is a new world. I have seen many new things in London. I would like time to think what to do with myself.

Nat: What? *(With irony)* Do you want a career in radio, in films?

Abe: Perhaps. I don't know.

Nat: Why don't you start work with me, then look around you, if you find anything better.

Abe: But I wouldn't find anything better. Look at this kit. I can see you have prepared it beautifully for me. It is too much. If I take this, I will never let it go. I am so selfish, but I wish to know what else I could be. Does this make sense? I expect I shall come crawling to you for the chance, but could you give me some time to think? To let me believe that I'm making my own choice?

Nat: Time, how much time?

Abe: A matter of weeks. Everything is open to me now. If I come down to your shop I would like it to be because I want to come to your shop.

Nat: You are making a choice now. Once this is behind you, you will not go back.

Pause.

Nat: Rube, I have found you a job.

Rube: Where?

Nat: Working in a huge place. The Guinness brewery. Actually I didn't get you the job, Cait's father did. We are very grateful to them, you can start on Friday.

Rube: What will I be doing?

Nat: Loading kegs onto the delivery trucks to start. That should build you up. But there's lots of jobs there, you may find yourself moved around.

Rube: Thank you. Thank you Cait.

Cait: It was no bother.

Nat: How was it with Hyam?

Abe: To be honest, not good. He was not a very old man you know. We may as well have come with you, the crossing to London was as bad for him as any attempt at America. He smoked continuously. He spoke of you often.

Nat: I thought of him.

Abe: He is very proud of you. Very fond of Cissy. He said that you are the head of the household. He said that he was sure that the family could not be in better hands.

Nat: Let us light a memorial candle for the soul of our dear father. I have said the mourners' kaddish for him *(Just getting his attention)*, Rube, I would say part of the memorial prayer with you.

Cissy: It's time we were going. We have to see the priest on his round. Apparently it's good manners if you've just moved in. Cait, will you show me the way?

Cait: Of course.

Nat: When will tea be?

Cissy: Not for a few hours. Six. It's a herring stew.

Abe: Goodbye Cissy, Cait.

Rube: Goodbye.

While they are on the stairs, and going out the door.

Cait: I'm not really sure where Fr McCree will be.

Cissy: It doesn't matter. I'm letting them say a prayer for their father in peace.

Cait: Cissy. Why did Rube need a job, why doesn't he work for Nat?

Cissy: Rube is a schlemiel. It is not his fault. He has no talent.

While their dialogue takes place **Nat** *says, 'Together for our father , and the brothers chant the prayer. They are facing east.* **Abe** *falters slightly.*

Nat: You are a little out of practice Abe.

Abe: Thankfully one doesn't say the memorial prayer very often.

Nat: It may be one day that we have need of a shul *[synagogue]* here. Then the people of the tribe of Levy will be needed for the readings.

Abe: I'm sure you will be available.

Nat: All of the the Levy should.

Rube: *(Interrupting)* Where do we put our belongings?

Nat: That shelf. Clothes in this box. *(**Nat** opens letters which **Abe** has given him)*

Abe: Nat, your letters.

Nat: *(Reading)* You saw Tottenham play.

Rube: *(Sings)* Glory, Glory Tottenham Hotspur.

Abe: Many times.

Nat: £6,000 for a footballer.

Abe: He was always injured.

Rube: And we were relegated.

Nat: *(Reading the spine of a book)* William Morris on Unions.

Abe: The Arts and Crafts man.

Nat: The English socialist.

Rube: *(Looking out of window)* Which way is that?

Nat: South. You see that tower. That's the hop store, for the Guinness factory.

Rube: *(Uncertainly)* It's good to have work.

Nat: Look, *(Produces bottle of Guinness)* a Hebrew version. Isn't that something?

Abe: Very decorative.

Nat: Hebrew is a practical language.

Abe: Well, not for ordering groceries.

Nat: There are plenty of kosher shops around. Or has your interest waned a little?

Abe: I am always pleased to find new shops.

Nat: And with what do you plan to buy your buying?

Abe: I will find a way. I am not afraid of work.

Nat: Just afraid of working for me?

Abe: I thought the idea was to work *with* you.

Nat: An apprentice is still an apprentice.

Rube: Will you stop bickering?

Nat: Sorry Rube.

Abe: *(Joking)* You don't expect us to get on?

Rube: We have to work together. I mean in a manner of speaking.

Abe: I know what you meant.

Nat: That is what I'm offering him.

Abe: Truce, truce, Nat, give me time.

Nat: Alright. In this room we won't fight. And if we do *(To Rube)* you can referee.

Rube: I would rather contribute.

Nat: *(Uneasily)* You will be bringing in a wage.

Rube: I know. But I think I could be of some use to the business as well.

Nat: In what way?

Rube: Well, while we were in London I learned to keep books, for the Maccoby's store.

Nat: I don't keep books, like that. I don't need books like that.

Rube: But I learned something about bookkeeping. If you are clever, like their previous boy, you think, 'I will remember this bill and write it in later', or 'I have added up this column twice and it balances so I will not do it a third time.' But if you are slow, and write everything down as it happens, if you don't trust the sums in your head, then you cannot risk being careless or lazy.

Nat: You have not been in this country. This country is different to England.

Rube: With straight books the money comes in and out and you know what you can afford, what you need. But if you still think it is all craft, trust and waiting to be paid …

Nat: No, no. These people understand. If I make a promise to a man, I will keep that promise, until the Day of Atonement. They appreciate that, and the promises they make in return they will keep, unless they say, 'Sure, I'll have it for you in the morning', then I know they are lying. We understand each other. The day I arrived in Dublin was the same day as the Papal Nuncio, the envoy of the Pope, his mouth. This was a great thing for them. It set their church's approval on their long fight you see. They had bunting up in every street, electric lights, parties. Fate was at work in that the day we arrived was the day the city celebrated. They were so happy. I was in O'Connell Street when the Papal Nuncio went past, *wumph*, ten thousand Irish knelt as one. I could see tops of heads from Parnell Square to O'Connell Bridge, until I was dragged down. I was taught by a nun to ceili and she had to hitch her habit above her ankle. I hope you still have a few tunes or you will be ashamed. If they have no money they give in kind and in kindness. It is a whole different way.

Rube: I know I am no craftsman, but I think I could help run the business.

Abe: Why not? There is no harm.

Nat: I tell you, there is no need, only I know the full accounts.

Rube: I will help you keep track. For the future. I am grateful for the job, but let me be useful. I'll keep a ledger.

Nat: There is no need.

Rube: Nat. You needn't pay me unless I make you money. You can look after yourself, but what about the government?

Nat: I don't understand ...

Rube: I could make sure your taxes are right. You cannot pay your taxes with gifts of sideboards, or if you did you could get into trouble. I have dealt with men in offices. I could help look after you.

End of scene.

Scene Two

Doris Hughes *is alone in the room. She is standing with her back to the audience, looking out of the window. She is smoking. She is a solid-looking woman who is actually young, but could pass for a few years older. She does not seem nervous or curious about being in this strange house.* ***Cait*** *enters.* ***Doris*** *turns. It is October.*

Cait: Are you Doris Hughes?

Doris: Yes. When are the bailiffs due?

Cait: Any time. They're coming downstairs.

Doris: I know. You get a better view from here.

Cait: Do you think we can stop them?

Doris: Perhaps, with some help. It's been done before.

Cait: Have you done it before.

Doris: Yes.

Cait: What happened?

Doris: *(With a slight smile)* I got let off with a warning.

Cait: They go easy on women.

Doris: That's not true.

Cait: Protestant women, with an education.

*We see **Abe** and **Rube** coming in the front door (which isn't locked).*

Doris: Ní miste do gach uile bheann a bheith páirteach i ngluaiseacht na saoirse. *[The struggle for freedom involves all women.]*

Cait: Ach ceapaim go bhfuil cuid acu níos saoire ná an chuid eile. *[But seems to make some more free than others.]*

Doris: Real freedom for women can only come with freedom for all workers.

*Abe and **Rube** enter.*

Rube: Cait, there are—

Cait: Abe, Rube. This is Doris.

*Pause. **Cait** is not going to make any more explanations.*

Doris: Of the Cumman na mBan. I'm here to help keep out the bailiffs.

Abe: Is it that bad?

Cait nods.

Rube: What are you going to do?

Doris: Reason them into seeing their real duty.

Abe: Which is?

Doris: Not to serve the interests of the capitalist property-owning barons, but to show solidarity with their working-class comrades.

Abe: Are you to be evicted?

Cait: No. Just to have all our furniture repossessed.

Rube: Can you renegotiate terms?

Cait: Not any more.

Abe: This is within the law?

Doris: It is quite against the law to try and bar them.

Abe: But you're only going to try and talk them out of taking the furniture.

Doris: I'm going to start like that.

Rube: There must be a different way of settling this. If Nat were here—

Abe: We can't break the law.

Doris: I'm not asking you to.

Abe: I mean we can't get into trouble. We can be deported.

Rube: We should not be here.

Abe: We are technically in America.

Rube: Nat and Cissy jumped ship at the wrong port.

Abe: It was night. They thought it was New York.

Rube: The captain told them it was New York.

Abe: It was Cobh harbour.

Rube: There are no visas for us to go anywhere anymore.

Doris: *(Who has been keeping an eye on the window)* Time to go.

Doris moves determinedly out. Closely followed by Cait.

Rube: We are not to become involved.

Abe: True.

They pause, look at each other. Then go to the window.

Rube: There are no men there to help them.

Abe: Doris seems to be making her points clearly though. *(Touches glass)* She's making the windows rattle.*(Pause, suddenly very angry)* Bastard goyem.

Abe rushes out down the stairs.

Rube: Abe! We are not …

He starts to follow uncertainly. End of scene.

Scene Three

Cissy is alone with the crib. It is winter. She starts to sing a lullaby, 'We Live on the Edge of Town . It is sentimental and centres on what the baby will be when he is grown. **Nat** *enters the front door, he is coming home from work. He hears her singing. He moves quietly up the stairs. He waits behind the door, timing his entrance perfectly to enter at the second verse, which he sings in Yiddish.* **Cissy** *joins back in the chorus in English which they sing in harmony.*

Nat: Sweet Polish dreams.

Cissy: Sweet Irish dreams.

End of Scene

Scene Four

Rube *is alone in the flat. He is trying to dance, which requires all his concentration. He clips the edge of the table, which nearly upsets the samovar. It is February.*

Rube: *(Frustrated and angry)* Don't hit the table. Don't hit the table. Don't hit anything.

Cait has been hovering. She enters.

Cait: What are you up to?

Rube: We have to go to a wedding.

Cait: Whereabouts?

Rube: Little Jerusalem. I think it's called Portobello properly. The Goldsterns. They took Nat and Cissy in when they first arrived. It is their second daughter who is getting married. I'll have to dance at it. Everyone will have to dance at it.

Cait: How do you dance?

Rube: I'd show you if I could. *(He makes clumsy moves)* Like this.

Cait: Would it help if you had a partner?

Rube: It would.

Cait: Where do I put my hands?

Rube: Up here.

Cait: Just put them where they should be.

Rube: We're not supposed to touch. We don't touch our dancing partners.

Cait: Then what's the point?

Rube: Try it. Here, like this. Keep your arms up. *(They move around)* That's the first lap of the room where I haven't hit anything.

Cait: Try a foxtrot. Only we'll have to touch for that. Here *(Puts hands in place)*. Back and side and—

Rube: I'm going to tread on your feet.

Cait: No you're not. Now. *(Hums foxtrot; they dance well)* You've done this before.

Rube completes the dance. They split.

Cait: What makes you say you're clumsy? You're not at all. How's the job going?

Rube: It's fine thanks.

Cait: No it's not, it's hell. Da was in the loading bay for twenty years.

Rube: They all miss him.

Cait: Like I'd miss the sound of coughing in the mornings. They all hated him. He was a foreman. It wasn't so bad when he was just a worker, but when he got in charge of things. Put it like this, do you like your boss?

Rube: No.

Cait: So three full kegs got rolled onto him and smashed his hip. Nobody was sorry. Nobody had made a mistake. Can I ask you something?

Rube: Yes.

Cait: What's a schlemiel?

Rube: *(Very still)* A fool. Some one who's unlucky. Some one who will not complete a task.

Cait: Would you like to be a cabinet maker?

Rube: There's like and there's able and they're two different things. I get too enthusiastic you see. Yzaak, he's our uncle, would ask me to plane a bit of wood, and I'd shave and I'd shave, and I'd think, 'Next push and it'll be flat', but I'd never see if I'd got it in the vice wrong, or if the blade was angled, but I wouldn't want to stop. Then no more wood.

Cait: What about dancing?

Rube: I never had the concentration for it. I'm only practising out of fear. It's our first big event and we'll both be required to show off for the mothers.

Cait: Who told you you can't dance?

Rube: I just can't. You should see Abe and Nat.

Cait: I'd rather see you. *(Pause)* You can dance.

Rube: No.

Cait: Yes. I'm telling you you can. You have everything it takes. It's only because you've been told that you can't. Is there anything you like doing?

Rube: Nothing useful. Nothing grown-up.

Cait: What is it?

Rube: I like to make up stories.

Cait: I thought so, from looking at your face when you were talking to Padraig. Tell me a story.

Rube: They're for children.

Cait: Tell me the last one you told Padraig.

Rube: This is the story of the Princess and perfection.

Cait: *(Being lifted onto the table)* Janey!

Rube: Once there was a princess who said that she would only marry the person who brought her the perfect gift, because, she said only that person would love her perfectly. The first gift was a diamond necklace made with flawless gems which dazzled her eyes with their rainbow of colours.

She took each gem and inspected it in turn. She ground each gem beneath her heel, they were perfect, but she threw it back. 'This gift contains no love', she said, 'the clasp is cheap'. The second gift was an Arab stallion of great haughtiness, who barely deigned to tread his hooves upon the ground and had a neck with an arc that matched the grace of the prow of a ship, but she found fault with that too, for it had no saddle and harness fit for a princess. And so she went on and on, each gift becoming more precious than the last and each dejected suitor suffering and sighing more than the one before. Finally there came a man, and he said, 'This is my gift. If we marry, I shall leave you in peace to run the country, and whatever you decide shall become law, I want none other from you than you call me husband.' And this the princess accepted, for she decided that the perfect gift was to be allowed to run her life as she saw fit.

*During the story, **Rube** has been doing some acting out. The implication of which is that **Cait** is the princess and he, the suitor.*

Cait: Did they have a wonderful wedding?

Rube: The country was not sober for three days.

Cait: And did they kiss?

Rube: They did. For they had come to be *(Very close to **Cait** now. Slowly)* very much in …

They kiss. They don t really stop except for the dialogue.

Cait: You're not a fool. You're not a schlemiel.

Rube: I have watched you by the pump, in the street.

Cait: You can do whatever you want.

Rube: Coming home from work. I run to the end of the street.

Cait: You're as clever and talented as the rest of them.

Rube: Then I loiter so slowly and hope you will be there.

Cait: I made sure I was there.

Rube: I had never thought to hold so much beauty.

Cait: So much dirt.

Rube: I mean it. Princess. With you I could—

Cait: What do you want?

Rube: I want to be useful. I want to be needed.

Cait: What does that take?

Rube: I don't know. Money.

Cait: Then make money. Anyone with health can make money.

Rube: Can you keep a secret?

Cait: Of course.

Rube: *(He gets out a ledger)* Nat's books.

Cait: Nat doesn't keep … you look after his books?

Rube: *(Proud of himself)* He is very grateful.

They kiss again, just to make sure.

Rube: I know things about his business that even he does not.

Cait: What do you know?

Rube: That at any one time he has twice as much money as he thinks. Look. Nat works by saying, this is what I owe, and this is what I am owed and here is the balance. *(Cait looks doubtful)* But look here *(He pulls out loose papers at the back)*. What he should say is, this is what I have, and this is how long I have it for. See?

Cait: Yes.

Rube: *(Gets carried away with enthusiasm and desire to explain to a blank **Cait**)*. Look. He buys some wood in here. But he does not have to pay until here. You see? In the meantime he has the security of that wood. It has its own value. Plus the sale price of the item. He has both the security and the sale price, and he rarely has to pay his suppliers until after he has realised that value. And he makes no use of it at all.

Cait has been carressing the back of his neck. She kisses him. **Rube** *jumps. He has had time to think.*

Rube: My princess. This is not the right place. We should not. It is Nat and Cissy's home.

Cait: It's my Da's home, just about. It's the Corporation's home. That should have been my bedroom. Alright, we'll stop.

Rube: *(The books are still in his hand. He is thinking thoughts he has never had before)* I don't want to stop.

End of scene.

Scene Five

Doris *is in the flat again. She is sitting quietly, smoking, in the centre of the room. If anything she looks slightly more gaunt than when we met her first.* **Abe** *enters.*

Abe: Back for another fight?

Doris: No. I've come to see you.

Abe: Does it ever occur to you to leave a message?

Doris: Not really, I'm just out, you can lose social conventions in the 'Joy.

Abe: How are you?

Doris: Fine. A stone lighter. I got hard labour. Better than solitary.

Abe: I tried to get arrested.

Doris: I know. You did very well. I hope you cracked his ribs. You took your time about it though.

Abe: I thought it would look better to let him take the first swing. Why did they arrest you and no one else?

Doris: Because I belong to a troublesome organisation of women who start fights. It's 'unnatural' so they get upset. It's taken for granted that the neighbours will get involved, but they hate it when outsiders come over. And it's my seventh offense.

Abe: They didn't get much. Anything valuable was shifted out of the back. There was no real need to fight.

Doris: It's the principle.

Pause.

Abe: Would you like some tea?

Doris: No thank you, I made some while I was waiting.

Abe: What can I do for you?

Doris: It's more what I think I can do for you. I think there's something worthwhile in you.

Abe: What makes you think I don't know that?

Doris: But you're confused. Why did the bailiffs come?

Abe: To repossess the furniture.

Doris: Whose furniture is it?

Abe: Legally, the company the bailiffs work for I suppose.

Doris: Then why did we fight?

Abe: Because it wasn't fair. I've seen their type before. I came down because the odds were uneven.

Doris: So if there were more of us than them you'd have joined their side, to even things up?

Abe: What good does it do? You said yourself that they just arrest you, then come back.

Doris: But the issue is raised. I got to make a statement in court. What good is it for a country to liberate itself, to build houses for its own people if they're going to throw those people back out when they get sick, which is no fault of their own?

Abe: You came to see me to tell me that?

Doris: Not just that.

Abe: I'm pleased you've come. *(Pause)* I haven't met many women like you.

Doris: There are many women like me. You don't hear about us because we make too much sense. And the church and the government and the union bosses, when they're in their closed meetings, deciding our future, don't want people out on the streets making sense. They don't want to hear people saying there is a better way.

Abe: I meant I don't know so many women that I've been so instantly attracted to.

Doris: Pardon?

Abe: I went into that fight for you, not anything to do with the damned furniture. I want to help you, because—

Doris: Stop.

Abe: What's wrong?

Doris: You needn't feel obliged to make some kind of pass.

Abe: I assure you, it isn't an obligation.

Doris: I'm sorry. *(Pause)* You know nothing about me, or why I do what I do. Maybe I'm not very good at expressing myself. Everything I say sounds like slogans to you doesn't it?

Abe: A little. I have heard language like it before. The way you conduct yourself though.

Doris: Comes from the same place as the words. You have to understand. I'm willing to fight for people I don't know because of things that have happened to people I do. *(Suddenly)* Come to this meeting *(Hands him note)*. I think you will find it interesting.

Abe: Alright.

Doris: Goodbye, Abe.

She exits.

Abe: *(Looks at note, partly reading)* 'International socialism.' Perhaps we should have gone to the Soviets. You spoke so well of America, big brother. What we would find? 'Soviets in Ireland. Revolution in Ireland.' The world follows us. Revolution follows. Revolution all over the world.

End of scene

Scene Six

It is night. **Nat**, **Abe** *and* **Rube** *are on the stairs. They have been drinking. They are singing a Yiddish drinking song.*

Nat: Still, it really was marvellous.

Abe: What do you mean by 'still'?

Nat: Still nothing. It really was marvellous. What would I be meaning by 'still'?

They enter the flat. The table is put away and the two camp beds are put up for **Rube** *and* **Abe**.

Abe: 'Still' usually means, 'in spite of'. That we might be disagreeing.

Nat: Pff. What a death. A very classy death. Eleven minutes from first prick to last death rattle. Extraordinary.

Going to make tea.

Rube: *(Assenting)* Mmm.

Abe: I thought for the first time he deserved to live. He'd finally got it all worked out.

Nat: But there's the tragedy. To know what's right, to fight gallantly for it and to fall by treachery.

Makes as if to duel with **Abe** *with an imaginary sword.* **Cissy** *enters from bedroom wearing dressing gown over nightdress with bare feet.*

Nat: Where's the tragedy in dying when you deserve it? *(Deliberately childlike, eager to share his excitement)* Oy Cissy, you should have come. I mean we could have got Cait to mind Padraig. Four corpses at the end. Including a king, a queen and a prince. What a slaughter.

Rube: They were either poisoned or stabbed.

Nat: Or both. The queen was poisoned with a drink. *(Acts out the parts)* She just went 'Oh, oh' like a surprised girl and subsided. It was very sudden. She must have already been sick in her heart to have died that fast. But the prince.

Abe is getting settled down for bed.

Rube: He was stabbed with a poisoned blade.

Cissy: I see.

Nat: He was superb. The greatest. At one moment he would clutch at his wound and roar for the rip in his gullet. *(Cissy frowns in a 'Don t wake the baby kind of way. Nat quietens a little)* At another he would come over feverish, flushed and then pallid for the poison in his blood.

Looks to Abe and Rube for support.

Rube: He did.

Abe: Twice he got up from the ground. He staggered from one end of the hall to the other. The courtiers rushed this way and that to be by him at the end. *(Whoop of actorly breath)* He seemed to see angels, the ghost of his father. Fantastic visions. His eyes were rolling, he slobbered. Then he collapsed, clutched in the bosom of his dear friend, letting out this snarl, which became a rattle, which became a whisper of breath. Then the rest was silence.

Rube: Apart from thunderous applause.

Abe: Then he got up and bowed.

Rube: And died all over again.

Nat: Quite right. It was the most accomplished piece of dying.

Cissy: Well it seems morbid to me. I am going to sleep now. I'd appreciate quiet for Padraig's sake. *(Pause)* I'm glad you enjoyed the play. Goodnight. *(Exit)*

Rube and **Abe:** Goodnight.

Rube: Thanks for taking us.

Nat: *(Absently)* Thank Maurice Mickelberg. They were his seats.

Rube: Could he not go then?

Nat: No. *(Pause)* He fitted out the theatre. He's making his money in theatres and cinemas. I'm making a chess set for his son. I think the knights will have a cloak like the prince's. But I'm not sure.

Abe: Why not?

Nat: If the set is too flamboyant you might play emotionally and in chess, that's no good. There is only one design that perfectly expresses each piece.

Abe: So why are you making another?

Nat: I should copy? I've been commissioned, it wouldn't be right. So you think you have a career as a photographer's assistant?

Abe: *(Smiles)* I don't expect so.

Nat: It's better than being a projectionist. That kept you out every evening.

Abe: *(Defensively)* I came out with you this evening didn't I?

Nat: The first free night this week.

Abe: The meetings and training take up time, that's all.

Rube: This is a truce area remember.

Nat: So it is.

Abe: *(After trying to settle to bed)*. Always the way.

Nips off to the toilet, which is downstairs.

Nat: *(Noticing what **Rube** is doing)* So what do the books say?

Rube: That you are doing very well. That you have all the raw materials for the Forbes-Pattersons and have had to go no further into debt. Soon you will be in profit. But I expect you knew that. So, what shall we do with your fortune?

Nat: We haven't got it yet. But you should see the frame for the roll top desk. It will have secret compartments. I shall be looking to hide half an elephant in it, not just a few documents.

Rube: Yes, but when did not having money stop one from spending it?

Nat: Oh, I shall spend my fortune on an aeroplane journey around the world.

Rube: No, I mean really spending it.

Nat: Why, on what?

Rube: How much is the rent here?

Nat: Four shillings and fourpence, you know that.

Rube: And do you know how much it would be if you were to be paying off a mortgage?

Nat: Why should I have a mortgage?

Rube: Four shillings and sixpence.

Nat: So?

Rube: So I'm saying you should buy your house.

Nat: This house is shared, we couldn't just buy it.

Rube: There are simple rules for these things. I have spoken to the O'Shaughnessys.

Nat: But you would have to put money down. Solicitors.

Rube: I can arrange this. You would have to put none of your own money down. The Corporation is trying to make this a nation of home owners. They are giving these places away and what it will be worth will be many times what you paid for it.

Nat: We will sleep on it.

Rube: We are happy here?

Nat: Of course.

Rube: And you want Padraig to grow up here, his brothers and sisters, among the music, in these schools?

Nat: Yes.

Rube: Then make this your home. You will barely notice the difference, and when Padraig is the age you are now you will be able to say, 'I have done this for you'.

Abe: You're serious aren't you?

Rube: Of course I'm serious.

Nat: It is a nice thought, but …

Rube: It is the thought that played on Hyam. He had nothing to pass on. We never knew if we were going to be thrown out. We could call nothing ours. Isn't that so?

Abe: But he didn't complain.

Rube: Give me permission. I will look after all the paperwork. It will be a kind of present from me.

Nat: I know you are being kind.

Rube: Have I not worked well?

Nat: Yes.

Rube: Already I have saved you £3 in taxes. You don't have to change a single thing. You sign two forms, you forget about it, you have a house. Is this a good thing or not? Is it a good way for me to say thank you?

Abe: Leave it Rube, I'm tired. He'll never do it without consulting Cissy.

Nat: Why shouldn't I?

Rube: Surprise her. Look I'll leave the forms here. See how simple they are. You can sign them on the way out to work in the morning.

*As **Rube** says the last few lines, **Nat** exits.*

End of scene.

Scene Seven

Rube is in the flat. The crib is in the room. During the story he looks casually into Cissy s box, seeing what s new. He takes some papers out of a hidden panel in the dresser and checks through them, all the while telling the story.

Rube: *(Half-singing)* Little *(Pause)* Padraig, little *(Pause)* Padraig, little *(Pause)* victim. More stories. A new story. Here's one, here's one. A riddle. Once, not so long ago, a Polish Count was dining, with his friends, in his club in Krackow. They were all very wealthy, very important men you see, in their gentlemen's club. You have to imagine luxurious pannelled walls, stained yellow by tobacco. Heavy curtains, thickly woven carpets, gentlemen to the gentlemen making their way discreetly between the tables, bringing drinks, cigars, attending to the needs of their masters. And around a table, in a group of his peers, our Count, Count Oblivshoboblovski, or Bimblordorovitchski or one of those noble Polish names you know. He has a big round brandy-glass in one hand, a big fat cigar in the other and a big sagging belly behind his beautiful silk waistcoat. He is a little bald man with a florid complexion – red face – and a swollen nose, how should he be otherwise and be a Polish squire? He says, 'Gentlemen, as you know, I have recently come up to the city from my estates.' The others are very polite, very attentive, how are his estates faring? 'Not so well,' he says, 'I am having a deal of trouble with my farmers. They are not giving my stewards as much as they should be giving. They are lacking in … gratitude,' and he sucks his cigar, 'so do you know what I did?' They did not know what he did. 'I decided to hang one of them.' 'Bravo!' they cried, 'Quite right, capital plan.' 'But I had to decide which one of them to hang. A lesson had to be taught you understand.' They understood. 'I hit upon a plan. I took three hundred zlotys' – golden coins – 'and I went visiting. I went to the houses of three farmers, and each time I left, as if by accident, a little present of a hundred zlotys, and a few spies. And do you know what the farmers did?' They were all ears to hear what the farmers would do with such a large sum. 'The first one, he went on a spree. He bought lavishly, ale, meat, furniture,

linen, books, presents for his family, gifts for the poor, then
he tried to forget that it had ever happened. The second
man, he invested. He lent the money, he went into a venture
here, he bought half a mill to grind his corn there, he bought
better seed. Soon I hear that he is flourishing and my
stewards say he is giving me my tithes and more. Guilt and
gratitude in one you see. The third, before I was even in my
carriage, came running after me crying, "My lord, my lord,
you have left these hundred gold coins," and so he returned
them honestly. Now which one did I hang and why?' Little
sick baby, which one did he hang? After a final puff of cigar,
the count said, 'I hung the Jew for being a Jew.'

End of scene

Scene Eight

*Abe and Doris are entering the flat. Abe is carrying a box. They
look a lot more comfortable with each other. It is May.*

Doris: *(Entering)* If the valve was gone you'd hear the glass.

Abe: I just feel stupid. *(Calling into the room to see if anyone is
in)* Hello! Hello! The socket's down here somewhere. The
man in the shop showed me how to set it up.

Doris: Have you managed to turn that on?

Abe: Yes, I think so.

Doris: Then why are you fooling about with it?

Abe: There's no sound. Maybe. Is this the volume dial?

Doris: Give it a chance to warm up, leave it alone. Our one
takes about a minute.

Abe: Oh. Do you think they will like it?

Doris: Of course, why shouldn't they?

Abe: I don't know. Maybe they'll think it a little … that I
bought it to be showy.

Doris: Well, did you buy it to be showy?

Abe: I bought it because I can afford it, and they deserve something for waiting so long for me to decide what to do with myself.

Doris: So are you going to tell them what you are going to do?

Abe: One thing at a time. I'll have to tell them what we've done first.

A voice comes on the radio, 'The Thinking Man smokes a Peterson s Pipe etc. Then music.

Abe: Would Mrs Katzmeir care to dance?

Doris: Mrs Katzmeir is alone with her husband for the first time in a week. She would care to do bloody more than dance.

Abe: *(Darkening)* Anyone may come in at any time.

Doris: Would it matter? I suppose it would. You might at least kiss me.

Abe: Of course. I mean, a pleasure.

Doris: Would you remind me why I married you?

Abe: Because, we make sense together.

Doris: If we stay in Ireland you're going to have get to grips with 'irony'.

Abe: Who wants to live in Ireland?

Doris: But since we're here, what do you mean, 'we make sense'?

Abe: We belong together. We make each other strong.

Doris: And love.

Abe: Yes, that as well.

Doris: What, that old thing. Love. We got married to make each other strong and luckily we fell in love.

Abe: I wasn't sure *(Blurts)* that you believed in love.

Doris: Because I say things like: 'The family unit is a capitalist construct designed to maximise the potential value of the worker.'

Abe: 'The woman in wedlock is consigned to domestic slavery due to the inequality of wage remuneration.'

Doris and **Abe:** 'Which ensures that of any two workers it makes sense to them for the man to go to work.'

Abe: You can see how you might give that impression.

Doris: And so you think that somehow I think it's not socialist for a woman to love a man.

Abe: Yes.

Doris: We are told who we can love, by our parents, our teachers, our churches. We cannot love out of our sex, class, religion. Marriage law only gives us permission to love once in a lifetime. These are limits on love, given to us. In me, there are no limits. In the kind of country we want there are no limits. More love, not less, do you understand? Now, right here and now, I love you. I love you in private and in public. I love you, your body, your face, the way you bounce when you walk, the way you squint when you think. I love you. I love all of you, I married for that. Not to do what's right, or to prove some cross-cultural point. Now tell me you love me.

Abe: Oh my love. My wife. Thou art fair and there is no spot on thee. When you came to me first I was a boy. Naive. You have given me all that is strong, has purpose. I have had such dreams of you. Belly like a sheaf of wheat, breasts like doves. I am ashamed.

Doris: Never be ashamed. Not with me. Nothing is forbidden.

*Noise off. Enter **Rube**. They separate.*

Rube: Oh hello, I was asleep.

Abe: I called when we came in.

Rube: I must have been sound asleep. Hello again Doris. It's been a long time.

Doris: Good afternoon Rube. Pleased to see you again.

Rube: Have you come for dinner?

Doris: Yes, Abe has some news for the family.

Rube: Oh. *(Seeing radio)* What's this? Actually, I know what this is, I mean what's it doing here?

Abe: I bought it. It's for all of us. Will Nat and Cissy like it?

Rube: If you can get the Voice of Palestine on it I'm sure they will. Which dial is which? Oh it lights up.

Abe: Yes. The man in the shop showed me how to set it up. It's very delicate.

Rube: Don't worry, I've worked one before. You turn this don't you?

Abe: It depends what you want it to do. If you want to hear it make a noise, then it's this.

Rube: The little vertical bar is stuck. Shouldn't it go further to the left?

Abe: No. That's the end of the waveband.

Rube: But it looks like it should. There's space for it. Doris. Don't you think it should go farther?

Doris: I'm afraid I have no idea.

Rube: But you own one of these things. It might look familiar.

Abe: Rube, it's not supposed to.

Doris: I think Abe is right, 187 on the left, that's the same as our machine. You'll be able to tell by tuning through all the stations.

Rube: Could you find us a light music station? Something to impress Cissy.

Doris: I think, here.

Abe: But she prefers horse racing.

Rube: Try and memorise that, will you Abe?

Abe: Fine, yes.

Rube: Come and sit down Doris. Have this chair, I'd say that's the one you ought to have. Tea?

Doris: That would be nice, I was wondering if Abe had forgotten how it was made.

Abe: What? Oh sorry. Of course. Let's see. We're out of milk. We have buttermilk.

Rube: Not really suitable.

Abe: No, of course not.

Rube: I'll put my boots on.

Abe: No. No need. I'll pop out. You'll be fine for a few minutes?

Doris: I should expect so.

Abe: Back soon.

Abe exits.

Rube: You're not from this area. It's a splendid area. You can almost see the Phoenix Park. Come and look.

Doris: I'm not sure I care to almost see the Phoenix Park.

Rube: Sorry? Of course, silly.

Doris: I mean I don't care to be pushed around the room like a piece of furniture. If there's some one you'd rather I didn't see I could easily just close my eyes.

Rube: I ... it's not as you think. Not that I'm at all sure what you think. Cait.

*Enter **Cait**.*

Doris: Hello again Cait.

Cait: Doris.

Rube: Perhaps you should say what you plan to do.

Doris: What I plan? Nothing I think. Cait, do you want me to do anything?

Cait: No. I don't think so.

Doris: Don't look so miserable.

Cait: It isn't quite the way it seems.

Doris: Who am I to tell you what is and isn't done? We must have a private talk some time.

Cait: Yes. Bye. That would be nice. I'd like that. Goodbye Rube.

Rube: Bye Cait. Hurry. I'll see you as soon as I can.

*As **Cait** leaves, enter **Abe** and **Cissy**, with Padraig.*

Cait: Excuse me.

Abe: Hello again. Look who I've found.

Cissy: Good evening, you must be Miss Hughes I've heard about.

Doris: Call me Doris, Mrs Katzmeir.

Cissy: Cissy please.

Doris: This must be Padraig. Delighted to meet you.

Cissy: Say hello Padraig to the beautiful lady. I'm sorry I was not here when you arrived, Mrs Goldstern takes so long over a hand of rummy, you wouldn't believe. Now have either of these two boys managed to make you a cup of tea?

Abe: On its way. I'll just turn this switch on the way to the samovar.

Cissy: *(Indicating radio)* What is this Abe?

Abe: Just a little something I picked up.

Cissy: A very big something to be just picking up.

Abe: A little something I picked up with a part of the money for winning the Oliver Grogan scholarship. It's only second-hand.

Cissy: A scholarship. You didn't say you were entering for an award. What is it for?

Abe: A scholarship to go to Trinity College Dublin to study medicine.

Cissy: You're going to be a doctor. Congratulations! Doris, did you have anything to do with this?

Doris: The school of medicine wouldn't listen to me.

Abe: All my own work.

Cissy: Nat will be delighted.

A waltz comes on the radio.

Cissy: He should be here for this. I'll start straight away. You sit down, Doris. I'd ask all about you but I know you will be having to tell things three times over for Nat, so I think you'd better prepare yourself.

Cissy goes to get water for tea.

Rube: *(To Abe)* That's a very pretty ring Doris has.

Cissy is returning.

Doris: Thank you. I'm just getting used to it.

Cissy: Oh, are you engaged?

Doris: Married actually.

Cissy: Married. That's wonderful, you should have brought your husband with you.

Abe: She did. *(Goes behind Doris s chair)* Doris and I are married. We were married two weeks ago.

Cissy: Oh Avraham. What have you done?

Abe: Nothing. I have got married, and I have fallen in love, that is all.

Cissy: I see the need for a present. I thought you were a mature man.

Abe: The present is a present, not—

Cissy: Not a bribe. I see. *(Rube turns off radio)* You have come here with your Bush wireless, your new college colleague. Would it not have been better to have done neither and told us in advance what you were doing?

Abe: It was our decision. It wouldn't have made any difference.

Cissy: Then why not tell us? Do we mean that little to you?

Abe: No.

Cissy: I suppose you thought it was none of our business what you did with your private life.

Abe: That's not it.

Doris: It may not be my place.

Cissy: But you've made it your place. Excuse me, but has Abe explained to you what it means to our family? What it will mean?

Doris: He gave me some idea.

Cissy: When a Jew is no longer a Jew … What did your family have to say?

Doris: They disowned me immediately. But they've done that before.

Cissy: I see.

Doris: They were actually more shocked than you seem to be.

Cissy: I am not Abe's mother. You clearly do not want my advice or you would have sought it. I do not think any good will come of such a hole-in-the-corner way of handling such an affair. I shall wait for Nat to decide about you. *(To Abe)* Who was there?

Abe: Two witnesses.

Doris: Friends from College.

Cissy: A marriage should be an open thing. A celebration in public. This is sad. What good is …

*Enter **Nat**.*

Nat: Good evening.

Abe: Nat.

Cissy: Nat, you should—

Nat: Be quiet please. Sit down.

Cissy: I'll get on with—

Nat: Sit down Cissy. I have to … I am going to tell you something. When I went down to the shop I found … I found a smell waiting for me, a scent. The sweetest smelling scent. There has been a fire. My works, and the stocks of timber have been burnt down. That's not quite true. They are burning still if you would care to go down. It is a great attraction for the children. I have been interviewed by the police. They were waiting to question me. They were quite happy. They said it must be the sweetest smelling fire in all the world. They thought I had done it for the insurance money.

Pause.

Doris: You're not insured?

Nat: I have signed nothing. I should have signed something. Why should I be insured? Oh my wood. When they understood that I had no insurance they were very sorry for me. They let me go. Cedar, poplar, elm, ash, sycamore and apple, ebony and teak, pine. All my timber. No wonder. The sweetest smelling fire in all the world.

End of Act One.

ACT TWO

Scene One

The same room. Act One ended in May. It is now October, perhaps the last good day of summer. In the area where we saw Abe set up his bed there is now Doris s stuff as well. A large shapeless bag and a pile of books. It might be possible to curtain the area off. Cissy is in the kitchen area. Doris is sitting in her area, smoking and reading. Cissy is about to talk, then she takes Padraig from his crib and goes to settle him in the other room instead. Cait enters.

Doris: I thought you still went to Mass.

Cait: I do. I just needed some air. I thought Cis would be in.

Doris: She is.

Cait: Good.

Doris: Are you sick?

Cait: With Da around, sickness is a way of life.

Doris: We were going to talk.

Cissy re-enters, and notices Cait.

Cissy: Is it that late already?

Cait: I left Mass early.

Cissy: You're very bold.

Cissy exits again.

Doris: We were going to talk.

Cait: Yeh, well a lot's changed.

Doris: You mean me moving in with Abe?

Cait: I suppose.

Doris: Are you worried I'll tell him anything you tell me?

Cait: Not really. I've got things to think through for myself.

Doris: *(Affectionately)* Look after yourself.

Cait: Thanks. I don't really feel sick. I just wanted to leave. *(Suddenly)* But just because I can't stand church now and again doesn't mean I'm about to become some feckin' Bolshy.

Doris: Shame. *(She smiles)* Am I really that aggressive?

Cait: Intimidating. Yeh. At times.

Cissy returns.

Cissy: We will be having eggs in aspic, a meat stew with fried potatoes and almond cookies.

Cait: A meat meal.

Doris: So no milk.

Cissy: All that is left is the cookies. *(To Cait)* As you are here put this in your memory.

Cait: Have you always stuck completely to the laws Cissy?

Cissy: Should I have taken a day off?

Cait: Haven't you ever been tempted to break them? Just one little rasher?

Cissy: I have been tempted, but I would not be tempted trivially. It is maybe we are not allowed to eat pig because it is the most succulent and tasty of meats. It is not an easy demand, it is not easy to keep. It occurs to me that boys must suffer the mark of circumcision because it is not an easy demand.

Cait: Father McCrae said that we must all circumcise our hearts.

Cissy: Perhaps when His kingdom comes we shall all eat the same food. How are things between you and Abe?

Doris: Very well. On a purely social level. It is difficult you know, being frowned on by both families.

Cissy: I could imagine. Will we have enough hot water?

Cait: I'll put some more on.

Cissy: *(With meaning)* You can take your time, there's very little else to do.

Cait: Yes Cis.

Doris: You know Cait is really a woman, not a girl.

Cissy: Anyone who prefers Douglas Fairbanks Junior to Senior is a girl. You know that under the law, our law, women have certain rights.

Doris: Given by men.

Cissy: That aside. Your property is still your own. I know that is against the law of the land, but you must always think of yourself as an equal, in a contract. If Abe fails you, what was yours is still yours.

Doris: I've brought everything I own, it wouldn't be much of a loss, and I don't see enough of him to want to get rid of him. Alone that is.

Cissy: Why did you marry Abe?

Doris: Really?

Cissy: Yes really, of course really.

Doris: Why I love Abe? Well, this sounds very calculating, and not very romantic, but he was the first man I met who didn't mind how clever I was. I grasp ideas as fast as him, I read books faster than him, and he doesn't mind—

Cissy: Why should he mind?

Doris: All the men I ever knew minded. Even the ones who should have known better. Abe is the first who actually listens to what I am saying, and what I really am trying to say, not just the words.

Cissy: So it is a meeting of minds, and is he fulfilling his connubial obligations?

Doris: *(Surprised at the question)* Connubial obligations?

Cissy: What am I saying. *(As if trying to find the right words in English)* Is he satisfying you? It is written how many times you can expect him to have intercourse you know.

Doris: It is written.

Cissy: Perhaps if you read one of our texts, as well as your political works. If he were a man with no job and he had means you could expect a minimum of six times a week.

Doris: He is not exactly in a position … I mean.

Cissy: As Abe could be said to be under stress, we could lower it to five times.

Doris: Five.

Cissy: The least would be if he were a sailor, in which case you would have to make do with once every six months. I am just letting you know where you stand.

Doris: Abe is no longer Jewish.

Cissy: Once a Jew is properly trained there is no problem. Once a man is properly trained. Just ask him if he is capable of fulfilling his role.

Doris: You are … quite right. *(Laughs unexpectedly)* But the problem is more one of finding places to be together. Nat stares at us if we so much as touch. I don't feel married at all. Except for all the trouble. When it's outdoor weather like today, he rushes off to play his games. It's very difficult. How is Nat?

Cissy: Oh my Nat is an ox of a man.

Doris: I didn't mean.

Cissy: Oh you did, why not? I used to wake up in the summers and find that he had stripped the sheet off me. We slept naked. He would be awake, sitting in the chair, in the thick, blue light. Just watching me. He used to say that he was admiring the handicraft of God. That he could never make a joint that allowed for a curve like that, or a varnish that gave a finish of such smoothness.

Doris: Didn't it disturb you?

Cissy: Why? I encouraged him. Sometimes I would be awake and carry on pretending because I could hear the catch in his breathing and know it was because there was a square of moonlight creeping down my body, and he was following it. Do you know what it is like to have a man love you like that, to put a catch in each breath? To have him love your body. He married me for my brain too, he really did, but at night ... Then I'd stretch out and ... stop pretending to be asleep. How is your studying?

Doris: Fine, good. I have finished. I will get an MA from Trinity College soon. First woman from the Northside to do it. I won't get a job out of it, not unless we leave the country.

Cissy: Where would you go?

Doris: England, America. Anywhere there's work.

Cissy: What does Abe think?

Doris: New York. The teamsters and the longshoremen are there.

Cissy: What about his study?

Doris: You're right. He'll complete it. It's nice to think on though. We may know better today how serious we should be about going.

Cissy: Why?

Doris: O'Connor's giving a meeting. It should give us a good idea which way Fianna Fail are going. Maybe this country won't be worth living in. The constitution may be one of the most disastrous steps taken since *(Speech cut across by entrance of Nat and Abe)*

End of scene.

Scene Two

Enter Nat, Abe and Cait. Nat is smoking. He ignores Doris. Abe has a pair of boxing shoes which he puts away.

Cissy: At last. I thought you'd lost your appetite.

Nat: Shalom. For your cooking, never. I have been seeing Georgie Downes off.

Cissy: What did you say?

Nat: What was there to say? He stood on the 'Princess Maude' with this two daughters and they sang for me. They sang 'Over the Sea to Skye' until the song blended with the lowing of the cattle.

Doris: Hello Abe. I think you had better kiss me.

Abe: Of course, yes, why?

Cissy: You should kiss your wife, that's why.

Nat: He said perhaps he would find a new master as good as me back in Scotland. He was very sweet.

Doris: What have you been up to?

Abe: There was a kick-about after training.

A bath is prepared during the following scene.

Cissy: And who else have you seen today?

Nat: Oh Tomas Hardy and I have been comparing tunes. We combined one together. They are virtually the same you see.

Cissy: Would you sing to us while we get things ready?

Nat sings a combination of 'Mother McCrae and 'My Yiddisher Mamma ; his voice is rough. In the end he seems to swallow awkwardly. Abe takes up sewing one-handed.

Nat: That's no good, that wasn't it at all. I had it perfect before. Sorry.

Doris: *(Deliberately friendly)* It was lovely.

Cissy: Do you sing Doris?

Doris: Not really. 'The Internationale'. And the hymns I was forced to learn by ear. I thought 'Gladly the Cross I'd Bear' was an animal with a squint.

Nat: We saw a dancing bear in Poland, didn't we, Cissy?

Cissy: You did.

Nat: That's right, Cissy wouldn't watch.

Cissy: Patches of the poor thing's fur were torn out, you could see its shiny, black skin underneath, and they put this tiny, little clown's hat on it, tied up with a ribbon.

Abe: Animals will be exploited as long there is money to be made out of them.

Cait: What did the bear do?

Nat: Well it danced. Like this *(He roars)*. It more shuffled really. I don't suppose it was a very happy bear. It could also balance a ball on its nose.

Cissy: We should have enough for everyone.

The following sentences overlap in an easy conversational way.

Nat: Herman its name was.

Abe: Have you been in all day?

Nat: Or Hans.

Doris: Oh you've noticed I'm present.

Nat: I saw a wolf once, a wild one.

Cissy: Did you now?

Abe: Is the black thread around?

Cait: What?

Doris: Embroidery.

Nat: Yes. I helped some farmers hunt it. After the snows had melted.

Cissy: I wasn't aware that you could hunt.

Cait: Water's hot.

Nat: I was no good. I was savaged.

Doris: Left-handed today.

Cissy: I've never seen the scars.

Cait: Why do you do that one-handed Abe?

Nat: It was an old wolf, very hairy, very few teeth.

Doris: Work of course.

Cissy: I'm not sure I should be taking you seriously.

Cait: Do you make money with it?

Doris: Money? Heaven forbid.

Abe: I do this as a practice for casualty.

Nat: I am very serious; I got a particularly nasty suck.

Abe: You see, when some man comes in drunk after a fight with their face laid open you may find yourself having to hold them still with one hand and stitching them up with the other. The neater you do it the first time, the less of a scar it leaves when you take the stitches out.

Cait: Oh.

Nat: What will you do with that piece when it is finished?

Abe: I'd imagine it will make some one a fine Hannikah present.

Rube has entered, his clothes have improved. When he talks he dominates the centre of the room.

Rube: Good afternoon all.

Cissy: Hello Ruben.

Cait: Hello Rube.

Nat: Shalom.

Cissy: *(To Abe)* Do you want your bath?

Abe: Yes please.

He goes into the other room.

Cissy: *(Passes cake of soap over to Doris)* Make sure he's properly clean.

Doris smiles and exits. Nat watches the exchange with an unhappy look.

End of Scene.

Scene Three

Nat: How's the businessman?

Rube: Good, never better. We'll have enough for new curtains soon. I can get them made up cheaply if you want to pick a material, Cissy. Stew, excellent.

Cissy: Keep your paws off for the moment. It won't be long until we eat.

Rube: I've brought us some sliced beef.

Cissy: A luxury. It must have cost a bit.

Rube: No, not really. I was owed a favour.

Cissy: What kind of favour?

Rube: A favour from a man who has some beef.

Cissy: Where did you meet this man?

Rube: In a street. By a pub. Where I always meet people. It's not an important thing you know. It *is* kosher.

Nat: I for one am very grateful.

Rube: How are things with you Cait?

Cait: Very well thank you Rube. Can I read your book Cissy? I won't lose the place.

Cissy: Don't tell me how it ends. I'm glad you're feeling better.

Cait: Oh?

Rube: Were you not well?

Cissy: I thought you left Mass because you weren't feeling so good.

Cait: I just needed some air.

Rube: You should look after yourself better. I could get you a new cardigan.

Cait: It's not winter yet.

Nat: We look after her, isn't that right?

Cait: Yes, and half the children on the street. You're too generous.

Cissy: Every urchin needs a bowl of borsht.

Rube: That's why they swarm here, we're running a soup kitchen.

Nat: They descend as the locusts on Egypt. Before our people were freed to go home.

Cait: The Maloney brood may be ugly, but they're not insects.

Cissy: Nathan, that reminds me. On the way back from the pump today I saw something very peculiar.

Pause. **Nat** *is brooding.*

Rube: What?

Cissy: You remember how after we moved in our orange boxes vanished? And how later the children had planks to play hurley?

Nat: Very mysterious, I agree.

Cissy: Well now, today I go past, the planks have all disappeared and they are playing with perfect little wooden sticks. I wonder how they got those?

Nat: Ash, not any wood. They were improving, so—

Cissy: Did you think I'd be annoyed with you for the waste?

Nat: No. There was no waste. I picked through the fire. I had ash in for the tops of two desks, for the balustrade of the central staircase. I was reading up on how to get the bend for a rocking chair. Pff. What was left was enough ash for seven half hurley sticks. It was hardly a waste.

Cissy: I'm sorry Nat. I did not—

Nat: So I am expecting the boils next.

Cissy: No Nat.

Cait: What boils?

Nat: Job was afflicted with boils after losing his business and children.

Cissy: Padraig is still here and I am neither telling you to curse God or to die.

Nat: It would be fruitless.

Cissy: And both of us are staying.

Nat: Oh Cissy.

Rube: How's the boxing Abe? *(No reply)* The club under the shul is very good, but if he is to improve he must box on a Friday night. I don't suppose that will bother him now. He's a counterpuncher. Cait come here. You see a counterpuncher works like this. Throw a punch.

Cait: How?

Rube: Any way.

Cait: Like this?

Rube: *(Surprised by sharpness of blow)* Very good. You see. When you throw a punch you open your guard. Abe is so quick he could land his own in that space, and move off. He never loses to anyone he boxes a second time. Too clever.

Cissy: What happens when two counter-punchers fight each other?

Rube: Nothing. His first fight was stopped because neither of them would throw the first blow.

Cissy: Nat. That's ready now. We're off for an afternoon walk.

Nat: *(Daydreaming interrupted)* We are?

Cissy: Yes, you're going to take me to the park.

Nat: I've been to the park already. It's green.

Cissy: Well we can go to Nelson's Pillar. Are you ashamed of me, Nathan Katzmeir?

Nat: I'm very proud of you. I'm very proud of your cooking.

Cissy: We'll eat when we are back.

Cait: We'll wait.

Rube: We can all have a family meal.

Nat pauses. Uncomfortable.

Nat: Cissy's right. You must eat. But not my eggs in aspic.

Cissy: They'll leave the eggs, won't you?

Cait: Of course. The O'Carrolls have got oranges in. I'm sure they'd give you a few.

Nat is now ready to go.

Nat: Oranges? Come on Cissy.

Cissy: Stay here and eat, like civilised people, and we will be back soon. Keep an eye on Padraig. Goodbye.

Cissy and Nat descend the stairs.

Cissy: Nat. You make meals very difficult you know.

Nat: We are not a family. We will not eat as a family. Inviting those two into our bedroom.

Cissy: It is done Nat.

*Cissy and Nat leave, leaving **Rube** and **Cait** alone on stage.*

End of Scene.

Scene Four

Rube: Arrange the table.

*As **Cait** leans over the table, **Rube** stands behind her. He runs his hands over her shoulders, and starts to kiss her neck.*

Cait: Why d'you always start when we've got no time?

Rube: Because I can't resist.

Cait: *(Dancing)* That's nice. Rube.

Rube: Hmm?

Cait: This is silly but when I used to get water from the pump—

Rube: Where else?

Cait: No, but I used to spin around quickly when the bucket was full and I'd catch you there, lurking.

Rube: Casually loitering.

Cait: Whatever. Well I spin round now and you're not there.

Rube: I'm right here.

Cait: But not … you're not looking for me any more. Are you?

Rube: There have been so many meetings. So many men to straighten out. I thought I would be caught out. There was this agent—

Cait: Is it sorted now?

Rube: Nearly.

Cait: Can we tell them?

Rube: It has to be handled tactfully.

Cait: When did you last tell me a story?

Rube: What kind of story?

Cait: You know.

Rube: A while ago.

Cait: Three months ago. When it rained in Stephen's Green in June.

Rube: So if you knew the answer.

Cait: Will you start again, for me?

Rube: I haven't thought.

Cait: Promise.

Rube: I have told—

Cait: Promise, or I'll take back all the kingdom.

Rube: Finished. The end. They kiss. They live happily ever after.

Cait: Then why aren't we?

Rube: They'll hear.

Cait: No they won't.

Rube: *(Loudly)* Abe. Doris.

Cait: Why disturb them?

Rube: Finish the table!

Cait: I left Mass again today.

Rube: I never go myself.

Cait: I said I was sick this morning.

Rube: *(Pause)* Well?

Cait: Well what?

Rube: Well are you?

Cait: No. But if I was, what—

Rube: Then maybe it's time to stop. Quits.

Cait: It's not a fight contest.

Rube: But if it's so no good. I am not a prince.

Cait: Drop down to me this evening.

Rube: I'm busy this evening.

Cait: When will we see each other then?

Rube: Soon. Tuesday.

Cait: Why have you stopped looking for me?

Rube: Because I'm bored.

*Doris and Abe re-appear. **Rube** produces sweets from a pocket.*

Rube: Who would like a lemon drop?

Abe: No thanks.

Doris: I'd rather start dinner.

Rube: Go on. They're Cleave's. I bought Irish especially.

Abe: Why?

Rube: Isn't that what we're supposed to do?

Doris: Is it better to be exploited by an Irish millionaire or an English one?

Rube: Better not to be exploited.

Abe: The Nationalist card is to try to buy off struggle.

Rube: But I thought the Cumman broke the windows of shops that stocked English sweets.

Doris: Some do, but it isn't policy. We've got to make it clear. That might be worth doing if Ireland were a workers' Republic, but so long as it looks like being a carve-up between the bosses and the church.

Abe: Do you think we'll hear any more today?

Doris: Nothing exact but we should get more about intentions.

Rube: The three of us should eat anyway.

Abe pulls a wry face and nods.

Doris: The four of us.

Rube: *(looking at **Cait**)* That's right.

Cait starts serving.

Rube: We may as well do this properly. Although I'm not sure why. *(He begins meal in kosher fashion with him at the head)* Stew Doris?

Doris: Please.

Abe: Don't leave too much.

Doris looks askance at this seeming greediness.

Abe: Nat talks about food a lot, but he doesn't actually eat that much. Then he and Cissy get upset. It's better if they feel that he's eating as much as he can. Will you intervene at the meeting?

Doris: I shouldn't think so. There'll be no one there worth convincing. But if O'Connor makes another crack about the women in 1916 standing behind their men, I may have to say a few things.

Rube: I thought he actually fought.

Abe: He did, so?

Rube: So shouldn't he know?

Doris: He fought under de Valera, who was the only commander to refuse women arms.

Cait: Abe, there's more wrong with Nat than just the business burning, isn't there?

Doris: Which was stupid in practical terms if nothing else.

Abe: I'm a student doctor in my first year.

Cait: But you have been watching him.

Abe: I can't not.

Cait: And what do you really think?

Abe: I think Cissy's stew is worth our full attention.

Cait: Can a man be sick from a broken heart?

Rube: I don't think that's a medical idea.

Doris: Diseases have causes.

Abe: *(To Rube)* You may have a point. It could be a kind of shock. *(To Doris)* Has he addressed one remark to you since you moved in?

Doris: No.

Abe: He will not accept us.

Doris: It's not our fault.

Abe: Then whose fault is it?

Doris: Abe.

Rube: He is smoking more.

Cait: He says if he's going to have his money burnt he'll do it for his own pleasure.

Doris: He should have been insured.

Cait pauses for a fraction in her movements.

Abe: Easy to say that now.

Rube: It was not difficult.

Abe: You were looking after his books, why didn't you do it?

Rube: Silly man.

Abe: We are still at his table.

Rube: Technically.

Abe: Technically what? Technically nothing, he made it.

Cait: Cissy said to be civilised.

Doris: Won't Nat start up again?

Abe: That's it, precisely, he should. The job in the furniture factory. It's very kind of Mr Fagel, very kind, but it's breaking his heart. It's mass production, he's on a fixed wage. He knows he isn't really supporting us any more. He knows he's a nuisance to them now, because he drifts off over the machinery.

Rube: Buttermilk Cait?

Cait: Thank you.

Abe: It's all in the will. He won't get better unless he wants too. That's at the heart. If a man decides that's it, it is it. And he's carrying a terrible debt you know.

Rube: Doris? *(Offering milk)*

Doris: Pardon. Thank you.

Cait: How bad a debt?

Abe: Enough that he can only pay off the interest.

Doris: *(To **Rube**)* You bring in the money, don't you?

Abe: He does what he can.

Rube: Thanks.

Abe: Nobody has any spare money. *(He looks towards bedroom)* Padraig's condition doesn't help matters, he's not growing properly. *(Gets up to make to go and check on him)* He's underweight. Doris stop, what are you doing?

Doris: What?

Abe: This is a meat meal.

Doris: Oh stupid of me.

Cait: What?

Doris: Stop drinking.

Abe: Rube, what are you doing?

Rube: What? Nothing. Worrying about Nat.

Abe: I mean to bring milk to the table.

Rube: Cait is not a Jew, Doris is not a Jew, you are practically an atheist, and I don't mind.

Cait: But Cissy.

Rube: But Cissy isn't here. Are you going to start believing in this rigmarole after all?

Abe: No, but we should respect Cissy's kitchen.

Rube: I am growing fat respecting Cissy's kitchen. I would not dream of upsetting her, but she knows well enough what we get up to.

Abe: What do you mean?

Rube: Cait, time for the washing up.

Cait: Yes.

Doris: *(Helping, with a poisonous look at **Rube**)* Here.

*Doris and **Cait** are at the sinks. **Abe** and **Rube** are at the table. They can hear each other, but do not necessarily do so.*

Abe: I don't see what you're driving at.

Rube: Would you be happy if all the things that you have done in this flat were open to inspection?

Cait: *(To **Doris**)* I'm not sure what to wash in which.

Rube: Just wash the dishes before she arrives.

Abe: What on earth has got into you?

*Rube gets up to clean a dish himself. He pushes **Cait** out of the way. She goes to leave the flat. **Doris** follows her to the landing.*

Doris: Why are you putting up with this?

Cait: He's only like this in public.

Doris: Why?

Cait: So people don't catch on.

Doris: Does he treat you better in private?

Cait: Yes.

Abe: Rube?

Cait: I'm tired of waiting for him to—

Doris: For what?

Cait: For nothing.

Rube: Look at that, a clean dish. Was it done right or wrong?

Abe: How should I know?

Rube: Yet it is a clean dish. Do you think that it is unclean, that Cissy will tell, that somehow a God you don't believe in will have registered one dirty side plate?

Abe: Obviously, no.

Rube: I am sick of the mumbo-jumbo in this house. These rules are not for us. Yet we creep timidly. I hear that you are making quite a reputation for yourself in these political meetings.

Abe: So?

Rube: You fire up the halls. International Socialism. All power to the Soviets!

Abe: You don't have to say it with bitterness.

Cait: It seemed like the right thing.

Rube: And yet you obey every little superstitious custom of the house as if you were still a Yesshiva boy. Take Padraig's name.

Cait: *(Overhearing, and going back in)* Rube, after Padraig Pearse.

Rube: Not after Padraig Pearse. Not after any Irishman, correct Abe?

Doris: What's this about Padraig's name.

Abe: It's not his real name. He had a name before that.

Rube: What is his old name, his real name?

Abe: It is taboo. The rabbi changed it.

Cait: The rabbi said he'd get better if—

Rube: The rabbi. Is the rabbi wiser than your priest, I thought you were such a good Catholic.

Cait: Yes, but.

Rube: Then what have Dybbucks to do with you?

Doris: What was his other name?

Rube: Abe will not say. He knows it. It is written in this box. But he is scared of the evil spirit and will not say it.

Doris: Are you still superstitious like that?

Abe: No, not at all.

Rube: Then tell your wife his name.

Cait: No.

Doris: It doesn't matter to me in the slightest.

Rube: That's it then, if it doesn't matter.

Abe: Yzaak. He used to be called Yzaak.

Doris: There was no need.

Rube: Now you're miserable.

Cait: You made him so.

Abe: No. Rube is not making me miserable.

Cissy and Nat return.

Cissy: What is all this commotion?

Cait: *(Guiltily at sink)* Nothing.

Rube: Just something stupid.

Doris: Yes very stupid.

Cissy: *(Heavily)* Something, nothing very stupid, I see. Has Padraig behaved himself?

Cait: He's been very quiet.

Rube: How is Nat?

Cissy: Why don't I ask him?

Nat: Fine thank you.

Abe: No you're not. It is not something very stupid. Neither is it in God's hands. I think you are a sick man Nat. It is time to make yourself better.

Nat: What is this?

Abe: I too am sick. I am sick of watching you walk with this blindfold on. If I didn't depend on you, I should have spoken earlier.

Cissy: You are not dependent.

Abe: Yes I am. I have been ever since we made our decision to leave our country on nothing more than a dream.

Nat: We took a vote.

Abe: A vote to run and hide and be a victim.

Cissy: What has brought this on?

Rube: Justification of behaviour.

Nat: What behaviour.

Abe: Saying Padraig's name.

Cissy: Padraig!

Abe: Yzaak! Isaac! Two syllables just the same, a word, a token, not a magic spell.

Cissy rushes into other room.

Nat: A name is more than a word, it is the thing itself.

Abe: How about yellow jaundice, dyptheria, cholera, never mind the name, your child is sick.

Nat: Abe.

Abe: Your child may be dying because this city is rotten, and not because some demon from the old country is inside him. Not because he had the wrong—

Nat: Shut your mouth Abe.

Abe: And what will you do if he does die? Blame me, blame fate?

Doris: I don't think that we should talk—

Nat: And you shikse. Listen. There is a right and a wrong way of … do you think that by bringing misery here you are making things better?

Abe: It is possible to make things better.

Nat: Shut up. You have lived under my roof, and eaten my food. You put yourself out of the shul when you married out of the family. You are not a Godfearing man. But still we accept you.

Abe: I want you to get better Nat.

Nat: Don't talk like that to me. What you say you want, and what you do are different things. Do you think there is no connection between our actions? That there is no fate? Do you think that it was some unlikely chance that the day you came to tell me of your marriage was the day my business burnt?

Abe: That is exactly what it was. Do you think that no more unlikely things than that happen in the world?

Nat: The world that you and your ... want to change.

Abe: My wife, this is my wife. It is not our fault. We did not burn your wood store. How many Jews' businesses go up in smoke?

Nat: Not in this country. These are good people.

Abe: Can you answer for all of them?

Nat: I believe in these people.

Abe: There will be anti-semitism as long as it is in the interests of capitalists that it should be so. There will be no cures for diseases unless there is a public drive for prevention and hygiene, there must be prevention, and not selfish pointless mutterings of spells.

Nat: You're claiming the role of a practical man and educated scientist. And your head is stuffed with slogans, a vision of a world brotherhood of workers, which has never been seen.

Abe: In the USSR.

Nat: The USSR, do not talk to me.

Cait: *(To Rube)* Rube, stop them.

Rube: *(Excited)* If we stop them we'll never know who's right.

Nat: It will fail and fail again.

Cait: Please.

Nat: Our faith is older and stronger than any nation. We are a nation and a faith, this is no dream it is happening. It is you who are dreaming. Will you not accept that your vision is just as much founded on faith as my own?

Abe: It is a rational vision.

Nat: It is wild. It goes against all things human. You cannot even live with your own brother.

Cissy returns.

Cissy: Have you boys nothing better to do than shout while Padraig—

Nat: *(Obviously weak)* I'm sorry Cissy. Is he—?

Cissy: Looking for his father.

Nat: We were just running over old ground.

Cissy: I could hear quite well what you were running over, thank you.

Nat goes to look at Padraig.

Cait: Happy Rube?

Rube: I did not say those things. I am interested in all points of view.

Cissy goes over to crockery. She is visibly upset. She starts to pack it away.

Cissy: I had hoped that this would last longer.

Doris: What are you doing with the crockery?

Cissy: You can have it as a marriage present, it's no use to us.

Rube: I'll buy you a new one.

Cait: *(Suddenly, loudly)* You hypocrite.

Nat returns.

Rube: *(He warns)* Cait.

Cait: I don't care.

Rube: Cait.

Doris: You don't have to speak Cait.

Cait: It's not that, he said he was going to look after you all.

Rube: I am looking after them.

Cait: With Nat's money. The business *was* insured. In Rube's name. He kept the money and talked Da into letting him buy the house from the Corpo.

Nat is not taking this in. He sits down as if considering.

Abe: Then who are we paying the rent to?

Cissy: Rube?

Abe: You said he wasn't insured.

Doris: So there is no need for Nat to break himself in a factory.

Rube: So he has to work in a factory eh? What a hardship?

Cissy: What have you done?

Rube: The only thing left for me to do. When you put that toolkit under my nose and brushed my career aside, that was what started this. He didn't look after his own brother. I support this family. I am the man of the house.

Cissy: We do not need you. We can support ourselves perfectly. The people here know of Nat's kindness.

Rube: I too operate by kindness, a favour here, a favour there. It is good business.

Doris: What exactly has he done?

Cait: He kept his mouth shut when the fire happened. Then he collected the money without telling.

Rube: Nobody ever asked me.

Cait: We were behind with the rent, so he said to Da, if he'd let him buy the house he'd let him off the back rent, and I thought it would come out right.

Cissy: You must leave our home.

Rube: Our home. We can all stay here. I am paying the mortgage.

Abe: Rube. This is not you.

Rube: No? I have done things. Nat, I gave you the forms for the insurance. You ignored them. So I filled them in for us. The house is ours. It is a surprise for you.

Abe: You cannot treat people like this.

Rube: What, should I have married out too? We are the Levy. It is up to us to read the scrolls of the Torah. With only one sick baby in the next generation.

Cissy: We will have more children.

Rube: And if you don't? Who will be there to head the family if not me?

Cissy: Who could trust you when you swindle your own brother?

Cait: Who else are you making money from Rube?

Rube: What did you expect? I'm a Jew, a Jew. Look at these books eh? The world's classic poets. Longman's, great playwrights. Novels of the nineteenth century. You see, week in, week out we go to the library and we each get our two books to read. Abe, Doris, here are your political works, Cissy your Westerns, Zane Grey, don't ask me why. Nat you have no imagination, you are reading alphabetically and you are half way through Fielding. You know who I read when I first came to England. Who I couldn't wait to read? Shakespeare of course. Shakespeare and the great storyteller Dickens. This is how we learned to read. Do you know what I found in Shakespeare, 'my daughter, my ducats'? Chaucer, the Prioress's Tale, Dickens with his Jewish criminal low-life scum. Marlowe, Barabbas, he called him Barabbas, The Jew of Malta, 'When we grin, we bite'. English. I was so keen to learn to write in English. The tongue of the greatest, the best of writers. All Europe talks about English and the springs of the well are tainted by the Jew. Yes I have done this. I have had no other choice given me by the Irish, the language, or the family.

At the end of this speech **Cissy** *removes a concealed drawer from the dresser. It contains papers and money.*

Cissy: I'm afraid your woodwork isn't up to much. I spotted the join some time ago, but I thought that everyone deserved a secret cubby hole.

Rube: Those are my papers, books.

Cissy: And money.

Rube: That money is owed. I could get into trouble.

Cissy: You are already in trouble Ruben. Nat. Will you deal with your brother?

Nat: *(Quietly)* Yes Cis.

Rube: We can keep the household with that money.

Nat: Yes Cis. Rube, when I went down—

Rube: It just has to be used wisely.

Nat: Rube, you will listen. When I went down to the woodstore the fire was nearly out. The heat and the water made great gouts of steam rise. And in with the steam were the smokes of the woods. And I watched it all twisting together. And it has been twisting and I see it twisting now, do you understand? At the same time there has been a creaking. Timber bursting and the water sizzling into the spaces. That is a voice. You hear me, it has become voice speaking to me, while the steam and the smoke twisted. Up and up, I watch it lift until it becomes a staircase. A spiral staircase hanging over the city. Each step of a different timber. Not what I had. Each step of a timber from a different country. There is bog-oak, but also mangrove from the Amazon, eucalyptus from Ethiopia. Apple, damson, cherry, boxwood and sandlewood, sweet smelling cedar, plane tree, firs from the north, birch, alder and ash. And this is hung by one thread, one central column. Perfectly above the city. And that wood glows. It holds the shine of the breath of God.

Now I have heard all that you have said, and it makes it very hard for me to listen to that voice. But while you were speaking, about hard luck and what we have and have not done for you I have been listening to the voice of the water crackling in the fire. It says that our people are like a flower, we are seeds blown from nation to nation. And if we choose to grow sweetly, then the flower that we produce has the scent of God. But that is only the start. The voice says, climb. So I go to the top of the staircase and I look out. I see tower on tower, wall on wall, blue sky and the city. Jerusalem, Jerusalem. *(To Abe)* Yes we took a vote, but we were wrong. There is only one country for us. One city to build. There we are one and we are different. There there are orthodox Jews in black. Jews from the South in brightly stitched yamankas. African Jews. Jews from the East in heavy faces. Two rabbis clasping their beards in a fierce debate over a point of the law and there is none to disturb them. And coffee, hot coffee. And the smell. The ovens turn out breads. Poppy seed rolls, bagels, croissants, fresh aniseed loaves. And my fire, is the fire in the heart of the temple which does not consume the stuff that feeds it. There are masons there, brickworkers, carpenters. It is the craftsmen that will rebuild the city. Not the moneymakers, not the politicians. There is a right way, and you come with your trade and you contribute, you give, you do not ask where is my ten per cent, you do not whine at me and say the world is unfair, I have had no chance. You learn. If you do not have one talent, you find another. You do not say, we will only work nine and a half hours a day, not ten or we will down tools, we will work to rule. That is not how you build the city of God.

What you have done Rube, which you know is wrong, and what you are doing, Abe. These acts are like, like grease and fat, and it rolls down. It rolls down from the fire into the river. And all the wrong and bad and evil, all that we do stupidly and spitefully, is like this fat that drips. It oozes to the bottom of the ocean where it melts together and it becomes Leviathan. An unthinking mass of blubber. Now I have seen Jerusalem, and I can see Israel. And in the ports there are fires waiting. These are cooking fires. Out on the deep are fishing vessels. On the sea that gleams white over blue, we are on the hunt. Do you understand me? There will

come a day soon, and it is not dream, when we will build
Jerusalem, and we will go out hunting on the deep. Now
Leviathan may have become gross with the cruelty of man.
Larger than this house, these houses, be she as large as this
city we will fish her up. That same day we will roast and eat
Leviathan. That will be all, it will be over. Then there will be
no more betrayal. No more sickness. This is what I see. That
is what we must do.

Cissy: Nat.

Nat: *(To Cis)* We were wrong to come here. We're going to
little Jerusalem. Now. Then we will see about leaving again.

Cissy: Nat, what about Padraig?

Nat: What do you mean?

Cissy: It will not be long until we have to say the mourner's
kaddish for him.

Doris: It may not happen Cis.

Cissy: I have always known it would happen. No baby who
looks as he does will make it to yesshiva school. Every
woman on this street has lost a child. Nat, I don't want to be
the only woman to have lost her only child. Nat, you
understand. All this about Jerusalem.

Nat: Cissy, what I have seen I have seen clearly.

Cissy: Maybe we did get the wrong name. Doris says Pearse
made many mistakes. I would like a Jim for James Larkin.

Nat: I have heard clearly. If I am not to curse God—

Cissy: He said, 'The great seem only great because we are
on our knees, let us arise'. Don't you think that's very good?
Don't you want a Jim? Will you not look to your family
first?

Nat: If I am not to stumble, to reject what I have heard.

Cissy: I am not asking you for that.

Nat: Then we must accept what God wills.

Abe: Do you know what that is?

Nat: I think so.

Abe: You have really seen—

Nat: A city. I am a religious man. I do not choose in this, I am chosen. Why are you thinking that you may be chosen too?

Abe: No.

Nat: Are you sure? Wouldn't it be a great adventure.

Abe: Not for me.

Nat: We won't be seeing you at the shul?

Abe: Not except for the boxing.

Nat: Well brother, what will you and your wife do?

Abe: My wife, whom I love, and I will talk.

Nat: That's very good, you should love your wife. I do it myself.

Cissy: Please Nat.

Nat: Good luck then.

Rube: Nat, Cis. The money could be used to start up again.

Nat: We need nothing.

Rube: But only if …

Cissy: *(To **Rube**)* As this is your house, you can keep it.

Rube: You know I cannot afford it without that money.

Cissy: With ownership is responsibilty.

Rube: The O'Shaughnessys will be thrown out.

Cait: Don't even try Rube.

Cissy: This money was badly gotten. I shall leave it to fate to decide. Perhaps I shall bet it on a horse. Goodbye.

Rube: Nat.

Cissy and Nat leave to landing.

Nat: Starting again my bride.

Cissy: It is not so easy. I have not heard a voice.

Nat: I tell you, I have heard it sound like the trumpets at Jericho. It is a wonderful thing.

Cissy: *(Quietly, to herself)* Perhaps. *(Drawing herself together)* Everything will be well.

Cissy and Nat leave.

Doris: My wife whom I love.

Abe: Poor Cissy.

Cait: Do you believe him?

Abe: I don't understand.

Cait: You were tempted. Aren't you going to follow him to Jerusalem?

Abe: Jerusalem. Dangerous nonsense.

Doris: Not even slightly tempted?

Abe: They'll probably end up in Malta by accident. If they go at all. Build a city? Of course I'm tempted. But not that city. Don't we have a meeting to go to?

Doris: We could miss it.

Abe: Why? I want to see you get thrown out for causing an affray.

Doris: A pleasure. *(As they are leaving, to Cait).* You'll be alright?

Cait: I'll be fine.

Rube: Abe.

Abe: I don't know what you want.

Rube: Not this. It could have worked perfectly, for all of us.

Abe: There is no 'all of us'. You're a free man.

Abe and Doris leave. Cait and Rube together. Cait picks up the toolkit. They are staring at each other.

Rube: Princess.

Cait: I thought you were bored with that.

Rube: That is not how I meant it.

Cait: Do you think there's something left?

Rube: *(Pause)* Yes.

Cait throws chisel.

Cait: Here.

Rube drops it.

Cait: *(Slowly and deliberately)* Klutz. Clumsy Rube. Very clumsy. Rube the schlemiel, grown up.

Rube: I am no schlemiel.

Cait: You didn't have to be.

She leaves. Rube is left alone. He picks up the chisel that Cait threw. He smiles at it. He looks around the flat as if taking it in properly for the first time. He puts it gently back into the toolkit. He caresses the box. He throws it violently to the ground.

The End

The first draft of *The Ash Fire* was written when I was 24, and at a time when I had fallen passionately, and enthusiastically, in love with the idea that my ancestors had not, as I had presumed, lived their lives simply in order to create the circumstances under which I was born. My very existence, in fact, was due to an (extremely) unlikely set of accidents within the fits and starts of history, rather than the smoothly planned summary of time that I had taken it to be. I was astonished by the thought that people in the past did not know at the time that they even were living in the past.

I grew up in Chester. Chester is a small English city on the border with Wales. Like many border towns it has a distinct touchiness about its location. It is no more than a half-hour walk to get down into Wales, but Chester is firmly, prettily on its little English hill. I grew up secure in a world where Basildon Bond letters, stamped with the Queen's profile, were dispatched into red post boxes.

I knew, without it ever getting under my skin, that my father was not English, but both Irish and Jewish. He grew up in Cabra, Dublin in the 1930s and emigrated in the 1950s. But as he never made an issue of it, it never occurred to me that this meant that *I* might be in some way Irish or Jewish.

I moved to Dublin in 1984 only to avoid the Law Library of Birmingham University. I chose Ireland because the Chester Local Education Authority would give me a grant to go there, but not to any other English-speaking country. If money had been no object I would now be in Sydney, Australia. Or possibly Chicago.

My grandfather, Nat in the play, was an immigrant – from Poland to Ireland. His choice was even more arbitrary, and much more pressured than mine. My father was an immigrant – from Ireland to England. I was now an immigrant – back again. Suddenly I had the immigrant's understanding that some of the major decisions in life – where do I live? What shall I do? Where shall I find my true love? Where will my children grow up? What will I teach them? – are not answered by slow reflection but in sudden rushes, difficult rejections, arbitrary moments, bitter disputes, and passionate recklessness.

The play is crammed with true incident. But just as I no longer saw the past as a museum, with oneself wandering by, and them, static, on the other side of the rope, I wanted the audience to understand that the issues being raised, and the points of view articulated, were an urgent part of contemporary debate in any immigrant situation. Personally, I think that the experiences within *The Ash Fire* have become even more relevant in Dublin in the ten years since the play was first produced.

Gavin Kostick

Red Roses and Petrol

A Play in Four Acts

Joseph O'Connor

&

For my sister, Eimear

Red Roses and Petrol was first presented by Pigsback Theatre Company at the Project Arts Centre, Dublin, on 11 May 1995. It then toured to the Belltable Arts Centre, Hawk's Well Theatre, Garter Lane Arts Centre and Galway Arts Centre before transferring to the Tricycle Theatre, London, and Tivoli Theatre, Dublin. The cast was as follows:

Medbh Kathy Downes
Moya Anne Kent
Catherine/Young Moya Deirdre O'Kane
Tom/Young Enda Barry Barnes
Enda John Kavanagh
Johnny Paul Hickey

Director Jim Culleton
Set Designers Fiona Leech and Fiona Whelan
Costume Designer Marie Tierney
Lighting Designer Stephen McManus
Production Manager Brian Treacy
Stage Director Paula Tierney
Stage Manager Louise Drumm
Assistant Stage Manager Orla Hennessy
Administrator Kate Hyland
Project Arts Centre Director Fiach MacConghail

Red Roses and Petrol won the In Dublin 1995 Awards for Best Play, Best Director and Best Actress (Anne Kent). The play was presented by Theatre Newfoundland Labrador in association with Fishamble at the 2001 Gros Morne Theatre Festival. Film rights belong to Georgeanne Heller and Stephen Rea.

Photo (clockwise from left): Deirdre O'Kane, Paul Hickey, Anne Kent and Kathy Downes as Catherine, Johnny, Moya and Medbh © Colm Henry.

Dramatis Personae

Medbh Doyle, twenties to mid-thirties.

Moya Doyle, mother of the family.

Enda Doyle, father of the family, who appears on video recordings only.

Catherine Doyle, twenties to mid-thirties.

Tom Ivers, Catherine's boyfriend, from Wexford.

Johnny Doyle, twenties to mid-thirties.

Young Moya, (same actor as Catherine).

Young Enda, (same actor as Tom).

ACT ONE

Scene One

Lights up on a cluttered living room in a slightly battered suburban house. Two doors, one of which leads to the hallway, the other to the kitchen.

A large television in a corner with a video machine. As the play opens, the television begins loudly playing the Irish national anthem; and the RTE "closedown" sequence of rural scenery can be seen on the screen.

The room contains a tatty three-piece suite which has seen better days. A man s overcoat, black, is draped over the sofa. There is a trestle table arranged with bowls of fruit, bottles of wine and beer, stacks of glasses, plates of sandwiches covered with tinfoil. Many funeral Mass-cards sit on a mantelpiece or bookshelf. But perhaps the most striking feature of the room is that it contains so many books.

There are bookshelves groaning with thick academic tomes; more books are stacked around the room and on the windowsill. Books on the coffee table. An open suitcase full of books on the floor. There are several tea chests around the room and these, too, are half-full of books.

*A middle-aged woman, **Moya** Doyle, is kneeling on the floor, working her way through one of the piles of books. She is examining their titles – throwing some into a tea chest and making a smaller stack of others. She glances at her watch. Gets up. Begins to busy herself around the room. She arranges more dishes of food, more glasses, bottles of beer and wine.*

*Her daughter **Medbh**, an attractive woman in her late twenties, wanders into the room from the hallway and sits on the arm of the sofa. She is wearing jeans and a sweatshirt and is speaking on a cordless phone.*

Medbh: Stop! … Don't say another word you poxy wagon. I never said that.

Moya exits to get vase.

Medbh: (*still on the phone*) I never said that, you dope ... No ... Who else was there? ... Yeah? ... That fellah's too stupid to brush the dandruff off his shagging Raybans if you ask me ... Yeah ... And he'd fuck a frog if it stopped hopping for five seconds ...

Moya: (*Re-entering*) Medbh, please...

Medbh looks around for the remote control device, points it at her mother s back and presses, as though it is a Star-Trek weapon.

Moya, imperious, begins arranging a vase of flowers. She is softly singing the song 'The Leaving of Liverpool'.

Moya: So fare thee well, my own true love
When I return, united we shall be ...

Medbh: (*Still on the phone*) Yeah ... The mass is eleven o'clock, and then the cemetery at half twelve ... Are you coming back up afterwards? Ma'd love to see you. Well she's ... yeah. She's surviving. OK then, see you petal.

Medbh hangs up.

Moya: (*Still singing softly*):
It's not the leaving of Liverpool that grieves me
But my darling when I think of thee ...

Medbh: Mairead says hello.

Moya: Oh good, love. How is she?

Medbh: She's fine. Yeah. She's got a new job.

Moya: (*Not really listening*): Good.

Medbh: She said she d try and drop over tomorrow. She's not sure she'll be able to.

Moya is unhappy with the flowers and begins arranging them again.

Moya: Good.

Medbh: With her mother.

Moya: (*Still not listening*) That's good, love.

Medbh: And Elvis.

Moya: Good. (*She looks around the room*) All done now.

Medbh: Good.

Moya looks at her watch.

Moya: Look at the time, love. It's time for bed for you.

Medbh: I'm grand for a while, Ma. It's early enough yet ...
Do you want a cup of tea or something?

Moya begins fiddling with the flowers again.

Moya: Or inside in the kitchen. What do you think?

Medbh: MA! Do you want a cup of tea?

Moya: Haven't I been telling you for years not to be calling
me Ma. I'm not a feckin sheep.

Medbh: You're a dozy old mare.

Moya: Oh, I've a lovely family alright.

Medbh: (*In exaggerated Dublin accent*) Ah, sure God and all
his holy saints bless us, but you do, Juno.

They laugh together.

Moya: Terrible to be laughing...Would you not go on up
though, love? Tomorrow'll be a long day, you know.

Medbh: I was gonna to wait up for Catherine. Do you want
me to make you a cup of something?

Moya: I don't know what I want tonight.

Medbh: Well do you want a whiskey or something?

Moya looks at her watch.

Moya: I don't know where that sister of yours is. She should
have been here at half-past.

Medbh: It's foggy out at the airport. They were saying on
the news.

Moya: Do you think we're after doing enough though?
There'll be so many people.

Medbh: Ma. Would you stop fussing around. You're giving me a headache.

Moya: It'd be terrible if we ran out. There's nothing worse than a funeral where they run out of food.

Medbh: We won't run out.

Moya: I don't know now. People can eat a lot when they're upset... I remember at Uncle Liam's funeral they had one plate of sausage rolls between the lot of us. That's your Auntie Fidelma of course. Wouldn't spend Christmas, that one.

Medbh: How in the name of God would we run out?

Moya: ...Your poor father's the last of that whole family to go, you know. Out of all those children. Imagine.

Medbh: I know, Ma.

Moya: Do you think 'our friend' will come though? Do you think he'll change his mind?

Medbh: I haven't a clue, Ma. You know what he's bloody like.

Moya: Maybe if you gave him one more ring. He could come over in the morning; they have the early flights from London now.

Medbh: *No*, Ma... He didn't get on with Daddy, and that's not gonna be changed now. So don't involve me, alright?

Moya: A man would think he'd be entitled to have his own children at his funeral, whatever else about it.

Moya puts her hands to her face and begins to cry. Medbh goes to her and embraces her, sighing.

Moya: Well has he never heard of *mercy* in his life? Or compassion?

Medbh: (*Gently*) Ma. Stop it.

Moya: What went wrong with all of us? As a family? What did we not do for you that we should have done? We should all be together now. It isn't right Medbh.

Medbh: Ma, look, I know we're not exactly The Waltons, alright? But we're not The Addams Family either.

Moya smiles, in spite of herself.

Medbh: Ah stop your cryin' now, Juno.

Medbh caresses Moya s face. Moya laughs. Medbh points to the window.

Medbh: Joxer, Joxer. What is the stars?

Moya laughs again. She slaps Medbh playfully on the arm.

Moya: You're terrible.

She pulls away from Medbh.

Moya: They're lovely flowers they sent. From the university. One from the library staff and one from the Arts faculty.

Medbh: Yeah.

Moya: And a lovely note from Professor Thompson. Did you read it?

Medbh: *(Wearily)* I read it.

Moya: Such a lovely cultured man too. He always sings Gilbert and Sullivan at parties.

Medbh: Dad always thought he was a smarmy old bollocks.

Moya: Medbh, that's an awful thing to say.

Medbh: He did. He said he never read a book in his life. He said he was a culchie little chancer who plaumaused his way to the top.

Moya: God, I never remember him saying that.

Medbh: He did all the same. He said he washed his suits in the washing machine.

Moya: He was always good to your father anyway. Enda never would have done as well in there if it wasn't for Professor Thompson.

Medbh: Ah rubbish, Ma.

Moya: It's true, you know. There's not many from Usher's Quay had a job in a university library, I can tell you.

Medbh: Dad would have got on fine wherever he was.

Moya: Well I'm not saying that. I know that. But he was good to Enda. And Catherine too, when he was her tutor there.

Medbh: I remember sitting at the next table to Thompson once in the Belfield restaurant. And there was this young one with him, from Finland, with tits on her like she was deformed or something, and he was giving her the hairy eyeball, you know. And he says to her, 'Well of course, Guy de Maupassant is my favourite author'... And I thought, 'gee' is certainly something that gobshite knows all about.

Moya: That doesn't sound like him at all. Sure, he and Maureen are a lovely couple, considering Maureen's nerves. She'd take a bite out of a lightbulb, the same poor girl.

Medbh: Oh, it was him alright. Dirty looking eejit.

Moya: Stop spreading slander, Medbh Doyle. Now listen, come on and help me do a few more of these.

They both kneel, examine books and put them into tea chests.

Moya: Is Jerry coming back to the house tomorrow?

Medbh: Maybe. I dunno.

Moya: How do you mean, you don't know?

Medbh: I mean I don't *know*... Look, I may as well tell you, mother, now you're not to go ballistic on me.

Moya: What?

Medbh: We split up on Sunday night.

Moya: Ah no, Medbh love. Why?

Medbh: Ah, he was getting on my nerves. You'd swear we were married for fifty years the way he went on at me.

Moya: But he's very fond of you, Medbh. Anybody can see that. You've that poor fellow wrapped around your finger.

Medbh: Well he can be fond of someone else now, the big miserable bollocks.

Moya: You've a very hard streak in you, love. If you had a row or something...

Medbh: We didn't have a row Mother. He was just ... Ah, he wanted to be with me all the time, you know. Jesus, if I looked sideways at anyone else he'd nearly have a period about it. And we never went out with a crowd or anything, just him and me and his fucking ego and his "Oh Medbh, Medbh I love you so much."

Moya: God, you poor dear thing. Some girls would love that.

Medbh: We went to Mairéad's party a few weeks ago, and Charlie Foster was home from Australia ...

Moya: (*Knowingly*): Oh I see, said the blind man. I thought you'd a look on you when you came in that night.

Medbh: What do you mean a look?

Moya: I thought you had an expression. You and Charlie Foster were always thick as two thieves.

Medbh: Well I hadn't seen him since he got back and we just had a bit of a dance, you know, and your man nearly chews the head off me on the way home in the taxi. 'Don't you humiliate me in front of my friends ever again,' he says, in his Kerry bloody accent. Jesus I nearly smacked the ugly face off him.

Moya: He's got the measure of you anyway. You're a terrible flirt.

Medbh: I am not. The cheek of him talking to me like that.

Moya: You've a gamey eye. I've seen you in action often enough.

Medbh: He was useless in the sack too.

Moya: Medbh!

Medbh: Well he *was*, Ma. Jesus, the original three-minute hero. You could boil an egg by him.

Moya: Stop!

Medbh: Do you know what he says to me one night? 'It'd help me, Medbh, if I could think about someone else – you know, when we're making love.'

Moya: My God almighty.

Medbh: Yeah. I said, that's fine, petal; it'll make a change from you thinking about your fucking self anyway.

Moya: You did not say that.

Medbh: I did. And I told him he had a sweaty arse.

Moya: Medbh Doyle, I'll have to send you down to confession if you keep on talking like that.

Medbh: Bless me, father, for I have sinned. I'm after gropin' a fat sweaty arse. Do you know what Father Morton'd say, mother? He'd say, 'Oh, that's an awful sin now, love, for if it wasn't we'd all be doin' it.'

Moya: Stop now.

Medbh: And they *are* doing it anyway, half of them.

Moya: Poor Father Morton isn't like that.

Medbh: Sure he has a *face* like an arse, Ma. Even Annie Murphy[1] wouldn't do the bizz with Father Morton.

Moya shakes her head. She looks at her watch. She stands and goes to the window.

Moya: I suppose I could go on up and rest my eyes for a while, if you're going to stay up for Catherine. Maybe you'd give me a shout when she comes in.

---

[1] Ms Murphy was the girlfriend of Bishop Eamon Casey of Galway, mother of his son. Much in the news at the time the play was written, she has more recently faded from the attention of the public. Potential producers should feel free to improvise another name at this point, if required, and should not necessarily feel restricted to episcopal girlfriends.

Medbh: Yeah, why don't you. I'll bring your tea up to you.

Moya takes out a pack of cigarettes and lights one.

Moya: Where is that girl? Do you not think we should phone him again though?

Medbh: No I don't, woman. And why are you smoking that thing?

Moya: I just feel like the one. Don't be nagging me now.

Medbh: You'll give yourself cancer, you know. I'm worn out telling you. Or you'll have to have an artificial lung, like a big accordion, playing The Walls of shagging Limerick while you're breathing your last.

Moya: God, Medbh don't. And your poor father not even buried.

Medbh: He'd agree with me, you know. If he was here.

Moya: I hate to think of him down there in the church, all alone.

Medbh: I know, Ma. I know.

*Moya sits on the arm of the sofa and **Medbh** takes her hand.*

Moya: He often said that to me: 'You know Moya, it's, a terrible thing to be alone.' I remember one time we were in Majorca. Just after I lost the child. And there was this woman on the tour, who was an awful bore. But your father kept asking her to come on day-trips with us. And one night I said to him that I was fed up being with her. And putting up with her nonsense. And this terrible look came into his face. I'll never forget it. And he said to me, 'Moya, have you never heard of loneliness in your life?' God, I felt two inches tall then. I saw a really different side of him then. Loneliness.

Medbh: He'd a lot of different sides alright. There's some wonderful people in the world and Daddy was definitely two of them.

Moya: Don't now, Medbh. You know he was very fond of you.

Medbh: I know he was.

Moya: You know well what the problem was there.

Medbh: What?

Moya: You were too like him. That was the problem there.

Medbh: God, I *hate* it when you say that. I'm not a bit like him.

Moya: He'll never be dead while you're alive. You've the same wilful eyes anyhow. Look at you. You'd say night didn't follow day if you were let.

Medbh: Well it doesn't matter now anyway. Do you want that tea or not?

Moya: I suppose so, yes.

Medbh leaves. Moya rearranges plates of food and glasses. As she does this, she sings another bit of a song: 'The Lowlands of Holland .

Moya: Now then Holland is a lovely land
        And on it grows fine grain
        It is a place of residence
        For the soldier to remain.

As she sings, she kneels and begins sorting through a suitcase full of books. She removes some and finds a plastic bag underneath. She looks inside the bag and finds six or seven video tapes.

Medbh now enters with a tea tray. Moya continues examining the videos. Medbh puts the tray on a table.

Medbh: Listen … I'm sorry, Ma.

Moya: For what?

Medbh: For what I said. About Daddy.

Moya: No. You're alright, love. It's a difficult time for us all, God knows.

Medbh opens a can of beer for herself. She notices the videos.

Medbh: What's on those?

Moya: I'm after finding them here in the case. I don't know what they are.

Medbh: Do you think they're dirty ones?

Moya tuts. **Medbh** *comes back to her mother and kneels down. They continue working, examining books and putting them into a tea chest.*

Medbh: The thing is, about Daddy. He never forgave me for what happened with Luke.

Moya: Well that's best forgotten now, darling.

Medbh: I know. But I wish we'd been able to make up about it. If he'd just once in his life said he saw it my way.

Moya: He was set in his ways, love. It's great for kids now the way they're so open about everything.

Medbh: But … did you two really never do it before you got married?

Moya: My God, are you joking me? … There were times I wouldn't have minded, to tell you the truth. But he never even touched me until after we were married, that's the gospel truth. And we stayed virgins for a good while after that.

Medbh: *Really?* They didn't hang the sheet out the hotel window the morning after the wedding?

Moya: Indeed they did not. The only thing hanging out the window next morning was your Uncle Liam. No. It was six months before anything happened in that department.

Medbh: Seriously?

Moya: Well I mean we'd kiss and we'd hold each other. There would have been a lot of fondness there and gentleness. But we were shy, I suppose. Sure I never saw you father naked until after you were born. We'd make love with the lights off.

Medbh: Me and Jerry did it like that too, so I couldn't see how fat he was.

Moya: Stop it, you rip. Anyway, I liked it like that. It was more romantic in the dark.

Medbh: You big floozy, Mother.

Moya: God, floozy indeed. When I think of the little we knew. But I loved the sound of his voice in the dark. And the little things he'd say to me.

Medbh: (*Teasing*) Like what?

Moya: Well, you don't think I'm going to tell *you*.

Medbh: Ah go on, Ma.

Moya: Oh, look at the holy innocent, you know well what I mean.

Medbh: 'Moya, Moya. Undo the bleedin handcuffs, willya.'

Moya: (*Slaps her playfully*): You're far too curious now, for your own good.

Moya stands. She picks up the coat from the sofa.

Moya: It's nearly a shame to throw away his old coat, isn't it? When he loved it so much. Maybe Johnny'd like it.

*Moya hangs the coat on a door. She kneels beside **Medbh** again and they resume sorting books, putting them into a tea chest.*

Medbh: *Complete Poems and Sermons of John Donne?*

Moya: Yes. Poor Enda loved that one.

Medbh: *Poetical Works of Percy Bysshe Shelley?*

Moya: Yes… What class of a name for a man is Bysshe? Holy water was never poured on that anyway.

*Noise in the hallway. Enter **Catherine**, an attractive woman in her late twenties; her mode of dress notably more sophisticated and fashionable than **Medbh** s.*

Moya: Mum?

Moya: Catherine!

*Catherine throws her arms around **Moya**. **Medbh** comes to them. All three embrace, fighting back tears. **Moya** kisses them both.*

Moya: I didn't hear you coming in, love. How are you?

Catherine: I'm alright, Mum.

*Enter a young man, **Tom**, carrying two suitcases.*

Catherine: Oh Mum, this is Tom Ivers. He came over with me from New York. Tom, this is my mother.

*Moya is surprised at the presence of an intruder but hides it. She composes herself and holds out her hand, which **Tom** takes.*

Moya: I'm very pleased to meet you, love.

Tom: (*A bit shy, but courteous, with a rural Irish accent*) Likewise. And I'm sorry about what happened, Mrs Doyle.

Moya: Well it's a terrible loss Tom; for us and for a lot of people.

Tom: I know. I mean it must be.

Moya: Yes, we've all lost something very precious.

Tom: Well I'm … sorry for your trouble.

Catherine: And Tom, this is my sister, Medbh.

*Tom and **Medbh** shake hands.*

Medbh: Hi.

Tom: How's it going?

Medbh: Grand. Yourself?

Tom: Sound as a hound.

Moya: Well, you must be famished.

Catherine: No, I'm tired just. I ate a bit on the plane.

Moya: Well there's sandwiches and things. Maybe in a little while …?

Catherine: I'm fine really. How are *you,* Mum?

Moya: I'm keeping busy anyway. I haven't had time to think much. There've been all the arrangements and everything… but Father Morton has been very good, I must say.

Catherine: … I still can't believe it.

Moya: No, pet. Well, look, you'll have a bite of something now. I'll just go and put the kettle on. Or would you like a drink maybe?

Catherine: Maybe later.

Moya helps **Catherine** *out of her coat. She is wearing a fashionable and smartly cut dress.*

Moya: God, look at the style. Turn around and give us a gander.

Catherine turns.

Moya: Oh, you look a treat, Catherine. It's lovely to see you looking so well, isn't it, Medbh?

Medbh: (*Wearily, having heard this many times*) Yes, Ma.

Moya: (*To Medbh*) I wish you'd buy yourself a few clothes. You'd look lovely if you got yourself a few new things.

Medbh: Yes, Ma.

Moya: Amn't I lucky though, Tom? To have two lovely young women like these two?

Tom: You are.

Moya: You know, Tom, sometimes I think I'm the luckiest woman in Ireland.

Moya leaves.

Catherine: How is she?

Medbh: (*With sarcasm*) She's delighted. How do you think?

Catherine: I tried to get over sooner.

Medbh: Well, you're here now.

Catherine: So were you there? When it happened.

Medbh: Yeah.

Catherine: And?

Medbh: And what?

Catherine: Well did he say anything? What?

Medbh: Catherine, the man was *in a coma*. He didn't say anything... They rang us up at five in the morning to say he wouldn't last and we better go down. So we drove down to Saint Vincent's and by the time we got there he was nearly gone. And we just went in and sat with him for a while, waiting for the priest. Ma held his hand. And he didn't wake up again.

Catherine: So he had nothing to say?

Medbh: Jesus, no. He had nothing to say, Catherine. He was too busy fucking dying, you know?

Catherine: Alright alright.

Medbh: Christ almighty, what do you want him to say? The Charge of the fucking Light Brigade or what?

Tom snuffles with laughter. **Catherine** *glares at him. He is silenced. She looks back at* **Medbh**.

Catherine: I just thought he might have said something. That's all. I just thought...

Medbh: Well he didn't.

Catherine: Alright, he didn't. Forget it.

Medbh: You've been watching too much television.

Catherine: Christ. We're off already.

Tom: Should I wait outside or something?

Catherine: No no, you're fine. Stay there.

Tom: I feel like a stretch of the legs anyway. After the plane.

Medbh: You're alright, Tom. Sit down. I'm sorry.

Tom sits down.

Medbh: (*To Catherine*) I'm sorry, alright?

Catherine: It's OK... So. How are you?

Medbh: Tuesday was bad. I'm OK now.

Catherine: How was Mum?

Medbh: She was alright, I suppose, when it happened. I mean she knew it was going to happen, so... But then it was terrible seeing him. In the coffin, you know. She got a bit weepy then.

Catherine: Fuck.

Medbh: Yeah, fuck... And there was a big row down in Vincent's because she wanted to wash him, you know, and lay him out and everything. She told the nurse she did that for her father and she wanted to do it for Dad too.

Catherine: Jesus, really?

Medbh: Yeah, and they wouldn't let her. And when we went down to see him then, it was awful. Because it sounds stupid. But he looked like a dead person, you know? He didn't look like Dad...His hands looked so odd or something, wrapped around the rosary beads. And they'd combed his hair the wrong way across his head, to make him look like he wasn't bald. He looked like Jackie fucking Charlton lying in the coffin. It was terrible.

Catherine: I couldn't believe it when they rang me... I actually...do you know, I actually thought it was a joke, when they rang me in work. Some sort of sick joke. Isn't that terrible? And then I got the number of the hospital. I made them give it to me and I wrote it down, and I rang it straight back. But the same woman picked up the phone and she said no, it isn't a joke, love. I'm afraid it's true. Daddy's dead.

Catherine almost lapses into tears. Medbh goes and hugs her.

Catherine: No. I'm fine. I'm just ...I'm grand.

Medbh: I'm sorry for getting into a snot with you.

Catherine: It's OK. Forget it.

Tom stands and goes to the bookshelf. Catherine pulls away from Medbh s embrace and sits down.

Medbh: Do you've sisters, Tom?

Tom: Five.

Medbh: Ah well. You know what it's like, then.

Tom: What it's like?

Medbh: With sisters. You know.

Tom: Oh yeah. I do alright. There was some rows alright. With five sisters.

He takes a volume from the shelf. A photograph falls out of it. He picks it up, looks at it.

Tom: They'd fight like cats in a sack. Sisters.

Tom looks at the photo again.

Tom: (*To Catherine*) Is this one of you?

Catherine comes over, smiling.

Tom: It doesn't look like you. Is that a birthmark there on her forehead? Shaped like…a little crescent, isn't it?

When Catherine sees the photo her expression darkens. She snaps it from his hand.

Medbh: (*To Catherine*) Did you find something?

Catherine: Look. A fucking *photo* of your one! Jesus Christ, if Mum had found that.

Medbh: Give it to me.

Catherine doesn't hand over the photo, but pockets it.

Catherine: Christ almighty. Photos of her lying around the place like she was *his bloody wife.*

Medbh: Alright, alright. Calm down, for God's sake.

Catherine: I'm perfectly calm, thank you. I'm fine.

Silence

Catherine: What are all these stupid … books doing down here?

Medbh: She's giving them all into UCD. To the library, you know. We're just sorting through them.

Catherine: (*Surprised*) Is that what he wanted?

Medbh: I dunno. That's what she's doing anyway. She says he was happier in there than he was here.

Catherine: (*Meaningfully*) Little does she bloody know…

Silence descends.

Catherine: I wouldn't mind having a look through some time.

Medbh: (*Surprised*) Sure, *you* don't read, do you?

Catherine: (*Affronted*) Of course I read. Jesus Christ.

Medbh: Alright, alright.

More silence.

Catherine: Maybe tomorrow.

Medbh: Sure. Why not.

Catherine: So … any word from the college? About who's coming tomorrow?

Medbh: How do you mean?

Catherine: I mean, did you *hear* anything? Did anyone *say anything* to you?

Medbh: About what?

Catherine: About Dad. Is 'your one' coming?

Medbh: I don't know what you mean.

Catherine: (*Intensely*) Look Medbh, I spoke to Maloney. I rang him up from New York yesterday, and he says there's a rumour going around the college that she's going to turn up tomorrow. Here.

Medbh: Sure, he's only a fucking eejit, Catherine, I didn't hear anything about that. Alright?

Catherine: I hope there's no unwelcome guests anyway. I'm going to tell people not to come back to the house afterwards.

Medbh: *What?* … You can't do that, Catherine.

Catherine: I've phoned half of them about it already.

Medbh: …For fuck's sake…

Catherine: I'm not having her humiliated, Medbh. If that little bitch is coming along here to cause trouble…

Medbh: What trouble? Don't be so bloody dramatic for God's sake. Look, seriously, I didn't hear anything about it.

Catherine: You didn't talk to Maloney. He said *the whole college* is talking about it. She's *coming tomorrow.* I'm telling you. Can you imagine? Playing the spurned fucking mistress in front of Mum.

Medbh: (*Nodding towards* **Tom**) Look, Catherine. Do we have to talk about this now?

Catherine: It's alright. Tom knows all about it.

Medbh sighs.

Medbh: Well, look…let's just leave it for now, alright? She's uptight enough wondering whether Johnny's gonna show up.

Catherine: I can't believe he'd even *talk* about not coming.

Medbh: Well I rang him and ate the face off him. He said he'd think about it.

Catherine pours herself a gin and tonic, a whiskey for **Tom**.

Catherine: They were saying the flights from London were delayed. Out at the airport. We were lucky to get in at all. You should've seen the mist. I've never seen anything like it.

Enter **Moya**, *with tray of food.*

Moya: Here we are now. Tom, you'll have a bite to eat.

Tom: I won't, thanks, Mrs Doyle.

Moya: Indeed and you will. Sit over here and don't start any trouble.

Tom: Well, alright. Thanks.

*Moya puts the tray on **Tom** s lap.*

Moya: I like a man who eats, I must say. Enda always ate enough for an army. He'd eat two dinners if he was let and a sweet afterwards. But he never put on too much. No. He was lucky that way.

***Tom** begins eating under **Moya** s admiring gaze.*

Moya: So where are you from, Tom?

Tom: From Galway, Mrs Doyle.

Moya: Ah call me Moya for God's sake. You make me feel old with your Mrs Doyle. What part of Galway?

Tom: From Salthill there, Moya.

Moya: Oh Galway's lovely. Enda always loved Galway. For a Dublin gurrier, I mean... although he'd Wexford blood in him too. He used to say he was a Wexford Viking.

Tom: I don't know Wexford. But Galway's alright.

Moya: So you're a Connaught man, that's a turn up. You're a big secret now to us all. Catherine keeps everything quiet.

Tom: She does yeah. Sometimes.

Medbh: Always did.

Moya: And are you long over in New York?

Tom: Well I went in 85[2]. I'd a brother over there. In Queens.

Moya: And do you like it over there?

Tom: I like it well enough, I suppose. There's a lot to do in it anyway.

Moya: Oh there is, I believe. *I ve* never been. Enda was there once for a conference one time. The influence of Yeats on American culture it was called.

Medbh: Must've been a short fucking conference.

---

[2] Producers should feel free to change the date if they so wish.

Moya: Medbh, would you stop?

Tom: You'd never be bored in New York anyway. That's the thing.

Moya: Well it's terrible though, isn't it? The way some of the young people still have to go away now.

Tom: I suppose so.

Medbh: Some of them don't go far enough away, if you ask me.

Moya: It is terrible, Medbh.

Medbh: (*In her O Casey voice*) Sure the whole world's in a terrible state a chassis.

Moya: Listen to that big lump. I can't get her out of the house, Tom, never mind out of the country. If she goes down to the pub on a Friday she nearly sends me a postcard.

Medbh: Stop you.

Moya: Well it's true. She's nearly welded into that couch. I don't think it's normal for a girl of her age. Do you think it's normal, Tom? For a girl of her age I mean?

Tom: I don't know.

Moya: Well, I don't think it's normal for a girl of her age. Myself and Enda would be stuck in here like Darby and Joan, watching the Late Late or something on a Friday and the queen bee over there wouldn't stir either.

Tom: I don't go out much myself actually.

Catherine: (*Laughing*): Yes you do.

Tom: Not that much. I used to go out a lot more.

Catherine: You're always out when *I* call you anyway.

Moya: And what does your brother do over there, Tom?

Tom: He has a bar, Moya. A little place on Second Avenue. The Easter Rising it's called. He's in it nine or ten years now.

Moya: Oh that's great. An Irish bar, is it?

Tom: Well, I suppose so. But it's not…it's just a bar, you know.

Catherine: It's a gay bar, mother. Tom's brother is gay.

Moya: (*Shocked, but hides it*) Is that right? How interesting.

Catherine: What's interesting about it?

Moya: Well…I'm interested, that's all.

Tom: Well yes. It's not a gay bar as such. We get the odd gay person in there.

Catherine: Listen to him. They're so gay in there their hair is on bloody fire.

Tom: That isn't true now, Catherine.

Catherine: Jesus, they're *gay*. What's the big deal?

Moya: I used to know quite a few of the gay people, you know, Tom? I used to act a bit when I was younger, and of course you'd meet a lot of them in the theatre. I always got on well with them. I found them very funny.

Tom: Really?

Moya: Oh yes. Very humorous.

Tom: I suppose they are.

Moya: Well, they were such gentlemen too – great company. I used to pal around with a fellow called Seanie Darcy I think it was. He made costumes in the Gaiety, for the opera, when it was on. Such beautiful costumes, all silk, you know, and lace. God, Seanie could make anything with his hands. And he was…y'know… that way inclined.

Catherine: God almighty. That way inclined.

Moya: Well he *was*, love. Does your brother have a friend, Tom?

Tom: A friend?

Moya: A special friend.

Tom: Well yes, he does.

Moya: That's nice for him. I remember going to see this play at the Gate once with poor Seanie. It had Hilton Edwards in it and Micháel McLíammóir, and as you know, they were, well ...(*She can t say it*)...and anyway, it was called 'Home is the Hero'. Oh, it was fabulous now. And in the bar afterwards Seanie says to me, 'You know Moya, there was only one little thing wrong with that play, and that was the title.' And I said, '... What, Seanie? 'Home is the Hero?' And he said, 'Yes dear, with that pair in it, I thought it should have been called 'Here Is The Homo'.

***Tom, Medbh** and **Catherine** laugh, **Catherine** reluctantly.*

Moya: That's a good one isn't it, though?

Tom: Did you go to plays with your husband, Moya?

Moya: We went sometimes, dear, but Enda wasn't a great man for the theatre. He'd no patience, God love him. He used to say, the theatre's all very well, but half the time you'd nearly go mad with the feckin boredom in it.

Tom: (*With genuine interest*) Catherine was saying he was a poet.

Moya: Oh well, poet ... Well, he worked in the library, dear, you know, in UCD. But he wrote poems alright. More when he was younger. More when ... he had one in *The Sunday Tribune* last year. It was a bit ... heavy though. I couldn't really get the meaning of it.

Tom: I'd love to see some of his poems.

Moya: God, I don't even know where they'd be, love. There's a rake of papers to be gone through.

Catherine: I could help you do that.

***Moya** caresses **Catherine** s face.*

Moya: Of course, love. You can give me all the help you want. I'd like that.

Tom: It must have been interesting, I'd say. Being married to someone who wrote poetry, I mean?

Moya: No, not really, dear... Enda was always very...he kept to himself about it, do you know? He always said he'd write one for me. A love poem, if you don't mind. Oh, the things he was going to say in it. But he never did. All those years together and he never got around to it.

Tom: That's a shame.

Moya: Yes. But who needs poems though, when I have these two ladies? And my son too? Aren't they more a part of him really? When you think... Because I remember a poem Enda showed me once, by Ben Jonson, you know. And he says in it that his little son is his greatest work. And I thought that was lovely.

Medbh: Johnny's some poem alright. A terrible fucking beauty is born.

Moya: Listen to that one, Tom. She hasn't a good word for anyone tonight.

Catherine: So what's happening tomorrow, with Daddy?

Moya: How do you mean?

Catherine: Well is everything taken care of?

Moya: Taken care of?

Catherine: God, Mum. I mean, is there a grave sorted out and everything?

Medbh: Jesus Christ.

Catherine: What? I'm just asking if there's a grave, for God's sake.

Moya: Well there's something I have to tell you, Catherine. Your Daddy said he wanted to be cremated, love.

Catherine: Did he really?

Moya: Yes, he did. He said he didn't want to be put into the ground. He was laughing about it when he said it, but I knew he meant it. He told me ideally he'd rather we just lurried him down to Connemara in an old potato sack and left him up the side of a mountain for the eagles to eat. He said to me, 'Moya, if I'm going into the food chain, I want to go in that bit higher up than everyone else.'

Medbh: But then he said he'd settle for cremation.

Moya: And he asked me to say, about the ashes, that he wanted them divided up between you and Medbh. And Johnny of course. I know it sounds a bit funny, but that's what he said.

Catherine: Ah Mum, you're not serious.

Moya: Why not?

Medbh: That *is* what he said. He said it to me too.

Catherine: Oh well, I suppose if that's what he wanted.

Catherine goes to the suitcase full of books and begins rummaging through it.

Moya: It's a big thing now, Tom, the cremation. It used to be they wouldn't do it in Ireland.

Tom: Why was that?

Moya: God, I don't know. Was it against the church or something? I think it might have been. Of course the things that were against the church in those days, you'd need to be up early in the morning to do anything *not* against the church.

Catherine finds the videos in the suitcase.

Catherine: What's on these?

Moya: Oh, I don't know love. I found them in his wardrobe and I'm after been wondering what to do with them.

Catherine: Have you played them?

Moya: Well, I didn't like to.

Catherine: Why not?

Moya: God, I don't know, really. I thought they might be private.

Catherine: Sure, don't be silly. Mum. Maybe he wanted us to look at them.

Moya: Of course he didn't. Weren't they hidden away.

Catherine: Mum, for God's sake. Maybe he left something behind. Maybe he wanted us to find them. After he was gone.

Medbh: Christ almighty. You really *have* been watching too much television.

Catherine: Well, people do that, you know.

Medbh: In your dreams they do.

Moya: I wasn't sure anyway. And I don't really want...

Medbh: I'm sure they're just to do with the library, Ma.

*Catherine goes to the video machine, inserts a tape and begins to play it. Her father **Enda** s face appears, speaking intensely. The fact of his appearance is more important than what he is saying.*

Enda: ..And when I looked at him, I thought. Doctor Malone, you're no friend of mine, and you keep your bloody advice. And back into the library then. And the conversation was all tripping along quite nicely when Mrs D comes tumbling in pulling out tufts of her blue rinse. Murder over theology...

Catherine: (*Laughing*) Look! Look, Mum! It's gas, isn't it? Tom, look, there's Daddy.

Tom: Yeah. I can see the resemblance right enough.

Enda: ...You see it every year of course, I did warn them this would happen. What happens is, when exams start coming around the damn theology students start borrowing everything in sight and cutting chapters out of them.

Catherine presses stop and takes out the tape.

Catherine: Do you think they're all of him?

She puts another one in and presses play.

Enda:.. Big night anyway, went to the faculty end of term brouhaha. The chaplain was there. Father Joe, he insists on being called. One of those trendy ones, liberation theology and so on, bomber jackets, very Nicaragua, intense look, sandals with no socks, mo-ped. I mean it's all very well...

Catherine: Is it some kind of diary or what? We should look through them properly, mum?

Medbh picks up the remote control and presses stop.

Medbh: I don't want to look at them now.

Catherine: Medbh, I was looking at that...

Medbh nods meaningfully towards her mother.

Medbh: Catherine, maybe we'll look at them *some other time.* Is that OK?

Catherine: Well, yeah. But there's loads of them. Do you think they're all of him? I mean, they'd be worth looking through.

Medbh: Some other time, alright?

Catherine: Jesus, alright, alright. I just thought it was odd, that's all ...So listen, Mum, when's Johnny coming over?

Moya: God, that *is* gas though, isn't it? Why do you think your father did that? I never knew he did that.

Medbh: Do you not remember, Ma? When he said they got the video camera in the library?

Moya: No. When was that?

Medbh: It was just last year, woman, don't you remember? And he said he'd been messing with it, trying to get it to work and he nearly broke it?

Moya: I don't remember that at all.

Medbh: Good God, Ma. You're little Miss Parallel Universe, aren't you?

Moya: I don't remember that now, I must say.

Catherine: Mum! *Johnny.* When's he coming over?

Moya: What? Oh, I don't know if he is, love. He's very busy in work. He said he'd try his very best.

Catherine: Busy in work? My God, he's entered the workforce.

Moya: Yes, he's got something working for some outfit or another, some computer place I think it is. But I can't get over that now, your father putting himself on those tape things.

Catherine: Busy in work. I've heard everything now.

Moya: Well, he *is* very busy now. And you know what he's like. My fellow keeps to himself, Tom. He's a bit like yourself that way, I'd say. Isn't he, Medbh?

Catherine: He is not like Tom. Selfish little bastard. He doesn't keep to himself enough for me.

Moya: Don't say that about your brother, love.

Catherine: He is, Mum, and you know it.

Moya looks at her watch.

Moya: Well I don't know if he is coming now. I suppose the last of the flights'd be in now. Or maybe we could ring the airport?

Medbh: They'd be in, Ma. There's no point.

Catherine: So. Which room do you want to put us in?

Moya: Who, love?

Catherine: Myself and Tom, of course.

Moya: ...Yourself *and* Tom?

Catherine: Well unless Gabriel Byrne shows up, myself and Tom, yes.

Moya: (*Forced laughter*) God, it's great now, isn't it, for you youngsters. Which room do you want us in? Your poor father not even buried and his house already turning into the Folies Bergères.

Catherine: Mum, look, we're sleeping together, alright, and we're over the age of consent, so I mean…

Tom: (*Embarrassed*): Catherine, for God's sake.

Moya: Oh, you needn't lecture me about it. You're big and bold enough to do what you want, so I'm not arguing. I'm only saying.

Catherine: Well, let's not have a big debate over it.

Moya: God almighty, sure I'm only jealous. Come on then and help me make up the bed.

Moya and Catherine leave. Tom and Medbh are apprehensive of each other.

Medbh: You're red in the face, Tom.

Tom: Am I? God.

Medbh: Don't worry. Ma loves the slagging. She wouldn't mean any harm.

Tom: Oh no, I know that.

Silence.

Tom: So. You're Medbh anyway.

Medbh: I am, yeah.

Tom: You're Medbh. I've heard a lot about you.

Medbh: And the rest of the family too, it seems. Well, I've heard nothing at all about you, Tom.

Tom: Catherine talks about you a lot, so she does.

Medbh: Really? What does she say?

Tom: Just, you know. She talks about you. She's gas when she gets talking. You wouldn't get a word in.

Medbh and Tom speak the next two lines simultaneously.

Medbh: What does she say though?

Tom: It's hard to think of what…

Medbh: (*Laughs*) Sorry.

Tom: No. Go on.

Medbh: You were telling me what she says.

Tom: What she says?

Medbh: About me.

Tom: Oh yes. About you. Well she says you're a very strong person. Very steady.

Medbh: (*Laughs*) God, does she?

Tom: And she says you're very brainy. And you were very good at your studies. She says you're ate with brains. Like your Da.

Medbh laughs.

Tom: What?

Medbh: It's just your expression. What was it?

Tom: Ate with brains? Oh, my mother used to say that to us. 'Don't pretend to be a big thick,' she'd say, 'you're ate with brains'.

Medbh: It's nice.

Tom: I suppose it's a bit stupid.

Medbh: No, it's lovely. So how long have you known her now?

Tom: My mother?

Medbh: (*Laughs*) No. Catherine. How long are yiz an item now?

Tom: I suppose it's, what is it now? A year nearly. The best part of a year.

Medbh: God almighty, you must be some sort of saint, Tom.

Tom: I dunno about that.

Medbh: You'll get a lot of time off your spell in purgatory for putting up with that one.

Tom: I don't know. I'm fairly mad about her anyway. She made a great difference to me, you know. When I met her.

Medbh: She's alright I suppose.

Tom: She's a very strong person herself. Very considerate. She lets on to be an awful wagon sometimes, but she's a heart the size of a lorry. And she's a great dancer too.

Medbh: Really? I never knew that.

Tom: Oh God, yeah. Catherine? I met her in this place in New York called Rhinestone Cowboys, it's a line dancing place, you know. I used to go with a crowd, on a Monday, girls and fellas together, you know, just for the crack. And that's where I met her.

Medbh: I wouldn't've had Lady Jane down as a line dancer.

Tom: Oh no, she hates it. She likes the rap music, you know, and the rave music. She was only working there.

Medbh: She was working there?

Tom: She was waitressing, yeah.

Medbh: (*Taken aback*): Was she? …I thought she was working for some lawyer.

Tom: Was she?

Medbh: That's what she said. She was working for some lawyer. The office was in the Empire State Building.

Tom: Well, she was working in Rhinestone Cowboys when I met her. And we just clicked I suppose.

Medbh: Well, she looks well on it anyway.

Tom: It's gas about them videos, isn't it? Your mother seemed a bit uneasy about playing them.

Medbh: Yeah. Well. I suppose it's a bit strange for her.

Tom: Sure, of course it would be. Were you close to your Dad?

Medbh: We had our ups and downs, you know, in the family, (*She laughs*) I guess you do know, since blabberbeak upstairs told you.

Tom: Every family has those though. And I suppose you don't want to be thinking about them at a time like this.

Medbh: No. Exactly.

Silence.

Tom: It's a terrible thing for you all anyway.

Medbh: Yeah. Listen, Tom, you're very good to come over.

Tom: Well, I wouldn't let herself come over on her own. Because I remember my own father dying. He died when I was only eight, you know. And my uncle said to me the day we buried him, 'Tom, this is the worst day of your life'. And it's important that somebody says that to you. 'This is the worst day of your life, son – you'll never really forget today.'

Catherine comes back in.

Catherine: Well. You two look like you're getting along well.

Tom: We are. Sure, why wouldn't we be?

Catherine: Is she flirting with you, Tom? Medbh's an awful flirt, everyone says it.

Medbh: Shut up you; you'd get up on a stiff breeze.

Catherine: Do you want another drink, Tom?

Tom: Alright.

Catherine pours him another whiskey, makes another gin for herself.

Medbh: So how's the Empire State Building anyway?

Catherine: How do you mean?

Medbh: How's your office, in the Empire State Building?

Tom: That's not where your office is.

Catherine: No it isn't. It's on 46th and Eighth. Sure, you know that.

Medbh: You wrote to Ma that you were working in the Empire State Building.

Catherine: (*Laughs*) No I didn't.

Medbh: You *did*, Catherine. I mean I don't care or anything. But you did say you were working in a lawyer's office in the Empire State Building and that you could see all the way down to The Statue of Liberty from your window.

Catherine: You're dreaming, Medbh. I never said that.

Medbh: Catherine, for fuck's sake, you know you did.

Catherine: I did *not.*

*Enter **Moya**.*

Moya: Well, I don't know about anyone else, but I'm bushed now.

Catherine: Would you not go on up to bed. Mum?

***Moya** looks at her watch.*

Moya: I think I'll wait up a little more. They sometimes have an old film, Tom, on ITV late at night. I love the old black and white films.

Medbh: Ma, it's well after midnight.

Moya: Go on. Leave me here. I'll be fine.

Catherine: You shouldn't be by yourself.

Moya: Go on, for the love of Mike. I'm not a baby.

Medbh: I'll stay up for a while anyway. I'm not tired.

Catherine: (*To Tom*) Will we head up, so?

Tom: OK.

***Tom** gulps down his drink. **Catherine** kisses her mother.*

Catherine: Goodnight, Mum. Try to get some sleep.

Moya: Goodnight, pet. Oh I'll sleep alright. I don't have a fine big hunk like Tom to keep me awake all night.

Catherine: Mum!

Tom: Night, Moya.

Moya: Goodnight now, love. It's lovely to have you here with us.

Tom and Catherine leave.

Moya: Well....what do you reckon?

Medbh: He seems alright.

Moya: Do you think? There's no sign of a ring anyway.

Medbh: I'm sure you had a good look.

Moya: Mmmm. We're not exactly weighed down with the brains, are we?

Medbh: Don't be such a wagon, will you?

Moya: Sure, once they're happy I suppose.

Medbh: Jesus Ma, if I ever bring a fella back here and you say that I'll brain you with a shovel.

Moya: What?

Medbh: 'Sure once they're happy'. Why don't you just say he's thick as shite in a bucket and be done with it?

Moya: I'm not saying that. Now. Put another one of those videos on.

Medbh: Are you sure?

Moya: Yes. I'd like to see him now. You don't think there's anything to what Catherine was saying though?

Medbh: Not at all, Ma. I think he was just messing.

Moya: It's curious, though, isn't it?

Medbh inserts a tape and turns on the video. She opens a can of beer for herself and pours a whiskey for her mother.

Enda can be seen again, his face close to the screen as he switches on the camera. He walks away from it, turns to face us, runs his fingers through his hair.

Medbh: Where's that? Is that his office, Ma?

Moya: God, I don't know. I was never in it in my life.

Enda: Hello? Hello there? Testing one, two, three.

Medbh: Look at the state of him. It's gas, isn't it?

*Suddenly **Enda** begins clicking his fingers and swivelling his hips.*

Medbh: God almighty. What's he doing, Ma? Jesus. Is he going mad?

Enda: (*Singing 'Heartbreak Hotel' in exaggerated Las Vegas croon*)

> Well since my baby left me
> I found a new place to dwell
> It's down at the end of lonely street
> Called Heartbreak Hotel
> And I'll be
> I'll be so lonely, baby
> I'll be so lonely
> I'll be so lonely I could die.
>
>
> Although it's always crowded
> Ya still can find some room…

*Medbh and **Moya** laugh all the way through the song. **Enda** suddenly loses his place in it. He scratches his head.*

Enda: What's the blasted words to that anyway?

*He approaches the camera and turns it off. **Medbh** leaves, taking cups with her. **Moya** touches the screen. Lights fade.*

Scene Two

*White noise dissolves into the sound of the sea, waves breaking on rocks. Lights up as **Young Moya** runs on. She hides behind a pillar.*

Young Enda: (*Offstage*): Moya, Moya. Where are you? Come and look at the sea.

*Enter **Young Enda**. He s breathless.*

Young Enda: Where've you gone, Moya?

Young Moya jumps out.

Young Moya: Here! Are you blind as well as daft, Enda Doyle?

They laugh and hug.

Young Enda: God almighty, you're always running away from me. I think you don't love me at all.

Young Moya: I never said I did, did I?

Young Enda: You don't. You've clicked with some else, my girl.

Young Moya: Oh, you'd love to be rid of me so easily.

Young Enda: Stop that talk. I'll always be here. You know that.

Young Moya: You're only saying it to get on my soft side.

Young Enda: Do you know what day it is today? It's the fifteenth of June, 1964. Do you know what that means? We're together three whole months today. And you forgot.

Young Moya: Of course I knew that, you lump.

Young Enda: And I'm after getting you a present too. Here. Close your eyes first.

Young Moya closes her eyes and holds out her hands. He takes her hands and kisses her on the lips.

Young Moya: Stop that messing, you scut, or you'll be sorry.

Young Enda: No, here. Close your eyes again.

He gives her an old book.

Young Moya: God. What is it?

Young Enda: Can you not read, love? It's *The Love Songs of Connaught*, by Douglas Hyde, the first President of Ireland.

It's the most beautiful magical book, Moya. And that copy's nearly a hundred years old.

Young Moya: Is it really? Well aren't you the awful fool wasting your money on something like that.

Young Enda: Mr Cohen in the shop said I could have it on the never never. It's so lovely and old. He got it from an old lady who came in, and she got it from her grandmother! And I'd wish you all the happiness and all the dreams and all the love…all the hopes that anyone ever felt who held that book in their hands, Moya. And more.

Young Moya: I'll clatter you in a minute. The way you talk.

Young Enda: It's so beautiful though. Look at this one here.

Young Enda leafs through the book, looking for a poem.

Young Enda: My grief on the sea
How the waves of it roll
As it comes between me and the love of my
soul.

Isn't that just gorgeous, Moya? That's how I feel about you. When I'm away from you.

Young Moya: God almighty, the rubbish you go on with. And you needn't think you'll plaumaus me so easily. I'm not one of your English ones whose head you'll turn playing the poor Irish gom.

They hug again.

Young Enda: God help me. I'm completely at your mercy.

Young Moya: Oh listen. The dying swan.

Young Enda: And I'll always be here to help you.

Young Moya: I'm sure you will. Till the right girl comes along. If you haven't got her stashed away somewhere already.

Young Enda: Are you astray in the head or what? I'll always love you Moya Rogan, I cross my heart and hope to die.

She runs off. He pursues her.

*Lights up suddenly on the living room. The video is playing again, with the sound turned down so that **Enda** s voice is a barely audible mumble. **Moya** is watching it. She cannot bring herself to turn it off. She touches the screen for a moment. Then turns off the lights and leaves the room. The room is dark now, except for **Enda**'s face on the video, which fades slowly to complete darkness. Sound of funeral bells.*

ACT TWO

Scene One

*Sound of funeral bells continues. Lights up on the living room, with daylight through the window. The room is as before. The only difference is that six or eight chairs have been arranged around it. A video tape of **Enda** is playing, with no sound.*

*Enter **Moya**, **Medbh**, **Tom** and **Catherine** all dressed in black. **Catherine** is holding her mother s hand. **Moya** is carrying an urn. **Moya** looks at the video screen.*

Moya: (*To **Medbh***) Did you leave that on, love? When we went out?

Medbh: No. I didn't go near it.

Catherine: Neither did I.

Moya: Sure, somebody must have.

Tom: I could've sworn it was off when we left for the church. I thought I checked it.

Moya: Well, it didn't switch itself on, did it?

*They look at each other and shrug. **Medbh** switches the machine off. **Moya** goes into the kitchen. The others take off their coats and sit down. **Medbh** hangs the coats up. [Her father s coat is back hanging on the door]. She prepares a round of drinks and hands them around. Then she sits down too. Silence for some moments. **Catherine** lights a cigarette.*

Catherine: That's strange though, isn't it?

Tom: What, pet?

Catherine: The video being on.

Tom: I must be wrong. I mustn't have checked it.

Catherine: Sure, I saw you. You turned off the plug.

Tom: That's what I thought. But I mustn't have.

Catherine: You did, Tom. You know, I've read about things like this.

Tom: Like what?

Catherine: Paranormal things.

Tom: Would you stop messing for God's sake.

Catherine: I read an article about it. They say when a person dies, and if they've left something unfinished ...if their aura doesn't want to return to the void it can stay behind. Here.

Tom: Would you cut it out, Catherine? Their aura.

Catherine: Well that's what I read. If there's something the person should've done, and they didn't do it, some of their energy stays behind. In the place where they lived, or the place they worked, and...

Tom: Catherine, stop it now.

Catherine: Well, how would you explain it?

Tom: I just turned off the wrong plug.

Catherine: (*Laughing*) You didn't, Tom... You know you didn't.

He ignores her. Silence.

Catherine: So... Did you see her there in the church?

Medbh: Leave it, will you.

Catherine: The way she went on. Moaning and crying like that. Jesus.

Medbh: Catherine, please.

Catherine: She better not turn up here, I'll tell you that much.

Medbh ignores her and concentrates on her drink. And now makes a big effort.

Medbh: Well, it was a lovely Mass.

Catherine: God almighty, I thought it was awful.

Tom: It was grand, I thought.

Catherine: The priest was a bit cringemaking wasn't he?

Tom: I thought he was sound as a hound.

Catherine: God is like a librarian? On the last day he'll gather up all the books and put them on the one heavenly shelf? I mean, Jesus Christ, is that out of a Daniel O'Donnell song?

Medbh: It's from John Donne actually. One of his sermons. It was one of Dad's favourites. Did you not know that?

Catherine: Was it? Well, I thought it was morbid. And that folk group, strumming away like that. God, it was embarrassing. I mean half of them were wearing *trainers*. And the acne on the altar boy. He looked like he'd shaved himself with a fucking cheese grater. And when we went to the crematorium, Jesus.

Medbh: What?

Catherine: I mean the tape playing 'Bridge Over Troubled Waters' when they put the coffin in.

Medbh: Well what did you want? 'Come On Baby, Light My Fire'?

Catherine: I thought your one would have to be fucking hospitalised at that stage, the big act she put on.

Medbh: Catherine…

Moya suddenly comes back in, carrying three lunchboxes and a spoon.

Moya: Well, I've a job to do now, before everyone arrives.

Catherine: What?

Moya: I've a promise to keep. I have to divide up the ashes.

Catherine: God, Mum. Do you have to do it now?

Moya: Why not?

Catherine: Couldn't we do it later?

Moya: We'll do it now, and that'll be an end to it.

Moya places the urn on a table and unscrews the lid. She reaches into the urn with a large spoon, takes out a spoonful and begins to fill up the lunchboxes.

Moya: Come on now. Gather around.

Catherine: Jesus Mum, *you can t do that!*

Moya: What?

Catherine: You can't put Daddy into a bloody lunchbox!

Moya: Well, I've nothing else, dear.

They watch with a mixture of horror and fascination while Moya performs the operation.

Medbh: Which one's mine?

Moya: (*Pointing*) That one.

Medbh: (*Playfully, like a child*) How come you're giving her more than me? Gimme a bit more.

Moya: Would you have a bit of respect, for God's sake.

Medbh: (*Fighting back laughter*) Sorry, Ma.

Moya continues the delicate operation.

Medbh: Can I lick the spoon?

Moya: Medbh Doyle, I'll skelp you in a minute.

Catherine: Well, I don't care. I'm not bringing Daddy back to New York in a lunchbox. Tom, hand me over my bag, will you?

Tom retrieves the handbag. Medbh puts the other two lunch boxes on a shelf out of the way.

Moya: (*Nodding at handbag*) You're not putting him in that?

Medbh: (*In Lady Bracknell mode*): A handbag?

Catherine: Of course I'm not.

Catherine takes an envelope out of her bag. She pours the ashes from the lunchbox into the envelope. She peers into it.

Catherine: It's hard to believe that's all that's left of him.

Moya: Well that isn't all that's left, love. I mean, we remember him, don't we? That's the important thing.

Catherine: Well, I know that.

Moya: And aren't you here? Big lump?

Catherine: I suppose so.

Moya kisses her. Catherine puts envelope back into her bag.

Moya: As long as I have you, he'll never be gone. Isn't that right, Tom?

Tom: That's right Moya.

Behind them, from the interior of the house, **Johnny,** *a young man enters, naked except for underpants and bathtowel. He is carrying the rest of his clothes over his arm.*

Johnny: Well, well.

They whip round, startled.

Johnny: What a pretty picture. The Catholic family united in grief.

Moya: (*Startled*) Jesus! Johnny.

Johnny: How are you, Maw?

Moya: Oh Johnny. You put the heart *crossways* in me!

Johnny: I was just taking a shower.

They embrace. **Moya** *buries her face in his shoulder.*

Moya: Johnny, it's just lovely to see you son.

Johnny: And grand to see you too, little grey-haired mother.

Moya: Oh Johnny, son.

Johnny: And look, sweet Jesus, the two ugly sisters as well. My God, everyone's here – and even *the Da* s here, on the silver screen anyway.

Moya: Was that you switched it on?

Johnny: Who else? Good old Enda, eh? Tripping the light fantastic. I've been watching them all morning and he didn't crack one fucking joke.

Medbh: Catherine thought they were a message from Daddy.

Johnny: Well, she would. Wouldn't you pet?

Catherine: I didn't say that.

Moya: But could you not have got over earlier, love? You're after missing everything. What kept you?

Johnny begins to dress himself.

Johnny: I got tied up, Ma. Jenny tied me up.

Moya: You're a terrible brat. Would you cover yourself up, for God's sake, I was long enough looking at you. I knew you'd be here though. I said a little prayer last night and I knew you'd be here.

Johnny: Very good.

Moya: Didn't I say that to you, Medbh? That he'd be here.

Medbh: Yeah, you did.

Johnny: And you were right! Now, any chance of a drink there, Mother?

Moya: Of course, love. What would you like?

Johnny: (*Nodding at Tom*) Who's this? I'll have a whiskey.

Moya: (*Archly*) Are you sure now? You wouldn't rather a glass of milk?

Johnny: I'm sure, Mother dear.

Moya pours him a large glass of whiskey and hands it over.

Catherine: Johnny, this is Tom. Tom, this is my brother, Johnny.

They shake hands.

Johnny: Tom, Tom, the piper's son. I'm thrilled to meet you, Tom. Tell us, do you pluck your eyebrows?

Tom: Sorry?

Johnny: Tweezers, you know. Do you pluck your eyebrows?

Tom: No I don't.

Moya: Don't be ridiculous, love. Of course he doesn't.

Johnny: Really? Well, they're beautiful Tom, if I may say so. You'd want to see the eyebrows on some of the creatures that sister of mine has brought strolling in here through the years. Jesus Christ, one of them just had *one big eyebrow* across his forehead. He was like something out of the circus. He was like a big fucking muppet in a Dunnes Stores suit.

Tom: Is that right?

Catherine: Don't mind him, Tom.

Moya: No, don't Tom. You leave Tom alone, you brat. Oh now, look, there's no ice. Wait till I get some.

Medbh: I'll get it Ma.

Moya: No no. I'll get it.

Moya leaves. Johnny goes to the bookshelf with his glass.

Johnny: So. How was it?

Medbh: You could have been there.

Johnny: I got held up.

Medbh: What are you talking about?

Johnny: I got held up in London.

Medbh: My arse. You would have been here if you wanted to be.

Johnny: Well, I don't like funerals. I'm not the type.

Catherine: It would have meant a lot to her.

Johnny sits down on the sofa with a book in his hands.

Johnny: So Tom. I suppose you've fucked my sister?

Medbh: Jesus, Johnny.

Tom: Sorry?

Johnny: You heard me, Tommo. You and Sis there, have you been looking at the mantelpiece or stoking the fire? I actually prefer looking at the mantelpiece myself. I mean most fireplaces look the same after a while, don't you think Tom?

Tom: I... don't know... I don't know what you mean.

Johnny: Oh, we don't know. We're not allowed to have an opinion, no? By the creature from the fucking black lagoon over there?

Catherine: Don't mind him Tom. Johnny specialises in trying to be outrageous. It's because he has no friends.

Johnny: That's right. No friends.

Catherine: No friends. No prospects. No nothing.

Johnny: Not like you, dear.

Catherine: That's right. Not like me.

Johnny: That's right, Tom. Not like Catherine, the most popular girl in the class.

Catherine: Fuck off.

Medbh: Don't start, the pair of you.

Johnny: And such a command of the English language. What a tongue.

Medbh: Johnny, please.

Johnny: A lot of people have been on the receiving end of that tongue of course. But we don't talk about that.

Medbh: Johnny!

Johnny: Well, anyway, here's to innocence.

Johnny drains his glass and pours another. Silence in the room, while he thumbs through a book.

Johnny: (*Reading rapidly*) It is now sixteen or seventeen years since I saw the queen of France, then the Dauphiness, at Versailles, and surely never lighted on this orb ...

He throws the book down.

Johnny: Orb my bollix.

Silence.

Johnny: So. Will we check out of a bit more of the old video collection? *The message from beyond the grave?*

Catherine: Fuck off.

Johnny laughs.

Tom: So Johnny. Is it London?

Johnny: Is what London?

Tom: Is that where you are? I mean, where you're living?

Johnny: It is where I am, yes. You could say that, though I don't know if you'd call it living. But anyway, no, nice try Thomas, but back to the point. I suppose you've given her the old lash by now, have you?

Tom: I don't really think you should talk about your sister like that.

Johnny: Oh no... Naughty boy... Nice little Tom doesn't think I should talk about my sister like that.

Catherine: You're a fucking pitiful bollocks you know. You always were and you always will be.

Medbh: Catherine, please.

Johnny: I'm only joking, Jesus. Smile and give your face a fucking holiday.

Catherine: You're not funny.

Johnny: Tom, I say, old man, I'm most awfully sorry. Truly. Je suis desolée.

Tom:... No, you're alright.

Johnny: (*To Catherine*) See? I'm sorry, and all's forgiven.

Catherine says nothing.

Johnny: And Sister Medbh the Rave. How's that long streak of misery of yours. Jerry from Kerry? With his brother Terry?

Medbh: We broke up.

Johnny: Good Christ! Tom and Jerry! That's just occurred to me. (*To* **Catherine**) *You re* getting up to mischief with a Tom, apparently, and you (*he means* **Medbh**), for your part, are fucking a Jerry.

Medbh: We broke up.

Johnny: Tom and bleedin Jerry. My God, if I could only find Minnie Mouse, we'd be laughing.

Medbh: More like a hundred and one dalmatians in your case.

Johnny: Very good, my dear. Yes, there've been a few canines, I have to admit that, a few Crufts champions over the years. Your Jerry, however, is such a prime fucking specimen of Chippendale manhood, isn't he?

Medbh: We split up, I told you.

Johnny: Oh yes. You split up. We're not very good at relationships Tom, in our little clan. It's all to do with our difficult childhoods, you see. My psychiatrist was only telling me the other day. There I am, whingeing on his couch, you know, and he says, Johnny, those voices you keep hearing, Johnny, they don't mention anything about my fee, do they? And then he says you have difficulty bonding. Bonding. And I don't like that word. It makes me think of superglue. It makes me think of handcuffs and chains and big women with LEATHER TITS, Tom, what does it make you think of?

Tom: I don't really know.

Johnny: Yes. What a surprise. Tom doesn't really know. Well big German women with nipples like organ stops is what it makes me think of, and I say all this to Doctor Murphy, the Sigmund Freud of Palmer's Green and he says

it's all Mater and Pater's fault. Old Catherine there would
have loved him. She thinks everything is Mater and Pater's
fault too, don't you dear?

Medbh: Shut up, Johnny. For Christ's sake.

Johnny: No no, let's remember the dead. Here's to the
faithful departed. From me and my inner child.

He takes another large slug from his glass, then refills it again.

Medbh: Not today, Johnny. Please.

Johnny: Yes, you're right. We don't want to put Tom off
now, do we? He looks like a promising one. The latest in a
very long line of course, but a good one. And I mean,
alright, our dear sister has been through a few hands but
who can blame her? Isn't that right, dear? Or am I
embarrassing you?

Catherine: You're embarrassing yourself.

Johnny: Because you have to kiss a lot of frogs before you
find your handsome prince; and we've trawled through the
old swamp in our time, haven't we, Sweetheart? Searching
for Kermit on eighty grand a year.

*Moya comes in with a saucer of ice and an ice bucket. She puts the
ice bucket on the table and comes to Johnny.*

Moya: Now. (*She pours ice from the saucer into his glass*) There
you are. Would you not have a sandwich, pet? You're
looking fierce thin.

Johnny: I am not looking thin, Mother.

Moya: Indeed you are. God, look at you. You'd see more
meat on a butcher's bike on a Friday afternoon. That Jenny
isn't feeding you properly. Is she coming over so I can tear a
strip off her?

Johnny: She can't Ma. She's not well.

Moya: (*Demeanor changes*) What's wrong with her?

Johnny: Well, you're not to throw the head, but she had an
accident the other day.

Moya: Oh my God, you didn't tell me that.

Johnny: I didn't want to worry you, Ma.

Moya: Johnny, for God's sake. Was it serious?

Johnny: Well, it *is* serious actually. She was... over in Paris on work you see, for a few days, and she's in the office anyway and she hears bells, outside in the street. An ice cream van. And she fancies an ice cream. Because it's a hot day. So out she goes. And wham. She gets run over. By the fucking ice cream van. They had to amputate her leg.

Moya: Jesus, you're joking me.

Johnny: No I'm not. They had to amputate her leg. Up to the thigh.

Moya: My God almighty. The poor dote.

Johnny: (*Reliving the painful memory*) I got this message in the office, and it didn't even say which fucking leg. And I had to ring the hospital in Paris. I mean, *Quelle jambe, monsieur le docteur? Le droit ou le gauche?* Is that right? I mean, the Leaving Cert doesn't exactly prepare you for these situations, does it?

Catherine: I don't know how *you d* know.

Johnny: What?

Catherine: About the Leaving Cert. Since you failed yours twice.

Johnny: (*Now very upset*) Jesus...thanks a lot. Here I am pouring out my heart about my poor crippled girlfriend...

Tom: Jesus. That's terrible though.

Moya: Sacred Heart.

Tom: That's really terrible.

Johnny: It is. Oh, it is.

Johnny bows his head as though he is about to cry. He puts his hand to his face. Suddenly he starts hopping up and down on one leg. He collapses with laughter.

Johnny: Ah Joxer, she gave her leg for Auld Ireland! Look at the fucking mugs on you.

Medbh: (*Throws a cushion at him*) You poxy bastard.

Moya: You dirty gurrier. How is she really?

Johnny: She's fine, Mother. Still spreading my balls on toast.

Moya: One leg indeed. I didn't believe you for a minute. And when are you going to marry the poor girl?

Johnny: These London girls never want to get married, God love and preserve them. It's something in the water over there. And neither do I. It's a perfect arrangement.

Moya: Tom, this fellow of mine doesn't believe in marriage. Did you ever hear the like?

Tom: I didn't, no.

Johnny: Oh, I believe in marriage, Tom. I mean if I'm going to get old and sad and fat anyway, I'm bloodywell taking somebody with me.

Moya: We'll see. You'll want to get married when you have kids.

Johnny: Yes. Well don't hold your breath, Mother.

Moya looks at her watch.

Moya: God now, I can't understand why nobody's here. I suppose they're still in the pub.

Johnny: They'll be here, Mother, don't worry.

Catherine: I think it's all nonsense anyway, this coming back to the house afterwards.

Moya: Ah, it's not, love. People want to pay their respects.

Catherine: I think it's nonsense. I'd be just as happy if they all left us alone.

Johnny: (*Loadedly*) Would you really?

Catherine: I would actually.

Johnny: Really?

She turns away from his mirthless gaze and says nothing. His mask goes back on.

Johnny: Well I had a wonderful taxi driver from the airport anyway. He had one of those things on his seat. With the beads you know. And I said, is that any good? And he said, (*caricatured Dublin accent*) 'Oh yeah, it is, pal. It stops yeh sweatin'. Because in the summer, the heat does be fuckin dreadful. And the shirt does be stickin to the seat. And the sweat, my *Jayzus*, does be rollin down yer back. And it gathers there, in the small of yer back, and it trickles down between yer cheeks. And I do have piles, yeh see, terrible piles…And sweat, by its very nature, is salty.' That's what he said to me. 'Sweat, by its very nature, is salty. And it does tear the arse ourra yeh.'

Everyone laughs.

Moya: Isn't that lovely talk, Tom?

Catherine: Will you leave Tom alone, for God's sake.

Moya: What?

Catherine: You're asking the poor man to do a running commentary on everything.

Moya: God, I am not. Am I Tom?

Tom: Not at all, Moya.

Johnny: Well, here we all are together. Anyone know any jokes?

Catherine: I don't think it's a very good time for jokes.

Johnny: Oh really? Well, Jesus is walking down the road one day…and he meets this adulteress and…

Medbh: Johnny.

Johnny: What? It's a good Catholic joke too.

Moya: All the same.

Johnny: And there I was on the plane thinking, thank God I'm going home to dear auld holy Ireland, where I can tell my Catholic joke and people will get it. They don't get it over in England, you see, being a shower of Proddy pagans.

Tom: I wonder would I get it?

Moya: And why wouldn't you, love?

Tom: Because I'm a Protestant.

Johnny: Are you, Tom? But you're from the countryside, aren't you?

Tom: I'm from Galway.

Johnny: And do they have Protestants in the countryside?

Moya: Of course they do, my God.

Johnny: Really? (*Mock amazement*) Well, take me back to Tennessee. And do you live in one of those big houses?

Tom: What?

Johnny: You know, those big houses the country Protestants live in? The ones they used to write novels about. Skulduggery in the scullery.

Tom: No, we don't.

Johnny: Burnt down, I suppose.

Tom: What?

Johnny: Burnt down in the liberation struggle. The struggle for Irlanda Libre?

Tom: No.

Johnny: Fell down of its own accordion.

Medbh: Will you shut the fuck up, you big eejit.

Medbh hands around more drinks. Moya looks at her watch.

Moya: God, it's nearly four already. I think I'll just go out to the road to see if anyone's coming.

Johnny: Will I go with you, Ma?

Moya: Not at all love, I'm fine. You stay here.

Moya throws on her coat and goes out. Silence in the room.

Johnny: So. Are the two ugly sister's going to tell me why nobody's here?

Catherine: (*Feigning innocence*) I don't know.

Johnny: I see... So. Catherine's the eldest anyway, Tom. She was The Da's pet. She used to look after us, didn't you Catherine.

Tom: Is that right?

Johnny: Yes, that's right. But she wouldn't remember.

Catherine: I do remember.

Johnny: She used to slap us around the place when our parents were out.

Catherine: I did not.

Johnny: Oh she did. Before she learnt how to validate her anger and express her assertiveness. Back then she used to validate her anger by kicking seven shades of shite out of us, Tom. Her little power thing, you know. She used to get off on it. I remember the look in her eyes when she used to do it, you've probably seen it yourself Tom, from time to time, or at least I hope you have.

Tom: She's a bit fierce sometimes alright.

Johnny: She is, as you say, (*Mockingly imitating his accent*) 'a bit fierce sometimes', Tom, the way the reverent Ian Paisley is 'a bit fierce sometimes'. She used to get on top of me with her legs on each side of my chest, you know the way Tom, and she'd slap the face off me.

Catherine: I never did that.

Johnny: And sometimes she'd wait till her friends were here, and she'd do it then. She'd sit on top of me, with her legs over my chest, you know? And you know what she's like Tom, when she has her legs on a person's chest.

Catherine is now upset and fighting back tears.

Medbh: Leave her alone, why don't you?

Johnny: That's exactly the way I'm gonna fucking leave her, don't worry. That's exactly the way *she ll* end up.

Catherine begins to cry.

Johnny: Smoke gets in your eyes, darlin'. Occupational hazard for a martyr.

Medbh: Stop it. Can't you see she's upset.

Johnny: (*A nursery rhyme*) I wonder, I wonder, said the duke to the dame, why they all threw a wake, but nobody came.

Catherine: You don't care about anyone's suffering, do you?

Johnny: You think you've a monopoly on suffering? You think you fucking invented it?

Catherine: It's just perfect for you, isn't it. Scrutinising the fucking world from that armchair. Why don't you just crawl into your bottle and fucking stay there?!

Moya comes back in, in time to hear the end of Catherine s last outburst.

Moya: Will you stop it! Will you stop accusing each other.

Silence. Johnny pours himself another large drink. He lights a cigarette.

Johnny: I'm sorry.

Moya: Good God, what are you like? I don't know what your father would say if he were here.

Johnny: Oh I know what he'd say. He'd say nothing.

Moya: What do you mean?

Johnny: He'd say nothing – the way he always did when there was something on his mind. And then he'd stand up and put on his jacket and he'd say he was going out. The way he always did.

Moya: You're very hard on him.

Johnny: Oh yeah, sure. Very hard. First sign of trouble, Tom. On your marks, Daddy. Get set, Daddy. Go, Daddy.

A hundred miles an hour right out that door. Unless it was Catherine, of course.

Moya: Please Johnny, don't talk like that.

Johnny: Oh right, he was a fucking saint, was he?

Moya: There's very few people are saints.

Johnny: He sure wasn't one anyway.

Moya: He wouldn't have claimed to be.

Johnny: He wouldn't have *claimed* anything. He would have waited for the rest of us to find out.

Moya: I sometimes wonder whether I was married to the same man you talk about.

Johnny: As well you might.

Moya: You seem full of terrible stories about him. I don't know where you get them.

Johnny: Oh really, Ma. Don't you? Well, let's tell a few stories, will we? Seeing as nobody knows any jokes. *I ll* start. I used to rob shops, Tom, when I was a kid. My very expensive psychiatrist has explained to me that this was all my parents' fault, because they didn't give me enough attention. But I didn't know that at the time. I thought I used to rob shops because I was a robbing pure little bastard. But here I am anyway, in Eason's bookshop, one day, and up the jumper goes this big book of poetry. Yeats's poems. Father's Day is coming up, you see, and I've no readies for a present for The Da, so. Up the jumper goes Willie B. And I'm on my way out the door, tap on the shoulder. Up to the manger's office quick march. Why did you do it, says he. I'm disturbed, says I. The manager rings up The Da. The Da comes in firing on all cylinders, guns blazing, I mean, open for fucking *business*, Tom. He beat me from one end of Abbey Street to the other. And you know what he did then?

Tom: What?

Johnny: He took me down to the cop shop himself.

Moya: Stop, Johnny.

Johnny: Down to Store Street. And I'm crying. I mean, I'm seven. And I'm so scared that I'm pissing in my pants, Tom. And I'm begging. 'Please, Daddy, please, I'll never do it again.' And what does The Da do? Up to the counter, knocks on it, knock, knock, knock. Big woollyback culchie guard sweating Irish Stew into his armpits. 'What can I do for your honour?' Would you ever lock this pup in a cell for the night, says The Da, to the copper. 'I couldn't do that sir, tis against the regulations'. Out to the car, another few punches in the kidney, then home for round two. Good story isn't it? Will I go on? Do you want to hear what happened when I failed the Leaving Cert? Or maybe Catherine's told you already.

Moya: (*Passionately*) Your father never had the chances you had. That was how he was brought up. *In a hard world, Johnny.* I'd like to have seen you in it for five minutes. Times were tough then, and he worked like a dog for you and you never gave him a thought.

Johnny: (*A bawl of rage*) And what about ME?! ... What thought did he fucking give *me*? Or YOU, when it fucking mattered?

*Moya gets up and leaves the room. **Johnny** lights a cigarette.*

Medbh: Thanks very much, Johnny.

Johnny: What?

Catherine: Can't you just have a bit of respect for him? For once in your life can you have respect for something?

Johnny: Respect. Beautiful.

Catherine: He was her husband, for Christ's sake. He was your father.

Johnny: He was a cold vicious bastard and you know it.

Medbh: Don't say that, Johnny.

Johnny: Oh the dutiful daughter. What about you and yer man?

Medbh: Me and who?

Johnny: You know, that fucking long streak of misery who knocked you up and then disappeared. Luke the fucking fluke. A little grandson to dandle on his knee. You weren't so complimentary about the old man back in those days.

Medbh: Daddy didn't understand the situation, that's all.

Johnny: Oh, Daddy understood the situation all right.

Medbh: He didn't.

Johnny: He understood when he found out that junior wouldn't be arriving after all.

Catherine: Johnny, for God's sake.

Medbh: I don't want to talk about that now.

Johnny: You broke his watery excuse for a heart when you did that. So don't throw stones, Medbh.

Medbh: You've a fucking neck on you calling him cold. He wasn't as cold as you when you feel like it.

Johnny: Oh, he was cold alright. Yes. He was cold. And what hurts *her* over there, what drives dear Catherine absolutely crazy, what makes her rip her fucking highlights out and dance on them… is that I loved him anyway. And she was his pet. And she didn't. And she just can't figure that out.

Catherine: Don't you say that. I loved him too.

Johnny: Oh yeah, you did alright. And that's why nobody's here today, I suppose?… Look at you. You wouldn't know anything about that, would you? Well anyway, he beat the shit out of me, Tom, when I was bad, and I loved him anyway, and I think he was right. And *when* he was beating the shit out of me I knew it was his sick fuck way of telling me he loved me, the poor bastard, and when *I* have kids I'm going to beat the shit out of *them* too in his memory. In fact, it's the only reason I'm *gonna* have kids!

Catherine is now in tears again.

Tom: That's enough, Johnny, for God's sake.

Catherine: I loved him too… I loved him too..

Johnny: What would you know about love?

Catherine: As much as you anyway.

Johnny: My Jesus, you're in trouble then.

Catherine: What the hell is the matter with you? Do you have to do this?

Johnny: Oh no, I don't have to. But it fills in the time. While we're waiting for all the special guests to arrive.

Catherine: I loved him. At least I told him I loved him.

Johnny: Oh great. Divvy out the fucking medals. CALL THE FUCKING PRESIDENT.

Catherine: Did you ever tell him you loved him in your life?

Johnny: 'Daddy, daddy, I wuv you.' You told him that to embarrass him. You told him that because you fucking hated him.

Medbh: She did not. Don't say that about her.

Johnny: Sisterly solidarity, Tom. I'm sure you've read about it in *Cosmopolitan* while you're waiting for the dentist. And here it is in real life.

Catherine: I was very fond of Dad.

Johnny: He embarrassed the shit out of you and you know it.

Catherine: He did not.

Johnny: When did you ever have a friend in the house when he was here? He embarrassed you, and that shower of middle-class *cunts* you call friends. My Christ, Catherine and her friends. I used to come home from school and find a load of them sitting around perming each other's hair and listening to Wham, and if you shouted 'Fiona' in here you would've have been trampled to death in the stampede.

Medbh: And you're the humble proletariat, I suppose.

Johnny: Oh, I'm not saying *that* now, Joxer. I leave that to you and your revolutionary thespian mates. Medbh studied *acting* you see, Tom, in Trinity College Dublin. She and her little pals used to put on plays in some basement on the Northside for the working class, you know. God now, they really had the bourgeoisie shaking in their shoes.

Medbh: There's nothing more middle class than using 'middle class' as an insult.

Johnny: My Christ, listen to Forrest Gump over there. Get that out of a fucking Christmas cracker, did you?

Catherine: You shagged off to London first chance you got and started shoving coke up your nose just to teach him a lesson. That's how much you loved him.

Johnny: And you're a total stranger to the prohibited substance, of course, aren't you? Look at you. Last time I saw you, you were developing a *third nostril*. How much of it did you bring in with you this time? You didn't know that, did you Tom? Last time she was here, last Christmas, she brought half-a-pound of Colombian nose-candy home from the Big Apple with her, just to help her over the festive season. Her fucking handbag was like Diego Maradonna's. Not that I blame her, of course. I mean I am a great believer in Einstein's theory of relativity myself, of course – time goes by a lot more fucking slowly when you're with relatives – but still, but still. A white Christmas is certainly what Catherine had. But you wouldn't know about that.

Tom: I do know about that.

Johnny: Oh do you?

Tom: We've talked about it. I know about it. I think your sister's a very brave person. For trying to deal with her problems. Instead of boring everyone to death about them!

Medbh: So do I.

Johnny: Oh you've talked about it. How sweet. How fucking therapy. Sure get it out, Catherine. We'll *all* have some. I'm sure you've brought another big bag of it.

Johnny goes to grab her bag. Tom grabs his wrist.

Tom: You've some mouth on you, Johnny. You'll get yourself in a lot of trouble one day.

Johnny: Oh bejayzus, the rattlin' boy from the old bog is gonna teach me a lesson.

Tom: It's an awful pity *nobody ever did.*

Catherine: Leave it Tom. He's only trying to annoy me.

Johnny: If I was trying to annoy you, you'd be fucking annoyed, dear. And you'd stay annoyed.

Catherine: Big man, aren't you?

Johnny: I can press *your* buttons any time I like, honey, and don't you ever forget that.

Medbh: Shut the fuck up, the two of you. Ma's coming.

Moya comes in wearing a dressing gown over her clothes.

Moya: I thought I heard the door. Is anyone here?

Johnny: No, Ma. Nobody's here. Yet.

Medbh: Just us, Ma.

Johnny: But you never know who might turn up later, of course. Do you, Catherine?

Moya: Is everything alright? Have you been crying, Catherine, love?

Catherine: No.

Johnny: Nobody's crying, Ma. Everything's great. Just shooting the breeze, you know. Just chewing the old familial fat.

Johnny gets up and goes to the window.

Johnny: And there's plenty here to chew, Juno. Plenty here to chew.

Lights out. Music

Interval.

ACT THREE

Scene One

Lights up on the living room. **Tom, Medbh** *and* **Johnny** *are lolling in the middle room, smoking and drinking. Tom s jacket is off.* **Catherine** *is sitting away from the group looking moody.*

Tom *and* **Medbh** *are singing together.*

Tom *and* **Medbh:** Well if I was a small bird and had wings
that could fly
I would fly o'er the sea where my true love
does lie
Seven years and six months since he left
this bright shore
He's my bonny light horseman who I'll
never see more.

As the song ends, **Johnny** *claps and whistles. Enter* **Moya** *from the street. She looks at her watch.*

Moya: It's after seven already. And no sign of a soul.

Johnny: Don't worry about it, Ma. Aren't we all here? And aren't we *singin* ?

Moya: It's getting late, though.

Catherine: Stop worrying, Mum.

Moya: I can't figure it out. I thought there'd be loads here by now.

Medbh and Catherine avoid Johnny s glance.

Johnny: Will we have another song?

Catherine: I think we've had enough singing actually.

Johnny: But sure isn't there always supposed to be singing at a good auld Dubbalin wake?

Catherine: God stop, will you. You sound like one of the fucking Furey Brothers.

Medbh: You know, Catherine, I sometimes think you walk around with a fucking corncob up your arse. If you sang a bit yourself it might loosen you up a bit.

Catherine: I do sing, when I want to.

Medbh: Well, I've never heard you.

Catherine: Well, I do. What would you know about me anyway?

Medbh: I've never heard you singing, that's all I'm saying.

Moya: Catherine always used to sing when she was a girl. She'd a lovely little voice, Tom. Enda always said that. And he loved singing himself, of course. All the old Wexford rebel songs.

Johnny: Ah yes, of course. The Sunday drive into the country, Tom. We'd set off after the lunch in a convoy of five thousand cars, every car in Dublin, all full of mammies and daddies and little kiddies all smacked out of their head on the angel dust in the roast beef, all off to see the woollybacks of the County Wickla. And when we got there, there'd be three million bewildered suburbanites all lined up and staring into the Sally Gap like they were waiting for the second fucking coming or something. And then Catherine would sing on the way home.

Catherine: Well I don't want to sing now.

Medbh: Don't be so stubborn. Just sing, for fuck's sake.

Catherine: I don't *want* to, I said.

Medbh: Alright, *don t* then, Jesus.

Moya: Oh stop it, the pair of you. You're like a couple of fishwives.

Johnny: Will you have a drink, Ma?

Moya: What? Oh, I suppose I might have a small whiskey.

Johnny: Oh, a ball of malt there me auld scout, for the mother of all the Behans.

Medbh pours drinks.

Medbh: Do you want something to eat, Ma?

Moya: No no. I wouldn't be able.

Moya sits beside him. Johnny kisses her on the cheek.

Johnny: I'm sorry for rowing with you earlier.

Moya: (*With mild sarcasm*) I'm sure you are. You look fierce sorry alright.

Johnny grabs her hand and swings it while he sings.

Johnny: (*singing*) Ah sure, Dubbalin can be heaven
Wid a coffee at eleven
And a strowill in Stephen's Green
There's no need to worry
There's no need to hurry
You're a king ... and Tom's brother's a queen.

Moya pulls her hand away, laughing with the others, including **Tom.**

Moya: Stop will you. You're as odd as two left feet, you are.

Medbh: Are you alright now, Ma?

Moya: I'm grand love. I'm tired that's all. I haven't slept the last few nights. I've been having strange dreams.

Catherine: Have you been dreaming about Daddy?

Moya: No, love. I don't think so. I dreamed I was in a big old house all on my own. There was a child's laughter coming from one of the rooms. But the house was so big I couldn't find where it was coming from.

Johnny: That'll be tuna.

Moya: What?

Johnny: Tuna sandwiches. They always give me strange dreams too. Does it give you strange dreams Tom?

Tom: No, it doesn't.

Johnny: Whaddyamean, no?

Tom: Well, I don't like tuna.

Johnny: Well no wonder you don't have dreams then.

Tom: I have dreams alright.

Johnny: Do you dream about Catherine, eh?

Tom: I did dream about her once.

Johnny: Oh God, tell us. Wait now till I get another drink. Give us a whiskey there, darling.

Catherine pours him one.

Johnny: Ah give us a bit more, will you.

Catherine pours him out more. He takes the bottle from her and fills his glass.

Tom: You don't want to hear.

Johnny: I do, Tom. Tell me.

Moya: Sure, tell us, Tom.

Tom: Well... I was walking by the sea. It was down near home. And it seemed to be early in the morning. There was... nobody around. It was just me, by myself, and I could hear the seagulls. And the sound of the waves on the beach. And suddenly, I saw her about twenty feet away from me, out in the sea. Catherine. Up to her waist in the water... You were calling out to me, and I went to try to get to you. And I couldn't. I kept walking through the water. And running then. But the more I ran, the further away from me you were.

Johnny: That's it?

Tom: That's it. She was up to her waist in water.

Catherine: I wonder what that could mean.

Moya: It sounds very deep.

Tom: What? The water?

Moya: No love. I mean it sounds very ... it sounds spiritual or something. Would that be the word?

Johnny: You were probably pissing. She used to do that, you know Tom, when we were kids. She used to piss in the sea and in swimming pools. It was ferocious.

Catherine: (*Laughing*) I did not.

Johnny: She did. It was too *too* embarrassing. And she crapped in a swimming pool once. In Leisureland, in Galway.

Catherine: I did not, you little fucker.

Moya: Catherine. Language, please.

Catherine: I didn't though.

Moya: Sure don't mind that galoot. I know well you didn't.

Johnny: She did. There we were, Tom, all trying to drown the bejayzus out of each other, and all of a sudden her face goes all funny, and out it comes. This big turd, you know, like the battleship Potempkin. Floating on the top. Jesus Christ I couldn't believe it.

Catherine: (*Responding, but more teasing than vicious*) And what about *you* that summer? We were in the Gaeltacht, and he got off with this big lump from the Northside. She was six foot tall and ugly as sin, with a big brace on her teeth. She had a head on her like a giraffe. And when he got off with her he got his tongue stuck in the brace. I could hear him screaming. And I ran into the room and there he was. And Bean Uí Costello ran in, roaring and shouting at us not to be speaking English. And he was hopping around, trying to get his tongue out.

Johnny and his sisters laugh at the memory.

Johnny: My eyes still water, whenever I hear Irish spoken, Tom. People sometimes think it's national pride.

Moya: My God now, I never knew any of this. There we were thinking it would help your education.

Catherine: Oh it did, Mother.

Moya: Aren't dreams funny though? The things we keep hidden away, you know. I remember giving out to Enda, about all the old rubbish he had in the study. And he said, it's like your dreams, Moya. Everything is filed away somewhere, and you never know when it's going to come out.

Johnny: Good old Pops. Zen as ever. The Maharishi of Usher's Quay.

Tom: It kind of bothered me though, that dream. I didn't know what it was about. And I woke up in a sweat over it.

Catherine: The garden's a bit of a mess, Mum, isn't it?

Moya: Well with Enda being sick, love. We've let it go to pot a bit. Enda always took a great pride in his garden, Tom. He always loved it. He never had a garden as a boy, you see. Not that I did either, God knows. He was happy as Larry out there, just doing the grass. And he used to go down to the garage every Saturday with one of the kids. With Johnny usually, and they'd bring the can, you know, for petrol. For the lawnmower. And it was the kind of an old-fashioned garage where they sold messages as well, you know. And he'd buy me roses. Red roses every Saturday. Do you remember that, Johnny?

Johnny: Yeah. I remember they didn't have them one week and he nearly threw the head.

Moya: And then when the kids had grown up, we'd just go down together Enda and myself: like a couple of old duffers. And Mister Clancy down in the garage got to know us over the years. Red roses, Mister Doyle, he'd say, and a can of petrol. A funny combination, isn't it?

Silence.

Tom: And how did you meet your husband, Moya? If you don't mind me asking.

Moya: God love, it's so long ago I nearly don't remember.

Medbh: She does so remember, don't mind her. It was at a dance, wasn't it?

Moya: No it wasn't actually, if you're so smart.

Medbh: How was it, then?

Moya: It was over in London, Tom, in digs, you know. God it was thirty years ago. I was in a little play over there. *Juno and the Paycock* by O'Casey. And it was only a small part now. I was Mary, the daughter, even though this shower call me Juno sometimes, for slagging. There were dances back then, in the Hammersmith Palais. All the Irish would go on a certain night. I was kind of home away from home.

Tom: And you met him there?

Moya: Well no... What happened was that Enda and his pal went along one night. And they met some girls, and they danced the night away I suppose. And he arranged to meet them the next morning and drive down to Bournemouth.

Johnny: Bournemouth, you know. The Da was a flash old bastard, wasn't he?

Moya: And anyway, next morning when they turned up to collect the two ladyfriends, wasn't the one Enda had his eye on not there. She was sick or something, so she'd sent along her friend in her place. And her friend was an awful looking moose apparently.

Catherine: Mother!

Moya: Well she *was*. That's what I was told anyway. So didn't Enda decide he didn't want to go after all. And there I was walking down the Fulham Palace Road, just minding my own business and he pulled up beside me and asked me the time, as bold as you please. He had a Dublin accent, and so I asked him where he was from. *(A bit of silent mimicry from **Johnny** and the girls, who ve heard it all a million times.)* He was from Usher's Quay and I was from Bride Street, in the Liberties. He lived about ten minute's from me at home, imagine. But if I hadn't gone to England I never would've met him. You wouldn't do it now. Get into a car with a strange man. But he had a very kind look about him.

Medbh: And what happened so?

Moya: We went to Bournemouth for the day. All the way down in the car he sang some stupid song that would have been in the hit parade at the time. It might have been Frank Sinatra. Or Elvis. Yes. Because Elvis was going then. Elvis was…and we had our lunch in a restaurant called English. I remember that because it seemed so funny to me, that there'd be a restaurant called that, when I didn't know a restaurant called Irish. Anyway, we talked for so long that they were putting the chairs up on top of the tables. And oh, he made me laugh so much. He'd have you in stitches. We walked along the seafront and we bought rock. And then we went to Mass at tea-time.

Catherine: You went to *Mass* on your date?

Moya: We certainly did. God, you wouldn't miss Mass. Not for Elvis himself.

Johnny: Mass is something we papists have, Tom.

Tom: I know what Mass is, thanks.

Catherine: (*Pointedly*) He knows what Mass is because he was at one today.

Medbh: And what happened then?

Moya: What do you mean?

Medbh: On the way home? Did he get the tongue in?

Moya: Stop that. Your father was a gentleman. He dropped me off home at the digs and he said – I'll always remember – Moya, I must say, I've had a very pleasant afternoon and I'd be disappointed now if I couldn't see you again.

Johnny: Oh a magnificent way with the words, all the same.

Moya: Well one week then, he asked me if I wanted to meet him beforehand. That was the big thing. That was when you knew you were going together, when you'd meet the fellow outside and he'd pay you in… And we just clicked really. And when the play was over then, I didn't come home to Dublin. I got a little job, in a hotel in Earls Court. And he worked in a bookshop on the Charing Cross Road. And the times we had then in London.

Catherine: And did you love him straight away. Mum? When you met him, I mean?

Moya: God, pet, I don't know. I *liked* him as soon as I met him I suppose. And then before I knew it...Well, I remember we had a row once, and I came on home to Dublin on the boat. And my mother asked me: do you love him, Moya? And I thought: to say I loved him would be like saying...like saying that it was rainy today. So I went back to him.

Moya fights back tears.

Tom: That's a lovely story, Moya.

Moya: That's the way it was, I loved the children's father and he loved me. We had our ups and downs over the years, of course. But that's the way it *was* in those days. It wasn't something you thought about. Some people now, they want moonlight and roses the whole time..

Catherine: It wasn't always like that though, was it?

Moya: Well, no. But that isn't something that needs to be discussed.

Catherine: But you know that time when you had all the rows...

Moya: Catherine please, not today love.

Catherine: God, I'm just saying, there were rows weren't there? I remember you not getting on well sometimes. That's all I'm saying.

Moya: But, sure, every marriage is like that, pet. You'll see when you're married yourself. Please God. Every marriage... it's such a very hard thing to get to know a person. My God, you're young, you're beguiled. And then you find you change. And everything in your life changes. You're not the same people any more. You think love is the feeling in your tummy. That lovely feeling when you're falling through the air. But it isn't.

Medbh: So what is it?

Moya: It's when… it's when you start to think, another person is real.

Catherine: (*Laughs*) I don't know what you mean.

Moya takes her hand.

Moya: No. Well you will, pet, please God. You know sometimes when I think about all of you… I see myself at your age. And I remember all the hopes I had. All that hope is a great thing. You should make the most of it. Because it won't always be like that.

Medbh: Deep, Ma.

Moya: *You* know exactly what I mean though. You all do.

Medbh: I know. I do.

Moya: (*Looking at her watch*) So now, God it's so late. And I'm talking too much. As usual, says you. I think I'll go in and make us all a nice pot of tea.

Moya stands and goes to leave.

Moya: Tom, go and make another one for yourself, for God's sake. You needn't stand on ceremony here.

Tom: Thanks, Moya.

*Moya goes to leave. Silence in the room. **Tom** makes his drink and goes to the window. He peers out. It s raining hard.*

Tom: Well, it's another terrible night out there anyway.

Medbh: Is it?

Tom: My God, you wouldn't send a dog out in it.

*Silence. After a moment, **Medbh** makes an effort.*

Medbh: The weather's been fucking poxy this year, Tom. I remember Dad saying to us when we were kids: Saint Patrick used to pray that Ireland would sink into the sea with the rains, seven years before the end of the world. I think it must be happening.

Tom: I was only just saying that to that girl in the church today. I can never remember the weather being so bad.

When I lived in Ireland, I mean... I mean, yes, you'd have your hard winters, but now half the country's flooded, she was saying. All the farmers down the West are up in arms about it.

Medbh: Yeah, so I believe. Which girl was that?

Tom: Oh, just... that girl, you know.

Medbh: Which?

Tom: That one your father knew.

Catherine turns and glares at him.

Catherine: You *spoke* to her?

Tom: (*Laughs anxiously*) Well, I just said hello, Catherine. It was after the mass when you were talking to everybody, and I just slipped out for a fag. And she was there by herself, and the girl was upset... I mean, I had to just say nod and say hello.

Catherine: You're joking me.

Tom: (*Laughs nervously*) What, Catherine? ... I only gave her time of day, for God's sake. Sure I only said hello and goodbye to the girl, that's all.

Moya very suddenly comes in with a tea tray.

Moya: Which girl was that, Tom?

Tom: ...Nobody, Moya... Just this girl who was at the funeral.

Moya: (*Laughing, to Catherine*) You'll have to be up early the morning to keep tags on this fellow, love. He's an eye for the ladies I see. Tell us, was she good looking. Tom?

Tom: Well, I was only talking to her for a second.

Catherine stands suddenly and goes to the window

Moya: Oh God, would you look? There's going to be a big lovers' tiff now. She wants you on a short leash anyhow, Tom.

Catherine: Tom does and says exactly what he likes.

Tom: I do not, Catherine.

Catherine: Oh, you do alright.

Tom: I said I'm sorry, Catherine. Don't be embarrassing me now, in front of everyone.

Moya: My God, Catherine, stop. Look at the puss on you. What's ailing you, sweetheart? The poor fellow was only being polite, for heaven's sake. There's no harm in that. Tell us, who was she anyway, Tom?

Tom: I don't know who she was.

Moya: (*Harrassing him playfully*) Well, what did she look like then?

Tom: I didn't really see.

Moya: (*Laughs*) Go on, tell us. I won't say a word.

Tom: I ... I think she might have had a mark on her face.

Medbh: I... don't think I saw anyone like that.

Silence. Moya sips her drink.

Tom: Well, I just said hello, that's all. She seemed to be so upset, and I only ... Would you not come back and sit down, Catherine?

Moya: (*Laughs, a little too loudly*) Do you know, now that you mention it, I think I saw you. A girl in her twenties. Yes, with the birthmark? Sure I saw you myself in the porch, he was just chatting dear. I know all about her actually. Tom, you were only being mannerly, weren't you Tom?

Tom: (*To Catherine*) Will you not sit down, love?

Moya: She's just some girl from the college, Tom. Daddy was giving her a hand with her studies. With advice, you know. On books. He had so much knowledge, but he was generous about it too. He got on great with the students.

Moya takes another sip of her drink.

Moya: Enda was always very popular. Very good with people. Always very...

Catherine: Mum, for Christ's sake…

Medbh: Leave it, Catherine.

Catherine: What difference does it make now? Why can't we all just tell the truth?

Moya: What do you mean, love?

Medbh: She doesn't mean anything.

Tom: Catherine, please, I'm sorry if I've done anything I shouldn't.

Moya: Tom, you've done nothing bad at all, love. She's some girl who Daddy was helping out with her studies. It's very simple. Now, sit down there and we'll have a cup of tea together and not be rowing.

Catherine: *Stop this!*

Moya: Stop what, love?

Catherine reaches into her pocket and takes out the photograph she removed from the book the day before.

Catherine: What's that?

Moya takes the photo, looks at it for a few moments.

Moya: It's a photograph. So what?

Catherine: It's a photograph of *her*, Mum. Of that girl. It was in a book over there on the shelf.

Moya: Well, isn't that nice? … Is it a crime to have a photograph of a person now?

Catherine snaps it out of her hand.

Catherine: Are you blind? (*She turns it over and reads aloud*) To Enda, with all my love and thanks, from Helen.

Moya: Well what does that mean?

Catherine: Don't you really *know* what it means? Don't tell me you don't, Mum. I don't believe it. You lived with the man for thirty years, you must know.

Moya: (*Laughs*) What?

Catherine: You know well. Don't laugh at me, you do know. That's why nobody's here, Mum. You must know that. It was all over UCD when I was there. It was the laugh of the whole place. Big big joke. Big laughs all round. And when Medbh was there too, before she left. That's *why* she left, Mum. Because she *had* to, with all the talk.

Medbh: I did not, Catherine.

Catherine: That's not what you told *me.* It is *so* and you know it. People used to laugh about it, Mum. Everyone in the place laughed about it. Why do you think nobody's here?

Moya: God, I haven't a clue. Wasn't I only just saying that..?.

Catherine: How would *anyone* come here? When they've no idea what might happen today? When they've no idea what bloody scene they might fucking see if she turned up here?

Moya: You'd want to calm down now, my girl, you're losing the run of yourself, isn't she, Tom?

Catherine: *Don t* tell me to calm down. Do you know what it was like for us? They'd point at us and they'd laugh when we were passing by in the corridors…

Moya: Stop it, I said.

Catherine: 'There's Enda Doyle's daughters, oh, you know the story on him and your one, don't you? Been going on for years now. Do you think the wife knows? Does she just pretend *not* to know, do you think?' What do you think that was like for us?

Moya: Things were good for you. Good for you always. We worked bloody hard so they would be. And this is the thanks…

Catherine: Good for us? *Good for us?* When your father is fucking some little tart who's young enough…

Moya lashes out and slaps her in the face.

Moya: You little bloody bitch! How dare you! That's a terrible thing to say about your father. If you knew the love he had for this family, the sacrifices, the trouble he went to.

Catherine starts to cry.

Moya: *(Furious)* Do you know what it was like for him? When he was your age he'd been working fifteen years! There's not one of you kids now would know the meaning of responsibility! Perfection is what you want. The world handed up to you on a bloody plate. Nothing else will damn well do, and then you blame everyone else for everything.

Catherine runs out in tears. Medbh runs after her.

Moya: My God almighty, there's lovely talk for you now.

Tom: Moya, look, I didn't... I mean I really...

Moya: I'm sorry now, Tom, that you've been embarrassed. I don't know what must have come over her. I just don't know. I think we're all a bit tired, that's all, and I don't mind people having a drink, but I won't have that kind of talk.

Johnny goes and puts his arm around her shoulder,

Johnny: Relax Ma.

Moya: I'm *perfectly* relaxed, thank you.

Silence. Moya looks at her watch.

Moya: I think I'll just go out to the road again, and see if anybody's coming.

Johnny: Leave it Ma. Sure nobody's coming now.

Moya: You don't know that. They might be here any minute.

Johnny: Ma, it's lashing rain out there. Go on up and have a rest and if anyone comes I'll call you.

Moya: Well, I'm sorry now if I've embarrassed anybody. I'm sorry if I made a fool of myself.

Johnny: You haven't, Ma.

Moya: But we didn't do everything we did, your father and me, to have that kind of filthy talk in the house.

Johnny: I know, Ma.

Moya: You wouldn't hear it in a whorehouse.

Tom: I'm sure Catherine didn't mean any harm.

Moya: *(Freezingly cold)* Tom, you're very welcome here, but I'll thank you not to hand me out lectures on my own family if you please!

Moya leaves the room. **Tom** *slowly sinks his head in his hands.*

Tom: Jesus.

Johnny: *(After a moment or two)* So. Do Protestants have mothers, Tom?

Tom: You're very smart, aren't you?

Johnny: Not as smart as you, pal. We've all just seen how fucking smart you are.

Tom stands and goes to leave.

Johnny: *(A conciliatory sigh)* Listen … stay and have a drink, why don't you. It's done now.

Tom: I'm tired. And I've had enough to drink.

Johnny: Well, look… I'm sorry for having a go at you, alright? I get a bit puerile sometimes, my psychiatrist says. I suffer from depression, you know. But I'm puerile too, he tells me.. Fifty quid a session and I'm puerile. Look it up in the dictionary, Tom.

Tom: No it's OK, Johnny. I got my Leaving Cert, you know?

Johnny: *(Laughs softly)*: Good man.

Tom leaves. **Johnny** *swigs from his glass. After a moment he gets up, goes to the television, inserts a video tape and presses play. His father s image appears in the screen,* **Johnny** *raises his glass in mock salute.*

Johnny: Look at me. Da. I'm on *toppa da woild.*

Enda: And the fields were laid out like bedspreads or something, as far as the eye could see, all the way down to Galway Bay. There were birds too, great big cormorants I suppose, that you get down there in that part of the world. And we stopped in Spiddal, for our tea. It was quite cold and there was that lovely smell in the air, of turf, and the salty tang of the sea. Mass was on in the church and you could hear the choir singing. And the people in the shops were all talking in Irish. It was such a lovely sound to hear, the sound of people all talking in Irish.. And Moya asked me to say a poem for her...

Suddenly, **Medbh** *runs through the room in tears and grabs her coat,* **Johnny** *presses pause on the remote.*

Johnny: Medbh!

Medbh runs out into the rain. **Johnny** *looks at the screen*

Johnny: You're missing a *really fun day*, Da. Do you know that? And isn't it just like you to cause all the trouble and then not be here? Isn't it?... Do you know what I'd really like now, Da? A big load of coke. A big fucking *pillowcase* full of it...What do you think Da? Do you think that sister of mine's brought anything over with her, do you? Help her through the stress? Will we take a look, Da?

Johnny *begins rummaging through* **Catherine** *s handbag. He pulls various items out of it and scatters them around. He finds the envelope containing his father s ashes. He opens it. Takes the envelope to the table and spreads the ashes out into lines on a plate.*

Johnny: I knew me big sister wouldn't let me down, Da.

Johnny grabs a mass card and tears off a piece of paper. He rolls it up and snorts one of the lines of ashes. He stares at his father s face on the screen.

Johnny: Well, Da... you know now... You know if there's anything up there now. You said you knew for sure, but you always wondered. You wanted everything to be sure. And wanted everyone to be sure about *you*. But they weren't. Because you had your little secrets, didn't you Da? Oh, you had your secrets alright.

Johnny brings a can of beer with him, sits down on the floor and presses the play button.

Enda: And then one day, didn't we all drive up to Cleggan and got the ferry out to Innishboffin, Moya and the girls, and the young lad, and the sea was so… the colour of amethysts, it was, and so clear and cold when you put your hand in the water. And we came out to the island and looked at Grace O'Malley's castle, and I told the young lad all about her. Grace O'Malley, the pirate queen, and I thought then, as I looked at it, of a line I once read somewhere…'And when Alexander saw the breadth of his domain, he wept, for there were no more worlds to conquer…'

Johnny presses pause.

Johnny: Enda Michael Malachi Doyle. You poor old fucking phoney.

Lights fade. Sound of waves breaking on a shore. Sound of thunder.

Scene Two

*Enter **Young Enda** and **Young Moya**, hand in hand. **Young Moya** is in preoccupied mood.*

Young Enda: The sea looks beautiful tonight, Moya, doesn't it?

Young Moya: It looks the same as it always does.

Young Enda: But look at the lights out there, the way they move on the water. That's France over there, you know. And look at the moon up there.

Young Moya: *(Melancholy)* I think the moon is looking for lovers.

Young Enda: My God, that's ripe talk, if your mother heard it.

Young Moya: It's in a play, you fool. It's in *Salome*, by Oscar Wilde.

Young Enda: Is it now? Well, come here and give us a kiss then, Salome. Before I lose my head over you.

Moya dodges his advance, with genuine irritation.

Young Moya: Stop, would you. I'm not in the mood.

Young Enda: You're in cranky humour tonight.

Young Moya: Don't be saying that.

Young Enda laughs softly.

Young Moya: What's so funny all of a sudden?

Young Enda: Nothing, nothing. 'But why did I laugh tonight?' That's in a poem by John Keats.

Young Enda: God Enda, all your talk of books and poems. And what do you know about anything? For all your books?

Young Enda is a little shocked. But he laughs gently again and takes her hand.

Young Enda: Nothing. I know nothing at all. And I don't care. I'll burn my books!

Young Moya softens, in spite of herself.

Young Moya: That'll be the day alright. You're mad about those stupid old books of yours.

Young Enda: Will we get married, Moya?

Moya s demeanor changes again. She turns away.

Young Moya: God, you're very serious aren't you.

Young Enda: We could go home to Ireland.

Young Moya: (*Laughs dismissively*) How could we do that?

Young Enda: We could try, couldn't we?

Young Moya: That's only dreaming, Enda. There's nothing at home now, you know that.

Young Enda: That's not true, love. There's plenty of opportunity at home these days. I was only reading in the paper the other day, where they said that. The new government at home.

Young Moya: If there's so much bloody opportunity what's everyone doing over here?

Young Enda: But things are changing at home now, Moya. That's what everyone says. They're building houses, left, right and centre. Things are on the up now, I read about this job a while ago, in the university in Dublin. Junior Library Assistant. I thought it'd be a handy enough sit if I could get it. And I did the interview when I was at home over Christmas. And guess what?

Young Moya: What?

Young Enda: I got it, Moya... I'm after getting it. We can get married now, and go home to Ireland.

Young Moya: You've everything figured out, haven't you?

Young Enda: I love you, Moya.

Young Moya: You say you love me and you don't even talk to me about something like that. How do you know that's what I want to do? Did that ever dawn on you for a minute?

Young Enda: ... I'm sorry, Moya. I thought I'd surprise you. I thought it was what you wanted.

Young Moya: Oh did you now? You're bloody clairvoyant as well, are you?

Young Enda: I'm sorry, Moya. You know I do love you.

Silence.

Young Moya: Well, you know I'm fond of you as well. God help me.

She turns to him. He kisses her.

Young Enda: We could be happy as anything together, you know, over at home where we belong. And I'm so fond of you, Moya. I really am.

Young Moya: I know you are.

Young Enda: If I've let you down some way...

Young Moya: You haven't let me down. I just...

She hugs him desperately.

Young Moya: Don't ever leave me, Enda, sure you wouldn't?

Young Enda: How would I leave you? Haven't I just asked you to marry me?

Young Moya: Please don't ever leave me though.

Thunder rumbles.

Young Enda: Come on, love. We'll catch our deaths.

*Lights fade to darkness as **Young Enda** and **Young Moya** run off. Sound of thunder continues.*

ACT FOUR

Lights up on the living room. It is late at night. Continuing thunder and lightning outside. The sound of heavy rain.

*Johnny is asleep on the floor behind the couch, so that he cannot be seen from the door. On the frozen video screen, **Enda** s face is distorted into a smile. **Medbh** comes in from outside, her clothes soaked. She takes off her coat and dress and throws them over a chair. She takes her father s coat from the hanger and puts it on. Then she goes to the table, which is still full of food. Takes a bottle of beer and opens it. **Johnny** wakes up.*

Johnny: Who's there?

Medbh jumps.

Medbh: Jesus. Johnny. You scared me.

Johnny: What time is it?

Medbh: It's midnight. Jesus, my heart.

Johnny: Fuck. Midnight, is it? Where were you?

Medbh: I went down to Dooley's to see Charlie Foster.

Johnny: Fuck. Dooley's. What are you going to that kip for?

Medbh: Dooley's is alright.

Johnny: Good Christ. *Dooley s.* They used to search you for weapons on the way into that place, and if you didn't *have* any, they'd kick the shit out of you.

Medbh: It's good crack down there now. It's changed a good bit since you've been away.

Johnny: And how's Charlie? I heard he was home for a few months.

Medbh: He's grand. I've been seeing a bit of him, you know. Since he's been home from Oz.

Johnny: Oh yeah? Which bit of him have you been seeing?

Medbh: Don't slag me, Johnny. Please.

Silence.

Johnny: Is it serious?

Medbh: Ah, I like him alright. I'm a bit gone on him.

Johnny: Well, Charlie's a great bloke.

Medbh: Yeah he is. He's gas.

Johnny: I've a lot of time for Charlie.

Medbh: Yeah. Me too.

Johnny: Well, why do you look like a bulldog sucking piss off a nettle? What's up with you?

Medbh: He… asked me to go to Australia with him, Johnny. He asked me to go over with him, to live, you know. He's set up over there. In Melbourne. He wants me to go with him. He's going back next week.

Johnny: Are you going?

Silence.

Medbh: No, I'm not.

Johnny: Why not?

Medbh: I don't really know. But I'm not. I've been thinking about it a lot lately. I've been stringing him along, I suppose. I told him I'd tell him tonight for sure.

Johnny: *Go* Medbh. What the hell are you hanging around this dump for?

Medbh: Stop.

Johnny: Christ Medbh, get on that plane and go. Don't even think about it, just do it. Sure, Charlie's been mad about you since we were kids, you know that.

Medbh: I know, and I'm…I don't know if I've got what it takes. To go all that way. I mean, it's Australia, Johnny. It's the other side of the world… And then if it didn't work out.

Johnny: What are you talking about?

Medbh: Who'd look after Ma? Now she's on her own?

Johnny: That's only making excuses, Medbh.

Medbh: Well would *you* fucking do it? Would you and Jenny come home to look after her?

Johnny: ...What about Catherine?

Medbh: She'll never come home now. You know that. Her and Tom are getting married next Christmas. She told me earlier.

Johnny: Has she told Ma?

Medbh: She's gonna tell her tomorrow. She wanted to wait until after the funeral.

Johnny: Big of her.

Medbh: She's doing so well now, Johnny. Would you not give her a break?

Johnny: I'll give her a compound fucking fracture.

Medbh: It wasn't easy for her, you know. When she went to New York first she was still in a bad way.

Johnny: Yeah, well, we've all taken a few drugs in our time.

Medbh: Not the way she did, Johnny. You know that. You know what she was like. She was so mixed up about everything. All the rows at home, they hit her very hard. You remember all the rows they had when we were kids. But she's done a lot of work on her head over there.

Johnny: Work on her head. I love it.

Medbh: Well, it's true.

Johnny: I know. Look, I love her like a sister, OK? Just not one of mine.

Medbh: She loves you a lot, you know.

Johnny: She's a funny way of showing it.

Medbh: Well, so do you.

Johnny: I suppose I do. It's a family trait.

Medbh: Do you want a drink?

Johnny: Yeah. I suppose.

Medbh gets two cans of beer and a pack of cigarettes.

Medbh: So did anyone come while I was out? From the pub or anything.

Johnny: Don't, Medbh. You know nobody came.

Medbh: Johnny, I. ..How did you know?

Johnny: When I got in this morning the phone was ringing. It was some professor from the college. He wanted to know if it was true we didn't want people coming back to the house. It was a very revealing conversation.

Medbh: It wasn't my idea. Catherine was worried there'd be a scene. If that girl turned up. You're not to throw the head with her, Johnny, please.

Johnny: I'm not. I'm not. Maybe she was right.

Medbh: All the food Ma made.

Johnny: She's other things on her mind now, besides food.

Medbh: Do you think it's true, Johnny? About Dad and that girl?

Johnny: What does it matter now? Things aren't always what they seem.

Medbh: People did say it, you know. In UCD. You'd see them together all the time too. I remember bumping into them together in the bar once. And he looked right through me.

Johnny: Medbh, let's leave it be.

Moya comes in, wearing a dressing gown and pyjamas. She is carrying a shopping bag.

Moya: I thought I heard a noise.

Johnny: It's only us, Ma.

Moya: God, you're up late.

Johnny: We're only shooting the breeze.

Moya: Did anyone come, no?

*Johnny catches **Medbh** s eye.*

Johnny: Yeah, yeah. A few people came by from the college. From the library I think. I went up to you but you were asleep.

Moya: God Johnny, you should have *woken me*. What'll they think?

Johnny: They only stayed for a quick drink.

Moya: Still, though. I feel awful now. Who were they?

Johnny: I can't remember. A few dry shites in suits.

Moya: God. Was Professor Thompson here?

Johnny: I didn't catch the names.

Moya: I feel desperate now. What kind of tinker will they think I am?

Johnny: Well don't feel desperate, Ma. They were fine. They understood. They only wanted to drop in.

Moya: Were you out, Medbh, love?

Medbh: No, Ma. I just ran down to Mairead for an hour.

Moya: Look at you both, drinking and smoking away. It's like a speakeasy in here. Where's the other two?

Medbh: They're in bed, I think.

Moya: They're not. I looked just now. And I wanted to apologise for losing the run of myself earlier. It's a terrible thing to let the sun go down on your anger.

Johnny: She had it coming, Ma.

Moya: I'm ashamed of myself now, I must say. I don't know what came over me. I don't feel very big.

Medbh: I don't know where they are.

Moya: I hope they're alright anyway. It's not much of a night to be walking the streets.

Medbh: I think I'll turn in anyway. I'm jacked. Goodnight Ma.

Medbh kisses her mother.

Moya: Goodnight, pet. And thanks for all your help.

*Medbh kisses **Johnny**.*

Medbh: Goodnight sweet prince.

Johnny: Yeah, yeah. Get thee to a fucking nunnery.

*Medbh leaves. **Johnny** and **Moya** are alone together.*

Moya: It's so good to see you, love. You look well.

Johnny: I'm always well, Mother. You know that.

Moya: No you're not. Nobody's always well.

Johnny: Well, I am.

Moya hands him the shopping bag.

Moya: Look in that for me, love. I haven't my glasses. I'm sorting them out for the library. Daddy's books. Just read out the names on them.

Johnny takes out a handful of books and reads their titles.

Johnny: There's a Collected Yeats. Heaney, Auden, Philip Larkin…

Moya: They can have all those. Put them in the box.

Johnny throws them into the tea chest, behind the sofa.

Johnny: Milton, Marvell, Thomas Kinsella, Paul Durcan…

Moya: Those too.

He throws them into the chest and rummages again in the bag.

Johnny: What's this old one? *The Love Songs of Connaught*, by Douglas Hyde…

She thinks for a moment. But then:

Moya: That too.

Johnny: It looks old, Ma. It might be worth a few quid.

Moya: Not at all. Give it in to them where someone might read it.

Johnny: It's too good for the library, Ma.

Moya: Indeed it's not. What good is a book that noone reads?

Johnny: OK. If you're sure.

Johnny throws it into the tea chest.

Johnny: That's all.

They sit down together on the sofa.

Moya: Well, we'll have a good time, all of us together, now you're over. And a bit of a chat. Sure, I hardly ever see you now you're over there.

Johnny: Yeah. Look, I meant to tell you earlier, Ma. I'm going back tomorrow.

Moya: *What?*

Johnny: I've to go back to London tomorrow. First thing.

Moya: But you've only just got here, Johnny. Stop play-acting now. I mean you can't go back tomorrow when you've only just got here.

Johnny: There's some stuff I have to do.

Moya: What do you have to do? Would you not stay for a while?

Johnny: I'm going back.

Moya: Don't go, son. Please.

Johnny: It's Jenny… She's pregnant.

Moya: I'm sure she is. If this is another one of your spoofs.

Johnny: I wish it was. She is, Ma. She's three months gone.

Moya: Well. Isn't that great? Why didn't you tell me before?

Johnny: What's so great about it?

Moya: Well I mean, if that's what you want. That's wonderful news.

Johnny: It's not what I *want*. A mortgage and nappies and driving out to the country on a Sunday to see all the woollybacks. All that. I wanted her to get rid of it.

Moya: That's a big decision, Johnny.

Johnny: What's so big about it?

Moya: That's not an easy thing for any woman. You know that yourself. You know what Medbh went through.

Johnny: No. Well she wants to keep it anyway. So that's what we're doing. We're keeping it.

Moya: Would you not stay and just relax for a few days.

Johnny: I'm going tomorrow, Ma. I'm going home.

Moya: Why are you going? If you don't want that life?

Johnny: You know why.

Moya: Why? Tell me?

Johnny: Because I wouldn't do what he did.

Moya: What do you mean?

Johnny: You know well what I mean.

Moya laughs.

Moya: Johnny. I'm sure I don't.

Johnny: *Don t*, Ma. He told me about it years ago.

Moya: What did he tell you? What?

Johnny: He told me about Helen. I *know* you know.

Moya: I'm sure I don't.

Johnny: The girl yer man Tom was talking to in the church. You know well who she was.

Moya: ...He told you about it?

Johnny: He had to.

Moya: Why did he do that?

Johnny: I'm the executor of the will, Ma. He wanted to look after her. It's not much. There's the house, a bit of life insurance for you. A few bits and pieces. And there's just a small covenant in it for her. To pay off her college loan.

Moya: You're the executor?

Johnny: Yeah. Gas, isn't it?

Moya is silent for a few moments.

Moya: And he told you everything? ...My God.

Johnny: Are you shocked?

Moya: I always meant to tell you about it, love... You of all of them. I thought you'd understand. He was so young. His head was turned. It was just after I lost the child. There was... a distance between us then, I don't know why. We weren't getting on and it was a thing that happened before we had the chance to settle down again. You shouldn't judge your father for that.

Johnny: I'm not judging him. That's more than he did for me.

Moya: And the woman got pregnant on purpose. She trapped him.

Johnny: Oh yeah. Sure she did.

Moya: There's a good word for what she was, Johnny, but I wouldn't use it. She was well-known for it.

Johnny: She had a hard enough time, I believe. When Dad left her by herself to have the kid.

Moya: (*With sarcasm*) I'm sure she did.

Johnny: Sure, you know she did. Didn't he tell you that?

Moya: Your father and me had more to talk about than that one, believe you me. She needn't think she'll see anything your father had anyway. She needn't think that for a minute.

Johnny: She's dead, Ma. She died a few years ago. Over in England.

Silence.

Moya: And I'm supposed to feel sorry, am I? She wanted to ruin everything. For me and your father, and for you and your two sisters. And she would have too if she'd been let.

Johnny: My *three* sisters, Ma. Remember your Chekhov. My three sisters. Helen's as much Dad's daughter as Medbh or Catherine.

Moya: You needn't Helen me. She's no sister of yours.

Johnny: Ma, for God's sake.

Moya: She's *nothing* to this family and anyone who says she is needn't think they'll get the time of day from me!

Johnny: Alright, Ma. Relax.

Moya: I loved Enda and he loved me. That was the way it was. We were married and that was the way it was.

Johnny: I know he loved you. He told me that.

Moya: ...Did he?

Johnny: Yeah. He did.

Moya: Did he really say that?

Johnny: Yes.

Moya: He changed, Johnny. After we were married. I couldn't see it at first. But then he just stopped telling me he loved me. And I'd tell him all the time. I'd say it in the mornings when I woke up beside him. And he'd feel all warm and drowsy, you know, the way men do in the mornings. And I'd just say Enda, I love you. Just that. And all he ever said to me was, I know you're fond of me anyway, for you put up with me. And if he'd just said it to me even sometimes, I would have been so ...comforted. But he didn't. So then after a while I just stopped saying it to him too.

Johnny: Well he never said it to me either.

Moya: He never even wrote me a love poem. Not even one of his silly bloody poems. It wouldn't have been much to ask, would it, son? For all those years.

Johnny: No. It wouldn't.

Moya: There was once when he said… It was shortly after *you* were born. He was so happy when you came along, Johnny. After the two girls. There was a lightness about him then. There was an air of something…He came into the kitchen one morning with you in his arms, sleeping, and he said it in Irish. *A stóirín, tá grá agam duit.* Darling, I love you. I can see his face still. And we put you to sleep in the cot. And then we went upstairs and we made love.

Johnny: You've a great memory.

Moya: Well I remember that day well… Because it was the last day we ever made love.

Johnny takes her hand and squeezes it.

Johnny: He didn't deserve you, Ma.

Moya: He deserved a lot better than me.

Johnny: They don't come any better than you and that's the truth.

Moya: That woman… Did she ever get married afterwards, do you know?

Johnny: Yeah. She did. She married some Scottish bloke, apparently. He worked in a bank. She was living over in Manchester. And then Helen found her a few years ago. Through the agency, you know. And that was how she found Dad.

Moya: He never told me that. I mean, he told me she'd found him, of course. It brought it all up again. But nothing else.

Johnny: No. Well, I think he didn't want to hurt you.

Moya: And have you met her? The girl?

Johnny: I've seen pictures, that's all.

Moya: Catherine and Medbh. Please don't ever tell them. What your father told you.

Johnny: Why not?

Moya: I don't know. Because I asked you not to?

Johnny: I wouldn't have anyway. Not now. They'd've rushed us off to family therapy or something. We'd all have been on the Oprah Winfrey show in the morning. Or Jerry fucking Springer.

Moya: Oh son, I get a laugh out of you anyway. I wish you'd stay for a while. Would you not?

Johnny: I can't.

Moya: Would you not ring Jenny and get her to come over?

Johnny: I said I'd go back to her.

Moya: Well, if you have to. But there'll always be a home for you here. You and anyone you want, love. You remember that.

Johnny: Yeah, well I have to go. So there's nothing more to be said. So I'm going on up to bed. I'm a poet, Ma, like himself.

Moya: (*Laughs*) Sure, you can't, son.

Johnny: Why not?

Moya: There's only your father's bed free.

Johnny: That'll do.

Moya: You can't sleep in your father's bed.

Johnny: Why not?

Moya: It wouldn't be right.

Johnny: I'm not the sentimental type, Ma. You know that.

Johnny goes towards the door.

Moya: Johnny?

Johnny: What?

Moya: Nobody came, did they? ... From the pub.

Silence.

Johnny: They did, Ma. A few of them from the college. I didn't know who they were. They only stayed for a quick drink.

Moya: Really?

Johnny: Truly.

Moya: Well, I wish you'd woken me.

Johnny: Well, I should've. I'm sorry.

Johnny goes towards the door again. He pauses in the doorway.

Johnny: I love you, Ma... You know that, don't you?

Moya: Yes son. I know that.

Johnny leaves. Moya stands and begins clearing up plates of food. After a moment or two, she begins to cry. She drops the plates, holds her hands to her face and sobs violently, then tries to gather her composure. She goes to the interior door. She takes a look at the room. She turns off the lights and leaves the room, her body shaking with tears. She closes the door behind her, and as she does so, the video switches itself on. The screen shows Enda s face in tight close-up. He stares at the camera for a moment, then begins to speak. It is obvious from his declamatory style that he is speaking a poem.

Enda: A Christmas Eve. I could not sleep
         And so threw on some clothes and came in here
         And sat dazed at the desk and tried to type
         A word or two; and sensed an oddly rare
         Nocturnal kind of pleasure, as outside
         The midnight blackbirds gossiped in the yews.
         Hard rain and storm relentless on the roads.
         The ghosts of long-gone dreams, the clacking keys...

Enter Catherine and Tom from the outer door. They ignore the video, smile at each other, steal silently and slowly over to the sofa hand in hand. They lie down on the sofa and embrace. They begin to kiss passionately, as the volume of the poem rises.

Enda: And then I heard you cry out as you dreamed.

I stood, framed in the door, and gently called you.
Next, scared to cross the threshold, lest you stirred,
A century passed before I came and held you.
You said my name. I felt your body quiver.
Moya love, you opened doors I thought I'd closed for
ever.

Thunder rolls. On the video screen, **Enda** *stands up. He walks
towards the camera. He pauses for a moment, before looking closely
into the lens. He laughs, gently. On the sofa,* **Tom** *and* **Catherine**
are still kissing.

Enda *laughs softly again, switches the camera off. White noise on
the screen. Fade to darkness.*

The End

Moya Doyle is the matriarch of the family. In her youth she was an actress. She is a woman of some passion and imagination, but the limits of her marriage have not provided her with outlets for those. Often she talks in a kind of charmingly vacuous way; she is not a good listener or a quick thinker and doesn't always get the point at once. (When Tom tells her his brother's bar in New York is called The Easter Rising, Moya has to ask 'Is it an Irish Bar?' when its name has indicated that it could hardly be anything else.) She is a warm-hearted, compassionate and humane woman who really should have married somebody else. But she specialises in denial of a most extreme kind. She is one of those people who have constructed a mythical narrative of their lives: 'I was happily married. Everything in my family was fine. I loved my husband and he loved me.' As though she believes that if she repeats it often enough it will become true.

If people in families are cast into roles then **Medbh** (pronounced Maeve) is the family clown. Like many such actors, her humour is a defence mechanism. Though she is very attractive she pays little attention to her appearance or clothing – she might almost be a bit of a slob. She is quick-witted and sharp-minded, very bright and funny. But in some ways she is also this family's greatest victim. Not only has she not escaped the house (when both of her siblings have managed to do that) but we learn that what at first seems a comically awful love-life is actually a history which includes considerable pain. Her relationship with her mother is as close and real as any relationship could be in this damaged family – in many ways they are more like girlfriends than parent and child.

Her sister **Catherine** was the apple of Daddy's eye. Stylish, suave, cosmopolitan in her views. But perhaps there is an element of superiority about her – the girl who self-consciously left home and 'made it big' in New York, perhaps feeling that she had something to prove (though we learn she is capable of deception about that too). She probably sees many aspects of her Dublin life as a bit embarrassing. She might even resent the genuine closeness which Medbh has with their mother. Having had a drug problem and undergone therapy she is at least moving towards an honesty about her family's past, though she can also be selfishly and clumsily confrontational about expressing it.

Johnny is an explosion on legs. Absolutely full of anger and rage. If Moya is 'Red Roses', Johnny is 'Petrol'. And if Catherine is the family member whose therapy has led her to a version of the truth, Johnny is that most dangerous of things, someone who wants to tell the *whole* truth, sparing nobody. Often he spits out his words in a kind of passionate torrent. And yet Johnny – not the others – is the one who finally tells Moya that she was loved. I think of Johnny as being in two 'modes' during the play. There is high-octane Johnny who enjoys the more than slightly sadistic pleasure of washing the family's dirty linen in front of Tom – loving every moment of this performance – and behind that there is the family member who is probably the most damaged and hurt, but also the most realistic. The Hamlet of the Doyle clan, he too 'puts on an attic disposition'.

It is important that **Tom Ivers** is not played as a buffoon, but a thoroughly decent and dependable fellow who really does love Catherine. Yes, we have a bit of a laugh at his expense, particularly when we meet him first, but behind his shyness Tom is utterly reliable and truly concerned for her.

TEXTUAL AND PERFORMANCE NOTE

Red Roses and Petrol was commissioned by Pigsback Theatre Company and first performed in 1995, directed by Jim Culleton. After an extended run at the Project Arts Centre it had a national tour, a transfer to London and a transfer back to Dublin for an extended run at the Tivoli Theatre. Since then it has been professionally performed in London, New York, Boston and San Francisco, with dozens of amateur per- formances in Ireland and around the world. The version of the text presented here incorporates a number of useful cuts made in some of the play's professional performances and is thus a little shorter than the version appearing in the first published text (by Methuen Drama, 1995, ISBN 0 413 69990 0).

The action of the play involves the on-stage use of a video machine. To avoid causing heart attacks and other distresses to the actors, the VCR is usually controlled from off-stage.

It is important for the second stanza of Enda's closing poem to swell in volume. In the original production, to achieve the desired 'haunting' effect, loudspeakers not previously used in the proceedings (set around the theatre) were used from the line 'And then I heard you cry out…'. *Very* slight echo could also be used.

In the original Pigsback production the parts of Young Enda and Young Moya were played by the actors who played Tom and Catherine, thereby creating a deliberate ambivalence near the end of the piece. Who are the couple on whom the play closes? Young Enda and Young Moya, representing the hurts of the past? Or Tom and Catherine, the new lovers, whose relationship perhaps offers some hope for the future? Perhaps they stand for both couples simultaneously, as was the author's original intention.

Other productions have omitted the two scenes in which Young Enda and Young Moya appear. If such a cut is indeed made (and only in that eventuality) it is necessary to include the following lines in Act One (page 190; after Medbh's line: 'Sure. Why not?'):

Tom: (*Now reading a title*) *The Love Songs of Connaught* by Douglas Hyde.

Catherine: Load of rubbish. Should have dumped the whole lot years ago.

Medbh: (*Gently admonishing*) C'mon Catherine.

Catherine says nothing.

Medbh: My father gave that one to my mother, Tom. In their courting days, you know.

Tom: (*Reading reverently*)*:* My grief on the sea/how the waves of it roll ...

Medbh: (*Interrupting and continuing, she s heard it a million times*) As it comes between me and the love of my soul. Yeah.

Tom: (*Laughs; and then gently, to Catherine*) Sure you couldn't throw out a thing like that, pet.

Catherine: Oh sure. The happy couple. Let's all pretend.

Medbh: I'll ... put it upstairs. Ma'll want to keep it.

She puts it to one side. Silence descends.

Catherine: So. Any word from the college? About who's coming tomorrow?

Joseph O'Connor

From Both Hips

A Play in Two Acts

Mark O'Rowe

From Both Hips was first produced by Fishamble Theatre Company on 25 June 1997 at the Little Theatre, Tallaght, and then transferred to project @ the mint and the Tron Theatre, Glasgow. The cast was as follows:

Liz Marion O'Dwyer
Adele Clodagh O'Donoghue
Paul Ger Carey
Theresa Fionnuala Murphy
Willy Sean Rocks
Irene Catherine Walsh

Director Jim Culleton
Designer Bláthín Sheerin
Lighting Designer/Production Manager Nick McCall
Stage Director Jennifer Crawford
Stage Manager Orla Hennessy
Producer Maureen Kennelly
Project Arts Centre Director Fiach Mac Conghail

From Both Hips won the BBC/Stewart Parker Trust Award for Best First Play in 1997.

Photo (l-r): Clodagh O'Donoghue, Fionnuala Murphy and Marion O'Dwyer as Adele, Theresa and Liz © Paul Gaster

Dramatis Personae

Liz

Adele, her sister

Paul, Adele's husband

Theresa, Paul's girlfriend

Willy, a policeman

Irene, his wife

ACT ONE

Scene One

*A sitting room in a normal, working-class house. Stage left, the hallway to the front door. Up right, the door to the sitting room. Up left, stairs leading off. A table and chairs. A sofa. **Liz** sits on the sofa reading the paper. **Adele** stands in the centre of the room, looking around. She exits. She returns. She exits again.*

Liz: Adele! (*Calling*) Adele! What are you doing? C'mere!

Adele: (*Entering, just inside door to kitchen*) What?

Liz: See what it says here?

Adele: What? (*Exits*)

Liz: (*Calling*) Where are you going? Will you stop going in and out? Come back in, will you?

Adele: (*Offstage*) What?

Liz: Come back in and sit down. (***Adele** enters and stands there.*) What are you doing?

Adele: I'm looking for the ship.

Liz: Well, just ask me. It's inside on top of the press. It's grand. Sit down.

Adele: No, I'll stand. What does it say?

Liz: It says … You're making me very nervous, there.

Adele: Good. Go on. Read. Tell me.

Liz: Something I never knew. Something very surprising. Dogs …

Adele: Mmm?

Liz: … Dogs. Right here, some professor. Dogs are incapable of love.

Adele: Dogs?

Liz: ... Some professor, here. Although they appear, he says, loving and affectionate, they actually don't have any emotions. It's all ... the way they act, their behaviour. It's all instinctual.

Adele: Yeah?

Liz: That's not really fair, is it?

Adele: Why not?

Liz: Well, love's a two way street. I wouldn't want to be giving love to something if it wasn't going to love me back.

(*Pause*)

Adele: Mmm.

Liz: You know?

Adele: Were you thinking of buying a dog?

Liz: No, no, God!

Adele: Well, then.

Liz: But I know people who have dogs. Ciara and Joe have one, and thing ... Theresa Nolan. She's fairly into her dog, actually. She comes out sometimes, she reeks of it, you can smell it off her clothes and all.

Adele: Reeks?

Liz: Bits of brown hairs on her jumper. Yeah, reeks, Ah, I'm a bit addled now, damn!

Adele sits down and lights a cigarette.

Adele: What's wrong?

Liz: I feel like I should do something about it.

Adele: Do some ... What?

Liz: I feel like I should tell them.

Adele: Who? Theresa Nolan?

Liz: She's fairly into her dog. Ciara and Joe ... Who else do I ...?

Adele: Tell them what? That their dogs don't love them?

Liz: Yeah. They should know.

Adele: Ah, Liz.

Liz: If I don't tell them, they could go on through life living a lie. Their dogs don't love them, even though they love their dogs. That's a lie, they're being cheated, they should be told. On the other hand ...

Adele: On the other hand, ignorance, Liz.

Liz: What about it?

Adele: Ignorance is bliss.

Liz: It's ignorance, Adele. Nothing good comes of it. I'm saying if I tell, it'll hurt. It'll hurt at first.

Adele: Could.

Liz: Nobody likes being told they're in an unrequited relationship.

Adele: You wouldn't call it a relationship. (*Pause*)

Liz: Are they communicating, Adele?

Adele: I don't ...

Liz: In some way, a dog and its master, mistress. Its owner. Are they, like, aware of each other?

Adele: I suppose.

Liz: Well, then they're communicating. It's happening over a period of time, then it's a relationship. There's physical contact going on? Yes. In Theresa Nolan's case, a lot, judging from the stink on her, then it's a close relationship. Jesus! She feels love, the dog feels nothing, she's being made a fool of. Her dog's working the dark trick on her.

Adele: The what?

Liz: The dark trick. And she's not the type of girl who has many friends. It's probably the best friend she has. She's playing the fool for her dog and she doesn't even know it, she thinks it's two sided and ... You all right? (***Adele** is* *distant)* ... She's getting nothing in return. Are you all right? *(Beat)*

Adele: Hmm? *(Beat)* Yeah. I'm just ... I'm kinda ... I'm like ... Just give me two minutes.

Liz: Are you sure?

Adele: *(Flustered)* No, no. Just gimme ... I have to get my head ...

Liz: Okay.

Adele: ... Just two minutes, give me.

Liz: Okay. You sure? Do you want me to get something for you?

Adele: Yeah. No. I'm fine. It's just ... Okay. All right. That's it.

Liz: I'm say ...

Adele: Go on. Tell me the rest.

Liz: I'm saying ... You all right?

Adele: Sorry. Yeah. My mind was just ... This way, that, up, million directions. Go on.

Liz: It's all right ... Well ... For some people, you love someone and they don't love you. But they *like* you. Some people can live with that. That's enough for them. Least there's some emotion going on, okay? But a dog ... doesn't ... feel ... anything. What do you think?

Adele: Well, are you sure it's true?

Liz: It says it right here in the *Echo*, Adele.

Adele: But, that doesn't make it ...

Liz: *(Interrupting. Getting up)* I'm gonna ring Theresa. To hell with the other two, Ciara and ... They've got each other, anyway.

Adele: You're gonna ring, what are you gonna do?

Liz: I'm gonna ring Theresa.

Liz picks up the phone and dials. Adele puts her cigarette out.

Liz: (*Into phone*) Hello? Theresa. How are you? It's … Who d'you think it is? It's Liz. Yeah, how's it going?

Adele exits to the kitchen.

Listen. What are you doing? Nothing. Good. Come over to Adele's house, will you? (*Pause*) Because … Just come over and you'll find out. I need to tell you something. That doesn't … (*Pause*) That's no excuse, you just told me you weren't doing anything, so come on. Half an hour or so. All right? (*Pause*) Bit of company since you're bored. (*Pause*) Yes, it is important. Yep. Okay. See you then.

Liz: (*Calling to kitchen*) I told her to drop down. (*Pause. Calling*) Adele! (*Adele enters with a glass of water and a pill. She takes the pill, chases it with some water*) Should you be taking that now?

Adele: Just the one.

Liz: You only took one a while ago, Adele.

Adele: It's just the one, Liz.

Liz: I wasn't comfortable about breaking it to her over the phone, so I asked her to drop down. (*Pause*)

Adele: The dog?

Liz: Rather in person. So if she needs a hug or something. She might need a …

Adele: You're gonna tell her her dog doesn't love her?!

Liz: I couldn't do it over the phone, she's on her own there. She might need a bit of support, a hug, some comforting words, someone to listen and help, to tell her …

Adele: But, what about …?

Liz: … everything's …

Adele: … you shouldn't …

Liz: … everything's going to be all right. To calm down, to …

Adele: What about ...?

Liz: To pull yourself together. (*Pause*)

Adele: What about Paul? (*Beat)*

Liz: We'll *be* here.

Adele: *And* Theresa?

Liz: The more, the merrier, a bigger welcome, Adele.

Adele: He's only expecting you and me.

Liz: He'll be delighted to see her. Paul's fond of Theresa, he'll be delighted.

Adele: But, he's only expecting ...

Liz: Yeah! So, that's ... That'll be the surprise. Paul'll come home and there'll be three of us here to see him instead of two, a bigger welcome, the more, the merrier.

Adele: He might want some peace and quiet.

Liz: And if he does, we'll give it to him. *After* we welcome him and he sees he's got friends. Theresa has to be told.

Adele exits with glass of water to the kitchen.

(*Calling*) Sooner the better she finds out she's being tricked.

Pause. **Adele** *returns, lights another cigarette.*

Adele: You should have met her somewhere else.

Liz: I thought of that, but I want us to be here, the more, the merrier, three's a crowd, but four's a party.

Adele: He might not want a party.

Liz: Just for when he comes in. He can hang around and chat for an hour, have a brandy and do what ...? Head off to bed or watch telly or ...

Adele: 'Cos he might want to.

Liz: You give us the signal and we'll head off. Say 'Geronimo'.

Adele: Geronimo?

Liz: That's the password. Say. 'Geronimo' and I'll take that as my cue.

Adele: See, we shouldn't … Paul's … we shouldn't …

Liz: I know.

Adele: … He's …

Liz: … We'll head off. If he wants us to head off …

Adele: … You'll …

Liz: … We'll go up to the pub.

Adele: That might be best.

Liz: Yeah. You haven't been alone together for more than five minutes in ages. Be nice for you to get re-acquainted. You can have an early night. Go to bed. Make the beast with two backs.

Adele: Liz!

Liz: The *beautiful* beast with two backs.

Adele: (*Embarrassed*) We'll be … We won't be …

Liz: The beautiful beast of true love …

Adele: … Stop, Liz.

Liz: (*Pause*) … with two backs.

Adele: Liz! (*Pause*)

Liz: Are you looking forward? (*Pause. **Adele** looks distant*) Adele.

Adele: What?

Liz: Are you looking forward? Are you all right?

Adele: I'm anxious.

Liz: Did I upset you, there?

Adele: No, I'm just anxious.

Liz: Where's his present? Bring it in, put it on the table, so he can see it when he comes in. He'll say, 'Whose is that?' And you'll say, 'It's yours.' (*Pause. **Adele** looks distant*)

Adele: Yeah.

Liz: Go on. It's on top of the press. Go.

Adele: Yeah.

Liz: Go and get it.

Adele exits and returns with a model ship. Unmade. Still in its box.

Liz: Put it there on the table.

She does.

Liz: No. Like this. (*Repositions box*) So he can see the name of it and all. Lovely. (*Pause*) Has he ever done one before?

Adele: Not since I've known him. Wait … Lemme … Before, may …? Just thinking …

Liz: No?

Adele: Has he …?

Liz: No? No?

Adele: I don't think so.

Liz: Good. No? Good. It's a good choice. Something to pass the time.

Adele: Was a good idea.

Liz: It is. (*Of model*) Did you ever?

Adele: Never.

Liz: I heard that fifty percent of those things never get finished. Fifty percent.

Adele: Fifty?!

Liz: Half of them. Of every one of those things that gets bought. So, you'd better warn him.

Adele: Paul'll finish it.

Liz: I'm sure he will.

Adele: He wouldn't start it if he wasn't going to finish it.

Liz: Yeah.

Adele: Wouldn't see the point. He'll enjoy that.

Liz: He will. Something to pass the time. Two weeks?

Adele: Yeah.

Liz: Probably *take* him two weeks.

Adele: And even if it takes longer …

Liz: I know. He'd probably take another few days off.

Adele: Just to finish it. Yeah. (*Pause*)

Liz: Perfect present.

Adele: Yeah.

*The telephone rings. **Adele** answers it. While she s on the phone, **Liz** goes over to the model ship, turns it on its side, then puts it back the way it was. She looks at the door. Moves the ship forward on the table, so that it ll be in a more advantageous position.*

Adele: Hello? No, no, he's not in at the moment. Can I …? No, yes, I'm sure. (*Pause)* I don't. If you want to try … (*Pause*) Well, I don't know if … (*Pause. She hangs up. Pause*)

Liz: What?

Adele: I don't know.

Liz: Who?

Adele: Some man.

Liz: Who was he?

Adele: Paul. (*Pause)* Looking for Paul.

Liz: For what?

Adele: Bit sinister.

Liz: Who? The man?

Adele: Said he was going to call around. Bit scary.

Liz: When?

Adele: Later was all he said. He didn't sound too happy.

Liz: How'd he sound?

Adele: Not happy.

Liz: How?

Adele: Sinister.

Liz: Sinister.

Adele: He didn't tell me anything else. Ah, God!

Liz: It was probably just a friend of his.

Adele: (*To herself*) Angry, maybe?

Liz: He sounded angry?

Adele: Sounded sinister.

Liz: And you don't know who it was?

Adele: No.

Liz: You sure? You know his friends.

Adele: No. I don't know this one.

Liz: Surely ...

Adele: Not this one. A scary voice, it was.

Liz: Sinister.

Adele: I hope he's not in trouble. (*Pause. She looks distracted*)

Liz: You all right?

Adele: Hmm?

Liz: What'd he say?

Adele: Just ... (*Pause. She looks distracted/upset*)

Liz: What? Adele?

Adele: Two mi ... I'm fine. I'm just ... I'm kinda ... (*Pause*) I wonder.

Liz: It'll be grand.

Adele: That's strange. (*Pause*)

Liz: Listen, why don't you ...? That's a bit drab. Why don't you dress up a bit for him?

Adele: This?

Liz: Bit drab, Adele. What about your black trousers I borrowed on Thursday?

Adele: Dress up?

Liz: Impress him even more, and the sexy white cardigan. Just to give him a real welcome.

Adele: I ...

Liz: Go on.

Adele: Should ... The woolly one?

Liz: He'll love it, go on. Yeah. The woolly white one and the black trousers.

Adele: I should dress up for him?

Liz: He'll love it. A bigger welcome. We'll have the model there, Theresa'll be here to make up the numbers, the more, the merrier, a bit of style from you. Go on. It's a statement, says 'I love you.'

Adele: Will he know that?

Liz: 'Course he will. (*Pause*)

Adele: Yeah. (*Pause*)

Liz: Who'd have thought that, huh? 'Bout the dogs.

Adele: Mmm.

Liz: They can't love.

Adele: Yeah.

Liz: For their appearance, you'd think they'd a ton of love. Waging their ... And their actions. Wagging their little tails and snuggling, and licking your face. (*Sighs*) Instinct.

Adele: Yeah.

Liz: It's a shame. I'd say it's gonna be a big disappointment to a lot of people with dogs.

The doorbell rings.

Theresa. Get some spirits out, there.

She exists to hall door. We hear it opening. **Adele** *exits to sitting room.*

Theresa: (*Offstage*) How are you, Liz?

Liz: (*Offstage*) Theresa. Come in. Come in. Listen. I'm sorry to get you down in such a rush.

Adele *returns with a bottle of brandy and glasses. She stands in the centre of the room, listening.*

Theresa: (*Offstage*) Is it important?

Liz: (*Offstage*) It is, yeah. Gimme there ... (*Pause)* Just hang it there. Grand. How are you?

Theresa: (*Offstage*) I'm fine. Is Adele here?

Liz: (*Offstage*) She's inside. How are you?

Theresa: (*Offstage*) I think you'll need to sit down first.

Silence. **Adele** *remains standing. Frozen in the centre of the room.*

Blackout.

Scene Two

A typical sitting room. **Paul** *sits on the sofa with a walking stick in his lap.* **Theresa** *enters with two cups of tea. She gives one to* **Paul.**

Theresa: There you go. (*She sits down.* **Paul** *drinks. Winces.*) All right?

Paul: Bit hot. (*Blows on it)*

Theresa: Do you want me to put some more milk in it?

Paul: No. (*Drinks)*

Theresa: Good to see you. How's the leg?

Paul: Crap. It's not my leg, it's my hip.

Theresa: How is it?

Paul: Crap. (*Pause. Drinks*)

Theresa: Thanks for calling in, Paul, I was getting to miss you. Getting a bit lonely. How are you?

Paul: Where's your telly?

Theresa: I was broken into.

Paul: When?

Theresa: Last night. The telly and the video.

Paul: You were broken into?!

Theresa: They didn't touch anything else. Just the …

Paul: And where were you?

Theresa: In bed, fast asleep. I didn't hear a thing. Just the telly and the video. They must've known there was somebody upstairs.

Paul: Broken into. Jesus.

Theresa: I'm scared.

Paul: The bastards.

Theresa: If they'd come upstairs …

Paul: Telly and the video.

Theresa: I didn't hear a thing.

Paul: Did you call the cops?

Theresa: Yeah, I went down this morning.

Paul: No help, I bet.

Theresa: Nothing. I had to fill in a few forms, but they told me …

Paul: They told you, I bet, the fuckers. They told you there was nothing they could do.

Theresa: I never wrote down the serial number, and even if I had, they'd ... The robbers would've filed it off by now, some family has a new telly and video. And the worst thing they said ...

Paul: Useless bastards.

Theresa: ... Worst thing, and it's kind of sad ...

Paul: What's that?

Theresa: The people who have it now are probably quite poor, not well-off, and they bought it, like, whatsit? Hot. A hot video because they couldn't afford a new one. But they wouldn't be, like, criminals. Just a family trying to get by.

Paul: They should be strung up.

Theresa: But, they'd be decent otherwise.

Paul: The coppers.

Theresa: They do their best.

Paul: They do, all right, the fuckers!

Theresa: Since ... I've been a nervous wreck all day. I feel ... Do you know? If someone breaks into your home ...

Paul: We've an alarm.

Theresa: If someone breaks in ...

Paul: (*Interrupting. Not listening*) Some of the nurses in there, Theresa. (*Pause*)

Theresa: They take good care of you?

Paul: Excellent. Some nice nurses.

Theresa: Nice?

Paul: Good-looking. Sexy nurses gear. I don't know what it is about them.

Theresa: Mmm.

Paul: Some gorgeous looking things. (*Pause*)

Theresa: I think it's … Could be they're taking care of you, so … They're … You know, that's what's so attractive about them. Because they're there just for you and they're taking care of you. Maybe that's why they're … You know?

Paul: They're fucking gorgeous is what it is. I asked one of them out this morning. (*Pause*) I'm meeting her tonight. (*Pause*)

Theresa: Did you?

Pause. They look at each other.

Paul: Just testing you.

Theresa: You didn't?

Paul: 'Course I didn't.

Theresa: Oh.

Paul: Testing you, I was.

Theresa: Right.

Paul: 'Course I didn't.

Theresa: Why?

Paul: Why?

Theresa: Yeah.

She moves closer and closer as they speak.

Paul: Because … Yeah, they took care of me. Grand. But none of them were my special friend.

Theresa: Your special friend.

Paul: Yeah.

Theresa: And who's your special friend?

She leans on him.

Paul: Aagh. Fuck. Get away.

Theresa: Oh, God.

Paul: Get away. Ouch!

Theresa: Sorry.

Paul: Fucking hip!

Theresa: I'm sorry.

Paul: Jesus!

Theresa: Are you all right? I'm sorry, I didn't mean to …

Paul: Fucking hip!

Theresa: (*Pause*) I'm sorry.

Paul: You don't take good care of me. (*Pause*)

Theresa: But I'm your special friend. I want to take care of you. (*Pause*) Is it bad?

Paul: It's bad enough. I need this fucking thing, don't I?

He shows the walking stick.

Theresa: (*Loveydovey speak*) But you have your special friend, now.

Paul: My special pal.

Theresa: Your special pal who'll help you and who'll look after you.

Paul: Who'll tend to me, yeah?

Theresa: Who'll tend to you specially.

Paul: Better than the nurses?

Theresa: Much better. The way only a special … (*Kisses him*) pal … (*Kisses him*) can … (*Kisses him*)

Paul: Ah, God. Get away.

Theresa: What?

Paul: Get away, the … Wash your face.

Theresa: What?

Paul: Smell of dog off you.

Theresa: Oh, no.

Paul: I told you before.

Theresa: I forgot.

Paul: Wash your face. That's the most unhygienic thing you can do.

Theresa: I can't help it. He likes to lick my face, he likes to be cuddled.

Paul: You stink of it. Come on. Theresa!

Theresa: I was lo … (*Pause)* Fuck you! Fuck off if you don't like it. (*Pause)*

Paul: I don't like it.

Theresa: Well fuck off, then, you're only out of hospital.

Paul: All I'm asking you is to wash your face.

Theresa: You're not coming into my place and ordering … That's the rudest thing. My face isn't smelly. How dare you come in … How … I was playing with Toby. If you don't like it … If … Well, fuck off, then, if you don't like it. (*Pause)*

Paul: Do you want me to go then?

Theresa: (*Realising she s gone too far*) No, I don't wa …

Paul: Head off on my merry way?

Theresa: No, it's just like …

Paul: Say if I was eating garlic … I know you don't like garlic.

Theresa: No. I don't.

Paul: So, if I was eating garlic, you'd ask me to brush my teeth and I wouldn't say no, because I know you don't like it.

Theresa: If you were …

Paul: Garlic. Same thing here. I don't like the smell of dog, it's the exact same thing. (*Pause)* It's just it's polite, like, it's a bit of consideration.

Theresa: Mmm.

Paul: The smell or the taste. It's the same thing. I *want* to kiss you.

Theresa: Yeah.

Paul: I *like* kissing you, but ...

Theresa: I know. (*Pause*)

Paul: Go on. (***Theresa*** *exits.* ***Paul*** *gets up slowly.*) I'm gonna make a phone-call. Is that all right?

Theresa: (*Offstage. Calling. Loveydovey*) Only if you're still my special pal.

Paul: You know I am. (*He makes a face, takes out a piece of paper and dials a number.*) Know who this is? Is ... No. Put him on. *Him.* You know who. Put him on. (*Pause*) Yeah, fuckface, how are you? (*Pause*) Yeah, I just got out, so this is where it begins, do you hear me? (*Pause*) Well, I'm sorry. I'm sorry, but, you know ... (*Pause*) That's your problem. We all have stuff to deal with. (*Pause*) My heard bleeds. (*Pause*) Listen. You listening? Right. Carefully, now. Fuck her and fuck you. Fuck the pair of you. I'm out and the wheel is in motion. Do you hear me? The wheel is turning.

He hangs up and limps backs over to the sofa. He eases himself down painfully, takes a sip of his tea. Enter ***Theresa***.

Theresa: All done.

Paul: Good. Are you gonna get a new telly?

Theresa: Suppose I'll have to.

Paul: Good.

Theresa: Who were you ringing? Adele?

Paul: No. The bloke.

Theresa: What did you say?

Paul: I told him the cogs are spinning. Don't say anything, Theresa. Don't open your trap, I don't give a shite.

Theresa: Don't talk to me li ...

Paul: I don't give a flying fuck, that's where the line is drawn. Anyone who has any objections ... Anyone who has ... They can ... Look at me. (*Pause*) Theresa.

Theresa: What are you going to say?

Paul: In the papers, the *Echo*?

Theresa: Yeah.

Paul: That's not for your ears. You'll find out when you read it.

Theresa: Tell me.

Paul: It's a surprise. Tony Kelly's column. You'll see it when you read it. Look at me.

Theresa: What?

Paul: Look at me. I want you on my side. This is just so he knows what he's let himself in for. Do you know I can't even sign on? I've another two weeks before I can go back to work.

Theresa: But you're going to get compensation.

Paul: I don't care. I don't give a fuck. I want *him* to pay. Those fuckers think they're all powerful. I'll show him it can be personal sometimes.

Theresa: Doesn't mean you have to harass him. You're making whatchamicallit telephone calls.

Paul: I'll show the fucker. I'm gonna, in a few years, when I'm older, I'll be the one of those poor fuckers who can't walk when it rains.

Theresa: You won't.

Paul: 'Course I will. A bum hip.

Theresa: Bum?

Paul: A bum hip. A hip that 'plays up' when it rains. And it always fucking rains. Ever hear the phrase 'An old war wound?' That's what it'll be like. And it'll be 'Playing up.' I'll be a what's the word?

Theresa: Infirm?

Paul: Fucking retard's what I'll be. (*Pause*)

Theresa: Your old war wound.

Paul: Yeah.

Theresa: I think that's romantic.

Paul: You would. (*Pause*)

Theresa: How long are you staying? Do you've to …?

Paul: Adele? No. After.

Theresa: Oh.

Paul: I'm dreading going home. (*She looks at him*) But I'm not staying here. I'm going for a drink. I've a few things to sort out.

Theresa: Who are you going with?

Paul: On my own. I need to be on my own for a few hours. Away from nurses and doctors and … I've plans to make. I'm gonna be busy for a while. Preparing and planning. Did you wash your face?

Theresa: Yep.

Paul: C'mere. (*She approaches*) Be careful, now.

They kiss.

Theresa: Let's go upstairs.

Paul: I can't.

Theresa: A quickie.

Paul: I can't.

Theresa: Why not?

Paul: 'Cos of this. I can't with this.

Theresa: Try.

Paul: What do you mean try? I can't. Next few weeks, now, I'll be impotent.

Theresa: Not impotent.

Paul: Yes, impotent. Technically, I'm impotent. I'm an impotent man. A man whose manhood doesn't work.

Theresa: For the next couple of weeks.

Paul: Yeah. For the next couple of weeks. It still gets to me. I'm proud of my cocksmanship.

Theresa: And so you should be.

Paul: And I like to use it. Not that it's my cock that doesn't work. It's my hip. I can't move. There's nothing wrong with my virility.

Theresa: Sure, don't I know.

Paul: It's just my hip.

Theresa: I know. (*Pause*) Is she expecting you?

Paul: Who?

Theresa: Adele.

Paul: She's got her sister over there.

Theresa: Liz?

Paul: They can keep each other company. One of them's bad enough. Adele's hard to take these days.

Theresa: You'd think she'd be a bit more … capable nowadays.

Paul: I'm doing the best I can.

Theresa: I'm sure you are.

Paul: But, when you can't even talk to your wife properly …

Theresa: I know.

Paul: And, now, since this thing … (*Holds up stick*) I'm doing my best.

Theresa: I know you are. (*She hugs him*)

Paul: Watchit. Watchit.

Theresa: Sorry.

Paul: Anyway, different things affect different people in different ways. Nah, I'm gonna go for a drink, do some thinking.

Theresa: Right. (*Pause*)

Paul: We must be the unluckiest people in the world.

Theresa: You're lucky you've got me around.

Pause. He looks at her.

Paul: What the fuck is that supposed to mean? I'm lucky.

Theresa: No. It just means …

Paul: I'm lucky I've got … I should be …

Theresa: … That's not …

Paul: … I should be grateful to you?

Theresa: No.

Paul: … That you're around?

Theresa: That's not what I meant. Stop. I was messing. Jesus! It's good that we can …

Paul. That we can what?

Theresa: That we can have a good time together. That's all I was saying. It was a joke.

Paul: Last thing I need's bloody jokes. (*Pause*) Some of the nurses in that hospital, though. (*Pause*)

Theresa: I'm a bit, Paul.

Paul: What?

Theresa: I'm a bit scared. Over this burglary.

Paul: What burglary?

Theresa: The telly and the video. I feel …

Paul: Oh, *your* burglary. Why?

Theresa: In case they come back. What's the word?

Paul: Why would they?

Theresa: Whatsit? I feel …

Paul: There's nothing to take.

Theresa: Very funny.

Paul: Maybe *you* should be grateful that *I m* around. (*Pause*) Yeah. That's what I'll do. I'm gonna … You know Kevin? Tony Kelly's a friend of his, said he'd be interested. You know Tony Kelly?

Theresa: Is he the cri …?

Paul: The crime correspondent, yeah. Genius way with words, he has. Kevin said he's be interested in my version of events. Get in there now, I'm gonna talk about incompetency, I'm gonna talk about someone who doesn't do his job properly, who shouldn't *be* doing that job, who shouldn't 've been doing it in the first place. Detailed descriptions of events, and then I'll drop the bomb. (*Imitates the sound of an explosion*) The laughing stock of the country. He won't be able to show his face for a year.

Theresa: What *is* the bomb?

Paul: None of your business. You can read about it in the *Echo*. (*He raises himself from a sitting to standing position with the aid of his walking stick and a loud grunt.*) Jesus! (*Beat*) Shite! Gimme, have you …? Pen and paper. Just a piece of paper. I'll have to make some notes.

Theresa: A piece of …

Paul: Yeah. Pen and a piece of paper. Have you got it?

Theresa: Yeah. Hang on. (*She exists*)

Paul: (*Calling*) I'll go up and make some notes, I think it's better to write stuff down.

Theresa: (*Offstage*) Will a pencil do?

Paul: Have you no pens? (*Pause*)

Theresa: (*Offstage*) No. (*She returns*)

Paul: Right. Just gimme the pencil.

Theresa: And there's your paper.

Paul: Nice one. Right.

He turns towards the door.

Theresa: You going?

Paul: Yeah.

Theresa: Have another cup of tea.

Paul: Booze, I need.

Theresa: I've got wine and ...

Paul: ... A pint. From the pumps. Haven't had a pint in ...

Theresa: Hang on here for a while.

Paul: I can't.

Theresa: Well, can I come with you?

Paul: No. What did ...? Wasn't I just saying? I've to make notes, I've to be on my own, I've to get my head together.

Theresa: Well, I'll come up, have the one ... a glass, and then I'll leave.

Paul: Sorry, Theresa. No. Bit of solitude, gimme ... (*He kisses her)* Have to go. (*He hobbles towards the door)* Give you a ring tomorrow, all right?

Theresa: What time?

Paul: Some stage during the day. (*She opens the door for him)*

Theresa: All right. (*He kisses her)*

Paul: Or the evening. See you.

*The telephone rings. **Theresa** jumps nervously.*

Theresa: Paul!

Paul: What?

Theresa: Hang on a sec', will you?

Paul: (*Impatient*) Come one!

Theresa: Just 'till I ... (*Points at phone*)

Paul: Think it's the fuckin' burglars or somethin'?

She answers the phone. Paul waits at the door.

Theresa: Hello? Who is this? (*Pause*) Oh. (*Pause*) Nothing. (*Pause*) Why? (*Beat*) What, though? I'm a bit tired. (*Pause*) But, what? (*Beat*) I'm fairly tired. (*Pause*) Is it important? (*Beat*) All right. Yeah. Yeah. Yeah. Okay, see you.

Paul: Who's that?

Theresa: Oh, it's just ... A ... Just this ...

Paul: You cheating on me, Theresa?

Theresa: No, it's a girl I know, wants me to ...

Paul: Some bloke, yeah?

Theresa: A woman. A girlfriend.

Paul: Bit on the side?

Theresa: Paul!

Paul: I'm testin'. Am I allowed go now?

Theresa: Yeah.

Paul: Good.

Theresa: Thanks.

Paul: You're welcome.

Theresa: You okay?

Paul: Yeah.

Theresa: You sure?

Paul: I'm crippled and I'm impotent. I'm grand. See you.

Theresa: See you.

He exits.

Theresa *stands silently.*

Blackout.

Scene Three

Another sitting room. **Irene** *sits on her sofa.* **Willy** *paces behind her.*

Irene: Well?

Willy: Mmm.

Irene: Willy.

Willy sighs.

Irene: What was he like?

Willy: Like on telly. He listens, sits there in his chair, he says 'Hmm', and 'Go on', and treats you like a fucking child.

Irene *looks at him.*

Willy: Like a ... sorry. You'd end up believing you were a six-year-old. Where's Tommo?

Irene: He's in bed. If we decide to, Sandra said she'd come over and babysit, no problem. If we want to go out. I thought you might ... If you'd like to go out.

Willy: God!

Irene: Yeah?

Willy: Terrible.

Irene: C'mon, hardshaw. You'll get used to it.

Willy: Yeah. We can get used to anything, can't we. Doesn't mean that everything you get used to is good for you. There've been people found up the mountains in Canada've got used to eating dirty roots and smearing themselves in shite to keep warm. They've gotten used to it, but it doesn't mean it's good that they've gotten used to it.

Irene: That's horrible.

Willy: That's what they do, Irene.

Irene: What did he say?

He lights a cigarette.

Willy: They'd probably consider *us* uncivilised.

Irene: What did he say?

Willy: He asked me ... (*Takes a pull. Exhales*) He asked me what kind of things I was afraid of. He asked me about my history, he asked me about you, about my relationship with little Tommo, about ... Listen to this. About whether I ever get angry at him.

Irene: He's trying to cure you.

Willy: About whether I ever get angry at my son. There's nothing wrong with me, Irene. There's nothing wrong with me. They're testing me, the bastards, and guess what? Guess what? I'm failing. Treating me like a child. Talk about humiliation. He asked me about that day ...

Irene: You weren't humiliated.

Willy: I was humiliated. Grown-ups don't talk to each other like that. Grown-ups talk to each other like adults. We don't tell each other everything's going to be all right. We talk about adult things. We converse.

Irene: He's your doctor.

Willy: There's nothing wrong with me. You'd wanna hear the bloke. Talks with, you know that accent, it's Irish, but it sounds kind of English. Very ... Very ...

Irene: Yeah.

Willy: Kind of a newsreader accent, what the newsreaders have. Middle of the whatcha ... session, his wife rings up, think it was his wife. All of a sudden, he's speaking like anyone else.

Irene: His professional manner.

Willy: Like you or me.

Irene: Right.

Willy: Hangs up the phone and all of a sudden, he's on the telly again, reading the news. Talking like I'm a baby, asking stupid things.

Irene: But there's things they probably need to clear up.

Willy: Yeah. To clear up. Like how incompetent I was, how much stress I was under, like ... Do ... He actually asked me do I suffer from stress or nervousness? In general life, like. I'm the most relaxed man in the world. I only get worked up when ... you know ... (*Takes a pull. Exhales*) something deserves getting worked up over.

Irene: Well, he obviously doesn't know you yet.

Willy: And the accent. Don't forget the accent, disappears when he's on the phone. Trying to determine my mental state.

Irene: Your mental state's fine.

Willy: My career.

Irene: I know.

Willy: I'll be ...

Irene: Everything'll be okay, Willy.

Willy: And this fucker, this other fella. I don't know what I'm going to do. It was an accident.

Irene: Well, he can't be much of a human being ...

Willy: An accident.

Irene: ... He can't ... If he can't see that.

Willy: What to do, what to do? I'm gonna be thrown out, I know it.

Irene: We'll see.

Willy: I'll get the sack. Wait'll you see. The lads were all acting different in the station today.

Irene: I'm sure they're all rooting for you, Willy.

Willy: It's a joke. *I m* a bloody joke. Promoted for two weeks. Two weeks and I screw up. My fifteen minutes of respect.

Irene: Everyone respects you.

Willy: I ... This psychia ... psychologist, whatever he is, I asked him, what about this bloke? Could he be, like, a big threat, because, I tell him ... Because he's scaring me. He says I have to tell him about what happened between us, if he's going to be able to help me. I tell him he wouldn't understand. He says he's a psycholo ... psychiatrist ...

Irene: Psychologist.

Willy: Psychologist. It's his job to understand. See what I mean about talking like I'm a child? It's his job to understand. In his ... In his fake newsreader voice. I says not this. You won't understand this. I'll tell you whatever you want to know, but not this. He says I have to tell him what happened between us. I can't tell him, Irene. There are some things ... What's important at the moment, he tells me, is that we ... we determine your mental state and try to make you better. Now, that's a contradiction. Why try to make me better if he doesn't know whether anything's wrong with me or not yet? Which there isn't.

Irene: I know there isn't.

Willy: Don't worry about that. Well, I'm sorry doctor, but this bloke's a threat that exists. Don't worry about that. You're not helping, by the way.

Irene: I ... What?

Willy: You're agreeing with me ...

Irene: Because you're right.

Willy: ... you're ... And saying nice things, no, not because I'm right. Comforting. Thanks and all, but you're not helping. Comforting words aren't going to help. Action will help. That's all'll do anything for me. A plan of action.

Irene: But there's nothing you can do at the moment.

Willy: Except smile.

Irene: Yeah. Smile and tell the truth.

Willy laughs to himself. Pause.

Irene: Maybe it was the wrong thing.

Willy: What do you mean?

Irene: The work you're doing. I always thought you were right for what you *were* doing. When you were in uniform. Talking, you know, to people, communicating and helping people. You're more ...

Willy: I'm what?

Irene: When you're here with me. Or even ... You're more ... gentle.

Willy: Gentle?

Irene: Or ... Yeah. Or ... You communicate well. You know, since ... I've been thinking. You're nice to people. I didn't think it was right in the first place, you on that squad. The DS. It's not you, you know? It's aggressive. It's not the kind of job that your character would suit. (*Pause. Willy gives her a dirty look*)

Willy: I don't know what you're saying.

Irene: I'm saying ...

Willy: You're saying I'm not cut out for it?

Irene: No, I'm just ...

Willy: Well, now, thank for that bit of loyalty there, love. You're saying I'm not man enough for the job. One minute, you're calling me hardshaw, the next ...

Irene: Ah, now, Willy, now.

Willy: No, now, Irene. You think the other lads are cut out for it, but poor Willy can't hack it. How can you ...? How can you tell, anyway?

Irene: Willy, don't be silly, now. I'm not saying anything ...

Willy: Casting aspersions on my manhood, thank you very much. My own wife. I made a mistake. I'm not chicken. I'm not a fucking wimp. I made a mistake.

Irene: I know.

Willy: How do you know if I'm man enough for the job or not?

Irene: Your character I'm talking about. Your character.

Willy: I'm of a … Less than manly character, that it?

Irene: I don't know why I'm …

*The telephone rings. **Irene** answers it.*

Irene: Hello? (*Long pause*) I'd … All right. (*To **Willy***) It's him.

***Willy** takes the phone.*

Willy: Hello? (*Pause*) I'm fine. (*Pause*) Can you not …? I have a family. (*Pause*) I'm trying to take care of my family. (*Pause*) Can you not …? I may lose my job. My wife … (*Long pause. Hangs up*) The fucking bastard!

Irene: Willy!

Willy: The fucker! Do you know what he just said to me? The f …

Irene: Calm down. This is stupid.

Willy: (*Raging*) The … Do you … Ffff …

Irene: Come on!

Willy: He … Fuck her and fuck you. That's … The … He's talking about you! He's … The ffffffollox!

Irene: Calm down, Willy.

Willy: Fuck you, he said. To *you*. He said fuck *you*. I'll … if I could … I should've done worse. I swear to Christ, I should've done worse. If I could go back …

Irene: Don't say that, Willy.

Willy: Fuck him! Making ... Making phone calls to our house? Insulting you? My ... My wife in my own house. If I could go back, I'm telling you ...

Irene: Sit dow ...

Willy: The ...

Irene: Will you sit down? Sit down. Here.

Willy: The ffffcccc ...

He sits down. She goes to the cabinet and takes out a bottle of whiskey and a glass. She pours the whiskey and brings it over to him.

Irene: Drink that. One go. (*He does. She pours another*) Go again. (*He takes it off her. Sips it*). Now. You're going to ... Are you listening? You're going to calm down and think rationally. These things that are happening to us are ... Are you listening to me?

Willy: Mmm.

Irene: Look at me, then. These things that are happening to us are bad. Yes. But what we're going to do is use our heads and not, do you hear me? Not lose our heads. Not let ourselves get worked up. We cannot let trials like this get to us. We've had fairly bad times before and we got through them, didn't we? We may not get through this easily. We may have a few losses. The job, or some money ... I don't know. If you told me what the hell he was planning. (*He gives her a look*) No, but we'll do it like ... what you were talking about. Adults. Like civilised human beings. Willy. (*Pause*)

Willy: I just ... I ... When I saw him coming towards me, I ...

Irene: I know.

Willy: I reacted. In a situation like that one, like the one I was in, you see, I'm telling you, you see someone racing towards you, you can't just ...

Willy: I was caught off-guard, but when they don't seem to understand is that I reacted the way I was taught. The way I was supposed to. They send me to a bloody psychi …

Irene: Psychologist.

Willy: To a bloody psychologist? Any one of the others would have done the same thing. (*Pause*) You know? (*Pause*)

Irene: Tell me what he's going to write about you.

Willy: I can't.

Irene: Of course you can.

Willy: I can't. It's not … It's not me being … I physically … I actually physically can't tell you. (*Pause*) Can you understand? (*Pause*) Any of the other lads would've done the same thing.

Irene: Bad luck is all it was.

Willy: I'm not incompetent.

Irene: I know.

Willy: I did the right thing.

Irene: I know you did.

Willy: I'm trying my best to take care of you.

Irene: I know you are.

Willy: But I'm failing.

Irene: No you're not.

Willy: But I am.

Irene: You're not. Willy. You're not. We'll be okay.

Willy: It's him that needs the psychologist, not me.

Irene: We'll be okay, Willy.

Willy: Christ! When I think about what he just did.

Irene: So what?

Willy: And what he just said about you.

Irene: They're only words, Willy. (*Pause*)

Willy: Yeah.

Irene: (*Silence.* **Willy** *takes a drink*) Is that really true, what you said?

Willy: What?

Irene: That they, those people, up in the mountains?

Willy: What?

Irene: To keep warm.

Willy: The Canadians?

Irene: They smear … all over. Is that true?

Willy: Their shite. Yeah.

Irene: They don't wear clothes.

Willy: No. They smear themselves in their own shite. Saw it in the *Echo*, some professor.

Irene: God!

Willy: Professor of Canadian Mountain Tribes or something.

Irene: Ah, Willy!

Willy: Something like that. Had a column, there last week.

Irene: I couldn't do that.

Willy: Smear shite?

Irene: Yeah.

Willy: If it was cold enough, Irene, you'd smear yourself in anything.

Irene: The stink.

Willy: They'd probably like the stink. Wouldn't be a stink to them.

Irene: Mmm.

Willy: Soap, now.

Irene: Soap?

Willy: Soap, you see. Something like soap, or something we'd see as clean …

Irene: Ah, yeah.

Willy: Yeah? They'd probably gag if they smelt it. This is what your man was saying. Differences in cultures. (*Pause*) What's the story on tonight? What are we doing?

Irene: I don't know. We could go for a drink.

Willy: Yeah.

Irene: Or we could stay in.

Willy: Couple of pints'd be nice. Chat … Have a bit of a chat.

Irene: Yeah.

Willy: About … Not about …

Irene: No.

Willy: … About normal, everyday things.

Irene: That'd be nice. About … We could finish our …

Willy: The Canadians, yeah.

Irene: You could tell me a bit more.

Willy: That'd be good.

Irene: That's interesting.

Willy: Was an interesting article. Yeah. Want to try and forget about this fucker for a while. (*Pause*) Well, will we go out, then?

Irene: Yeah. Do you want to?

Willy: Yeah, if … We'll go out.

Irene: Yeah. (*Pause*)

Willy: I like you.

Irene: Really? I like you. (*Beat*) Hardshaw.

Willy: Couple of pints. (*Pause*)

Irene: What time is it? I'll run up and have a quick shower. Will you give Sandra a ring and ask her to come over? Tell her he's already asleep.

Willy: Right. Hurry up.

Irene: And, we're desperate.

Willy: Right.

Irene exits. **Willy** *goes to the phone, takes a piece of paper from his pocket and dials a number. He waits.*

Willy: Hello. Paul Bolger, please. (*Pause*) That's strange. (*Pause*) Hmm. Are you sure? You're sure. All right. Have you any idea where he is? (*Pause*) All right. That's ... no, that's fine. I'll call over later. (*Pause*) No, I'm a friend of his, I'll call over later. I'll be over anyway. (*He hangs up. Picks up his glass and drains it. Goes over to door. Calls.*) Irene!

Irene: (*Calling. Offstage*) What?

Willy: Nothing.

He takes his coat from the chair and exits. We stay on the empty room.

Irene: (*Calling. Offstage*) What?

She comes into the room. Looks around.

Irene: Willy? (*Pause*) Willy?

She stands in the centre of the room.

Blackout.

Scene Four

Adeles *house. Breakfast room.* **Theresa** *sits at the table.* **Liz** *pours a couple of brandies and sits down.* **Theresa** *is understandably nervous.*

Theresa: Is ... Paul's coming home tonight, isn't he?

Liz: He is. Adele's looking forward to it.

Theresa: Mmm. How's his form? Is he …? How's his walking?

Liz: I don't know. Says he'll probably have to use crutches for a while. But few weeks, he'll be back to normal. See the ship?

Theresa: Yeah.

Liz: What d'you think?

Theresa: Yeah.

Liz: Drink. (*She drinks*) Right. The reason I asked you down …

Theresa: Mmmhmm.

Liz: I didn't want to tell you over the phone, because I thought it'd be better face to face.

Theresa: All right.

Liz: The reason …

Theresa: Yeah?

Liz: It's too impersonal over the phone. It's something important that … To say it …

Theresa: You can't?

Liz: It's better to be in person, face to face, one on one, having another … To have a person, because … When I tell you, you'll understand.

Theresa: (*Pause*) Okay.

Liz: It's … something like this, eye contact is needed, the presence of … and to be able to see the other person, physical and all the other.

Theresa: Right.

Liz: All right?

Theresa: Yeah.

Liz: Drink. (*She drinks*)

Theresa: Now. (*Pause*)

Liz: This is a bit … (*Pause*) It's like … You see? This is the … in the first place, the reason I asked you to come down, because being told something like this over the phone … Anyway. I was reading the … Some … No. Nothing. It might be a shock to discover this. It's a shock, I'm sure, to find out that the love you're giving, you know? The love you're giving is one-sided and not being reciprocated and … Are you all right? Are you all right? Drink. Have a drink. (*They both drink*) I was talking about this subject to Adele. I don't want to … Not that it's any of my business. I don't want to see you made a fool of. You're living a lie and I think it's about time you found out about it. (*Pause*) He's incapable of love. (*Silence.*) Some … it's true. Instinct. That's all it is. By his nature, he has the incapacity to love. It's … It's in his genes, it's all instinct. Are you okay? I've been through it myself. I don't know. I'm just saying forget about love because it's an impossibility. (*Pause*)

Theresa: (*Thinking she s been rumbled*) How did you know?

Liz: Know what?

Theresa: Know about us? How come you knew?

Liz: I can smell him off you. Sometimes you've got hairs on you. What do you mean?

Theresa: (*Confused*) Hairs?

Liz: His hairs.

Theresa: I … (*Pause*)

Liz: It's all right. C'mere. Do you want a hug? Come over here.

Theresa: No, I'm all right.

Liz: You don't look all right. Sometimes a hug …

Theresa: No. No. The … (*Pause*) You can smell him off me?

Liz: Not bad. It's nothing you have to be embarrassed about. (*Pause*)

Theresa: I feel like a gobshite.

Liz: Theresa, you didn't know. It's all right. Sure, I only found out tonight.

Theresa: Does Adele know?

Liz: Yeah.

Theresa: Oh, Jesus!

Liz: I told her when I saw it, she was here with me. Don't worry, you're not a gobshite. She doesn't think so either.

Theresa: (*Pause*) What did you see?

Liz: In the paper.

Theresa: The paper?

Liz: Some professor or other.

Theresa: How does he know?

Liz: He knows because he's a professor. C'mere. Do you want a hug?

Theresa: No. What do you mean, he knows because he's a professor?

Liz: He kn … 'Cos he's … He studies animals. A … Behaviour. He's a, a Professor of Animal Behaviour or some such.

Theresa: How does he know about me?

Liz: He … He doesn't know about you. Your dog. Your dog, he knows about.

Theresa: My dog?

Liz: (*Pause*) Yeah.

Theresa: Oh! (*Pause*) My dog.

Liz: I'm sorry, Theresa. To have to … be the one to tell you.

Theresa: My dog doesn't love me is what you're …

Liz: Sometimes if we … I'm here for you. If you want a hug, to talk about it, if you want to cry …

Theresa: Toby.

Liz: (*Pause*) Toby doesn't love you. (*Pause. Drinks*) Who the hell did you think I was talking about?

Theresa: No, I kne ...

Liz: Did ...?

Theresa: Toby. I knew. Toby.

Liz: You thought I was talking about something else?

Theresa: No. I knew you were talking about Toby. Sure the, the hairs he leaves on me, etcetera.

Liz: Yeah!

Theresa: He's an awful shedder. (*Pause*)

Liz: How do you feel?

Theresa: I feel all right. I don't know. I didn't know.

Liz: No, well like I said. I only found out tonight, myself. It's a horrible thing to discover.

Theresa: Hmm.

Liz: Horrible. But, what? Would you rather have known or not have known?

Theresa: (*Pause*) Known.

Liz: That's the way I'd feel. That's the way I'd feel. You don't want to go around living a lie. (*Silence.*) Who did you think I was talking about?

Theresa: No one. I ... Toby. I knew.

Liz: No, you didn't.

Theresa: I did.

Liz: Do you have a secret?

Theresa: No.

Liz: Do you have a ...

Theresa: Stop, would you?

Liz: … No?

Theresa: I wish I …

Liz: You sure?

Theresa: I wish I did. (*Pause.* **Liz** *drinks).*

Liz: So do I. What do you think of the ship?

Theresa: Very nice.

Liz: Paul's coming-home present. (*Calls*) Adele! (*To* **Theresa**)
It's a very difficult one.

Theresa: It's big, isn't it.

Liz: (*Calling*) Adele! (*She goes to doorway*) Adele!

Adele: (*Offstage*) Yeah?

Liz: I was just showing Theresa the … Oh, very nice!

Adele: (*Offstage*) Yeah?

Theresa: Adele!

Adele: (*Offstage*) Stop.

Liz: No. God …

Theresa: That's gorgeous.

Liz: … look at you.

Theresa: Adele Bolger!

Liz: The word glamour is about to be redefined. Come here.

Theresa: Come in.

She enters wearing a sexy white top and black trousers.

Liz: Give us a twirl. (*She does so*)

Theresa: Beautiful.

Liz: Absolutely.

Adele: Are you sure?

Liz: Will you …? 'Are you sure?' Get out of it.

Theresa: Adele, it's gorgeous.

Adele: This'll be the first time …

Liz: First time you've worn that combination.

Adele: Yeah.

Theresa: Lovely.

Adele: I've worn both of them before, but separately.

Theresa: Right.

Adele: In different combinations.

Liz: He'll love it. (*Beat*)

Adele: (*Cheerfully*) I think I'll … (*Points at glasses*)

Liz: Yeah, yeah. Sit down. I'll get the glass, you vixen.

Adele: Ah, stop. (*She sits on the couch. Liz gets a glass from the press*)

Liz: Here we go. You staying, Theresa?

Adele: I'll …

Liz: Gimme your glass. (*Pours*) The more the merrier, am I right, Adele?

Adele: Yes.

Theresa: I think I might just …

Liz: (*Filling her own*) The more. The merrier. (*To Theresa*) How do you feel now? (*To Adele*) I told her.

Adele: Oh. How do you feel?

Adele starts to light a cigarette. She offers one to Theresa.

Theresa: I'm fine. I'm … (*Shakes head at cigarette*)

Liz: If you wanna talk about it …

Theresa: No. It's not that bad.

They move to the couch.

Liz: I just thought you should know.

Theresa: No, I appreciate it.

Liz: Good.

Adele: Cheers!

Liz: Cheers!

Theresa: Cheers! (*They drink*)

Liz: So. Any news?

Theresa: I was …

Liz: (*Interrupting. To **Adele***) What time is it?

Adele: Twenty to.

Theresa: I … think I should be …

Liz: Any scandal, Theresa?

*Liz takes the model ship off the table and puts it against the wall to make more room. The girls go into chat mode. **Liz** returns to her seat.*

Theresa: I was broken into last night.

Adele: Ah, no.

Liz: No way. What did they get?

Theresa: Yeah. Telly and the video.

Liz: Ah, God.

Theresa: Yeah.

Liz: The bastards.

Adele: Were you upset?

Theresa: Well, I'm a bit scared since.

Adele: Living on your own.

Theresa: This is it.

Liz: Did your dog not bark or …?

Theresa: No.

Liz: Didn't …

Theresa: They came in the front.

Adele: Jesus. Must be ...

Theresa: It's sort of freaky. Like, since. Say at night-time ...

Liz: ... Uhhuh. Yep ...

Theresa: ... On my own ...

Liz: ... Must be terrible.

Theresa: Yeah.

Liz: What do you think of Paul and his injury?

Theresa: It was terrible, wasn't it.

Liz: It was, all right. He'll come hobbling in, now. See all of us waiting, one two three, bottle of brandy, his new model ship, Adele's sexy attire ...

Adele: Ah, Liz.

Liz: Stop. You know you look great.

Adele: I look all right.

Theresa: You look great.

Liz: You look great. (*Pause)*

Theresa: To think that they were downstairs.

Adele: Mmm. (*She s a little distressed. Pause)*

Theresa: It's frightening to think that, while you're asleep, anyone can come in and wander around your house. Your things. Personal ... I was trying to think of the word. Someone in my house, it made me feel ... (*Pause)*

Adele: You should get an alarm.

Liz: (*With bottle)* Filler-upper, Theresa?

Theresa: Eh ... Well, I don't really know if I should be ...

Liz begins filling the glasses anyway, starting with **Theresa** *s.*

Liz: Gets you a bit looser, warms up the blood, gives you a nice buzz.

Adele: Makes it easier to talk.

Liz: Loose lips sink ships, but what the hell?

Pause. ***Theresa*** *picks up her glass.*

Theresa: What the hell? Cheers!

Liz: Cheers!

Adele: Cheers! (*They drink*)

Theresa: Should I get an alarm?

Liz: An alarm.

Adele: We have one.

Theresa: I suppose …

Adele: Make you feel safer.

Theresa: That invasion of privacy …

Adele: Paul got one installed in March, we never had a problem. The box … You can see … You know, you can see it as you come in. Over the door. I'd say that's a …

Liz: A deterrent.

Adele: A … Yeah. Was reading in the *Echo*.

Liz: Sure it is. As much as anything else.

Adele: A deterrent. Just the sight of it. This professor, what was it?

Liz: 'Cos, yeah. 'Cos they see it.

Theresa: Right.

Adele: A Professor of Burglary Prevention, it was.

Theresa: I'm gonna pop down tomorrow, see if I can get one.

Adele: (*To herself*) Home protection?

Liz: Soon as you can, Theresa.

Theresa: Yeah. (*Pause. They drink*) Can I use your loo?

Liz: Sure.

Adele: Of course.

Theresa: My bladder's just …

Liz: Don't be embarrassed. We're all the same.

Adele: Go ahead.

Theresa: Thanks.

Liz: And don't forget to flush. (*She goes. To **Adele***) Did you get it?

Adele: What?

Liz: Did you smell it?

Adele: No.

Liz: Yes, you did.

Adele: Liz, that's not nice.

Liz: I'm just asking you.

Adele: That's not nice. (*Pause*)

Liz: But, did you smell it?

Adele: Yes.

Liz: I told you.

Adele: Right. Enough.

Liz: I told you you could smell it.

Adele: Right. (*Pause*)

Liz: Did you see the hairs?

Adele: What? Liz! No.

Liz: They're on her jumper. She a …

Adele: I di …

Liz: … She always had them.

Adele: No.

Liz: You didn't?

Adele: No, I didn't. You're mean.

Liz: Just observant, Adele. You'll see when she comes down.

Adele: Right.

Liz: Have a look.

Adele: Right. (*Beat*) No! (*Pause. Then in shocked tone*) No! (*Pause*) How'd she take the news?

Liz: Ssshhh! (***Theresa*** *enters*) Did you flush?

Theresa: Of course I did. I always flush.

Liz: I'm joking. Sit down. (*She sits*) I'm joking. (*To* ***Adele***) Is this the last bottle? (***Adele*** *shakes her head*) Stupid question. (*They laugh. Pause.* ***Theresa*** *leans confidentially towards* ***Adele***)

Theresa: How are you feeling these days, Adele?

Obviously she s said the wrong thing. ***Liz*** *comes to the rescue, interrupting* ***Theresa***.

Liz: You should get that alarm. Now that it's happened, they might think you're easy pickings. They might come back. Might come upstairs next time.

Theresa: (*Alarmed*) Yeah?

Liz: Get that alarm. Security is the best policy.

Adele: It is.

Liz: 'Less you *want* them to …

Theresa: What?

Liz: That right, Adele?

Adele: Which?

Liz: Up the old bedroom.

Theresa: Ah, no. No.

Adele: Liz!

Liz: Up the old bedroom. What?!!

Theresa: No way.

Liz: A good ravaging, now?

Adele: Liz!

Theresa: You wouldn't!

Liz: All depends, now, Theresa. All depends. I don't know.

*They are interrupted by the sound of a key in the door. Enter **Paul**. He hobbles in slowly on his walking stick.*

Paul: How's it going?

Adele: Heya. Paul.

Liz: Heya, Paul.

Theresa: Hello, Paul.

Paul: Heya, Theresa.

He makes to take off his jacket.

Liz: Hold it. Wait. Paul. Let me do that. (*She does*)

Paul: Thanks.

Liz: (*Helping him sit down*) Down. Now. All right?

Paul: Yep. Thanks.

Liz: No problem at all. Do you want some brandy?

Paul: Yeah. Nice one. Dropped in for a pint on my merry way already. (***Liz** goes to get a glass*) How are things?

Adele: Fine. How's your hip?

Paul: (*Dismissively*) Agh!

Adele: Does it hurt much?

Paul: No, sometimes. Not much. Something strange going on here.

***Liz** sits back down with glass and begins to pour for **Paul**.*

Adele: What?

Liz: Something strange, Paul?

Paul: Mmm.

Liz: Do you notice something, Theresa?

Theresa: Me?

Liz: Yeah.

Theresa: No.

Paul: Adele?

Adele: What?

Paul: Do you notice something strange?

Adele: I ... I don't know. (*Pause*)

Paul: Hmm. (*Pause. He looks **Adele** up and down*)

Liz: Ah, Paul!

Paul: (*Still looking at **Adele***) What?

Liz: Stop it.

Theresa: What?

Adele: I ...

Paul: Sexy as hell. (***Adele** laughs*)

Liz: Paul.

Paul: Look at you.

Adele: Well, you ...

Paul: Look at the sexy lady.

Liz: Isn't she?

Paul: Look at you.

Adele: You were coming home. (*Beat)*

Paul: For me?

Liz: Yeah.

Paul: Yeah?

Adele: I thought …

Paul: No. No …

Adele: … I thought …

Paul: You thought right, Adele. No. You thought right. (*To Liz*) I see you didn't make any effort.

Liz: Go to hell.

Paul: (*To Adele*) Stand up. (*She stands*) That's beautiful.

Adele: The combination.

Paul: That's what it is. Can I have a kiss? (*She kisses him, then sits down*) This is nice. (*He drinks*) How are things, Theresa.

Theresa: Fine.

Paul: Long time no see.

Theresa: Yeah.

Liz: Theresa was broken into the other night.

Paul: Yeah.

Liz: Robbed her telly and her video.

Paul: (*To Theresa*) Yeah?

Theresa: Just my telly and my video.

Paul: You were lucky. (*To Adele*) Look at you.

Adele: Stop.

Liz: I told her she should get an alarm.

Paul: You should. You should.

Theresa: I'm going to have a look tomorrow.

Paul: You should. (*He drinks*) Agh! (*Pause)*

Adele: Are you glad to be out?

Paul: Too right. The nurses in there.

Theresa: Nice?

Paul: Rough. You must be joking. Big ... Awfully rough they are. Picking you up and putting you down. Big matrons treating me like a sack of potatoes. (*To Adele*) I was telling you.

Liz: You poor thing.

Paul: (*To Adele*) You'll be gentle with me, won't you. 'Course you will. I need a gentle hand at the moment. You look gorgeous.

Adele: Thanks.

Paul: My special pal.

Adele: *My* special pal.

Theresa almost does a double take at this.

Liz: Adele. (*Makes a signalling motion with her head. Adele gets the model ship*)

Paul: What's ... For me?

Adele: Yeah.

Paul: (*Taking it*) Oh, brilliant.

Adele: (*Sitting down*) That's to pass the time.

Paul: Brilliant.

Adele: Liz picked it out.

Liz: I did not. (*Paul is opening the box*)

Adele: You did so.

Liz: Well, you paid for it.

Adele: *We* paid for it.

Paul: (*Taking out pieces and looking at them*) Well, thanks the pair of you. What do you think, Theresa?

Theresa: It's lovely.

Paul: Look at the size of those pieces.

Liz: What's that? A gun?

Paul: A cannon. Jesus. That'll take a while.

Adele: Well, it's to pass the time. (*Pause*)

Paul: Thank you. (*Kisses her*) Thanks.

Theresa: Maybe I should get something like that, now that I've no telly.

*Paul has broken the little cannon off its frame. He shoots **Theresa** with it, making the sound with his mouth.*

Paul: Size of them.

Liz: It's got every little detail.

Theresa: Have you ever done one of those before, Paul?

Paul: Not … When I was a little boy, I used to. But not in years.

Adele: Who were you in the pub with?

Paul: On my lonesome.

Liz: There's no stopping him, he's only out of the hospital.

Adele: Why were you on your own?

Paul: Ah, I just had to have a think about things. It's a big deal getting out and coming home. Make a few plans, I wanted to get my head together a bit. Just to … 'Cos whether I like it or not, life's gonna be a bit different from now on. Things changed the minute that fu … Soon as it happened. Isn't it amazing? Little event like that. An occurrence … Still … (*To **Adele***) We can talk about stuff later if you want.

Adele: Yeah. If you want. (***Paul** takes a drink*)

Paul: So, how come you're here, Theresa?

Theresa: We …

Liz: Paul!

Paul: I'm only asking. I'm not being rude. (*To **Theresa***) Was I being rude?

Theresa: No.

Paul: I wasn't. I was just asking. I didn't expect.

Liz: I asked her down.

Paul: You rang her, did you?

Liz: Yeah.

Paul: Right.

Theresa: Liz read something in the paper and she felt she should ...

Liz: About dogs, Paul. Do you know that dogs are incapable of love?

Paul: What?

Liz: This professor in tonight's paper says so.

Paul: (*Kissing Adele*) Thanks for the model.

Adele: You're welcome.

Liz: Dogs, Paul. It's not in their gene structure to be capable of love.

Paul: Dogs.

Liz: Here, it's ... (*Liz hands him the newspaper*) There.

Paul: (*Taking a quick glance*) That's rubbish.

Liz: He says so.

Paul: Doesn't make it true. What do you think, Theresa?

Theresa: Yeah, I ...

Paul: Doesn't make it true.

Liz: Well, that's why ... I wanted to tell Theresa. (*Pause*)

Paul: (*To Theresa*) That your dog doesn't love you.

Theresa: Yeah.

Paul: (*To Liz*) You're fucked.

Liz: It says so there, Paul.

Paul: (*To **Theresa***) She got you all the way down here. (*Pause. Reads*) A Professor of Canine Psychology. That should tell you. The only bloke worth reading in that rag is Tony Kelly. Do you ever read him, Theresa? Crime correspondent?

Theresa: Em … I don't …

Paul: Good bloody writer.

Theresa: Is he?

Paul: Genius, he is. Very good.

Adele: I have to go the weewee. (*She rises and exits*)

Liz: Don't forget to flush.

Paul: Look at her strut.

Liz: (*To **Theresa***) I'm only messing. (*To herself*) Where's the …? (*Calling*) Where's the other bottle, Adele?

Adele: (*Offstage*) What?

Liz: The other bottle.

Adele: (*Offstage*) What about it?

Liz: Where is it?

Adele: (*Offstage*) It's in the cabinet inside.

Liz: Right. (*To others*) You on for some more?

Paul: Pour away. (*She pours*)

Liz: The more, the merrier, huh?

Paul: Yep.

Theresa: That's enough. Thanks.

Liz: I'll just get another one.

*Liz. exits. While she is gone, **Paul** and **Theresa** look very uncomfortable. Each looks down at the table as if the other isn t there. **Liz** returns with another bottle of brandy and sits down.*

Paul: (*Drinks. Confidentially to **Liz***) How is she?

Liz: She's fine.

Paul: Everything's …

Liz: Yeah. She's grand.

Paul: Who bought the ship?

Liz: (*Beat*) I did. (*Beat*) She's grand. (*Pause*)

Paul: This fucking adventure's all she needs.

Theresa: Will I head on?

Paul: No.

Liz: No. No. Theresa.

Paul: Sure, you're here.

Liz: Have a drink. You've started. (*They drink*)

Paul: What do you think of this dog business, Theresa?

Theresa: The … What Liz said?

Paul: Yeah.

Theresa: I don't know. It wouldn't really affect me much. If … I mean, it's true. Then that's … I don't know if it'd make any difference to me. I like my dog.

Paul: Do you belie …?

Theresa: It's not a person, though. It's only a dog.

Liz: But you like it.

Theresa: Yeah.

Liz: You like it a lot.

Theresa: It's a dog. I like it as …

Paul: But do you believe about …?

Theresa: I like it …

Liz: A lot.

Paul: But do you believe what Liz said?

Liz: I didn't say it, I …

Paul: Well in the paper.

Liz: The professor.

Paul: Do you?

Theresa: Do ... I don't know. But, even if it's true ...

Paul: It's not.

Liz: It could be.

Theresa: It wouldn't affect me, I don't think. It's only a dog, so I don't really mind. Lovewise. Long as it's there, especially now after the ... the burglary, I'm glad there's somebody around. What's the word I'm trying to think of? Anyway, love me or not, he can still provide me with some company.

*Enter **Adele** looking upset again.*

Paul: Okay?

Adele: (*Sitting down*) Yeah. (***Paul** kisses her*)

Paul: Do you believe it?

Adele: (*Distant*) What?

Paul: About the dogs. Are you all right?

Adele: (*Upset*) I'm ... Yeah. Just a ... Gimme.

Liz: Adele?

Adele: I'm a bit ...

Paul: D'you need ...?

Adele: There's ... Gimme two minutes.

Liz: You all right, Adele?

Adele: Gimme ... Yeah. Leave ... (*Pause. Upset. To **Paul***) Someone rang.

Liz: Oh, that's right!

Paul: (*To **Adele***) Who rang?

Adele: (*Starting to cry*) Someone.

*Adele gets up and leaves the room, distressed. **Paul** gets up and follows.*

Paul: Adele!

Theresa: Should I go?

Liz: No, no, she's all right. (*Calling*) She all right, Paul?

Paul: (*Offstage. Calling*) Yeah, she's grand.

Theresa: I think I should go. I shouldn't really …

Liz: Stay where you are. She … It'll pass in a minute. (*Very serious*) Theresa. Adele's a bit ill.

Theresa: Well, should I not go, then?

Liz: No, no, no, you're grand. She sometimes gets a bit confused or addled or frustrated, something. She's all right. Paul knows. Bit sick. Kind of nervous … Stressful situations, you know? She has these fits. Falls down, so she needs to be, you know. Nothing major, now, it doesn't damage her or anything, but they take a while to pass. Kinda … (*Demonstrates a fit*) you know? But not dangerous.

Theresa: I …

Liz: She's fine, she's pills, she's not having one now. Stay put, we're having a few drinks.

There is a knock on the door.

Liz: Who's this, now? (*She goes out to answer it. We hear the door opening. Offstage*) Yes?

Voice: (*Offstage*) Is eh … Paul Bolger home, please?

Liz: (*Offstage*) Yyeees. Who shall I say it is?

Voice: (*Offstage*) I'm the man who shot him.

Blackout.

•

ACT TWO

Scene One

The same. A few minutes later. **Paul** *sits on the sofa.* **Willy** *stands. They are alone.*

Paul *and* **Willy**.

Willy: You were running. You were running, you were coming towards me.

Paul: Trying to stay out of trouble.

Willy: But, yeah, but when it happened, all I could think about was …

Paul: How powerful you were.

Willy: No. What?

Paul: We talked about this at the hospital. Think you've got the power and the right.

Willy: Right to what?

Paul: Rights to do things.

Willy: Do what?

Paul: Do stuff and all, going around shooting guns.

Willy: Shooting?

Paul: Shooting guns and all, going around in your cars, flying around skidding. I know youse.

Willy: I'd never shot my gun before, shot it at a person.

Paul: Going around, then.

Willy: What?

Paul: Going around in your cars, flying around.

Willy: Well …

Paul: Deny that, you fucker.

Willy: … Sometimes we …

Paul: Ah-ha. Think youse are it. Can you deny it?

Willy: … Sometimes we drive fast.

Paul: Right.

Willy: But we don't think we're it. 'Least I don't.

Paul: 'Cos you're not.

Willy: What?

Paul: You're not it.

Willy: I don't think I am.

Paul: Think you're Don Johnson or something?

Willy: It wasn't my fault.

Paul: Whose fault was it?

Willy: It was an accident.

Paul: Well, maybe if you'd've been a bit more careful, now. Don Johnson doesn't shoot without thinking.

Willy: It was …

Paul: Don Johnson takes aim.

Willy: Too much was going on. I didn't have time to think.

Paul: You'd more time than me. I didn't have any time.

Willy: I know.

Paul: Time enough to feel pain.

Willy: I'm sorry.

Paul: On my merry way 'round the corner. BANG! Time enough to go into shock, know what I'm saying? On my merry way home to my wife. You could've killed me. You could've easily hit me somewhere else.

Willy: I know, I …

Paul: In the head or something, got me. In the heart. Could've blown my head off, Jayus! In my eye or something.

Willy: If I …

Paul: Jayus!

Willy: If I could …

Paul: In my … Shut up, will you? Shut your mouth. You're in my house, have the common decency not to start interrupting me. As soon as …

Willy: I'm sorry, I …

Paul: … Will you? You're doing it again.

Willy: I'm sorry.

Paul: This isn't some gangster's … hideout you're doing a … thing on, this is my house. (*Pause*) What was I …? My belly. Shot in the belly can kill you. Shot in the chest, doesn't even have to be your heart. Where else? The eye, now'd be the worst. See what I'm saying? See how serious what you did is?

Willy: I know how serious it is.

Paul: What d'you want?

Willy: I came for … To ask you …

Paul: Ask me what?

Willy: To stop.

Paul: Never.

Willy: Please

Paul: I will never, I will never.

Willy: But …

Paul: I will never.

Willy: Tell me why, then.

Paul: You know why. Look at the state of me. I'm in flitters. My hip's in flits, I can't walk without my stick. In tatters, I am. See that? That's all I'll be doing for the next few weeks, now, 'cos of you. Sitting on my arse, trying to build the, whatsit?

Willy: H.M.S. Victory.

Paul: The H.M.S. Victory. Recovering. There's a few weeks of my life wasted, now. On that fucking thing.

Willy: That's a beautiful ship.

Paul: That's not what I'm on about.

Willy: I know it's not.

Paul: I know it's a beautiful ship.

Liz: (*Entering from up stairs*) Sorry, Paul.

Paul: What are you …?

Liz: (*Indicating brandy bottle*) Can I …?

Paul: Yeah. Go on. Hang on. (*Pours himself a glass*)

Liz: (*To* **Willy**) Nice, isn't it?

Willy: Lovely.

Liz: Should keep him occupied for weeks, now.

Paul: How is she?

Liz: Ah, she's fine. You know.

Paul: Good. How's Theresa?

Liz: (*Beat*) She's fine, too.

Paul: Good.

Liz: (*Taking bottle*) Jaysus, she's gas, isn't she?

Paul: Who?

Liz: Theresa. C'mere. Did you notice …? (*Looks at* **Willy**) I'll ask you after. (*Exits*)

Willy: Do you have a family?

Paul: None of your … No, I have a wife.

Willy: Her?

Paul: You must be joking.

Willy: Your wife …

Paul: Don't talk about her.

Willy: My wife.

Paul: Yours.

Willy: My son. It's not just me you're hurting. My family had nothing to do with anything. When they read it … They're going to be hurt and they did nothing.

Paul: That's life, man. It's like me being shot, you know? Kind of stuff happens.

Willy: What the hell were you doing there?

Paul: I told you before, a mate of mine lives there. The whole block isn't criminal. See, it's this kind of attitude, now …

Willy: I wasn't saying …

Paul: … This attitude, just because someone lives in a place…

Willy: I wasn't …

Paul: You think you can judge these innocent people who don't have the money to live anywhere else.

Willy: I don't.

Paul: And this kind of fucking attitude, now. This kind of attitude, going around firing your gun, could take someone's eye out.

Willy: Yeah.

Paul: Could you imagine? (*Pause*)

Willy: When you phoned my house tonight and what you said to me. To my wife. About my wife.

Paul: What did I say?

Willy: You said fuck her. You said fuck me and …

Paul: Fuck you.

Willy: What did she do to you?

Paul: Look. I said it. I meant I don't care. I don't know your wife, if she happens to get hurt, then … You know.

Willy: Let me tell you this. Let me tell you this, waiting to go out and get someone, it's not exciting, it's far from exciting. Maybe for the other lads. I'm telling you this, now…

Paul: I'm not particularly interested.

Willy: Let me tell you this. This is just now, to, if I could make you understand the, the … pressures … inherent.

Paul: Go on. Fuck sake!

Willy: That day, the day it happened was a Friday, we were sitting in the office, I was only on the squad two weeks, we were sitting in the office waiting for a phone call, could get a phone call from any number of snitches …

Paul: Snitches?

Willy: Yeah.

Paul: Like in …

Willy: In … On telly, yeah. That's what we call them as well.

Paul: Right.

Willy: We've warrants there for three or four dealers and we're waiting to see which one we'll get a snitch on. Sitting there filling in the warrants.

Paul: You fill them in first?

Willy: Just so we won't have to worry about it later. Still have to get the district judge's signature. So, the phone call comes.

Paul: Snitch.

Willy: One of the snitches. This fella, Maurice Joyce.

Paul: The snitch.

Willy: No, the fella.

Paul: Oh, right. Who youse're …

Willy: Who we're, yeah, who we're …

Paul: Uhhuh.

Willy: Snitch gives us the address and the squad goes mad, 'cos Maurice Joyce's wanted for murder on top of being a dealer. That couple shot up at Whiteoaks. Did you …?

Paul: I did, I read it.

Willy: Two of them shot in the head.

Paul: In *The Echo*. Tony Kelly column.

Willy: I don't want to go up against a murderer. I don't want to put myself in that situation. I'm telling you this, now. I'm telling you this so maybe you'll …

Paul: Right.

Willy: So you'll maybe …

Paul: So youse get the info. The tip.

Willy: The squad goes mad, we're gonna catch a killer, we'll get a curry after to celebrate. Off we go, straight to the detective commissioner's house, he's out in the garden trimming his hedge. We skid up …

Paul: Skid up, yeah? See what I'm saying?

Willy: I wasn't driving.

Paul: Strange, though, isn't it? Youse skid up.

Willy: We're in a hurry to get there, 'case he leaves.

Paul: Go on.

Willy: This is my first time, now. Judge signs the warrant, good luck lads, off we go.

Paul: Pull a handbreaker off, yeah?

Willy: I don't remember. We go to the flat. Maurice Joyce is the third floor. The lads are still discussing curries.

Paul: What's this about curries?

Willy: Whenever they do a successful job, they have a curry.

Paul: Very good. Pint's not good enough for them, no?

Willy: It's just a thing they do.

Paul: More elitist behaviour, you see? Handbreakers, curry, go on. Fuckers thinking they're it, go on.

Willy: We get out the battering ram.

Paul: Youse have a battering ram?

Willy: To knock the door down.

Paul: Right.

Willy: Knock on the door …

Paul: What are youse knocking on the door for if youse have a battering ram?

Willy: Have to knock on the door and identify yourself.

Paul: I'd just plow my way in, surprise them.

Willy: That's the rules.

Paul: That's a bit stupid now. Giving them a chance? I'd knock the fucking door down, catch them in the act, don't give them the fucking chance, the bastards.

Willy: I know.

Paul: Go on, go on. Youse knock on the door …

Willy: We knock on the door, tell them it's the DS, we've a warrant.

Paul: DS?

Willy: Drug Squad.

Paul: 'Course.

Willy: Then we knock down the door. Have to do it as quick as possible before they flush the stuff down the jacks or swallow it.

Paul: Right. After …

Willy: Run inside …

Paul: … after giving them a warning.

Willy: It's the rules.

Paul: It's stupid. Go on.

Willy: Get inside and there's no one there.

Paul: But your …

Willy: The snitch. I know.

Paul: He told youse a lie.

Willy: Well, they could've been there when he said, but …

Paul: Right. Right. In the meantime …

Willy: … Time we get the warrant signed and all.

Paul: Which is why youse fill them out at the station.

Willy: Save time.

Paul: Right. That's smart, now.

Willy: So, in we go.

Paul: Smart thinking. How many of youse is there?

Willy: Three men and one woman.

Paul: You're the woman, yeah?

Willy: No, I'm not the woman.

Paul: Does the woman have a gun as well?

Willy: No. She's there to …

Paul: Good. Go on. This is interesting.

Willy: I'm telling you this, now, so you'll know what I was … what I was thinking. My …

Paul: Yeah. Yeah. It's interesting.

Willy: … Kind of pressure I was under.

Paul: Youse get into the flat and there's no one there.

Willy: And there's no one there. Hear someone calling outside. Youngfella at the front door about sixteen, strung out to fuck, says, 'Is Maurice there?' Door's on the ground and he doesn't even notice.

Paul: No way.

Willy: Strung out to fuck.

Paul: Doesn't even notice the door!

Willy: He just wants a fix, so I tell him Joey's not here. So, he's, 'Ah, I'm dying for a fix, man,' giving it all that, and then, 'Ah, sure here he is.' Maurice Joyce and four or five other blokes come around the corner, the walkway, McDonalds bags in their arms. They spot us, we spot them, out with the guns, us and them. McDonalds up in the air, they scatter, everybody scatters, running downstairs into other flats, disappearing, firing their guns behind them. Guess what Maurice Joyce shouts?

Paul: What?

Willy: Youse'll never take me alive.

Paul: Jaysus!

Willy: Thing is, he meant it.

Paul: Murder rap on him.

Willy: Exactly. Rest of the squad flies after them and I was left standing there like a fool. All happened so fast, I'm left thinking, where the fuck did everyone go? Wondering what to do and then you come along. Flying around the corner, running towards me, running at me.

Paul: On my merry way home, that's all.

Willy: I panicked. Do I shoot, do I run?

Paul: Innocent me on my merry fucking way.

Willy: All in a split second. Do I fight? Am I gonna die? I pointed my gun and … I overacted, I panicked, it was all so fast, I pointed my gun and I fired. (*Pause*) Now.

Paul: (*Pause*) Now what?

Willy: I told you what happened. I told you how scared I was. D'you see the, the confusion, the pressure I was under? I was scared. I've admitted it to you. D'you see what kind of …?

Paul: Admitted what?

Willy: I was scared, I was confused, I …

Paul: Admitted what? I'm sitting here … I'm sitting here listening to you telling me how cool the fucking drug squad is.

Willy: What?

Paul: Your guns and your cars, skidding up to the judge's gaff, with your battering rams, you're boasting. Poor little junkie, too strung out to notice a broken door and youse use it as a course of mockery?

Willy: It's what happened.

Paul: Tony Kelly's got a way with fucking words, hasn't he. (*Pause*)

Willy: I've given you this. I've told you stuff I wouldn't even tell my wife.

Paul: What have you given me?

Willy: Something … I'm trying to … Something of myself.

Paul: Of your …

Willy: Yes, of …

Paul: You didn't tell me everything.

Willy: What?

Paul: What happened when you shot me, you know? What's this all about?

Willy: Well, you saw that.

Paul: I'd my mind on the bullets in me.

Willy: I told you, the pressure … The, the … I told you how I was …

Paul: I wasn't really concentrating.

Willy: The pressure … (*Pause.* **Paul** *stands up*)

Paul: You pissed yourself. The man from the drug squad pissed himself.

Willy: I don't want people to know.

Paul: I was lying on the ground with two bullets in me, did I cry? I took what happened like a man. I didn't lose control of my bladder like a woman.

Willy: Stop.

Paul: How can you live with yourself, no I won't stop. I have to let people know there's a woman in the drug squad, you sad bastard. Down on your knees, whinging like a three year old, going weewee like a baby. 'Awww. I'm sorry. I didn't mean it. Awww …!' Me down there filled with hot lead, I didn't wet myself. Oh, no. And I saw you tying your jacket around your waist, you sneaky fucker. Least I know how to bite the bullet. Least I can take it. Youse all think you're such fucking men.

Willy: Stop it. Stop that fucking …

Paul: What'll you do? Cry?

Willy: Just don't …

Paul: Weewee in your drawers? You baby, you woman. Don Johnson wouldn't've pissed himself no matter who he shot. Don's like me. Don can bite the bullet.

Willy: Don't print this. Please. My wife …

Paul: Ah, now.

Willy: I'm being punished. I'm seeing a psychologist.

Paul: Why?

Willy: Because ...

Paul: Because you go around shooting people?

Willy: No, because ...

Paul: Because you've a bed-wetting problem?

Willy: He tells me I could be suffering from whatsit? Post stress ... Post shooting something or other. They're trying to see if ... They're trying to see if I'm incompetent.

Paul: Incontinent.

Willy: Incompetent. Do you not understand?

Paul: Tony Kelly's good at the old word play, isn't he? I wonder how he'll write this up, now. See if he'll make up a bit of word play using them words. Incompetent and ...

Willy: What can I do?!!!

Paul: Listen to me. You're wasting your time.

Willy: If you could.

Paul: You're wasting your time, Mister Incontinent. Read all about it. Think you can come in here, showing off with your drug squad stories, thinking you're Don, with your guns and your cars and your fucking curries, thinking you're Don, thinking you're fucking great.

Willy: You're ...

Paul: Telling me stories? (*Long pause*)

Willy: You're jealous, you cunt.

Paul: What?

Willy: You're fucking jealous of me?

Paul: Of piss in the bed? Calling me a cunt in my own gaff?

Willy: What the fuck have you got to be jealous about?

Paul: Go and ask my ...

Willy: You were well in there. Right up to the end.

Paul: I was interested.

Willy: You're jealous. You cunt.

Paul: Calling me a ... Calling me a ... (*Impersonating him*) 'Awwww!'

Willy: You're ... You're ...

Paul: 'Awwww!'

Willy: I don't belie ...

Paul: 'Pssss. Pssss. I didn't mean it. Awwww!'

Liz: (*Off*) You fucking bastard! (*Enters from upstairs*)

Paul: 'Awwww!'

Liz: I said you bastard.

Paul: What?

Liz: (*Calling upstairs*) Get your fucking arse down here!!

Paul: (*To* **Willy**) You've to go. Talk's over. Finished.

Liz: Theresa!

Paul: (*To* **Willy**) You've to go. Talk's over. Finished.

Liz: Theresa!

Paul: (*To* **Willy**) Get out! (*To* **Liz**) What's up?

Willy: If I could ... Another time ...

Paul: What?

Willy: If I could ...

Paul: Read all about it. Tony Kelly. Crime correspondent. the *Echo.*

Liz: (*Calling upstairs*) Theresa! Get your hole down here!

Paul: (*To* **Willy**) Now! Out! (***Willy** leaves*)

Liz: How dare you? (***Theresa** enters from upstairs*)

Theresa: Em … She's em …

Paul: What's going on?

Liz: Guess, you thick.

Theresa: You're wrong, Liz.

Liz: I'm …

Theresa: You're wrong.

Paul: What the fuck is …?

Liz: I'm wrong?

Paul: Making a show of us in front of …

Liz: (*To Paul*) You fuckhead. (*To Theresa*) You certainly made a … (*To Paul*) You fuckhead. All she wanted … (*To Theresa*) You should've kept your big mouth shut.

Theresa: Liz. This is all … There's a …

Adele: (*Off*) Get her out, get her out!!

Paul: What happened? What are you …? (*Calling*) Adele!!

Theresa: You're thinking stupid, the wrong things.

Liz: Don't you …

Theresa: How can you …?

Liz: Don't do that.

Paul: (*Calling*) Adele!!

Liz: You're no man, Paul Bolger.

Theresa: What's she talking about?

Paul: Liz. What are you …?

Liz: You know fucking well. The dark trick. (*To Theresa*) The dark fucking trick. Get out.

Theresa: Paul.

Paul: You'd better head on.

Liz: Get out.

Adele: (*Off*) Get her out!!! (*Pause.* **Theresa** *exits house. Pause*)

Paul: What's going on?

Liz: What kind of a husband are you?

Paul: You're in my house, Liz.

Liz: What kind of a man …? I don't give a good fuck whose house I'm in. That poor girl up … That poor girl …

Paul: Liz.

Liz: Shame on you, you mouse.

Paul: What were you drinking?

Liz: Same as you. Shame on you. She's up there. She's up there. I'm trying to take care …

Paul: (*Calling*) Adele!! Adele!! (**Liz** *goes upstairs*) Adele!!

Blackout.

Scene Two

Morning. **Paul** *is sitting on the edge of the sofa in his underwear. A blanket thrown off him.* **Liz** *is making breakfast throughout scene.*

Liz: We all feel the same.

Paul: We don't all feel the same. I should have something flat to sleep on for my hip. I've to keep my back straight. (*Pause*) Look at the dip in that.

Liz: You should have slept on the floor, then.

Paul: Look at that.

Liz: I see it.

Paul: I'm not sleeping on the floor. (*Pause*) My bed's straight, now. Big pit in the middle of it. (*Pause*) Tough night, Liz.

Liz: Yeah.

Paul: Where's my stick?

Liz: Where'd you leave it?

Paul: Well, if I knew that … Ah, fuck it. What happened, Liz?

Liz: She opened her big mouth, how could you?

Paul: I'm only human.

Liz: Bit of self-control, Paul.

Paul: What happened?

Liz: We were upstairs talking about Theresa's burglary and she was telling us how scared she was when she's on her own. She was scared about this and she needed someone to listen to her, to understand, and she said … Bit of attention, you know? And she said, 'When Paul's there … ' That's what she said. 'When Paul's there … ' Then she shut her mouth and you could see she knew she fucked up. Course we copped it.

Paul: That could mean …

Liz: Copped it goodo.

Paul: That could mean anything.

Liz: But it doesn't mean anything, does it?

Paul: Going through a difficult patch, Liz.

Liz: So am I.

Paul: Difficult time in my life.

Liz: So am I, so's Adele.

Paul: With this bloke, this copper. I've to see things through.

Liz: See what through?

Paul: Ah, now.

Liz: See what?

Paul: Ah, now … You know?

Liz: See? D'you see, Paul?

Paul: What? (*Pause*) Can I've a …?

Liz: Get it yourself.

*She goes upstairs. **Paul** looks for his stick, then goes to his model ship. Sits down at table. Opens box. A knock on the door. He goes out and opens it. His and **Irene**'s voices are heard offstage.*

Irene: Hello.

Paul: Yes?

Irene: I'm ... Willy's wife.

Paul: Who's Willy?

Irene: Willy's the ... the man who shot you.

Paul: Sent you around, did he?

Irene: No, he didn't. Can I come in?

Paul: I'm only up.

Irene: Just for a minute.

Paul: I don't know. Wife of the enemy. Haven't got my wits about me yet.

Irene: I won't keep you.

Paul: Did he send you around?

Irene: No, he didn't.

Paul: I'm only up.

Irene: Just for a ...

Paul: Jaysus! (*Pause*) For a minute.

They enter.

Irene: I just wondered if you'd seen him.

Paul: I saw ...

Irene: You saw him.

Paul: I saw ... Last night.

Irene: He didn't come home.

Paul: To your gaff?

Irene: Yes. No.

Paul: Oh.

Irene: He didn't come home, I waited up all night for him, you see, you see, we were going to go for a drink and I went up for a shower and …

Paul: Look at that couch.

Irene: What?

Paul: Lie down on that couch.

Irene: I will not.

Paul: See how it dips in the middle?

Irene: I see it.

Paul: Good.

Irene: You saw him?

Paul: He was here last night, causing hassle.

Irene: How are you?

Paul: I'm crip …

Irene: Is he here?

Paul: No.

Irene: No?

Paul: He left.

Irene: How are you?

Paul: I'm crippled and I'm imp …

Irene: (*Interrupting*) No. No. I don't care. Did he say where he was going?

Paul: No. (*Pause*)

Irene: What are you going to write about him?

Paul: You'll see it.

Irene: Is it bad?

Paul: I don't know. You mightn't think so.

Irene: Why not?

Paul: You mightn't think so. That's you …

Irene: How bad?

Paul: … But him, now …

Irene: How bad is it?

Paul: It's bad enough …

*Liz enters with a jumper in her hand. She throws it to **Paul**.*

Liz: Here.

Paul: … For him.

Liz: Who's this?

Paul: (*Putting on jumper*) The copper's wife.

Liz: You're his wife.

Paul: He didn't come home last night and she's worried.

Liz: Oh, God.

Paul: We don't know where he went. (*Turns back to his model ship, begins examining pieces*)

Liz: Sit down. Go on. Sit down. He didn't come home?

Irene: I'm getting worried.

Liz: He's … Your husband …

Irene: Yes.

Liz: Sit down. (*Irene sits*) He's a policeman. Why should you be worried about him if he's a policeman?

Irene: He might …

Liz: That's it. I mean, if he's a policeman …

Irene: He might do something.

Liz: What might he do? Don't be afraid.

Irene: I'm afraid for him.

Liz: You're … Okay. I'm listening, you're afraid.

Irene: Yes.

Liz: You're afraid, you're alone. All right. You're alone, you've got a problem, your husband's missing, you need someone to talk to.

Irene: No. I nee …

Liz: I'm here, you can talk to me, a cup of tea?

Irene: No thanks. I'm not really …

Liz: Okay. Tell us where he usually goes. We can sort this out.

Irene: Em …

Liz: Where does he usually go?

Irene: He usually … I don't …

Liz: If you tell us that, then. If we know where he goes usually …

Irene: Yes, he … (*Pause*)

Liz: Well?

Irene: When?

Liz: What?

Irene: When? He usually comes home to me.

Liz: When he's upset?

Irene: He usually comes home to me.

Liz: I'm going to make us a cup of tea. (*She exits to kitchen. Returns*) You've someone to talk to, now. You've a problem, you've someone to talk to, a confidante, a cup of tea. Nice?

Irene: Em …

Liz: Nice? (*Pause*)

Irene: Yeah.

Liz: Nice. What are you afraid of? I'm Liz.

Irene: Irene.

Liz: Nice to meet you. (*Of Paul*) Don't mind him. Tell me what you're afraid of. He won't come back?

Irene: I don't know.

Liz: He'll come back.

Paul: (*Of ship*) Ah …! Jaysus!

Liz: Don't mind him.

Irene: Are you sure …? He didn't …?

Liz: I don't think so. Paul?

Paul: (*Of ship*) Fucking hell.

Liz: Paul!

Paul: What!

Liz: He didn't say where he was going?!

Paul: Are you making tea?

Liz: I'm making a pot. If you want some you can get it yourself. Did he say where he was going?

Paul: (*Pause*) I'll make myself some coffee.

Liz: Bit of domestic strife, Irene. Paul!

Paul: Who!

Liz: Irene's husband. The guard.

Paul: I don't know. No. Have we coffee?

Liz: A fair bit of drink was consumed here last night, Irene.

Irene: Really?

Liz: A fair bit. We're all a bit …

Paul: This thing's impossible.

Liz: You can have a cup of tea and afterwards you can ring home, see if he's come back.

Irene: Okay.

Liz: That sound all right?

Irene: Yeah.

Liz: Good. (*Exits to kitchen. Pause*)

Irene: (*To Paul*) Are …?

Paul: Mmm?

Irene: My husband.

Paul: Don't talk to me.

Liz: (*Offstage*) Don't talk to him. He's in the bad books.

Paul: My bum hip's at me.

Liz: (*Offstage*) Your what?

Paul: This thing's impossible, Liz.

Liz: (*Entering with tea*) A child.

Irene: Is he your husband?

Liz: You must be joking.

Irene: Whose …?

Liz: Upstairs. She'd a harder night than the rest of us, God bless her. That right, Paul? (*To Irene*) A hard old night. (*To Paul*) Paul!

Paul: Did you see the dip in that couch?

There is a knock on the door. Liz goes to answer it.

Willy: Hello.

Liz: Ah! Your wife's here. Come in.

Willy: My wife?!

Irene: Willy? (*They enter*)

Paul: The man who shot Liberty Valence.

Irene: Willy. I'm worried stiff, where were you?

Willy: Thinking.

Liz: Would you like a cup of tea, Willy?

Willy: No thanks.

Liz: Have a cup of tea.

Irene: Thinking where?

Willy: I spent the night at the station.

Liz: Told you there was nothing to worry about.

Irene: Ah, Willy.

Willy: I needed to be on my own.

Liz: You might as well …

Irene: You should have rang.

Liz: Cup of …?

Willy: I didn't want to talk to anyone. I went up to the station, had a few cups of coffee … It was quiet up there. I sat at my desk and just … just had a long, hard think. (*Pause*)

Liz: (*Pouring tea*) You might as well have a cup of tea.

Irene: And where did you sleep?

Willy: On my desk.

Irene: Ah, Willy.

Willy: It's good for the back.

Paul: It is.

Willy: Flat surface.

Paul: Flat. Yep.

Willy: I've slept worse places.

Liz: Well, he's back now, anyway. Sit down, Willy.

Willy: Sorry to be back again.

Liz: It's alright. Sit. (*He sits*)

Willy: Sorry for disturbing you.

Liz: No bother. Sugar?

Willy: No thanks.

Liz: There's the milk.

Irene: Doctor Kielty called, Willy.

Willy: That's nice of him, now, Irene.

Irene: He wanted to know why you weren't at home.

Willy: That's nice of him. And was he using his RTE newsreader accent?

Irene: He wa …

Willy: On the phone, it was probably his normal one, was it?

Irene: I don't remember.

Willy: Then again, he was talking in a professional capacity so …

Irene: He said you were suffering from post … Something related to shooting. Post shooting something.

Willy: I have to do something.

Irene: Post, related to …

Willy: I thought we could have a chat.

Irene: Related to trauma.

Willy: (*To Paul*) I thought we could have a chat.

Liz: I don't think he's in the humour.

Irene: I think you shou … Willy!

Willy: What?

Irene: I think you should come with me.

Liz: Paul?

Paul: I'm not in the humour. (*Goes out to make coffee*)

Irene: He said you're suffering from … Let's go home. He said he needs you to call in today.

Willy: Don't know if I'll be able to, Irene. May not be able to.

Irene: Why not?

Willy: May not be able to.

Irene: What's up with you, Willy?

Willy: Nothing's up with me, Irene. I'm just saying I may not be able to.

Irene: Why not? (*Paul enters*)

Willy: (*To Paul*) I've a proposition for you.

Paul: I'm busy. (*Sits at ship*)

Irene: Why won't you be able to, Willy?

Liz: Drink your tea, Willy.

Paul: (*Of ship*) Where'd you get this bloody thing, Liz?

Liz: Tell us your proposition, Willy.

Willy: I can only tell it to Paul. Paul.

Paul: What?

Willy: Can I just ...?

Paul: Fucking hell!

Willy: It'll take me just, that's all, two minutes.

Paul: All right. Tell me it.

Willy: Ah, now, we ca ... The women'll have to step outside.

Irene: Why?

Willy: It has to be private between him and myself.

Liz: Ah, well if that's the case ...

Irene: Why can't we hear?

Willy: Irene!

Liz: All right, Irene, they want to go mano à mano, head to head, let's go inside. C'mon, two's company.

Irene: What happened to sharing?

Willy: I'll share with you after.

Liz: Irene? They need privacy.

Irene: I'm going home.

Liz: Sure you can stay here. We'll go inside, have a yap.

Irene: I'm going home to our son, Willy.

Willy: Go on home to Tommo.

Irene: What the hell are you up to? And sleeping on your desk? What are you up to? I need you to … I need you … What are you doing here with these people?

Willy: I'll see you after.

Irene: Why won't you be able to call in to Doctor Kielty?

Willy: No 'Won't'. Just may not be.

Irene: Why not?

Willy: Not not. May not.

Irene: Tell me what's going on, Willy.

Willy: I'll see you after, Irene.

Irene: Do you not trust me? (*Pause*)

Willy: No. (*Pause.* **Irene** *heads for the front door*)

Irene: I'll be at home if you want me. Willy?

Willy: Right. You'll be at home. (**Irene** *leaves*)

Liz: There's no need for that, now.

Paul: You right, Liz? Come on.

Liz: No need at all. That's no way to talk. (*Exits upstairs*)

Paul: I hope you're not gonna start your boasting, now.

Willy: No. I was in the station last night, there was a copy of last night's *Echo*. Did you read it?

Paul: No.

Willy: There was an article, this woman, Professor of ...

Paul: I don't read that shite. I read Genius ...

Willy: Professor of ...

Paul: ... Tony Kelly. That's it. I don't know how you can read those fucking eejits.

Willy: The emotion professor. You know her?

Paul: I know her. I don't read her.

Willy: Solves problems.

Paul: Seen her picture, she's a dog.

Willy: A woman wrote in, her boyfriend had cheated on her, they were fighting all the time because of it, so the emotion professor told her, this was her advice, get out and sleep with someone else.

Paul: Do the same thing.

Willy: Balances things, makes her feel equal. Got me thinking ...

Paul: That was her advice?

Willy: Yeah.

Paul: Jesus!

Willy: So ... (*Pause*)

Paul: So ...? (***Willy** takes out a pistol and puts it on the table*) Jesus! Is that real?

Willy: I need it for my proposition.

Paul: Jesus!

Willy: All right?

Paul: Is it real?

Willy: Yes. Now. You ready?

Paul: That's a …

Willy: Yes. It's a gun. This article got me thinking. I want you to shoot me.

Paul: What?

Willy: Do the same thing to me as I did to you.

Paul: Shoot you.

Willy: What I did to you. Then we're quits. Like the emotion professor says. Balance things out so it won't be between us any more. Do the same thing to me.

Paul: Twice.

Willy: Twi … (*Pause*) If you, yeah, if you want. I don't want you to kill me, now. Shoot me. You can shoot me in the leg, the hip, like yourself, the arm …

Paul: Is it loaded?

Willy: It will be when you do it. Bit of balancing out.

Paul: Some action.

Willy: Bit of action to settle things. You shoot me instead of printing about the … You know, what I …

Paul: You pissing yourself like a baby.

Willy: (*Beat*) Yeah.

Paul: Can I hold it?

Willy: Get the feel of it.

Paul: (*Picking it up*) Heavy.

Willy: Yep. (***Paul** aims the gun at various objects in the room*) Well?

Paul: It's tempting, I can tell you.

Willy: Then do it and solve all our problems. I'm sick of this inaction.

Paul: (*Putting gun down*) And get arrested.

Willy: Sure how will you get arrested if we keep our mouths shut? All we've to do is get rid of the evidence, clean up the blood, get rid of the gun. You drive me close to the hospital, my car, we'll dump the gun in the river on the way. I don't know who shot me, I didn't get a look, someone I arrested. Long as we keep our mouths shut, who's gonna know?

Paul: It's tempting.

Willy: (*Taking out silencer*) Got this so it's quiet, who's gonna know? I saw enough of the bloke to know he wasn't limping, so how could it be you? Put something under me to collect any blood, we fuck that in the river as well.

Paul: It's fucking tempting.

Willy: Did you tell anyone yet?

Paul: About …

Willy: Yeah.

Paul: No.

Willy: Your wife?

Paul: No.

Willy: 'Cos if we do this, we're quits. You shooting me cancels out you telling on me.

Paul: Yeah. No. Nobody knows yet.

Willy: So, come on. (*Pause*) I made you a cripple.

Paul: Yeah.

Willy: I shot you.

Paul: If I …

Willy: Twice. I know you want to. Do this and promise me that's the end of it. Revenge.

Paul: There's … You're tempting me, Pal.

Willy: An eye for an eye.

Paul: You're tempting me.

Willy: Let's see if you've got what it takes to put a bullet in someone.

Paul: Oh, I could do it.

Willy: See if you're man enough.

Paul: I'm man enough to take it.

Willy: But are you man enough to dish it out?

Paul: More man than you.

Willy: Well, I'm man enough to take it.

Paul: Well, then I'm man enough to dish it out.

Willy: Well, then, show me, then. Show me and we're quits. Even things up, do the deed, do this. (*Pause*) Do it.

Paul *picks up the gun, aims it at the audience.*

Paul: All right. Yeah.

Willy: Yeah?

Paul: Yeah.

Willy: All right. (*Begins loading the gun*) Okay if we do it here?

Paul: 'Course.

Willy: Kid's at home.

Paul: How old's the kid?

Willy: Kid's six.

Paul: Nice. (*Pause*) Young one?

Willy: Youngfella. (*Pause*) Get this fucking thing over with, yeah?

Paul: Settle it.

Willy: Exactly.

Paul: Done?

Willy: You'll have to get rid of them.

Paul: Oh, that's right, yeah. (*Calling*) Liz?!! (*To* **Willy**) Hang on a sec'. (*Calling)* Liz?!!

*Liz enters with **Paul**'s stick. **Willy** puts gun in pocket.*

Liz: How's it going?

Paul: We're having a good chat.

Liz: So our peace talks are coming to fruition?

Paul: Yeah.

Liz: Brilliant. Here. (*Throws **Paul** stick*)

Paul: Where'd you find it?

Liz: (*To* **Willy**) And you're mean. Don't think I'm talking to you yet, speaking to your wife like that.

Paul: Where'd you find it?

Liz: Upstairs.

Paul: How's Adele?

Liz: Not good, Paul.

Paul: (*To* **Willy**) My trusty stick.

Liz: Bit upset.

Paul: I wasn't upstairs last night.

Liz: Well, that's where I found it.

Paul: Do youse want to go out to the pub?

Liz: Well, do youse? A drink, the right atmosphere, a serious discussion …

Paul: No, we'd prefer to …

Liz: Drink and an old chin wag?

Paul: We'd actually prefer to stay here, Liz.

Liz: We're fine here.

Paul: Well, we'd actually …

Liz: Youse go down. The right atmosphere, neutral ground, pints instead of shorts …

Paul: The atmosphere's grand here, Liz.

Liz: I don't know if Adele's in the right shape.

Paul: Nice hot whiskey, get her, huh? Do the trick. Adele likes the old hot whiskeys with the clove things. Willy and myself need to … Don't we?

Willy: Need to …

Paul: But why not you two …?

Willy: … To … here's the right …

Paul: It is. D'you know what I mean, Liz?

Liz: I don't, Paul.

Paul: 'Cos, like, if youse go down to the pub … (*There is a pounding on the door*) Who the fff …?

Liz exits to answer it. **Theresa** *enters,* **Liz** *behind her.*

Theresa: Liz! I'm sorry it happened, but I'm scared. Paul! I've no one else to turn to. They came, they came back last night, I'm on my own.

Liz: They came back?

Theresa: Last night. I heard noises. I can't stay there on my own again.

Paul: I'm a bit tied up, Theresa.

Liz: You're hearing things.

Theresa: No, Liz.

Liz: Are you sure?

Theresa: Paul. I'm sorry. There were …

Willy: Who's this?

Theresa: Who …? You're here again. You're a guard, aren't you?

Paul: Theresa, we're a bit busy.

Theresa: You're that same bloke who ...?

Willy: Yes.

Theresa: Why can't you do anything? You shot him so why can't you protect me? Why can't you catch these people?

Liz: Sit down there, Theresa.

Theresa: I'm scared, Paul. I'm sorry.

Paul: What about your dog?

Theresa: Toby's ... Against thieves?

Liz: Theresa.

Theresa: Against bandits and murderers? (*To Willy*) You bastard, you're all alike. (*To others*) And rapists? Toby doesn't give a fuck about me anyway. You said so yourself, Liz, the Professor said. He'll leave me to these, these villains. (*To Willy*) Do you know what it's like to have someone break into your own domain? To have them prowling around while you're helpless, asleep? They could've cut my throat. They could've had their wicked ... I feel violated. I feel ...

Liz: Theresa. Relax. Talk rationally, if you sit down ...

Theresa: (*To Paul*) I was violated and you don't care. Do you know how that feels?

Willy: I do.

Theresa: What? You ...? No, you don't.

Willy: I'm being violated the same way. Of course I know how it feels. Privacy. I'm going through ...

Theresa: But you don't know.

Paul: Violated?!

Willy: Yes, I do know. Privacy?

Theresa: You're a guard. How can you?

Paul: Fucking violated?!!

Willy: But I do.

Theresa: How can you?

Paul: Fucking violation, you're talking about?!! I'll tell you a few, one or two facts about violation. Violation's a bullet entering your body, piercing your skin and pushing its way inside you. Inside where it shouldn't be. Tearing through your flesh and shattering your bone and pushing its way right inside you. That's violation. Youse haven't a clue what you're talking about. (*Adele enters, stands in doorway*) What kind of a bullet was it?

Willy: Thirty-eight calibre.

Paul: Through my hip, missed the socket by millimetres, came out my arse. Another one through my pelvis, lodged inside me, had to be taken out. (*To **Theresa***) Someone broke into your fucking house? Try taking a bullet sometime, youse wimps! Youse're all so fucking sorry for yourselves, well what about *me*?

Adele: What about me? (*Pause*)

Paul: What about you? You don't know what it is either.

Liz: Paul!

Paul: Get over it. I got over this.

Liz: Paul! There's no need for that!

Paul: Should try taking a bullet sometime. (*Pause*)

Adele: Get out of here, Theresa.

Theresa: Someone broke into my house again. Adele.

Adele: Did you not invite them into your bed, you tramp?

Theresa: I'm ... I'm ... You're the ones who ... who've always ...

Adele: Get out, you fucking tart, you. I won't let you get away with this, I'm not taking this. Go home to your fucking dog ...

Theresa: Adele!

Liz: Adele, calm it.

Adele: The smell off her, Liz. Do you know you stink of dog? Do you know you've the smell of a dog in fucking heat off you? No wonder you've no friends.

Liz: Ah, Adele, now.

Adele: Get out of my house, the stink of you. The stink. Go to your dirty mutt, fucking, your moulting fucking ... mongrel, dirty hairs all over you. He's the only one who'll love you.

Theresa: Paul!

Adele: He's the only one who'll love you, my husband has nothing to say to you. Go to your doggie.

Liz: Go on, Theresa. I'll drop over later to check up on you.

Adele: What?

Liz: Go on, now.

Theresa: I'm afraid, Liz.

Liz: This is a bad time.

Theresa: I'm alone.

Adele: She's her dog.

Liz: I'll drop over to you.

Theresa: I'm scared.

Liz: I'll knock six times and shout 'Geronimo' in the letter box.

Theresa: Will you?

Liz: I will.

Theresa: Geronimo?

Liz: Six knocks and Geronimo?

Adele: (*Screaming*) GET OUT!

Theresa: Paul?

Adele: Come on. (*Walks **Theresa** to front door and puts her out*) Out! (*She comes back in*)

Paul: Jaysus! (*Beat*) You all right? (*Pause*) Listen, do you and Liz want to go down to the ... pub, have a bit of a ...

Adele: I hate you.

Paul: ... Hot whiskey with the ...

Liz: Ah, now, Adele.

Adele: No, Liz. No. And you dropping over to her?

Liz: Well, she's ...

Adele: She's bad.

Liz: ... She's scared, she's alone. I thought ...

Adele: I'm fucking alone. (*To Paul*) You're not the only person lives in this house. You're not the only person has it hard. We're supposed to help each other. We're husband and wife, we're ... I'm not taking it any more, we're supposed to help each other.

Paul: And we are.

Adele: You're helping yourself. You're helping yourself to the fucking ... what's her ...?

Liz: Theresa.

Adele: ... the smelly woman. The doggy woman.

Paul: You know it's hard for me, Adele.

Adele: You big baby. (*Pause*) You're such a baby.

Paul: What did you have to wear that gear for?

Adele: What gear?

Paul: The top, the sexy stuff, was that a joke?

Adele: What?

Paul: Parading yourself in front of me.

Adele: What's that got to do with her?

Paul: Theresa?

Adele: Why were you seeing her?

Paul: I was horny. (*Pause*) You know? (*Pause*)

Adele: But you know I'm not able to.

Liz: Able to what?

Paul: Of course you're able to. I'm your husband.

Adele: You spoke to the doctor.

Liz: Able to what? What's this now?

Adele: You know I'm sick.

Liz: Do I know this?

Adele: You told me you understood. You told me it was okay.

Paul: Well, I don't.

Adele: You promised me.

Paul: I know I did.

Adele: You said you understood.

Paul: (*Shouting*) Well, I don't understand. All you've to do is spread your legs!!! All you've to do is spread your fucking legs for your husband!!! For your man!!! That's all you've to fucking do!!!

Adele: I … I … If I …

Paul: Buying me a ship to pass the time?

Adele: … Paul …

Paul: You open your legs, that's all there is fuckin' to it. Is that so fucking hard?!!! I've to go off with the dog lady.

Liz: Adele.

Adele: Need … I need …

Paul: Is that so fucking hard to do?

Liz: What do you need?

Paul: With the fucking dog lady.

Adele: Need to … Just, if you gimme … I need …

Liz: Adele. (*Adele runs upstairs*) Adele! (*Liz runs upstairs*)

Paul: (*To Willy*) Are we right?

Willy: What?

Paul: We right? Let's go. You got the gun?

Willy: But your wife …

Paul: We right?

Willy: Right for what?

Paul: For this. Are we right? The gun. Come on. Gimme the gun.

Willy: But they're still …

Paul: Fuck them. You want to do it, we're doing it now, come on, give it to me.

Liz: (*Offstage*) Adele!

Willy: You sure? Is there something …?

Paul: Do you want to do this? Come on, we've to do it now. If we don't do it now, we're not fucking doing it.

Willy: (*Attaching silencer to gun*) Just wait 'til I …

Paul: Hurry up. Gimme. (*Takes gun. Liz comes downstairs and runs into kitchen. Hurried. Distressed*) She all right? (*Liz comes out with Adele's pills and runs up the stairs*) Liz! (*To Willy*) Right. What do I do?

Willy: Cock it.

Paul: Right. I know that. There bullets in it?

Willy: Is your wife okay?

Paul: She's fine. What next, is it loaded?

Willy: Where do you want me to stand?

Paul: Stand there. (*Goes to kitchen, comes back with towel*)

Willy: Are you sure she's okay?

Paul: Happens all the time. Stand there. (*Throws Willy towel*)

Willy: Are you sure she's okay?

Willy: What's going on?

Paul: Are we doing it or what?

Willy: We are.

Paul: Well, come on, well.

Willy: I'd prefer if you did it quickly.

Paul: (*Pause*) Hold your horses.

*Paul begins spreading newspapers on the floor. **Willy** helps him.*

Liz: (*Off*) Paul!

Willy: Aim it, by the way, when you're aiming it, aim it a couple of inches below your target because there's a kick and it can throw you off, okay? Don't want you hitting me in the wrong place.

Paul: (*Pointing at newspaper*) Know who that is?

Willy: Yeah.

Paul: Who?

Willy: Tony Kelly.

Paul: Genius.

Willy: You'll get me to the hospital?

Paul: I'll drive you straight after. Just let me get my ... (*Deep breath*) Okay.

Liz: (*Offstage*) Paul?!

Paul: Okay. (***Willy**'s looking upstairs*) Willy? Willy, are we doing this?

Willy: Yeah.

Paul: Where do you want it?

Willy: The leg, the hip, just not the middle.

Paul: Right.

Willy: Or the head.

Paul: The leg or the hip.

Willy: The leg or the hip.

Paul: Well, pick. Which?

Willy: What?

Paul: The hip or the leg?

Willy: Oh. The leg.

Paul: The leg.

Willy: Is it properly cocked?

Paul: (*Cocking it*) Yep.

Willy: All right, go. The leg, is it?

Paul: Yeah.

Willy: All right, go. (***Paul** aims*)

Liz: (*Offstage*) Adele? (*Pause. Louder*) Adele?! (*Pause. Hysterical*) Adele!! Adele!!

Paul: (*Lowering gun)* Just gimme a second.

Willy: Aim carefully.

Liz: (*Offstage*) Adele! Paul!

Paul: Just give me a second or two. Have to … work myself up.

Willy: Take your time.

Paul: Just give me a minute.

Liz: (*Off stage*) Paul!

Paul: You've never been shot before.

Willy: I'm about to.

Paul: It hurts.

Willy: Well, come on, then.

Paul: Hold your horses. (*Pause. Aims gun*) You all tensed up?

Willy: Yeah.

Paul: The right leg, right?

Willy: The right one.

Paul: You right?

Willy: Thanks for not telling them. About the ...

Paul: Forget about it. I'm not your friend.

Willy: I know you're not.

Liz: (*Offstage*) Paul!!

Paul: Good. Are you right? (*Pause*)

Willy: Okay. Two inches lower.

Paul: Two inches. Right. (*Pause)*

Willy: Ready? (*Pause)*

Paul: Yeah. (*Long pause)*

Liz: (*Offstage*) PAUL!!!

Willy: (*Almost simultaneously*) GO!!!

Blackout.

The End.

I wrote this play in 1996, made a bunch of copies and posted them to various theatre production companies I'd looked up in the Yellow Pages. I got a single reply – from Jim Culleton – and Fishamble produced the play in 1997.

Many thanks to Jim for having faith in it.

Mark O'Rowe

The Nun's Wood

A Play in Two Acts

Pat Kinevane

&

For My Father

The Nun s Wood was first produced by Fishamble Theatre Company on 12 May 1998 in project @ the mint. It then toured to the Backstage Theatre, Watergate Theatre, Cork Opera House and Belltable Arts Centre.
The production had the following cast and production team:

Rhea Normile Máire Hastings
Silvy Hogan Myles Horgan
Jaso McLoughlin Fiona Condon
Picus Normile Chris Kelly
Bellona Barry Emily Nagle
Circe Caroline Gray
With the voices of Pat Kinevane, Pat Laffan and Niall Tóibín

Director Jim Culleton
Designer Kieran McNulty
Lighting Designer Paul Keogan
Original music Laura Forrest-Hay
Production Manager Stephen Bourke
Tour Production Manager Lee Davis
Stage Director Paula Tierney
Stage Manager Meredith Hagar
Producer Maureen Kennelly
Project Arts Centre Director Fiach Mac Conghail

The Nun s Wood won the BBC/Stewart Parker Trust Award for Best First Play in 1998. The play was performed live with a simultaneous radio broadcast by the Sibiu International Theatre Festival, Romania, in association with Fishamble, on 7 June 2002.

Photo (l-r): Emily Nagle and Fiona Condon as Bellona and Jaso
© Colm Henry

Dramatis Personae

Rhea Normile, 63 years old

Picus Normile, 18 years old

Silvanus Hogan, 18 years old

Jaso McLoughlin, 17 years old

Bellona Barry, 17 years old

Circe, A Woman

The male voices of Aeneas McCarthy, Tim Hogan and Turnus Normile occur from offstage.

Music (mostly violin) occurs throughout.

Rhea Normile is in the present. All others live in August, 1974.

The action takes place on the island of Tinaglasha, off the south coast of Ireland.

The stage directions are vital.

Atmosphere is all.

ACT ONE

Slowly, all becomes silent and dark.

Hold the darkness for 20 seconds. Front of House music soothes.
The lights begin 'in long lashes to lace, lance and pair , like ropes of
illumination, erratic, resembling the urgent flickers of emergency.
The speed of the lights is treble / six times that of the sound. We
almost distinguish three forms, still, in grouplets of shock.

These figures weep. Two bodies lie flat and covered in the space.
These bodies are strictly indistinguishable. An amethyst blanket
covers one of the bodies. The bloodied hand of this corpse is framed
in a cube of light.

The Front of House music yet soothes us. Softer light creeps in. As it
does, the figures and the dead fade away.

A large tree dominates the stage-left area. It is a Scots pine. Other
trees, as large, stand beside and behind it. These are silvery beeches.
Stumps and logs are scattered about the remainder of the area to
facilitate. Baked terracota soil.

Music yet soothes. A shallow stream of water, an inch or two deep,
trickles upstage-right. A gravestone stands downstage-right. The
grave is overgrown and old. Semblance of a bench is situated beside
the grave. Suggestion of another older grave juts into this space,
discreetly.

A lady walks forward as the crowd clears. Her name is **Rhea**
Normile. She is beautiful, well-dressed, in dark colours. She carries
a large black handbag and gloves. She stands silent beside the main
grave. This lingers.

The music finishes – **Rhea** *is anxious, cameo prayer, blesses herself.*
Rhea *smiles. She speaks to the Grave.*

Rhea: Lily love. It's me a ghrá. Rhea. Jesus. *(She lights a*
cigarette) How are ya lovín'. Pardon the Smoke Lil. No
disrespect to ya a ghrá, but it helps the loosenin'. I never lost
it says you. Needs must when the Devil rides! No
Woodbines anymore though. They were rippin' the chest

outa me. Barkin like a hound, so I changed to these … Silk-Cut Ultra-somethin' … like suckin' air Lil. They do the trick though. *(Pause and smoke)* First of all Lil, I have to say sorry for not visitin' ye this long while. Distance is a fright. I'm back here for two days Lil. Sad times Lil. Poor Vesta Barry was buried only an hour ago, just around the corner from you love. An end of an era for sure. Ye'll be neighbours forever now Lily. Vesta and yerself. *(Pause. She fidgets slightly, sits)* I only barely made it to the funeral Lil. Sure if it wasn't for your nephew Silvy, I would never av known. Ye see … Jaso and himself got wind 'o the word somehow about poor Vesta and they rang me from Australia. Laugh isn't it. 12,000 miles away and they get the news first. Sure that's only to be expected, says you. They couldn't possibly make it home for the funeral, so they asked me to do the emissary thing, pay their respects for them, kill two birds and check up on your good self. Say hello like, and spruce up your plot. So here I am. All the way from the Whest! God, Lil, yer like a jungle. I'll fix ye later.

Enter two animated youths, **Silvanus Hogan** *and* **Jaso McLoughlin.** **Silvy** *is an uncomplicated buck of 18 years, a power-house of energy.* **Jaso** *is a sun-burnt, dappled-red girl of 17, a character not to be messed with!* **Silvy** *sings snippets of 70s pop songs. He is happy.* **Jaso** *drags on a cigarette. On route crossing the main space,* **Silvy** *smacks her bum.* **Jaso** *squeals and replies.*

Jaso: Try that again now Silvy and I'll box the head off ya!

Silvy: Are you comin' to the hop tonight?

Jaso: I'll think about it. I hates that GAA hall. Smell of sweat.

Silvy: I'll wear me Old Spice Jaso, you can sniff me instead!

Jaso: *(Exiting)* I will in me high hole!

Silvy *follows her off. Laughing.*

A young man, **Picus Normile,** *crosses the space. He is 18 years old, touching 19, handsome and rugged. He carries a hurley. He calls.*

Picus: Silvy … Jaso?

*Too late. They ve gone. He sits and smokes … **Rhea** continues.*

Rhea: County Mayo is grand. Life is tickin' away up there. Picus is livin' just down the road from me. He's a good son Lil, so he is. Crazy busy with the roofing company, his own, thank God. Tiling, asphalt, gutters. The more leaks the better says you! He's been at that now for the best part of twenty years, and it's a tough ould station Lil. Out in hail, rain and snow. Keeps him fit though. Sure if he was livin' down here he'd probably be idle. Place has gone to the dogs Lil. He's happy enough, I think. Still the walkin' image of his father. I didn't get a look in love. Sure I knew that the minute he was born. They planked him on my belly and him wriggling and wet … Not a trace of me. Even now, he still has the jet black hair, chocolate eyes. The spit of his father. The pup off him …

***Picus** exits. **Rhea** lights another cigarette.*

Rhea: So, *sin an scéal* … Vesta pushin' up daisies too now girl. She didn't suffer Lil. Out like a light, the creatur … her heart Lil, bang! She was all by herself in the house when it happened. Dagon, the husband was out golfin'. Some things never change. The loneliness of a death like that, hah? They're all at it down here Lil. Golf courses and driving ranges everywhere. Good for tourists no doubt. But not the remote island we lived on Lil. Tinaglasha is not the same a ghrá.

*The lights snap to the centre area. It is night. Two more young figures enter. **Picus** is dressed well. Dragging him gleefully on to the stage area is **Bellona Barry**. She is 17 years old. She is simply a beauty, but a touch of a vixen. They banter.*

Bellona: I saw ya, gawkin' at her, eyes on sticks!

Picus: Untrue.

Bellona: Julie Goggin! Come on Picus, your standards are plumettin'.

Picus: True.

Bellona: Pig in knickers. She's 28 at least.

Picus: True.

Bellona: Like that, do ya? Old fiddle like?

Picus: True.

Bellona: Stop that!

Picus: What?

Bellona: 'True, untrue' … You're a flirt boy.

Picus: Incorrect. I was only lookin'.

Bellona: Lookin' is lethal.

Picus: Lookin'?

Bellona: Lookin' sometimes spoils the view.

Picus: The view?

Bellona: The panorama, me!

Picus: 'Spose.

Bellona: She's an antique Picus. Too ould to dance at the hop … instead gets a job servin' the chicken suppers so she can rub against all the young fellas dancin'.

Picus: I wouldn't object to that.

Bellona: Rubbin'.

Picus: I'm partial to an odd rub.

Bellona: Ya shagger! What about moi?

Picus: You're sound.

Bellona: Hah? Sound! Just sound?

Picus: Sound. Safe.

Bellona: Safe?

Picus: Grappled to me.

Bellona: With a chastity belt, God help us!

Picus: I'll pick that lock when I come to it.

*A ripple of a pause. A look. A passionate kiss. **Bellona**, assertive, pushes him away. She sits and applies her lipstick, aided by her trusty compact and mirror.*

***Picus** produces a pocket knife. He goes to a tree and begins to carve 'P+B on the bark.*

Bellona: What have I got that Julie Goggin doesn't?

Picus: Me.

Bellona: Besides?

Picus: A rich Da.

Bellona: Stop. What?

Picus: Okay Eyes – you got the eyes.

Bellona: Go on.

Picus: Mouth.

Bellona: Explain.

Picus: Lush.

Bellona: And?

Picus: Smile.

Bellona: Yes?

Picus: Killer.

Bellona: Continue.

Picus: Throat.

Bellona: Describe.

Picus: Slender.

Bellona: What else.

Picus: Time up. That's enough head-pumpin' for one night.

Bellona: You're the poet of love.

Picus: We aim to please.

Bellona: Fuck ya!

Bellona feigns a pout. She lights a fag. They look at each other.
*Look away. A loving quarrel. **Rhea** speaks.*

Rhea: Picus never married, Lil. He was engaged a while
back to a girl from Westport. Didn't last. I suppose, he never
really got over Bellona Barry. He hit the drink very hard, but
he's been off it now for the past eleven years. I light candles
every day love, but I suppose it will always be a struggle for
him. I constantly warn him Lil, face the sun Picus, but don't
turn yer back on the storm. Ah, he'll be grand!

Picus and Bellona continue.

Bellona: So what are ya gonna soft-soap me with instead of
compliments?

Picus: Depends what ya want.

Bellona: Sweets.

Picus: Naw.

Bellona: Why not?

Picus: Ye'll get hefty. Want to keep ye like a waif.

Bellona: So what else … flowers.

Picus: Nope.

Bellona: There's no romance in you at all, ya brute.

Picus: Ah there is.

Bellona: Why no flowers so?

Picus: Comparisons.

Bellona: Pardon?

Picus: You, against the flowers, no comparison.

Bellona: Who's the better.

Picus: The more beautiful?

Bellona: Yes!

Picus: No question.

Bellona: Who?

Picus: *(Pause, fun, question)* You.

Bellona: Good choice Picus Normile.

Picus: I'm known for me taste.

Bellona: Have to eat to taste. *(Rises and goes closer to her lover)*

Picus: What?

Bellona: Have to have a meal, to appreciate like.

Picus: What's on the menu?

Bellona: Boil-in-the-Bag … me!

Picus: Melted on toast.

Bellona: Me, au gratin!

Picus: Your breedin' is comin' out tonight!

Bellona: What?

Picus: The grandeur, the French.

Bellona: I just landed in a palace. My breedin's another kettle of fish.

Picus: Far from au gratin I was reared.

Bellona: Doesn't matter. The ugly are often the handsome unfortunate!

Picus: Think so?

Bellona: Of course, Why else would I be hanging round ya boy?

Picus: The Lady and the Tramp.

Bellona: Too right. I like it like that.

Picus: Me too.

A look, a pause.

Bellona: Finish that for me later on.

Picus: *(Putting his knife in his pocket)* That's a rough sketch.

Bellona: Hungry?

Picus: For what?

Bellona: Nothin too fillin', just a starter.

Picus: Half a loaf …

Bellona: C'mon, down by Goggins. The phone box. Hope Julie sees us. We'll rub her nose in it.

Picus: Naw, Morrison's haggart.

Bellona: No way.

Picus: We'll be grand, chill the bod.

Bellona: Why the farmyard, Pic?

Picus: I know a spot.

Bellona: So.

Picus: By the windmill.

Bellona: And.

Picus: *(With frustration)* Aaahhhh!

Bellona: What?

Picus: It's romantic, romantic out.

Bellona: There's a lover in you alright.

Picus: Shag off.

Bellona: Wooing me. And the attention to detail too. Makin' sure the scenery is suitable.

Picus: Oh yes, the film set, the ambience.

Bellona: Yes, I've converted ya.

Picus: Converted me?

Bellona: 'Ambience!' Tres bien!

Picus: It just slipped out.

Bellona: A French slip.

Picus: Latin actually, from *Am-bi-ens*, ambient.

Bellona: Jesus, you've learned something from the Pres Brothers, hurling apart.

Music in … A "well done" kiss from her to him.

Circe *secretly watches them from the wooded area. She wears a black dress. She does not wear a veil.*

Bellona: C'mon! Before Da sends a search party. *(Bellona tenses)* Are ya sure it will be alright Picus? Morrison will throw a mickey fit if he catches us in his haggart.

Picus: We'll be out of sight.

Bellona: Now, no pantin' or shoutin', Picus.

Picus: Promise. I'll whisper everything.

Bellona: Sweet nothins.

Picus: Sweet Bellona Barry.

The pair exit. ***Circe*** *watches them leave. She carefully places a tiny egg on the soil, close to the wood. It is framed in a cube of light. She looks at the engraved tree. A pause. She slowly melts an exit amongst the trees. Music out …* ***Rhea*** *…*

Rhea: I'm doin' alright Lil – tippin' away – the widows pension is shite, but I'm toppin it up with an extra few bob from the baking. Keeps the wolf from the door. I'm still at the baking Lil. I have a sort of contract with the local café, big place. 'Dare's money in Buns'. I do all the Chester cakes – bread puddings, scones, éclairs and home-made jams … Christ, the jams Lil! *(Music is low)* D'ya remember Picus, and your nephew Silvy, out collectin' with the saucepans. Sure half of those blackberries were reekin' of greenfly and mould. I'd give Picus the pan, he'd call for Silvy and God love them, they thought they were providin' Manna for the whole starvin' population of Tinaglasha.

A new day. ***Picus*** *and* ***Silvy*** *enter. They walk with saucepans on their heads.* ***Silvy*** *has a fag in his mouth, his trusty transistor radio in his hand. Sounds of nearby bullocks are heard.*

Picus: *(Imitating mother)* 'Don't touch the wans near the ground.'

Silvy: Sure how will she tell the differ?

Picus: *(Mother s voice again)* 'The rats' piss is on them and you can't kill it by boiling even!'

They all laugh.

Rhea: I was always on to him about the rats!

Silvy: They all look the same.

Picus: She smells 'um. Nose like a beagle.

Silvy: Yerra if she's that fussy, tell her to gather 'um herself.

Picus: There's no spud pickin' this week. McCarthy called it off. So she sent me out doing this instead. Slave driver.

Silvy: I hope she pays ya.

Picus: Me bollocks. I give her half of my potato money, but all I get for blackaz is abuse. 'You're doing nothing this week, gallavantin' and loitering. The ground's too damp for picking spuds, the blackberries are bursting out on the briars, so get down the hilly field and help your mother –'

Silvy: I couldn't stick that naggin'. My Ma would probably be the same if she was alive.

Picus: Rhea is harmless I s'pose. She needs the spondoolicks.

Silvy: Poor aul bitch. How's she coping?

Picus: Alright. Nine years now come December's his anniversary. I try to keep the garden in shape for her, but she keeps tellin' me how 'your Father' would have pruned this or 'your Father' would have planted that.

Silvy: You've a lot to live up to, boyo.

Picus: Don't I know it. Ma is always on to me about buildin' the business again, ye know the gardening?

Silvy: 'Tis an idea Pic. Oul Turnus was fierce popular.

Picus: Sure he had loads a customers. Used to do all the local gardens. He did all the shrubs for the nuns in the convent below. His oul tools are still in the shed. I should think about it, I suppose.

Silvy: You're lucky she doesn't take all the spud money off ya.

*Silvy takes out four pears, eats one, silently offers **Picus** one. **Picus** accepts. They eat.*

Picus: I offered. She said she has enough from the baking. Keeps her head above water. It's grand. It's more cash for me. More mon, more fun.

Silvy: More fun, more looove!.

Picus: Don't have to pay for that, not Picus Normile. *(Thrusts pelvis)*

Silvy: I'd pay, by Jasus I'd pay – I'd sell me sister, if I had a sister.

Picus: I'd fla yer sister, if ya had a sister!.

Silvy: Anyway how d'ye get on with Bellona Friday night?

Picus: Yerself and Jaso left the hop before us … how did you get on?

Silvy: No go in that department. She wouldn't let me near her. But what about Bellona?

Picus: Ah she's goin' around with a major snot on her since. We had a mad jag up in Morrison's. Snook into his yard. We started getting off, lovely night. Feelin' each other up.

Silvy: Go on!

Picus: Got my hand on her tit and the other one down front.

Silvy: Ya langer!

Picus: Just into her knickers. Fantastic! She kept bitin' my neck, my hand was wet.

Silvy: Go on, go on!

Picus: D'ya remember the finger thing we saw in the magazine?

Silvy: Ya – Jesus – did ya?

Picus: I was about an inch away.

Silvy: I have a horn!

Picus: Pervert!

Silvy: So … Jesus … and—?

Picus: I was lookin' in her eyes. She has massive eyes. Anyway, just about to try the finger—

Silvy: Come on – did ya?

Picus: Naw.

Silvy: *(Devastated)* Ya nooble, ya fuckin' gowl, why not?

Picus: Oul Morrison caught us, Paisley was barking like mad.

Silvy: Vicious bastards, them elkhounds.

Picus: He smelt us a mile off. Morrison shoots, ye know, as per normal.

Silvy: How'd ye get away?

Picus: Bellona screams. Ran like a hare and down the avenue, what a laugh, haulin' her knickers up 'round her arse.

Silvy: Wish I was dem knickers – go on!

Picus: I had to hide in the barn till Morrison retreated. Close shave. I was only passin' the place a week ago, crossin' the 14 acre, the fucker, he shoots at me, again!

Silvy: They're only pellets.

Picus: I don't give a shit – a pellet in the arse is no picnic. He has a gammy aim anyway. I shouted across to him 'Hey Morrison, all you own is the house and the yard, the rest of the land is a free country.'

Silvy: Good man yerself!

Picus: Now, fuck off back into yer pigsty, and play with your cogs and chimes.

They both laugh. **Bellona** *and* **Jaso** *enter. The sound of a trickling stream is heard.* **Jaso** *sits and dangles her feet in the shallow water,* *extreme upstage. She silently examines and reads a list and semi-listens to* **Bellona**, *who has been speaking.* **Bellona** *is incensed …* *painting her nails, fingers and toes!*

Bellona: 'Twas awful Jas. I felt like a prostitute or something, I mean, I know 'twas two to tango an' all, but, ye know, I was so, what's the word …? embarrassed, no, no, lowered.

Jaso: *(Still half-listening)* Yeah.

Bellona: I'm just terrified in case Morrison saw me arse. That's what really gets me. I mean, if he saw me, he'll tell me Da. Ma is no bother, sure she's scared o' me, but Da will go ape-shit.

Jaso: *(Reading her schoolbook list)* He won't.

Bellona: Ye see Da's company insures Morrison's oul farm buildings and his little shack of a house. Da calls up to him once a month to collect the policy money. If Morrison lets the cat out of the bag, I'm in for it.

Jaso: Ye love invitin' disaster, Bellona, don't ya?

Bellona: I'm serious Jas. The last time I went out with Picus he nearly murdered me.

Jaso: The hop?

Bellona: No, fishin' last week. Picus and meself were down the Tender Quay. Picus walked me home and left me to the front gate. I sneaked in the driveway about midnight, and there was Da, waitin for me, like a lion. He grabbed the mackerel I'd caught outa me hand like a mad thing and slapped me across the face with them. Called me a slut, for being out like, so late.

Jaso: Fishy slut!

Bellona: Told me never to go near Picus again, or he'd streel me with his golf clubs.

Jaso: *(Half in conversation)* Sure fathers are fathers the world over, Bell.

Bellona: Well I don't know what mine has against Picus. It's like as if he knows some awful secret about him. He never says a word to Picus when he calls for me. Jesus, if he finds out about Friday night he'll throw an unmerciful gaga. Hope that oul Morrison keeps his clock-makin' mouth shut.

Silvy and Picus continue.

Silvy: (*Laughing*) Does he still fix 'um?

Picus: Oh yeah. Pocket watches and grandfather clocks. You can hear them clanging from the fields. He has shag all else to occupy himself.

Silvy: In fairness Picus, he can't stop people walkin' the land. He has no claim on that.

Picus: He thinks he does. Where d'ya get the pears?

Silvy: Auntie Lily's orchard. Slogged them this mornin'!

Picus: How is Lil anyway? Ma called in a few times to her, but she didn't answer the door.

Silvy: Yeah.

Picus: She wasn't at the Mission either.

Silvy: Ah, she's not feelin' the best. Just a bit under the weather.

Picus: Her hand?

Silvy: (*Pause*) Yeah … the usual.

They eat and lie back, relaxed. Rhea speaks.

Rhea: I had to give the jam to your brother Tim for the pony. Smell of rats! Tim grazed that pony at the back of your orchard, Lil. I don't know how you kept them apples to yourself. and sure mornin' noon and night all the kids were sloggin' plums and pears from ye. I miss your cookers now Lil. God they were spicy gems!

Jaso and Bellona chat on …

Jaso: Stop freakin' out over Morrison, girl – 'twas only your arse he saw. Not much differ between that and yer face.

Bellona: Ah stop takin' the mick', Jas.

Jaso: You should have flashed yer diddies at him girl, he would have keeled over, the oul nobber. *(Laughs)* Sure Silvy's Da saw mine the other night!

Bellona: What!

Jaso: 'Twas a riot. I was sitting starkers in the tin bath in the middle of the sittin' room floor. Lifebuoy soap all over me – scrubbin' meself after pickin' spuds.

Bellona: So, Tim Hogan … what happened?

Jaso: Hould yer whist till I tell ya. I never locked the front door. Ma and Da were gone out to the Mission. Tim barges in, thinkin' he was collectin' a bag of stale bread for the pony. Ma keeps all the scraps for him. He got more than mouldy bread. Me diddies and me monkey runnin' to hide, all over the room. Suds flyin', got the fright of me life. I was roarin' laughin' though, his poor face, shock, like a lamped rabbit!

Bellona: Jesus.

Jaso: I'll have to shove the china cabinet up against the door the next time I'm washin' in that oul bath. It's a crock of a thing anyway. It was leakin' as well, and I had to use the bicycle puncture kit to plug the holes. Sure better still, I'll come over to your place next time, and have a proper bath, in proper porcelain. *(Laughs)*

Picus notices the egg on the soil. He moves toward it.

Silvy: What's that?

Picus: Looks … it is, an egg … still intact!

Silvy: Show. *(Takes it and examines it with great expertise)* Yellowhammer's!

Picus: Too late in the season. *(Looks about)*

Silvy: It's a yellowhammer's. Forsaken.

Picus: That's weird … out here like … no nest.

Silvy: Thanks, Pic.

Picus: *(Hand out)* Back! Finders! *(Silvy hands it over)* It's all *mine*! Gift. I'll blow it out when I get home. Give us yer sock.

Silvy: *(Without hesitation, begins to take off his boot and sock, speaking as he does … an everyday occurance)* I have a hammer's already so you can stick it up yer arse!

Picus: Liar!

Silvy: *(Admitting)* Lucky fucker!

Rhea continues.

Rhea: I walked passed your old place this mornin. Ah Lil, a new bungalow instead now love, the old cottage … levelled. The Desmonds own it. Big vellux windows on top, a mock fountainy plastic thing in the front garden, and gnomes – everywhere – very scary. Sure the orchard is like a wilderness Lil. But guess what Lil, Your purple delphiniums are still there, tall as a child, still surviving in the thick of it all.

The girls continue.

Bellona: Seriously Jas, Friday night was a nightmare.

Jaso: Tell me about it. Silvy tried to ate the tonsils outa me. I told him I'd chop the goolies off him.

Bellona: I s'pose I shouldn't have, ye know, let Picus get, ye know, so excited. Thanks be to God, in a way, we were caught. Sure I'm in me flowers.

Jaso: Never stopped ya before Barry.

Bellona: You're disgustin' Jas.

Jaso: But it didn't, hah?

Bellona: What?

Jaso: Don't be actin' the Mary Immaculate now, Bell …

Bellona: *(Amused)* What are ya on about?

Jaso: You weren't 'disgusted' the time I caught ya with Aeneas Mc Carthy ... the two of ye at it like cattle.

Bellona: *(Flattered, feigning coy)* Go 'way outa that Jas—

Jaso: Oh yes, and his jelly bum flappin like a turkey's chin ... He's not called Aeneas for nothin'. Jesus you could land a plane on that arse girl ... huge ... still, I suppose, the bigger the hammer, the bigger the nail, hah Bell?

Bellona: Ah stop Jas. Listen ... hope you haven't told anyone about that. Ye promised?

Jaso: Relax girl, lips are sealed. But c'mere ... how was Picus anyway? A donkey?

Bellona: Jaso stop please.

Jaso: I'm only askin'.

Bellona: Well don't. OK? Look we never did it, alright?

Jaso: What! Ye're goin' out for over a year Bell ... losin' yer touch aren't ya? ... Get a move on girl.

Bellona: *(Pauses, looking puzzled)* I can't Jas.

Jaso: Whyso Bell?

Bellona: I dunno.

Jaso: Don't know what like?

Bellona: Can't explain it, like ... it's weird.

Jaso: What's weird about it? He's gorgeous. Take the bull by the horns, girl. Shag him senseless and Bob's yer uncle.

Music in.

Circe enters. She views the girls. She carries a sliotar in her hands.

Bellona: Yeah.

Jaso: There's no wind ... row!

Bellona: Wish I could girl.

Jaso: *(Getting tired of this endless debate)* But what is the problem exactly? If ya tell me he's a homo, or you're frigid … I'll die laughing.

Bellona: *(Deadly serious)* I can't exactly describe it Jaso. It's a very unusual feel. I want to be close to him, ye know, in everyway, but when we're near doing it, and we have got very near it on manys the occasion, I gets … panicky … guilty and panicky.

Jaso: God, that's strange alright …

Bellona: Yeah. No, it feels … *(Snaps)* … change the subject Jas OK?

Jaso*: (With understanding of her upset, not the cause)* Suit yourself girl. Sure you can talk to me anytime ye feel like it, genno?

Bellona: *(Kisses Jaso s forehead)* Thanks a million Jas.

Jaso: Now what books have you left to get?

They refer to the booklist. Music out. The boys banter on.

Picus: That's 23 eggs in all.

Silvy: 23 me hole.

Picus: *(Swiftly counting on fingers)* Robin, wren, goldcrested wren, blackbird, grey crow, jackdaw, stonechat, chaffinch, bullfinch, greenfinch, song thrush—

Silvy: 'Viscivorus'.

Picus: What?

Silvy: Mistle thrush.

Picus: Yeah – professor – 12, then, great tit—

Silvy: Hand down knickers!

Picus: *(Trying to concentrate)* Yes – 13 – blue tit, cold tit, magpie, barn owl, stock dove, pigeon, house martin, swallow, yellowhammer, hedge sparrow—

Silvy: Cuckoo *(Silvy smokes a fag)*

Picus: *(Dismissive)* That's 23 … no! Hedge sparrow!

Silvy: What's the betting – cuckoo?

Picus: It's definitely a hedge sparrow's. I got it four months ago.

Silvy: Never told *me* about that, ye schnake! Where?

Picus: *(They look to the distance, **Picus** pointing)* See over there, by the Stoat's Well?

Silvy: I do?

Picus: See the flock of gooseberry bushes, to the left?

Silvy: Yeah?

Picus: I watched the hen sparrow from up here, with Dad's old racing binoculars. No joy. The hen kept trickin' me. After a week she was gettin' slower on the wing. Meal after meal, the cuckoo chick had her exhausted, wore herself out—

Silvy: Foster mother – poor bitch.

Picus: I bate me way thru the brambles to the nest, with a hurley. The sparrow chicks were all dead, impaled on the thorns around the nest. The big bastard baby cuckoo chucked them out an' had the whole house to himself. Sitting like a swan. There was one unhatched egg, sky blue, a dud. That's the one I have.

Silvy: I believe ya – OK. But I have a swan's.

Picus: Illegal.

Silvy: Fuck illegal!

Picus: How much is it worth?

Silvy: Bellona naked on a sheep-skin rug!

Picus: Shag yourself. C'mon we better get some blackaz.

Silvy: Shake the bush for a short cut. *(**Picus** begins to exit)*

Picus: Very clever, and they'll all hit the turf and smell of rat's piss.

Silvy: Nose like a beagle.

Picus: C'mon pick.

Silvy: Ah pick me nose.

Picus: Ah pick me arse. *(Sock in the air)* Yellowhammer!

*Both laugh with loud fun, exiting. **Silvy** blows smoke. Focus off the lads and on to **Rhea**, as before – laughing, still chatting to Lily.*

Rhea: I'm stayin at the Commodore Hotel down town, no less! Very very! The lap 'o luxury Lily. Picus gave me the money. I asked him to come with me, but he's busy. Too many bad memories for him down here, I suppose.

The girls continue.

Jaso: 'La France en direct'.

Bellona: Me too.

Jaso: And am, this one … 'Stair na Litríochta'.

Bellona: Ye don't need to get that one … that's for the honours course.

Jaso: Grand. Thank God for being thick, look at the price of it!

Bellona: Jesus Jas, just lookin' at it now, I've a rake o' books to get. And copies and stuff.

Jaso: Join the club girl. Ye can only get a couple of them secondhand. Listen! I'm gettin' mushrooms tomorrow mornin', down Ballybrassil. I'm gonna sell 'um to The Mad Monk.

Bellona: How much will he give ya for them?

Jaso: 90 pence a basket – money for books girleen. Not that you need it or anything.

Bellona: Listen Jas, Da might be loaded, but he's an awful miser, girl. He cut back me pocket money after the mackerel fiasco. I need all the spare pennies I can lay me hands on.

Jaso: He keeps Vesta in great style though, doesn't he? She has gorgeous clothes, Bell. Ye didn't pick yer looks up off the street.

Bellona: Well there's no way, physically, I could look like her.

Jaso: I know Bell, sorry. *(Pause. Music in … violin.)* But she's always decked out lovely daw.

Bellona: Don't believe all ye see Jas. Street angel. Da's as tight as a screw girl. Gives her just enough to run the house. Pays her no attention at all. Golf widow supreme. She's worse to listen to him. God, what a marriage!

Jaso: So where does she get the money for the style so? Hope she's not on the game!

Bellona: She'd be better off. He's a grumpy oul bollocks. Naw. She makes a fair few bobs from the music lessons. Has about twenty students. All violin.

Rhea interjects.

Rhea: You passed away before the story ended that summer Lil. You missed all the dhrama! You were better off *a stór*. Nothin' the likes of those murders had ever happened in Tinaglasha. Sure at Vesta's mass this mornin', the suspicion was drippin off them all, starin' at me, when I was comin' down the aisle from Communion. I got the cold-shoulder at her grave too, so I schneaked away over here, to you Lily. It's great to have someone to talk to … me oul pal.

The girls continue … Circe watches them.

Jaso: Ye know, that's one thing I'd love to be able to play.

Bellona: Ye wouldn't say that if your Ma was playin' it, every day! Drive ye off yer game it would. I love gettin' out of the house. Give me ears a rest.

Jaso: Can you play?

Bellona: Are ya mad girl? She keeps on an' on at me though, to learn it. Jesus, I could think of nothin' worse.

Jaso: She is brilliant on it though Bell. I heard her playing at the confirmations last year. *Veni Creator Spiritus ...* massive!

Bellona: I know. Sure she used always play that for me to send me asleep when I was small. Lovely then, but I've had me fill now. *(The violin music stops.)* Anyway d'ya think the mad monk'd buy some mushrooms off me as well?

Jaso: Course he will. Sure he ates nothin' else!

Bellona: Nothin' else?

Jaso: Yeah. It's a kind of penance thing he does. Offers his fasting up to some God or other. Sure ever since he got kicked out of the monastery, he's gone off his chuck. *(Indicates the head)*

Bellona: Is that the Carmelite place down the Holy Ground?

Jaso: That's right. Ah he's a harmless poor eejit. They should've known better than takin' him in to be trained, in the first place. He's away with the fairies. Shadoodineena help us!

Bellona: L' habit ne fait pas le moine ...

Jaso: Translate for the benefit of your gobdaw friend.

Bellona: It's not the clothing that makes a true monk.

Jaso: Jesus, I'm as thick as plaited pig shite.

Bellona: What time in the mornin' so?

Jaso: About a quarter past seven.

Bellona: That's an unmerciful hour. I'll be only turnin' over.

Jaso: I'm goin' anyway. I'll give ya a shout.

They both rise and prepare to go home.

Bellona: That's very early though Jas?

Jaso: That's when the mushrooms are up.

Bellona: Alright so.

Jaso: Just jump out of bed and lash on yer slacks ... no make-up!

Bellona: A girl needs her make-up Jas. Never know who y'd meet!

Jaso: Vain cow.

Bellona: Mooo ... Moooo!

Jaso: See ya amárach Bell.

Jaso exits. Bellona is alone. Music up.

Bellona: Se ya Jas ... and thanks.

Bellona walks a smidgen. In thought, she stops. She takes a powder compact and mirror from her pocket. Circe waits, ... and watches. Bellona gazes strangely at herself in the mirror, lifts her blouse and touches her stomach, hips and breasts. This is tender and discreet. During this, Rhea has also taken out her own compact and bits from her bag, to patch up her make-up. She continues to speak.

Rhea: Would ye look at the state of me! Pollyfilla! Lookin' back Lil, twas the best thing we could have done. Gettin' away from here. A fresh start. Picus ... wasn't a healthy young fella ... lost loads of weight, went fierce quiet and into himself. Prison does that to a body. And Spike Island was an awful time for him. In custody.

Music out. Bellona is immediately startled by Circe, and drops her compact. Circe speaks.

Circe: Hello.

Bellona: Hello.

Circe: Circe.

Bellona: Bellona.

Pause.

Circe: Bellona ... I wonder—

Bellona: Yeah?

Circe: I wonder ... could you tell me, who ... who that young man with the dark hair is?

Bellona: Sorry ... who?

Circe: The young fella … you … I see you with … passing by sometimes? Is he your brother?

Bellona: No. That's Picus Normile, my—

Circe: Oh yes, the gardener's son.

Bellona: Yeah. But his father is dead.

Circe: Really?

Bellona: Yeah.

Circe: God rest him.

Another pause.

Circe: Thanks.

Bellona: Why like?

Circe: Well, nothing really, well … it's just, I heard one of the teaching sisters talking of him and praising his hurling … I found this sliotar in the wood.

Bellona: Oh.

Circe: Yeah. He hit it in here the other day … like a thunderbolt, just past my head … *(She smiles)* He's a bit of a hardihood.

Bellona: Yeah. That's Picus all out.

Circe: A strong puc.

Bellona: Yeah, he's brilliant. *(A further pause)* I'll give it to him if ye like.

Circe: *(Handing her the sliotar ball)* Thanks Bellona. What's *your* surname so?

Bellona: Barry.

Circe: Barry?

Bellona: Yeah.

Circe: Would you be Dagon and Vesta's daughter? *(Bellona nods a vague 'yes)* I see.

Bellona: Do you know them?

Circe: No. It's just that sometimes Vesta plays in the convent church. Benediction. Lovely.

Bellona: There's no accountin' for taste.

Circe: Sorry for holding you.

Bellona: 'Sall'rite.

Circe: The sliotar … thanks.

Bellona: No problems.

Bellona turns to go. Is stopped. Music in.

Circe: Bellona?

Bellona: Yeah?

Circe: Take care now.

Bellona: *(Puzzled)* Yeah.

Bellona exits. Circe watches her go. Circe too is about to exit but Picus enters. She hides a little. Watches him. He is still, but calmly looks about as if searching for someone. He looks to the turf beside the stream. He sees Bellona s compact and picks it up. Puts it in his pocket. He lights a fag. During the above action, Circe speaks … unheard by Picus.

Circe: The trees have memories, Picus. They're as old as the world. They sponge us in, they read us, and choose, discerningly. If we fascinate them, they remember. If we bore them, they remember too. But if we hurt them, they never forget. That's worse than a memory. It's an omen. Picus.

Circe exits. Picus remains, smoking and relaxed.

Rhea continues.

Rhea: He was cleared eventually, Thank God. The only thing to do after that court case, was to leave. We moved to my folks in Mayo. Left behind the disgrace of it all. *(Music out. Rhea brightens)* I tell ya Lil, Vesta Barry got a great send off today. The crowds were like the Pope's. No music in the church at all though – sure she stopped teaching and playing

after Bellona's death. It must have been terrible to lose a
daughter, and so young.

*Picus exits. **Rhea** lights a fag. Music in.*

A new day.

*The lights slowly, like a dawn, come up on the wooded area.
Grandfather clocks and watches tick and chime. This sound occurs
regularly during the following scene–the 'Silent Scene ahead.*

*The wood looks glorious, sunshine breaks, shadows, shade. Faint
singing is heard in the distance, singing prayers. The atmosphere is
Eden-esque. Tinaglasha is radiant. Eventually a lone 'Sister is last
to be seen. **Circe**. She too is radiant. She walks, takes it all in,
reads, and eventually decides to pluck bluebell and whitebell
flowers, with no fuss – an idealistic opportunity for solitude and
purpose. She gathers a lot, comes forward to the edge of the wood,
still gathering.*

Front of House. Music snaps out.

*Suddenly bang! bang! Shot-bursts are heard nearby. The distant
barking of a dog. She is startled, but not too surprised, used to this.
She looks about … nothing. The violin plays. She is just about to
return to her work, when **Jaso** and **Bellona** run by. They carry
baskets. **Jaso** leads, and laughs. **Bellona** looks contrastingly upset
and shaken, constantly checking behind her. Both girls slow up on
passing **Circe**, like naughty students running and caught on a
corridor. They take in **Circe**, who stands, with flowers. She notices
them. They all nod slightly, a greeting. The girls subdue their
excitement on passing her, but **Jaso** laughs and then exits. **Bellona**
is waylaid by a stone in her shoe. She rectifies this. **Circe** watches
her. Putting her shoe back on her foot, glances about for her
compact. The violin stops and **Bellona** hears—*

Circe: Bellona, is everything alright?

*Bellona looks back at **Circe**, puzzled … responds.*

Bellona: Yes Sister.

*Bellona exits. **Circe** watches her leave – she is still clutching the
vibrant flowers. She watches further. After a time, a church bell is
heard, calling, convent direction, 'prayers within . **Circe** remains*

standing, and watching. **Rhea** *takes a white handkerchief from her handbag. She springs to life, kneels on the handkerchief by the grave. She takes out a little garden fork, wrapped in newspaper, and busies herself.*

Rhea: C'mere till I tidy ya up Lil. Brought me own plough. Jesus, yer riddled with weeds *a ghrá.*

She plucks out the cankers. **Circe** *exits.*

A new day. **Silvy** *enters the light, followed by* **Picus**, **Jaso** *and* **Bellona**, *in darkness. They bedeck the stage with props for the scene ahead. As they work,* **Silvy** *shouts.*

Silvy: Auntie Lil. Are y'alright love. Lil? *(Pause)* Sleep away girl. I was just on the way to spud pickin'. Da said he'll call into ye later on. When he's collectin' the pony, alright? See ya so.

Silvy *retreats and joins the other lunatic youth behind him!* **Rhea** *continues as she works.*

Rhea: I went up to Dagon Barry in the church today. Just to sympathise. He looked straight thru me Lil ... just nodded ... wouldn't take my hand. I know Vesta never felt like that – she was always civil to me ... even after the deaths. Very strange atmosphere around all of today's ceremonies Lil. Like steppin' back 24 years, to Bellona's burial. And the burial of that other woman ... the Novice.

Music in ... transistor ... 70s fare. Blasted hot summer light, it s noon. One line of potatoes, soil and greenery are strewn across the stage. Full paper potato bags occur in groups of two to ten at intervals. The potato pickers are busy beside the wood. Tractor sound is heard at full volume, and fades into the wings. Transistor radio lies on the soil – all is a hive of action – the people bend, pick potatoes with buckets – some drag bags between their legs. **Picus** *works close to a lazing* **Silvy**. *Behind* **Silvy** *works* **Jaso**. *She is followed by* **Bellona**, *who is wearing yellow rubber gloves.*

The work goes on, heads down, pocket money to be made. **Jaso** *comments, in a shouting fashion, as if they are all at least ten yards of a distance from one another. The music is low.*

Jaso: *(To **Silvy**, holding her hurt finger)* Ouch! Am I cursed or what?

Silvy: *(Still lazing)* What's wrong baby?

Jaso: The rocks. This field is brutal. It's the worst yet. Every drill that's dug has boulders in it.

Silvy: What did ya expect … diamantes?

Jaso: But it has. There's shag all spuds as well. I'd nearly half fill the bags with stones and fill the tops with Kerr Pinks if I thought I'd get away with it.

Silvy: Yeah! And Aeneas McCarthy would sack ya, down on ya like a ton o' bricks.

Jaso: *(Looking cheekily back to **Bellona**)* Down on *me*? Ah no! I'm sure Aeneas'd much prefer to go down on someone else.

Bellona *throws a killer look, a shut-up **Jaso** gesture.*

Jaso: *(Continues)* And I keep finding all these bits of crockery, glass, chaneys and shit. *(Holds up a section of delft)* Wonder what was built here long 'go?

Silvy: Nothin'. That's all the games.

Jaso: The what?

Silvy: *(Winding her up)* The games. The Island games.

Jaso: What in God's name are you on about Hogan?

Silvy: We learnt it in History. The foreign sailors used to come up from the Quays long 'go.

Jaso: What sailors?

Silvy: Italians, Arabs 'n all.

Jaso: Arabs?

Silvy: Yeah. They used to trade tea and stuff for timber. Then afterwards the locals would challenge them to a competition.

Jaso: First I heard of it. Stop talkin' shite, ye big gallute.

Silvy: I'm not, sure I'm not Picus?

Picus: *(Supporting Silvy s lie)* He's not! The boats would dock at the town, and the sailors would treck up the hill, three mile, to here.

Jaso: To Tinaglasha! For what?

Silvy: The competition ye daw!

Jaso: Serious like? When?

Silvy: About 3000 years ago.

Jaso: What competition?

Silvy: The plate throwing – other games as well, hurling, races, boxing – that sort of thing. But the big event in them days was the plate throwing.

Jaso: Ye mean like a disc thing?

Silvy: Oh yeah! They'd all stand at the top of this field. A team of local men against a team of sailors and whoever threw the plates the furthest, won.

Jaso: Won what?

Silvy: The prize … the Tinaglasha plate prize.

Jaso: Silvy, cut the crap, what was it? *(She ponders a pause.)* It wasn't a plate was it?

Silvy: No.

Jaso: What?

Silvy: A virgin.

Jaso: *(As the others hide their laughs)* A virgin! Shag off!

Silvy: I swear. A local virgin. The sailors got to pick the prettiest virgin from the village, if they won.

Jaso: That's mad. Jesus. They'd be hard pressed now to find a trophy. Pretty or no.

Silvy: Too right Jas. *(Suppressing his joy of a lie)*

Pause.

Jaso: *(After moments of thought)* And Silvy?

Silvy: Yeah Jas?

Jaso: What if the local men won? What, like, would their prize be?

Silvy: Ah, I dunno, ah – a bar of Turkish delight!

Jaso: Ye crock o' shite—

Silvy: Or a crate of bananas …

Jaso: You're winding me up.

Silvy: *(Who connot hold it in any longer)* Ye'd swally dung Jas … *(Laughs hysterically)*

Jaso: Bastard!

Silvy: *(Others laughing too)* Gotcha McLoughlin!

Jaso: Bastard absolute. I'll get you for that – plate throwing me arse, I'll rip the ears off ya.

Silvy: I'd love an oul game with you Jas.

Jaso: *(Furious)* Watch it! It's often a man's mouth broke his nose!

Picus: *(Mimes throwing)* A couple of cups and saucers Jas.

Jaso: Shut it Picus.

Silvy: Or a few soup-bowls … weeeee … *(Laughing away)*

Jaso: Careful now Hogan, do ya want the tooth fairy to bring ya the jackpot? I'll ram this bottle up yer poopshoot.

Silvy: I'd prefer tea-bone china Jas.

*Laughs all around, except **Bellona**. **Jaso** is sour. All settle back to work. **Rhea** is active digging and fixing.*

Rhea: Vesta was put into the same plot as Bellona, and about six, no, eight plots up from them, under the Yews, over there *(Points)* is yer woman … Circe. The Nuns didn't bury her in their own convent cemetery. Just C.I.R.C.E. is all that's written on her wrought iron cross, DIED 1974. That's all.

*Rhea wonders. She goes to the partially exposed other grave near her, looks at it squintingly, sees the old urn like a vase thereon, thinks and then carefully picks it up. As she does, **Bellona** screams.*

Bellona: AAAAhhhhhh!

All: What?

Bellona: I saw … A fieldmouse!

*Everyone laughs loudly at **Bellona** s ridiculous distress … **Rhea** with the urn. She dusts it off and speaks.*

Rhea: I dunno who's in this plot Lil. Can't make out the headstone for love nor money. Sure they won't be needin' this says you!

*Rhea returns to Lily s grave, wipes and semi-polishes the urn. **Silvy** pipes up.*

Silvy: *(Who is last to begin work, draws a line to mark his boundary with his foot)* Come beyond this line Jas, I'll give ya a batin'!

Jaso: My drill's gettin' bigger all the time. Stop movin' the line ya langer.

Bellona: It's awful chalky soil though.

Silvy: Yerra take off them gloves Farrah Fawcett.

Bellona: I'm not ruinin' my nails for no farmer. Jas, I've lost me sizer. Give us yours will ya?

Jaso: Don't bother gradin' them girl. Scoop 'um all up … the big 'n the small.

Bellona: Eeuch – I got a rottener. It's all hollow, look at the yellow pus in it.

Holds up the devil s potato!

Silvy: Like my spots Bell.

Bellona: You're an animal Silvanus Hogan.

Silvy makes an animal noise.

Jaso: The Neolithic Man … Jesus!

Tractor noise stops abruptly.

All: *(Straighten up, look to tractor in wings)* Hurray!

Picus: Shite – The Massey broke.

*They all split. **Picus** and **Silvy** in one group. The girls to another.*

Silvy: Magic – rest *(**Silvy** lies beside the grave and sings Frankie Valle number to **Jaso**)*

> My eyes adored ya
> though I never laid a hand on you,
> My eyes adored you
> like a million miles away from me
> you couldn't see how I adored ya
> so close, so close and yet so far

Jaso: *(Rude gesture with one finger held up)* Swivel!

Bellona: Yeees, great, tupperware box. *(Searches for it)*

Silvy: Got any orange left Picus? I'm gaspin' …

Picus: Naw, sorry – shit! *(Anger at stoppage)*

Jaso: I'm starved, an me backs crippled. *(Lights a fag)*

*Silvy has now gone to the stream for a handful of water. He drinks, and then splashes it, orgasmically cooling down. He then returns to **Picus**. During this action, **Rhea** speaks.*

Rhea: I'm ashamed of me life Lil. I arrives, empty handed. Not a bloom for ya. With all the rush o' gettin' here. I'll get ye some juice in a jiffy.

Silvy: *(To **Picus**)* Look at the puss on you. What's wrong moaner?

Picus: No tractor, no work ya langer.

Silvy: So?

Picus: No money. Talkin' never brought home the turf.

Silvy: Relax boy. There's only three weeks left, then it's back to school so enjoy the rest. *(Lights a fag)*

Picus: School books equal money Silv.

Silvy: Money equals 'Da giz a few bob for the school books will ya.'

Picus: Not in our house.

Silvy: You'll be alright, Aeneas'll get it going. *(Calls off)* Hey, McCarthy, get the finger out and dig dem drills boyfriend.

Jaso: Shut up ya prick. Aeneas, take your time boy.

Silvy: Are ya tired Jas?

Jaso: No – hot.

Silvy: Want to be made hotter?

Jaso: Ah go away and play with yourself Hogan.

Bellona: Jaso, that's filthy.

Jaso: Shag him. He's a La La. I want to doss girl. Not in the mood for labour. I'm passin' out with the heat. I've done 7 bags this mornin–that's enough. The sum total of 70p and I couldn't give a scutter.

Silvy: More cash to be made Jas, between this and the mushrooms ye'll be rollin' in it. Catch shit while it's flying.

Jaso: Rather catch the sunshine darling. *(Takes off her shirt. Silvy wolf-whistles)* Wish he'd plug his hole. What a spastic!

Bellona: But you're scorched Jas, you'll toast girl.

Jaso: *(Slapping liquid on her body)* That's the general plan.

Bellona: What – what's that?

Jaso: Home-made Ambre Solaire.

Bellona: What is it?

Jaso: Cooking oil.

Bellona: Mad bitch.

Jaso: No worries Bell, I'll be mahogany after the holidays. It's worth all the peeling. *(Shouts)* I'll be the colour a Picus one a these days!

Silvy: Want a hand putting that on Jas?

Jaso: In your dreams sweetheart, you wouldn't have a clue how to handle the body of a WOMAN!

Silvy: *(With wild encouragement)* Up ye get Jas, Top of the Pops! Top of the Pops Jas, song, song, *Precious Moments* …

Bellona joins in on this jeering, ad libs galore. Silvy switches off the radio. In full splendour, Jaso bursts into song–greeted by egging cheers and whistles. She raucously performs a Three Degrees number in front of and on top of, her seven full bags of potatoes.

Jaso: *(Sings)*

> Oooo aaaaa ha precious moments,
> When will I see you aaa gain?
> When will we share, precious moments?
> Do I have to wait, for everrrr?
> Do I have to suffer, and cry the whole day thru?
> When will I see you againnnnn?
> When will our lives be as one?
> Are we in love or just friends?
> Is this the beginning, or is it the end?
> When will I see you again …

Tumultuous applause and 'get-ups' on her finish. Aeneas shouts from the wings – very loudly: 'Half-hour break everyone, tractor s banjaxed!'

Picus: Shit. The one day I needed the money.

Silvy: I told you already, relax. Relax or fuck off, cos you're ruinin' me siesta.

Picus: I'm goin' into the shade.

Silvy: Shade, oh no, shade, no no no please, keep it away from me. Nothin' like the late potato, August sunny sun sun.

Picus: Yeah. If ya want to look like a lobster.

Silvy: Ah gwan off into the shade with yer parasol ye oul woman.

Picus ignores him and walks up to Jaso and Bellona s area. As he does, Rhea speaks, polishes and smokes.

Rhea: You're in a lovely private spot here Lil. Nobody back or front of ye.

*Picus approaches the lassies. Both are chilled out, reading Jackie magazine, sunning and eating from the tupperware lunchbox. **Jaso** is filthy and drinking from a large glass bottle. **Bellona** tenses.*

Picus: Hey Jas, great performance. Sexy chic.

Jaso: 'Opportunity Knocks' here I come! Wanna slug?

Picus: Naw thanks.

Jaso: Alright. Never let it be said love.

Aside.

Picus: Hi Bell.

Bellona: *(Sternly)* Hi.

Both: I / You.

Picus: Can we talk?

Bellona: *(With sarcasm)* Might get shot.

Both: Ah come on Bell how was I to know?/Don't start me now Pic, I'm angry enough as it is.

Picus: Please Bellona.

***Jaso** knows trouble is 'at mill . She rises and leaves them, lowly singing.*

Jaso:
> We had joy, we had fun, we had seasons in the sun,
> But the wine and the song, like the seasons are all gone …

***Jaso** rests at the stream. **Picus**, taking the compact from his pocket, continues.*

Picus: Here.

Bellona: Where d'ya get that?

Picus: I found it when I was lookin' for ya the other day. To talk.

Bellona: *(Takes it)* Thank you.

Picus: *Now* can we talk?

Bellona: I'm too warm.

Picus: Well stew on.

*Picus takes one of **Jaso** s sandwiches and walks to the shade, by the wood. Sits, eats the sandwich. **Rhea** is rising and moving to the stream, vase in hand. She stoops to the stream. **Rhea** fills the vase, cupping her hands and transferring the water as she speaks.*

Rhea: The nuns Lil. Walkin' the wood. The wood! God! You wouldn't know it now girlin', loads of pokey new houses built all around it. But Lord, it was a haven years ago. All beech. From the edge of the village right down to the convent, like an island, in a sea of corn, beet and potatoes. The bluebells, the ivys, the nettles. The echo was eerie there Lily … They say beech has the longest echo of any woodland. I forgot the Scots pine, fostered by the grove, tall as the rest of them, but allowed to grow there, for some reason or other.

*Pause. The vase is full. **Rhea** looks at the stream. **Jaso** walks forward to the stream. She does as **Silvy** has done earlier, cooling herself with animated splashes of water. She looks at the stream. Examining it carefully, she speaks loudly back to the others in the field.*

Jaso: C'mere. I dunno why they ever christened this, Tinaglasha Stream. I mean, I thought Tina-Glasha meant 'Green Fire'. Sure it's soakin' wet, no colour, crystal fuckin' clear.

***Rhea** and **Jaso** in tandem, move from the stream, **Jaso** to the field, takes out a sandwich. **Rhea** to the grave. She places the vase on the grave.*

Rhea: Christ Lil, I gets shockin' poetic with a few fags in me. (*Circe enters the wood, carrying a fold-up canvas stool, and a book. She sits. **Rhea** takes from her bag a sandwich wrapped in tissue*) Doggy-bag Lil. I got the porter to make this for me. The sea air down here gives me a ferocious appetite.

*She eats in tandem with **Jaso** and **Picus**. Focus back to **Picus**. Solo.*
*Finishes his feast. Behind we see **Circe**. She walks very slowly and*
*is in obvious thought. **Picus** is unaware of her. She glides past.*
Silently, she soaks the shade. Time taken here is crucial, languid.
***Circe** sits once more. Languid. **Bellona** goes to her bag. She takes*
*out the sliotar. Eventually she sidles up to **Picus**. Both awkward.*

Bellona: Here.*(Tosses the sliotar at him)*

Picus: What's this … swap city?

Bellona: One of the Novices, from the convent. She gave it
to me the other night, said you lobbed it in the wood. Nearly
knocked her block off.

Picus: Who?

Bellona: Just one of the novices. Circ … ye know the wan
that's in the wood a lot.

Picus: Jesus, they don't miss a trick … thanks.

A pause … tense.

Bellona: Look Picus. Let me speak and then you can have
your say. OK? *(Picus nods)* Friday night, I was upset. You
told me it would be safe to …

Picus: Fla?

Bellona: *(Nasty)* Stop it Picus. *Let* me speak, please. *(Pause –*
he nods yes) You said no one would see us. You promised me
that. And I warned ye not to try anything heavy on. That's,
that's why I am, I am, a bit, upset.

Picus: You were bitin' my neck.

Bellona: What!

Picus: You were bitin' my neck, and groaning.

Bellona: I was not – *(Pause)* that's not the point.

Picus: It wasn't all me.

Bellona: I know, but it's a bit …

Picus: I didn't know in advance that Paisley would sniff us
out. I wasn't to know Morrison would appear. He's all gong

and no dinner. He shot just to frighten us, that's all. *(Pause, softening)* Bellona, it was a laugh too – ya must admit that.

Bellona: Oh yeah, hilarious. Nearly killed, and my pants down to my knees, that's a scream Picus! Jaso and meself were gettin' mushrooms yesterday morning, in Ballybrassil. We passed his haggart, and he fired at us too. Twice in the one week is a bit ridiculous Picus. The man's a lunatic, and you're not exactly the full shillin' either.

Picus: OK. OK. Hold it. I take the blame for the … location. No go area, accepted. But I'm not to blame for the smooch? We've been going out for over a year Bell.

Bellona: Ya. I know. *(Pause)* I need time Picus.

Picus: 'I need time' – time, for what? What a heap of shite. You're beautiful Bell, You're a cracker, and I'm not exactly Quasimodo either. It's natural to want to do that.

Bellona: I know all that Pic, but I want to be sure.

Picus: You're unbelievable Bellona. 'Sure' of what? That I'm not a bastard, that I'm not flaing around. I'm not! I haven't touched another girl since I started with you. And I don't want to touch another girl. I want to touch you.

Pause. **Bellona** *is flattered, but distant.*

Picus: *(Moves away, oddly)* And ye know what else? I think you want me too. I think you *wanted* to do it. It's summertime Bell, it's very warm, and you wanted me too. *(Pause)*

Bellona: *(In a whisper)* Sorry Picus. Something feels, not right.

Long pause.

Picus: Go on.

Bellona: Something feels wrong. Picus. Something feels odd. The wrong is odd. I need to think, OK … Why.

She very, very slowly gets up, leaves, and joins **Jaso***, who has returned from the stream.*

Jaso: How are things in Glockamarra?

*Bellona does not respond, but instead goes to her bag and takes out the amythyst blanket we have seen earlier. She walks seductively past **Silvy**, dragging the blanket over his sprawled body. **Picus** sits, puzzled, alone. Summer haze, and dazed. Silent buzzing summer. He sits in peace, but unrest. **Jaso** smoothes more oil on. **Silvy** with the radio, raises volume. The field is alive with the still innocence of them all. **Picus** stares at **Bellona**. **Bellona** strews the blanket majestically on the hot soil. Then, with tease, removes her top, to her bra, lies back on her stomach. Temptress? The picture lingers. **Rhea** speaks. She fidgets with her dentures.*

Rhea: Sorry Lil, I got a bit of lettuce stuck in me falsies … 'should have got the dearer ones the last time, these are the bane of me life. Too much gum, not enough tooth. 'Member the day I first got them fitted …

*Circe reads on. **Rhea** … enjoying her sandwich, sits up, relishing the fun remembrance that is imminent. **Rhea** is animated. **Silvy** pipes up.*

Silvy: C'mere Bell, d'ye hear.

Jaso: *(Cautious of his proximity to **Bellona**)* What Silvy?

*During the imminent exchange, **Silvy**, **Rhea** and **Jaso** harmonise their story, unaware of each other s fluid continuations.*

Silvy: Young Willy Hegarty was attacked yesterday …

Rhea: We were all outside Hegarty's house, waiting … you and me Lil, horsin' inta Curly Wurlys—

Jaso: Howso?

Silvy: He was missin for about six hours—

Rhea: His mother distraught!

Jaso: Shi— God help us.

Silvy: He came back wrecked, staggering up the road.

Rhea: His clothes in shreds, blood down his face and legs—

Silvy: His eye in trouble—

Jaso: That's shockin'—

Rhea: Father at the ready to welcome his son—

Silvy: Dymphna with the wooden spoon for reprimand—

Jaso: Did they flake him?

Rhea: Well they both hugged the bejaysus out of him—

Silvy: 'O Son a ghrá, cá raibh tú?'

Rhea: Mad Republicans

Silvy: 'In the wood'—

Rhea: 'Cén fáth a Mhic?' asks Ould Hegarty—

Silvy: 'For to get the hawk's egg'—

Rhea: Says the spailpeen—

Silvy: 'The hen attacked me … The he-hawk did too, so I waxed down the pine, broke branches, twigs 'n all'—

Jaso: Poor creatur, nearly hacked the maneens off himself—

Rhea: 'Ó a stór tar isteach ya poor boy,' says Dymphna—

Silvy: Ould Hegarty blew a gasket.

Rhea: 'What's that ya whelp?' says he, eyeing his son's hand—

Jaso: What did he have?

Silvy: A piece of elder wood, leaves still attached—

Rhea: And a clump of elderberries in his other tiny fist—

Silvy: 'Just elders Da … I was rubbin' them on me legs to ease the burns'—

Rhea: 'There's blood on yer legs'—

Silvy: ''Tis blood outa me cuts father'—

Rhea: 'Did ya spill it on the elder?'—

Silvy: 'No father'—

Rhea: Slap – Ould Hegarty lashes him …

Jaso: Sure Jesus love us!

Rhea: 'Did ya spill it on the elderwood?'—

Silvy: 'No, promise father'—

Rhea: Slap eile from Ould Hegarty—

Bellona: Some men are desperate cruel!

Rhea: 'Ye spilt it on the elderwood ya little f-ing brat'—

Music in.

Silvy: Ould Hegarty started roaring in Irish …

Rhea: 'Beidh na coillte lán d'olcas as seo amach'—

Circe: 'The woods will host evil from here on in'.

Jaso and Silvy laugh and lie back. Picus springs to furious life.

Picus: Oh fuck this.

He goes into the wood. Circe finishes reading and sees him. Embarrassed, coy, she stands. They are a distance apart, yet close enough to talk in a comfortable volume.

Picus: You're *(Recognising her)* … thanks for the sliotar …

Circe: That's OK.

Picus: Sorry for nearly …

Circe: Knockin' me out? *(Smiles)*

Picus: *(Coy)* Yeah.

Circe: Don't worry about it … Picus.

Picus: Am?

Circe: Yes?

Picus: Ah … how d'ye know my name?

Circe: Oh, you're sister told me, Bell …

Picus: Bellona … oh she's not me sister.

Circe: Sorry … anyway, I have to go.

She makes to go.

Picus: Right … am … thanks again …I shouldn't be in here anyway … bye.

Circe: Relax! *(Smiles at Picus)* The beeches look beautiful today don't they?

Picus: Yeah.

Circe: Like giants … bye.

Picus: Bye.

*Circe exits. She has left behind a piece of pink paper. **Picus** comes to a standstill. Watches her leave the space. Electric pausing here. Energies bounce all over. **Picus** notices the paper … too late … she s gone! Slowly, he lifts the note from the wood floor. Reads it. Pause. He almost freezes, reacts to the note. Tableau. The tractor noise loudly resumes. **Aeneas** voice calls … 'Back to work – lazy bastards .*

Silvy: Jesus I fell asleep – Christ I'm scalded, why didn't ye wake me?

Jaso: *(Rising from the soil)* Ye only nodded off a minute ago ye langer.

Bellona rises silently, then Jaso speaks.

Jaso: Where ye get the hippy rug thing?

Bellona: Found it in the hotpress this mornin'. Grand for keeping the creepie crawlies off me.

Jaso: Except for that creepie crawlie. *(Points to Silvy, laughs)* Christ yer like the Princess and the Pea.

Bellona: Jaso. 'Member yesterday mornin, that nun in the wood? The wan with no veil?

Jaso: Yeah, What about her?

Bellona: Ah nothin'. She kinda says hello to me now like, when I passes by.

Jaso: So?

Silvy: Jesus I'm sizzlin'.

Bellona: It's just like, I don't know her. But she's very, familiar like.

Jaso: What's her name do ye know?

Bellona: Cir … Circles or somethin' looper like that.

Jaso: She'd know ya thru' the teachin' nuns below in the convent. They probably do nothin' else but bitch about their problem students.

Bellona: Yeah.

Jaso: You're the swat girl, I'm sure dem mickeydodgers have nothin' but praise for you. Someone robbed a sandwich off me!

A shout offstage is heard. A loud shout … 'Silvy, Silvy . It is a man s voice, Tim Hogan s voice. **Silvy** *reacts.*

Silvy: That's me Da. What the fuck's wrong with him. Ouch! Here Jas, pick my drill will ya?

Jaso: Shit Silv. I've enough to do.

Silvy: I'll be back in the minute.

Jaso: Ould Tim can wait.

Tim's voice: *'Come up outa that field will ya Silvy. Silvy, come on out … now !*

Silvy: Please Jas. It's sounds urgent OK.

Silvy exits in a rush, struggling with his sun-burn!

Jaso: *(Puzzled, then calls to* **Picus***)* Normile. Business as usual, c'mon.

Hub-bub continues. **Bellona** *puts on her gloves. All resume picking potatoes as per beginning.* **Picus** *remains still.*

Bellona: What was all that about?

Jaso: Haven't the foggiest girl.

Jaso and **Rhea:** *(Simulteneously, with shock)*

Jaso: Jesus me finger!

Rhea: Christ shag off!

Music in.

Jaso: *(Nursing her hand)* Fuck them plates anyway. *(Bellona grabs Jaso's hand and holds it up in the air, leading her to the stream)*

Bellona: Keep it up, keep it up girl.

Rhea: *(Nursing her arm)* Oh Lil, I got a sting. The sauce in the sambo. I think 'twas a wassie. Look, I'll leave the mess here. There's a new chemist by Goggins. I'll go off and get a plaster or somethin'. Jesus sorry Lil. I'll be back in a little while a ghrá.

*Looking at her stung forearm, **Rhea** gathers her handbag and nursing her wound, begins to cross the stage to exit. The girls are turned upstage at the stream, nursing **Jaso**'s wound. **Picus** looks about. Then once more to the note. As he does, the noise around him fades, as do the lights, and a voice-over replaces the din. As the voice over, **Circe**'s voice begins. Light remains only on **Picus**, and the lone amethyst blanket which lies unoccupied.*

Voice Over:

> My love for you is deep and wild,
> Don't tell a soul, I beg you please
> To keep the secret of our child
> Eternally, amongst the trees.

Front of House. Music creeps underneath this Voice Over.

As it ends, the lights fade.

End of Act One.

ACT TWO

*Front of House. Music in. The theatre goes slowly dark. Hold the black for 20 seconds, and the music swells. Lights grow slowly and the Front of House music crossfades to violin. **Silvy** is found standing, alone over Lily s grave. He is dressed in a black suit, just about fitting him. Shirt and black tie are elegant.*

His nose is red. He is in deep thought.

*The violin plays a sacred tune, the 'Tantum Ergo , beautiful, low and a funeral knell is heard. **Rhea** enters with two small brown paper bags, and a handful of glorious purple delphiniums, long stemmed and majestic blossoms. She stands beside **Silvy**. Both unaware of each other.*

Rhea: Christ Lil, ye'll die laughin'. I called into yer oul place after the chemist. The Desmonds were out, no answer, so I plucked these for you. Don't worry … I left a few stems growin', for luck.

***Rhea** places the flowers next to the grave. She takes out the plasters and begins to apply one. **Silvy** blesses himself.*

Silvy: Listen ah … Thanks for everything … Auntie Lil.

*Music out … he exits, crossing **Rhea**. She speaks.*

Rhea: Anyway … Silvy and Jaso send all their love from Australia. They keep in touch with Picus and meself in Mayo, fairly regularly. *(She plucks surrounding vegetation for her flower arranging.)* They're livin' in Adelaide. Silv is still workin' with the horses. He builds speciality fencing for racecourses and corrals out there. They've two kids. Jaso finally got a little girl to pamper, and she's nursing away, all the time. So they've made a good life for themselves Lil. Weren't Silvy and herself lunatics long 'go? He lost a second mother in you Lil.

*She arranges the delphiniums carefully. **Silvy**, **Jaso** and **Picus** enter, carrying items. **Silvy** s tie is undone. He carries a very large cardboard box full of papers and junk. **Jaso** carries another box, a*

primus and an old chair. She has a small bandage on her finger.
Picus also carries boxes and another chair. They pant.

Jaso: Thanks for the primus, Silv.

Silvy: Sound Jas.

Picus: Ya bum McLoughlin.

Jaso: Gift horse, Picus. I won't have to trudge to the
scullery anymore, when I'm bathin'. Just have a pot boilin'
beside me, for rinsin' me hair. *(Checks the primus)* It needs a
new nipple daw. I'd gobble a fag, Jesus I'd ate one …

The lads rest on the chairs.

Picus: Silvy, you OK lad?

Silvy: Yeah. Thanks.

Picus: You should have told us, Silv. That she was poorly
like. When ya ran off the other day, sure we didn't have a
clue what was up with ya.

Silvy: Sorry lads, but Lily like, she was fierce private in that
way. She asked to be left alone … to rest like. Da found her
sprawled on the floor daw.

Picus: Alright Silv boy.

Jaso: Well, you're on the ball Silv. Couldn't ya leave the
cleanin' out for a few days ye know?

Silvy: Best to keep goin'. Handfuls make a load.

Picus: Jesus Silv, at least change yer clothes. She's only just
laid to rest boy.

Silvy: I'm grand Pic. Want to make a head start on this
stuff. Her house is a tip. She threw rubbish all over the place,
didn't know the difference.

Jaso: Senile like?

Silvy: Yeah. Her mind musta gone haywire the few days
before she got the stroke.

Jaso: That happens.

Picus: God help us.

Jaso: *(New idea)* Why don't ya get yer Da's pony – sure you could shag a load of her stuff on the cart. Save ya round trips like?

Silvy: Ah, I don't want to be botherin' Da. He's too upset to go near her things.

Jaso: Poor oul Tim.

Silvy: He's taken it awful bad.

Picus: But bringin' them back to your house will upset him even more Silv.

Jaso: He has to ye lapsy! The stench in her cottage is rank. She went to the toilet everywhere – for the week.

Silvy: No control. I'll sort thru' the milieu in our own back shed.

Jaso: You're as tough as nails Silv, fair dues to ya. *(They all go to exit. **Jaso** lets drop a box of papers and photos)* Oh merciful Jesus, I'm sorry Silv. I'm an awful spagy!

Silvy: No probs Jas, I'll be dumpin' the most of them—

Jaso: Ah look Silv, This is lovely. *(Picking up a photograph)* Look Picus, your mother and Lily. *(Looks at rear of photo)*

Rhea *has taken out the same photo. She too examines it.*

Rhea: Taken in 1955.

Silvy: Lil'll be about … *(Calculating on fingers)* … 30 there.

Jaso: Really? God she looks much older.

Silvy: Always did. Old head—

Jaso: And they stayed friends ever since. Christ there's hope for us all!

Silvy: Yeah.

Jaso: Yer Ma Picus, Jesus, Rhea was a smasher wasn't she?

Picus: Yeah.

Jaso: Trust the Mayo woman, 'Gid help is' to come up with the style.

Silvy: Give it to yer Ma Pic.

Picus: Thanks Silv. She was fierce upset today too.

Jaso: Look at the hairdo …

Rhea: Mad.

Jaso: Like a model. And Lily in the drip-dry nylon frock.

Silvy: She wore nothin' else. Desperate oul maid all her life.

Rhea: Ah Lil why didn't ye ever tell us you were sick love. We could have looked after ye a ghrá.

Jaso: Never married Silv?

Silvy: Naw.

Jaso: Poor oul thing. Lonesome washin' that has no shirt in it hah? Poor oul thing.

Silvy: No poor about her. She has a few bob rottin' away somewhere.

Jaso: Seriously? How so?

Silvy: Compo – years ago.

Picus: Compo?

Silvy: Compensation. She lost her thumb in an office in Cork City. She used to organise flag-day thingamibobs for charity. Cuttin' sheaves of paper. Ye know, pamphlets, with a guillotine I think they call it. Wasn't lookin'. Chop! 200 flyers, a thumb and a fingernail.

Jaso: God between us 'n all harm. What?

Silvy: Said someone distracted her.

Jaso: What! That's unbelievable.

Silvy: I know, in fairness, sure she had shag all money before that.

Jaso: No Silv, I mean, unbelievable like, that she sued her bosses.

Silvy: Too right. Cats 'n dogs fight, but she won her case.

Jaso: But they were a charity organisation Silv. Seems a bit harsh like!

Silvy: What's wrong with that. Charity or no charity she was shagged! Was charity gonna stick her thumb back on? Sure she could never work again.

Picus: More power to her elbow.

Jaso: 'Spose so. Must have been brutal on her alright. Reefin' her paw like that. I mean it's bad enough loosin' a finger, but a thumb! Sure what's a hand without a thumb, 'tis just a shovel.

Silvy: Amazin' daw. When Da found her the other day, the only thing she could move, before she died, was that same hand.

Jaso: *(Can t help herself but laugh)* Sorry Silv ... Jesus I'm morto!

Picus: Here, help me pick up the rest of this shit.

Music in. 'Tantum Ergo once more. They all muck in, gathering. **Rhea** *arranges the flowers in the vase ...*

Rhea: Silvy's father wasn't long after yourself Lil. Four weeks later. Poor Tim pined away, I think. You were always a good sister to him Lil. Sure he had it tough, rearin' three sons all by himself. He left all the money between them and Silvy made good use of his share, in Australia. Oh Silvy! Mar a bhí ar dtús, mar atá fós.

During the above words from **Rhea**, **Silvy** *is pensive, in his own world, downstage. The others continue to gather the papers. Music out.*

Jaso: You're in for a gommel so Silvy ...

Silvy: *(Waking from dreams)* ... A gommel?

Picus: Lily's will like.

Silvy: Me hole. Da will get the lot. The cottage and the compo money.

Jaso: I bags these Green Shield stamps. *(Realises her brashness)* Sorry Silvy, I'm a grabbin' bitch!

Silvy: Keep 'um Jas. They're for the dustman if ya don't.

Jaso: Thanks a million Silv. Jesus, 'tis like a jumble sale!

Picus: *(Looking at a large book)* Wow!

Silvy: What Pic?

Picus: A scrapbook. All the old movie stars of the 40s. *(Flicks through the book)*

Jaso: Giz a sconce … Who's that?

Picus: John Hodiak in Hitchcock's *Lifeboat*.

Jaso: He's a fla. I'd smother me mother for him.

Picus: This is deadly.

Jaso: Look at the turban on yer wan's head … the state of her, and the price of turnips!

Silvy: Who's that babe?

Picus: Veronica Lake.

Silvy: She's a lasher.

Picus: Silv, this is fantastic. She has all the newspapers' dates written underneath.

Jaso: Smashin' handwritin, for someone minus a thumb. Sorry Silv.

Silvy: Keep it Pic, that or bin it.

Picus: Thanks Silv, I will. Never knew she was in to this.

Silvy: Me neither boy.

*Bellona enters, stops on seeing **Picus** and is tense.*

Bellona: Hi ya, you alright Silv?

Silvy: Yeah, thanks Bell, just clearin' out Lily's cottage.

Bellona: Want a hand or anything?

Silvy: I'm alright girl, thanks.

Picus: I'm away Silv. I'll leave this by yer front gate. Give ya a yowl later on OK.

Silvy: D'ya wanna come in and have a drink with Da and the crowd?

Picus: *(Awkwardly)* Naw thanks Silv. I promised young Willy Hegarty I'd call in and see how he is. Thanks for this, mate.

Silvy: *(Looks to **Bellona**)* Sound Pic, see ya so.

Jaso: Yeah, see ya Pic.

Picus exits. An awkward silence.

Bellona: Have I got scabies or what?

Jaso: What's goin' on?

Bellona: Nothin' girl. I'll explain the saga later.

Silvy: Listen girls, folly me alright, just drop them at the gate. I'll haul them in later on … thanks, g'luk.

*Silvy is happy to exit. **Bellona** is unhappy to have entered.*

Jaso: Right. Hope Silvy is OK. Lonely inside I'd say.

Bellona: Join the club.

Jaso: Just himself and the Da left now. Sure Lil was like a Ma to him. He's hidin' a lot. Poor bastard.

Bellona: *(Looking in the direction after Picus)* He's not the only one hidin'.

Jaso*: (Changing the subject)* Yer mother played lovely, 'The Tantum Ergo' … in the church!

Violin music in.

Bellona: Yeah. Mother fuckin' Ireland. She's in a big sulk at home.

Jaso: Cén fáth?

Bellona: Ah she's at me all mornin'. 'Member the purpily thing I was lyin' on pickin' spuds?

Jaso: Yeah!

Bellona: She's givin' me war over it. I left it in the field the other day. Went back to look for it this mornin'. It's gone. She's all fuss about it … pain in the tits.

Jaso: 'Sprobly buried now girl. Sure the tractors up and down would a mushed it to a rag.

Bellona: Yeah. I couldn't give a shit about it.

Jaso: C'mon, Silvy needs all the help he can get.

They both pick up the boxes, bits and chairs. They exit. **Bellona** *last. Music out.* **Rhea** *sits clutching the brown paper bags. She speaks.*

Rhea: Silvy was never the buck to hang around. After Tim's funeral he sprung into action again. He marched straight up to Jaso's father, announcing his wedding plans abroad. 'I'm takin' her with yer blessing or no', says Silvy, 'So t'would be best for all concerned if you consented'. A very eloquent Silvy. A very shell-shocked Mr McLoughlin. But it worked. And they emigrated. I remember wavin' them off. 'Twas as if they were leavin' forever. And ye know what Lil? They did, love.

Enter **Jaso** *and* **Bellona***. It is evening. Amber afterglows.* **Jaso** *s head is in* **Bellona** *s lap.* **Bellona** *in plucking* **Jaso** *s eyebrows for her. An attempt at a make-over. The following conversation takes place during this activity.* **Bellona** *is very upset. We join them in mid-conversation. Tweezers working like the clappers. The transistor radio is beside them. It plays at low volume.*

Bellona: I mean, he probably thinks I'm out now with Picus. He'll definitely gut me. Will you walk me home Jas, so he'll have no axe to grind?

Jaso: *(Wincing)* Ouch. No problems Bell. I'll tell him we were out together. Sure it's the truth.

Bellona: Thanks a million Jas.

Jaso: I can handle Dagon. God. It's crazy though. What did he say against Picus, exactly?

Bellona: I can't.

Jaso: C'mon Bell. Ouch. A problem shared, girl.

Bellona: Well Jas. He talked about Picus' father. 'Twas lousy. I mean the man would do cartwheels in his grave.

Jaso: What did he say, about him like?

Bellona: He warned me. He said that Turnus, that was his name 'Turnus' Normile, he said he was a gutty boy, fighting and stuff, an awful tramp. Years ago, when Rhea the mother, was pregnant with Picus, ould Turnus was on the ran-tan ... get up on a keyhole he would. Desperate for the drink and the gambling as well ... horses, ... and anything in a frock. By all accounts he was really handsome, looked just like Picus I suppose ...

Jaso: Ouch ... sorry ... sore.

Bellona: Sorry, nearly finished.

Jaso: Sorry. But am, did Mrs Normile know about his capers at all?

Bellona: Dunno Jas, 'spose not. Sure she hadn't much. She did everything and anything to make a crust, to rear the kids. She sold jam, and baked a lot. Any cash Turnus got from the gardening ended up in the pubs. He drank her dry. Gambled away the business.

Jaso: My God, I never knew that.

Bellona: Neither did I, girl. But me fuckin' oul fella won't stop goin' on about it. Said he'll lock me in if I hang around with Picus anymore.

Jaso: Not sayin' anything now or nothin' Bell, but like, there's no smoke without fire like. Every hound is a pup till it hunts!

Bellona: *(Gets upset)* It's not fair Jas. I mean ... how can I explain that to Picus? Things are bad enough between us like. I love him woegeous, ye know.

Jaso: But I thought you said it was weird like, Bell? Between ye like?

Bellona: I know I said that. I'm confused I suppose. I don't know what that weird feeling is. Too close for comfort or somethin'. Maybe it will sort itself out.

Jaso: Please God.

Bellona: Doesn't stop me wantin' him though. Like, he's, like, not like other fellas. He's deep Jas. I don't know anyone else, fellas like, like that. I know I've hurt him by not, well, ye know, lettin' him, like, go all the way with me, but … oh Jesus, I dunno what to do.

Jaso: Ouch, take it easy girl.

Bellona: Yeah. Sorry.

Rhea gathers herself and works on the eyebrows. Rhea takes a half of bottle of gin from a brown paper bag. She also produces a small plastic bottle of tonic water and a white paper cup. Rhea speaks.

Rhea: I was passin' the off- licence beside the chemist. Just a drop for old time sake Lil. Ah Lil.

She pours the gin and tonic slowly.

Bellona lifts the tweezers.

Bellona: There, finished Jas.

Jaso: Thanks Bell.

Bellona: Yer welcome.

Jaso: A friend's eye's a good mirror … well?

Bellona: Well they're a big improvement on the hedges ye had over yer eyes up to this.

Jaso: Thanks a lot ye cow!

Bellona: And c'mere, how many of ye are sharin' that jumper? I must give you some of my old cast-offs. You've been wearin' the same men's clothes for the past ten years girl.

Jaso: Keep yer cast-offs Bell. I have an extensive wardrobe to choose from at home. Six brothers. Hand-me-downs galore. Sure I could open a boutique girl, McLoughlin's Arcade!

Bellona: Jas, do us a favour now you will ya?

Jaso: 'Tis OK Bell, I know what yer askin'. I'll talk to Picus … alright?

Bellona: I wouldn't ask ya, Jas, only …

Jaso: No worries Bell … 'tis better I chat to him. Ní h'é lá na gaoithe, lá na scoilb.

Bellona: Translate for the benefit of yer gobdaw friend!

Jaso: Don't make hay on a windy day.

Bellona: Yer right Jas. I'd only be addin' fuel to fire. You go. Just, like explain the whole thing to him, will ya? Tell him I'll meet him on Thursday. He always goes to the cinema in the city on Thursdays. Tell him I'll go. We can chat then. I'll wait for him in the house. If he phones my house before three o'clock, lets it ring three times.

Jaso: A code like?

Bellona: Yeah. I'll know then to meet him at the ferry. Tell him to hang up after three rings, just in case me oul fella answers. 'Never know when to expect him to crawl home. Sure he can phone me from the box by Goggins.

Jaso: Is that all!

Bellona: Sorry for loadin' all this on ya Jas. Just tell him I'll be waitin' … alright.

Jaso: Hush Bell, 'what friends are for darlin'. *(Hugs her)* Now c'mon, I'll walk ya home to yer hi-falutin' parents!

They rise. They make to depart. Arms around each other.

Jaso: *(Returning to pick up the transistor)* Jesus, I nearly forgot this. Silvy'll go doolally.

Bellona: How did ya manage to rob it off him.

Jaso: I called into him this afternoon with some calamine lotion for his sunburn. While he was rubbin' it on, I lifted this.

Bellona: You're a hard case Jas. He'll miss it though. He always listens to Luxembourg about this time of night.

Jaso: Ah shag him. Let him sweat. *(She switches off the transistor and runs a wet finger over her brows)* I feel even more stunning now than I usually do. Thanks for the beauty therapy Bell. I'll have Silvy Hogan lickin' me wellies with excitement.

They both laugh and exit. **Rhea** *speaks and drinks.*

Rhea: I never told anyone this Lil, but shortly before the deaths, I noticed a 'change' in Picus. He'd go for walks, alone, at all hours. Up near Morrison's, or by the wood.

Music in.

Rhea: I saw the catkins on his clothes. He'd be preoccupied. Bellona and himself had a row around that time. They weren't together. I didn't see them out courtin'. I knew there was somethin' up.

Rhea *takes another swig from the cup.*

A new day.

The wooded area. Faint music underscores. **Picus** *wanders the wood. A wet day, but the sun shines chinks through a carpet canopy of deeper green. He waits, looks about, no one. Finally he sits, he is carrying a small branch, still with leaves – sycamore. He has a pen knife. He begins his intricate hacking, and carving work … takes lots of time over this! He is content, alone. Hence he hums. He wears wellies!*

Slowly, from Upstage, **Circe** *walks by. He is startled by her. She does not move.*

Pause for 10 seconds. **Circe** *carries a book in one hand. Music out. Silence. Finally …*

Circe: Excuse me.

Picus: Sorry.

Circe: A fright.

Picus: Me too.

Circe: *(Pause)* The Sisters are coming soon.

Picus: Oh.

Circe: The Reverend Mother as well.

Picus: Oh, Marcella … scary lady.

They hold each other s gaze.

Picus: I'll be off so.

Circe: T'would be wise.

Picus: That or die roarin'.

Circe: *(Small smile)* She's not that bad.

Picus: Bark worse than bite ha?

She smiles fully.

Circe: *(As **Picus** gets to his feet to leave)* How's your sliotar?

Picus: Fine, thanks. Sorry again … am … Sister.

Circe: Circe …

Picus: Right. Yeah. *(Pause)* See ya so.

Circe: Yes.

Picus: See ya. *(Leaving)*

Circe: Am?

Picus: Yeah? *(Awkward)*

Circe: Sorry for being so glib the other day. I rushed off.

Picus: That's alright!

Circe: *(Carefully)* Did you … stay long … in here?

Picus: A bit. The shade. Pickin' spuds … like the equator.

Circe: I know … The gleaners.

Picus: Yeah.

Circe: Cool in here … always is.

Picus: Yeah. Umbrellas. *(Pause)* So now.

Circe: *(Softening)* What are you up to anyway … Picus?

Picus: *(Defensive)* Nothin'. *(Realises, no threat)* Just hangin' about. No spuds today, ground's too tacky.

Circe: Day off so.

Picus: Yeah. *(Quotes Silvy)* I suppose we'd better enjoy the holidays, what's left of them.

Circe: What class?

Picus: Going into leaving cert.

Circe: Yeah, the big time.

Picus: Repeatin' it.

Circe: Dossin' all year were you?

Picus: No. Hurling – too much time training. Me mother's put a stop to that.

Circe: I don't know her?

Picus: Rhea. Rhea Normile. She's widowed, like.

Circe: Oh, sorry again.

Picus: 'Salright. Da's dead … a while now.

Circe: God rest him … how?

Picus: How? … oh … *(About to explain)*

Circe: Sorry for asking …

Picus: It's OK. His liver—

Circe: God rest him.

Picus: Yeah. Ma's from Mayo … originally.

Circe: *(Smiling)* The Whest!

Picus: *(Smiling back)* Yeah.

Circe: And where was your father from?

Picus: Oh here … born and bred in Tinaglasha.

Circe: Right.

*Both stand. Inexplicable feeling. She looks back toward the convent end of the wood. Checking, looks back to him. **Rhea** speaks.*

Rhea: Distance is a fright Lil. I couldn't face this town before now. Vowed never to come back here. But there's ghosts to be tackled Lily, things I have to tell ya.

Circe lightens the air.

Circe: What's that you're making?

Picus: Sycamore bow … and arrows.

Circe: Bit big aren't you?

Picus: For a kid, neighbour's child – he's only ten.

Circe: That's kind. *(Pause)* Stupid question, why sycamore?

Picus: It bends perfectly, and the shoots are ram straight.

Circe: The arrows!

*He nods yes. During this **Picus** takes string from his pocket, makes the bow and arrows with knife.*

Circe: *(Looking at action in the distance, distant voices are heard)* What are they up to?

Picus: Who? *(Remains sitting)*

Circe: Those children, across the 14 acre. They're pulling something?

Picus: *(Stands and looks out with her)* Oh that's furze bushes … gorse … for the 29th.

Circe: I'm lost … sorry?

Picus: The bonfire, for the stoat.

Circe: You've really lost me now. *(Smiling)*

Picus: *(As if she should know)* The 29th of August, next Thursday. There's always a party, in the village, and a bonfire. We throw a stoat into it.

Circe: But I thought bonfire night was in June?

Picus: It is, as well, but this is a local thingy.

Circe: You have me addled Picus.

Picus: Sorry.

Circe: Bonfires are usually lit on June the 23rd, I think.

Picus: Yeah, I think.

Circe: That's the vigil for the birth of John the Baptist. On the 24th.

Picus: Sorry, you've lost *me* now. *(Laughs)*

Circe: And you say that you light another on … *(Realises)* Ah, now I have it. The 29th of August is the anniversary of the *beheading* of John the Baptist, that's why, the gorse, and the fires?

Picus: Whatever you say. You're the religious expert. I only know it as the Feast of the Stoat, on the fire … and all that.

Circe: Sorry, I'm lecturing you. Habit of mine.

Picus: *(Indicating her skirts)* Habit!

Circe: *(Laughing)* I'll stop before I send you to sleep.

Picus: No, I mean, it's interesting, ye know, to, know.

Circe: Listen I'll just walk and read. You finish the gift. I'll alert you when I see the nuns coming. Sorry for disturbin' you.

Picus: It's your wood.

Circe: Not mine – the Order's.

Picus: Thanks.

*Violin music in. He makes and finishes the gift. Taking care. Glances at her as she glides so slowly around, reading, between the trees. **Rhea** speaks.*

Rhea: Poor Bellona. Dagon and Vesta were lacerated when she died. It was cruel Lil. They were childless for seven, eight years when they married first. No joy. But didn't they pick a real beauty when they adopted her?

Rhea *is still.* **Circe** *returns after some time. Birds sing, sparsely.*

Circe: 'Saw a young boy in here a week ago. Blond, curly haired. Ran off wailing and his clothes in tatters.

Picus: Oh that's young Hegarty, same kid. *(Points to the bow)* Willy Hegarty, Paddy and Dymphna's youngest.

Circe: Ah, the Gaelgóir family! He ran off distraught, blood on his legs … ran – then collapsed, then he'd walk two, three steps, collapse again. I tried calling him, but he ran.

Picus: Really?

Circe: Yes. He had a small clump of twigs in his little hands. I saw him break it off of the elder … over there.

Picus: Yeah, he was attacked by the hawks.

Circe: Hawks?

Picus: Hawk's nest – up there.

Circe: Never noticed that before.

Picus: Top of the Scots pine – vicious episode. Greedy little fellow wanted to be the first to have an egg.

Circe: Have – an – egg? *(Puzzled)*

Music out.

Picus: See Sister …?

Circe: Circe.

Picus: Circe. See, lots of us collect birds' eggs, a hobby, all different types. Steal 'um, sorry. *(Laughs)* Pin hole at either end, blow out the yolk an stuff, varnish the egg and store it in, protected like, in an old chocolate box or shoe box full of porridge.

Circe: *(Laughs)* Porridge?

Picus: Oats, oat flakes – a cushion like.

Circe: Isn't it late in the year for nests?

Picus: An expert too. *(Smiles)*

Circe: No no, just a wild guess.

Picus: These particular hawks are a bit of a mystery – the last to lay, every year. That's why it's a challenge like, to get their eggs – and the robber gets a fierce hefty pecking.

Circe: Seriously though?

Picus: Deadly – specially when the male joins in. Hegarty was lucky to keep his eye.

Circe: God forbid. Have *you* a hawk's egg?

Picus: No one around here has.

Circe: 'No one around here has!' No wonder. *(Smiles, Picus is taken in by this full smile)*

Picus: Yeah. *(Laughs, half-nervously)* I found a yellowhammer's over there last week!

Circe: Lucky you!

Picus: So what's the book?

Circe: Keats – poetry.

Picus: Oh yeah. Do ya read a lot?

Circe: Yeah, keeps me sane!

Picus: Sane … poetry?

Circe: Not yer cup o' tea?

Picus: So-so.

Circe: Choosy are ya?

Picus: Naw. But Keats is alright. Did him in school …

Circe: 'O what can ail thee, knight-at-arms. Alone and palely loitering?' *(Looks for him to finish)*

Picus: *(Embarrassed but willing to make a fool of himself)* 'The sedge has wither'd from the lake and no birds sing' … that's all, haven't a clue o' the rest.

Circe: Very apt – 'Knight-at-Arms'.

Picus: That's Keats for ya – forgettable.

Circe: I take it ye don't like reading that much.

Picus: Yep, prefer telly, cinema. I goes up to the city every week. It's cheap enough on the ferry, a short crossin' to Cork.

Circe: Ye like the pictures that much?

Picus: Yeah.

Circe: So! Favourites?

Picus: Nothin'.

Circe: Has to be somethin'.

Picus: Hard to choose …

Circe: Names? Come on! *(Having fun with this tennis match)*

Picus: Can't think.

Circe: Horrors?

Picus: Naw.

Circe: Westerns?

Picus: Sometimes.

Circe: Dramas?

Picus: Ish-ish. Depends who's in 'um.

Circe: Favourite stars then?

Picus: Jimmy Stewart, am, Fonda.

Circe: Like the oldies so?

Picus: Ya – 'suppose.

She checks to see if the convent approach is clear.

Circe: Sorry for, rushin' off, again, the other day. I had chores to do.

Picus: That's grand. We have to stop this 'sorry' business. *(Smiles)*

Circe: You're right. *(Smiles)*

Picus: I was just lazin'—

Circe: Right. *(Pause for 10 seconds. Music in)* Is Bellona your ... girl?

Picus: No ... am – my girl, well was ... sort of.

Circe: Sort of?

Picus: We're fightin' *now*.

Circe: She's lovely. Ye seemed to be talkin' *then*.

Picus: Did ya hear? *(Panic well-hidden)*

Circe: *(Looks at him, pause)* No. *(Smiles)* She is beautiful though.

Picus: We were just chattin'.

Circe: Sort of! *(She smiles, walks away a bit)*

Picus: Where 'ya goin'?

Circe: Back – time up – Marcella approacheth. *(Both laugh)*

Picus: Right.

Circe: Enjoy yer bonfire.

Picus: Ah, I'm not goin'.

Circe: Why not?

Picus: Couldn't be bothered.

Circe: Well ... nice talkin'.

Jaso enters, waits and watches.

Picus: Yeah – nice. *(She walks)* Hey Sis ... *(Rethinks)* Circe!

Circe: *(Turns with relish)* Yes cupid?

Picus: You're different, like.

Circe: How so?

Picus: Well for a start, ye've no veil.

Circe: You're sharp!

Picus: Are ya … a trainee – nun, like?

Circe: *(Thinks … smiles)* Sort of.

Picus: Do novices not wear veils?

Circe: Some do.

Picus: See ya around.

Circe: Yeah … soon.

Picus: I still say you're different.

Circe: Why?

Picus: No offence, but yer older than the other novices.

Circe: And wiser … thank God.

She exits in a hot slow wind. He watches her go. He leaves the wooded area. He takes the pink note out and reads it once more.

Music out.

***Rhea** speaks.*

Rhea: Vesta was dressed like a queen. The proud new mother, twin set and pearls. Dagon, in his seer-sucker golfin' gear. I recall, clear as glass, that day they brought Bellona home. They never warned anyone they had even, 'applied'– is that the right word?– for a child. They took Bellona out of the car. She was wrapped in that beautiful amethyst blanket, with an organza veil over her tiny face. A family at last.

***Rhea** drinks more. **Jaso** stirs. **Picus** hurriedly hides the note. **Jaso** and **Picus** exchange an awkward look.*

Jaso: *(With surprise and contained accusation)* Saw that.

Picus: What!

Jaso: Lots of smileens going on, Picus.

Picus: Being sociable. *(Funny silence – uncomfortable)*

Jaso: That's nice. *(Awkward pause … but smiles.)*

Picus: More to the point. What are *you* doin' up here –
following me?

Jaso: Oh yes, like a terrier.

Picus: Top marks for honesty.

Jaso: No-shit-Jaso. *(She holds out a white flower)* … here.

Picus: What's this in aid of?

Jaso: It's not from me, just in case ye think I have a secret
passion for ya or anything.

Picus: Who then?

Jaso: Dymphna Hegarty. I was askin' about where were ya.
Dymphna said you were gone to get weapons for Willy. She
saw ya head this way.

Picus: So why the flower? Don't tell me she's after my body.
A married woman … well, 'twould be an experience I
suppose!

Jaso: Don't flatter yerself Normile. She called me back and
asked me to give it to ya, if I saw ya. A gift. For being so
nice to Willy.

Picus: I'm sure that's lovely, but a flower … does she take
me for a poofter or what?

Jaso: Ya fool … It's a Moly.

Picus: What the fuck's a 'Moly'?

Jaso: It's a good-luck flower, Picus. Protection like.

Picus: *(Laughs)* Against what … Morrison's gun?

Jaso: Ah stop being so sarcastic Picus. She grows them in
her back garden. They're desperate rare. I'll keep it if you
don't want it. Protect me against Silvy!

Picus: *(Putting it in his pocket)* She's a weirdo alright. S'pose
I'd better hold on to it. All in good faith.

Jaso: Too right. Sure I wears me St Christopher medal all
the time. Got it at me Communion. 'Never take it off.

Picus: Not even when ye wash … ahhhhh … ye manky bitch.

Jaso: Dymphna's a laugh. She had colcannon stewing for the dinner, in the skillet pot. I spotted a big leaf of the cabbage in her dress, stickin' out of her bra. Jesus I could barely keep a straight face. She told me she does that to stop her boobs swellin', from feedin' the herds of babies she has.

Picus: Christ, she can keep her colcannon.

Jaso: Do you want a funt in the mouth?

Picus: Have ya got a fag for me.

Jaso: Here, lover boy.

*They smoke and are silent. **Rhea** speaks.*

Rhea: No welcome for the Normiles in Tinaglasha anymore Lil. But we have to be tough Lil hah? Nil bastardum carbarundum! Have to pay my respects to yourself and Vesta, exile or no. Sláinte Lil love. Oh, nature calls!

***Rhea** drinks and then makes her way into the wood. **Jaso** continues …*

Jaso: Seriously though, I followed ya.

Picus: Why?

Jaso: Follow?

Picus: Yeah. Is it urgent? Did I win the sweeps or something.

Jaso: *(Seriously and prepared)* Picus. I was chattin' to Bellona last night. She's in bits. She told me, well. She told me this. She said she loves you Picus, so much. She said she'd never met your likes, for all the right reasons. She said she's sorry.

Picus: For what?

Jaso: For not lettin' ya near her, like, nearer – if ya know what I mean.

Picus: C'mon Jaso, no-shit-Jaso, spit it out.

Jaso: Stop it Picus. Things like that, well, sex and stuff, makes me quiet sometimes.

Picus: *(Genuinely taken aback)* I'm surprised Jas!

Jaso: Lots would be ... look, she wants to meet ya on Thursday, an' explain a lot more to ya. You're to phone her at 3 a'clock, 3 rings and hang up. She'll know then to meet ya. Alright love ... See ya around big boy ...

Jaso goes to exit ...

Picus: So why are you here?

Jaso: She wants me to break the ice with ya first.

Picus: Well, spit it out Susie Sunshine.

Jaso: I spat.

Picus: C'mon Jaso.

Music in.

Jaso: Picus ... she heard something.

Picus: What?

Jaso: Don't get spiky with Jas, Picus, I'm only the go-between.

Picus: What did she 'hear' Jas, that I'm kinky, that I ties people up in bailin' twine – what?

Jaso: About your Da. *(Pause. Picus tenses immediately)*

Picus: And?

Jaso: She heard that, when he was your age, he—

Picus: What?

Jaso: He was, and these are *her* words Picus, he was as handsome as you, but a bit of a fly-boy.

Picus: So. What's that got to do—

Jaso: Her father told her—

Picus: That oul snob ... What?

Jaso: He said, that *your father*, and I don't know if you know Picus, that he was shaggin' around, years ago, behind yer Ma's back.

Picus: *(Gathering himself together)* Hold it right there Jaso, all respect to you, for having the courage to be a carrier-pigeon. Bellona is a shrewdeen, gettin' others to impart her gossip. I half-expected this.

Jaso: But Picus I offered to come and ta—

Picus: Her father is an oul woman. Whatever *my Da* did has fuck all to do with me …

Jaso: *(Fretting)* She knows that Picus love, but just list—

Picus: And if she thinks that I'm not good enough for her posh shaggin' family …

Has upset himself.

Jaso: She's only being careful Picus. She says it doesn't matter about your Da. She just wants ye to take it slow. It doesn't matter about your Da!

Picus: Bollocks! She's judging me. She's not trusting me, and she had no right to mention my father in any of this. God rest him, he may have strayed, but am I to pay for that? *(Getting furious)* I'll have a few words for Mr Dagon Barry in my own time. But you tell Bellona from me, she's a warmouth, a gossiping, shallow, vindictive fucking bitch. And if she ever comes near me again, *near* me – God help me, I'll slap her 'round Tinaglasha!

*He exits in a cold torrent with his bow and arrows. Music, minimally, with attitude. Shocked – **Jaso** is left alone. She glances to the wood. Holds look. Lights a fag.*

Jaso: *(To herself)* Merciful Jesus.

*Music up. **Picus** has left his knife behind. All light fades to a cube of light on this. Strangely, **Circe** returns cautiously to the wood. She looks about, watches **Jaso** s departure. Her hand enters the light, takes the knife and departs.*

*Music stops. **Rhea**, returns from the wood, but highly animated.*

Rhea: Tobar na hEasóige. The Stoat's Well. Every 29th of August, without fail, the trek to the Well. The Mad Monk would be there the first, at 6 a.m. The oul pagan Carmelite! Guaranteed to find the stoat, fresh dead, floating on top of the water, under the stone slab.

She laughs to herself.

The last day. Downstage, **Jaso** *and* **Bellona** *cross.* **Jaso** *is unusually subdued. She carries a white enamel bucket.* **Bellona** *is smiling. They are finishing a conversation.*

Bellona: God, I'm surprised Jas. I'm relieved though.

Jaso: So that's that girl.

Bellona: Was he, … calm like?

Jaso: Ah ya. I think he's alright. 'Did me best girl.

Bellona: *(Kisses* **Jaso***)* Oh thanks Jas love, you're a star.

Jaso: *(Brilliantly pretends)* No problems girl. Anyway look, I have to get to the well Bellona. See ya later on at the bonfire OK. I'll chat to ya then.

Bellona: Jesus Jas, I forgot all about it. Yeah … see ya there.

Jaso: *(Anxious to go)* Bloody right.

Bellona: And did he say Thursday, like today, was alright?

Jaso: What?

Bellona: *(Laughing voice)* The cinema. The phone call?

Jaso: I'm sure he will. I told him anyways girl.

Bellona: Please God. Jesus it's ten past two, wish me luck!

Silvy: Wait up ya black bitch ya!

Silvy *joins them. He is plastered in calamine lotion. He too carries a bucket.*

Jaso: *(Relieved)* Hi Hogan.

Bellona: Hi Silv.

Silvy: *(Catching up with them. Panting)* Hi guurlls.

Bellona: Bye Silv.

Silvy: *(Jokingly)* Did I fart or something?

Bellona: Relax Hogan. It's not you. I'm rushin' for a real man. *(She is exiting)*

Silvy: Must be on a promise, are ya?

Bellona: Amn't I always sweetheart. See ya later Jas.

Jaso: Alright. Christ!

Bellona goes, happy.

Silvy: Happy bunny, what was all that about?

Jaso: Girl-talk, nothin' … are ya going to the well?

Silvy: Naw, I'm goin to play hockey in me bucket, course I am! *(Grinning wildly)*

Jaso: Jack n' fuckin' Jill!

Silvy: *(Sing-song)* 'And now they have a daughter … '

Rhea speaks.

Rhea: The Mad Monk would take the first bucket of water, and then the whole village would follow. Sure if ye didn't partake Lil, it was like missin' Mass. Scandal!

*Violin music in. They exit toward the well. Buckets empty. Upstage right area. **Picus** stands, in bare feet in the stream. He stands facing directly out. Waiting. Purposeful.He looks through his father s binoculars and after much searching, focuses on someone at the back of the theatre, as it were. In tandem, **Bellona** stands downstage left. The violin music is loud and enchanting about her. She stands and looks about, dressed to kill! She waits also. No sign, she lights a fag, waits. Violin music all the while increasing in volume. A person seems to be drawing closer and closer to **Picus**. **Picus** watches, biding his time. He slowly lowers the binoculars. **Bellona** looks at her watch. Very agitated. No joy. Finally **Picus** shouts in a mockingly virtuoso style.*

Picus: If it isn't Dagon Barry! Want a hand draggin' that oul mattress Dagon? Draggin' it to the bonfire, are ye Dagon?

Bellona shouts off, as if to Vesta.

Bellona: Will you please shut up mother, I can't hear the phone!

The music abruptly snaps out.

Picus: Mr Barry, ye can relax the oul bones now. 'Cos I'll do ye a big favour and stay away from your daughter. Your princess … Bellona.

Bellona: *(Shouts off)* Was there a call for me earlier on?

Picus: Your mouth worked, Dagon.

Bellona: *(Shouts off)* I said did someone ring for me earlier on today?

Picus: Unlike yer prick, ye impotent dry-balled oul nancy …

Bellona: *(Shouts off)* Answer me!

Picus: Couldn't concoct a child of yer own …

Bellona: Mother I am totally pissed off of you and Da naggin' me about Picus.

Picus: Vesta and Dagon the barren elite!

Bellona: Now the best thing you can do is stay out of my way and stop interfering.

Picus: Got yer precious lamb daughter from a catalogue.

Bellona: Puttin' up with that golfin' bollocks. You're a weak pathetic bitch!

Picus: So do ye want a hand draggin' that mattress to the bonfire Dagon?

Bellona: *(To herself)* Ring.

Picus: God help us, but it's the only bit of heat it will have ever felt!

Bellona: *(To herself, close to eruption)* C'mon ring! *(A clock strikes three times. She shouts off)* You and your fuckin' blanket. I lost it OK. Big fuckin' deal!

*Music in. **Picus** reaches into his pocket and takes out the flower. He looks at it. **Bellona** takes off her jacket. Lets her hair fall and looks dejected. **Picus** then throws it in the stream and crushes it with his feet. They exit. Music out. **Jaso** and **Silvy** re-enter from the well, buckets brimming. **Silvy** grinning!*

Jaso: What's got you in such radiant spirits?

Silvy: Nothin'. *(Smug)*

Jaso: Nothin' me hole, look at the bake on ya, the smirk jumpin' all over yer face …

Silvy: I said, nothin! Hey, you're different lookin' … your eyebrows. *(Laughs)*

Jaso: Stop changin' the subject and come off the stage Hogan … what's stuck in yer craw?

Silvy: What?

Jaso: Yer like the cat that got the cream—

Silvy: *(Stops them both)* Jas. I … you won't believe my news. I can't hold it in any longer … I'll blow …

Jaso: What? I'll hit ya a dalk!

Silvy: I'm not goin' back to school any more.

Jaso: What!

Silvy: Listen Jas, I got a letter from my brother Pat in Australia. A job Jas, stud farm, stable work, riding out the horses … the pay is great and I get my own lodgings and everythin'.

Jaso: If this is a wind-up Hogan, I'll reef the tongue outa yer head.

She looks at his face. Sees his sincerity.

Jaso: You're serious … Jesus … you are …

Silvy: Funeral.

*Silvy takes out the letter. He hands it to **Jaso**. **Jaso** reads it. Her face tells all. Violin touchingly in.*

Jaso: Silvy!

Silvy: Isn't it great Jas – ha?

Jaso: *(Almost cries)* That is just wonderful news.

Silvy: I can't believe it myself. *(With sincerity)* Oh Jaso, honestly, I saw nothing ahead of me here. Let's be honest like. I'm no Einstein, and I know I've failed the summer tests already. I know I mess about, but I need a new way to go Jas, not like to spend the next couple o' years, in school again, flunkin' all the time. I want a reason … reason to, to work, to work for, Jaso, not to study. Just to do somethin' that I know I *can* do.

Lil is gone, Pat and me other brother John are in Australia, the only thing left here is me Da, and he *wants* me to go. He said he'll give me the fare and shit from Lily's will. He's sellin' her cottage to the Desmonds.

Jaso: Oh – Australia, Silvy. You lucky lucky lucky bastard. *(Both laugh)* C'mere to me ya big monster. *(**Jaso** hugs him fully. There is a beat, a look between them, still embracing)* I'll … Jesus I'm beetroot … I'll miss ya somethin' horrible Silvy.

There is a long, long moment. They smile at each other. They don t, uncharacteristically, laugh. They just look at one another. Hold.

Silvy: You're great Jas, ye know?

Jaso: Soft words butter no parsnips Silv.

Silvy: Can I kiss ye Jas?

Jaso: Ya know I hate ya.

Silvy: Without a doubt.

Jaso: I mean, I loathe ya.

Silvy: The feeling's mutual.

Jaso: You, you get right up my nose!

Silvy: Any chance of gettin' up your skirt.

Jaso: Ask me sister – I'm sweatin'.

Silvy: Fuck the marzipan, I want the icin'. By the way, I know ye robbed my tranny.

Jaso: Shit Silv, how d'ya know?

Silvy: Let's just say, I let ya.

A pause. They look at each other for a long time. A smile.

Jaso: Wanna throw a few plates?

Silvy: What's the prize?

Jaso: C'mere, ya chancer, till I ware the face off ya!

They kiss, so tenderly, and stop, and kiss again. Then they fall laughing to the ground, roll, and hug – both wince 'ah, mind me sunburn then both burst out laughing, crawl, and rise. They triumphantly exit, leaving the buckets behind.

Return to **Rhea** *– happy, with drink, upright, fresh.*

Rhea: Wasn't that water only diamond, Lil. You *had* to drink at least a pint of it, even the toddlers. Sure me own grandmother used to say 'Drink it for to have the stoat's sums'. That liquid cuteness was to protect us all, against the winter ahead.

Jaso re-enters alone. Shouts to **Silvy,** *who is off stage.*

Jaso: Stall the ball, relax, I have 'um. Mama shaggin' Toto.

She suddenly is distracted by action in the wood. She watches, discreetly. Soft Front of House music is heard beneath the silent scene ahead. **Circe** *and* **Picus** *enter. Passing thru the wood.* **Circe** *gathers more flowers, chatting to* **Picus,** *who strolls content behind her. He carries a box under his oxter. They both stop. Gather themselves, half kneel.* **Picus** *opens the box and takes out an egg and displays it to* **Circe,** *both chatting all the while. They laugh.* **Jaso** *exits.* **Circe** *suddenly is startled. Has to go, on realising the time, with a glance toward the convent. They wave each other off. Minimally. Smiles. He packs up his box and looking back at her* *exiting, he too melts off and out of the wood. Music out. Focus on* **Rhea** *once more.*

Rhea: The bonfire that night was always the highlight. The Mad Monk would throw the dead stoat on the flames at midnight. The white under-fur would go dark in a flash.

Front of House music crossfades. Celebration and singing are heard from the wings. An extremely red glow pervades from that area also. Bonfire lights. Jolly, drunk a bit perhaps, **Silvy**, **Jaso** *and* **Bellona** *are back a bit, centre-ish.* **Bellona** *is isolated but watches the pair. She is most definitely drunk.* **Jaso** *is in mighty form. She begins a bizarre dance, her left hand in the air, moving and circling* **Silvy**, *strange but fantastical choreography. Music low throughout. They both laugh.*

Silvy: What in Jasus name is the meanin' of all the gyrations?

Jaso: *(Still dancing)* My warning.

Silvy: What?

Jaso: Stoats do that, ya fool. If a hawk is swoopin' down to catch them, their tail distracts the attacker – black tip on it … the birds think it's a mouse, rat, or something tasty. The stoat might forfeit its tail, but the rest of it is saved.

Silvy: *(Still agog)* Meaning what?

Jaso: Thickhead! Meaning if anyone tries to steal my man … they might hurt me paw in the fight, but no preying bitch'll get her talons into my baby! *(Laughs and flirts with Silvy)*

Silvy: The oracle has spoken.

Jaso *makes a piercingly high pitched noise, still in motion, circling* **Silvy**, *in his disbelief!*

Silvy: What the fuck are ye at now ye la la?

Jaso: Stoats do this as well. They do a huntin' dance. Like shepherd dogs, and herd their victim. The poor unfortunate animal gets, like, spellbound by their display. They don't even have to kill it sometimes. The creatur dies of fright!

*On 'fright , **Jaso** jumps toward **Silvy**. She knocks him to the ground. He lies there. She cheekily tries to stop his messing and calls his name, first jokily, but then in a concerned fear. Just as she is about to get alarmed at his playing dead, **Silvy** comes to life and puts the heart across **Jaso**. **Jaso** jumps on top of him and they both hug and horseplay on the turf. This develops into lengthy kissing and such. This lingers. **Bellona**, knocking back drink, has been watching all the while. Eventually ...*

Bellona: So, ye finally got it together.

Jaso: 'Jaso get yer gun'.

Silvy: She's been after me for ages!

Jaso: Shi God help us – you don't be well with yer nerves Silvy.

Silvy: Huntin' me, badger batin'.

Jaso: Snared ya, screeeemin' like a bonjer rabbit! *(Both laugh)*

Silvy: *(Screams, mock snared)* That fire'll die, the rain's forecast. Someone's been dancin' under the ash tree ...

Jaso: Bhí fuinneamh sa stoirm a éalaigh aréir, Aréir oíche Nollaig na mBan, As gealt-teach iargúlta tá laistiar den ré, Is do screach tríd an spéir chughainn 'na gealt.

Bellona: So ye finally got it together.

Jaso: *(Laughing)* You said that already, Bell girl.

Bellona: So?

Jaso: No use boilin' yer cabbage twice.

Silvy: Don't mind her Jas, she's pissed.

Bellona: No.

Jaso: I am. Ha ha ha!

Silvy: *(With food)* D'ya want some sherbet?

Jaso: Naw thanks, I hate it when it foams up.

Silvy: *(Foaming)* That's what it's meant to do.

Jaso: I know, but it gives me the gawks! *(Jaso quotes)* 'I drinks the new and the old wine; with new and old wine, I heals infirmities.'

*They both laugh. She takes a swig from **Silvy** s bottle. Music in low. **Rhea** does the same from her cup. She lights another fag. Her lighter contrasts the darkness that has crept in about her.*

Rhea: They locked Picus up for three weeks altogether Lil. He was let out for the trial. Rattled the poor fella. Of course Dagon Barry, being a nob of a business-man had great connections. Hired a top solicitor. He was convinced that Picus was the culprit. Cheek of him!

*The wood. It is the same night. **Picus** sits at the base of the Scots pine. He smiles with glee. **Circe** is busy opening an amethyst blanket which is wrapped around a bundle of objects. She begins to arrange them on the cloth by **Picus** feet. The Music out.*

Circe: You're early. Don't look. Turn around!

Picus shuts his eyes and obeys.

Picus: I'm embarrassed!

Circe: Don't be. It's my treat.

Picus: For what though?

Circe: A surprise. For thanks.

Picus: *(Laughing)* For what?

Circe: Nothing in particular … for the company I suppose. 'Tis nice to have someone else, on the outside, to have a laugh with.

Picus: Will ya get into trouble.

Circe: For what?

Picus: Being out. Late … with a maaan!

Circe: A friend. No. What they don't know, won't trouble them. They're all with the sand-man now anyway. I'll sneak in later on.

Picus: Ye're mad, ye know that.

Circe: I wrote the book, boyo. If those trees could only speak!

Picus: What d'ya mean?

Circe: All words come from trees Picus. The ancient Irish alphabet. Each consonant stood for a month. Each month stood for a tree. For example ... April was the willow ... November was the elder. The words come from the trees, and return to the trees, on pulp, on paper, on gossamer!

Picus: Ohhhh!

Circe: Turn around! Let's call this – a celebration. Our celebration of the stoat's fire, and our private picnic to mark the beheading of John the Baptist. Now look!

Picus *opens his eyes.* **Circe** *lays beautifully beside the amethyst blanket bedecked with goodies!*

Picus: But you've gone to loads a' trouble. Look at all you brought!

Circe: It's absolutely no trouble whatsoever. Look Picus, I've had a really nice time, chatting to you over the last week. So the least I could do is to show my appreciation to you and your friendship and that is why I got this stuff ready and if you say one more time that you are embarrassed I will throw this cheese at you OK?

They both laugh. **Picus** *accepts defeat and puts his hands up.*

Picus: OK. OK OK ... I surrender. Thank you.

Circe: You're welcome. Now dig in. There's loads of cheese, bread, spread ...

Picus: Hope it's not jam. I'm surrounded by jam at home. Jamorama. Tis comin' out me ears.

Circe: It's honey. Courtesy of the 'holy bees' below. They produced tons of it this summer. So enjoy!

Picus: *(With formality)* Thank you once more.

Circe: Now eat! An empty bag won't stand.

Picus: Alright, here I go. Jesus, I'm that hungry, I'd ate a nun's arse thru' a wicker chair. *(Realising what he has said)* Oops, sorry!

They both breakdown once more, skitting and laughing. **Picus** *notices the blanket.*

Picus: Hey I recanise that!

Circe: What?

Picus: That's Bellona Barry's.

Circe: Oh is it? I found it in the field the other day. Sure you can give it back to her when we're finished.

Picus: Whatever.

Circe: Right. Oh stop.

Picus: What?

Circe: 'Can't have a banquet without the 'Draught of Vintage'.

Picus: *(Shocked)* What! Where did ya get that?

Circe: Where else? There's lashins of it in the sacristy.

Picus: Ye mad thing! Grazia tibi ago!

Circe: They won't miss this drop. Anyway, we're paying homage to a Saint.

Picus: And a stoat!

She pours them wine. **Picus** *notices her hands.*

Picus: Nice hands.

Circe: Yes. At least they're soft, not like your gardener's paws.

Picus: You're sharp. *(They laugh)*

Circe: C'mon Picus, make a pig of yourself!

Picus: All I'm short of is a snout and a troff of acorns!

Circe: Good health Picus … *(Holds her goblet up)*

Picus: *(Flabbergasted, but enjoying)* … Good health Circe.

Circe: To the wood, the stoat, the Baptist … *(Looks up)* … and the moon.

Picus: To the moon! The silvery egg of the night! *(Picus holds up the bread)* O salutaris hostia!

Circe: Stop!

They drink, and laugh … then eat. **Rhea** *again.*

Rhea: Picus had an alibi. Thank Christ. Oul Morrison saved his skin. Morrison said that he saw Picus that night, passin' the haggart, goin' home from the wood. A couple of minutes later he said he saw Bellona, on her way into the wood. Then, he heard a scream. Like a banshee. He timed it all. Picus was stunned Lil. Of all people to come to his defence. Morrison. Thank God for his watches and clocks.

Return to **Silvy,** **Jaso** *and* **Bellona.** *The couple are busy snogging and laughing.*

Music in. **Bellona** *retorts …*

Bellona: 'Spose ye think ye're lovely.

Jaso: *(Jibes)* I'm gorgeous, why?

Bellona: Oh, the couple of the year.

Jaso: Do I detect Mrs Big Fat Jealousy Pants?

Bellona: What ya say?

Jaso: Joke, Bell.

Silvy: Young love, blind as bats.

They mess and huddle, playful – linger for 20 beats.

Bellona: *(Shouts)* Cop on will ya!

Silvy: *(Alarmed)* Take it easy Bell.

Bellona: Cop on I said.

Jaso: What's atein' *you* girl?

Bellona: What's atein' *me?*

Silvy: Yeah, you're like a little Jack Russell there all night, yelpin'.

Bellona: Oh yeah?

Jaso: And bein' sarcastic. When ye throw dirt ye lose ground lassie.

Pause.

Bellona: Ah shag off!

Jaso: I won't Bell.

Bellona: Well I won't either Jaso, shag off!

Silvy: Ladies, now.

Bellona: 'Ladies now', shut your cake-hole Silvy.

Jaso: What in God's name's *your* problem?

Bellona: I'll tell ya my *problem*. The two of you. Cooin' and bill-in like shaggin' swallows, drivin' me mad. Insensitive bitch.

Jaso: Don't look if it annoys ya.

Bellona: Ye'd swear ye were goin' out for years, flauntin' it to all an' sundry, pettin' before the whole gatherin'.

Jaso: Listen Bellona, I makes no apologies for Silvy and me. OK … we're only enjoyin' ourselves.

Bellona: Every aul shoe gets a sock I suppose!

*Double take from both **Silvy** and **Jaso**, they retort overlapping. Together …*

Silvy: What? Hop off now … what?

Jaso: Watch yer gob now girl!

Bellona: I'll say what I like. The truth. Ye're well matched, two oul goms, two oul eejits, sure no one else would touch ye.

Jaso: *(Controlled)* Take that back Barry.

Bellona: *(On a roll)* … and ye'll probably rot here, for the rest o' yer lives. 'Silvy I love ya – I love you too Jaso' – two boring, ugly nobodies.

Jaso: *(Trying hard to hold her temper)* Take that back.

Bellona: Ate shit and die Jas.

Jaso: Take that back, ye trollop.

Silvy: Bellona, come on.

Bellona: The beautiful couple – when all fruit fails, welcome haws. *(Laughs)*

Jaso: You listen, Miss *fucking* Rubber-Gloves. I know your gripe. Just because Picus doesn't want ya anymore doesn't mean you can sling your shite at us.

Bellona: What!

Jaso: So clamp it, Barry, or I'll rip the Jasus head o' ya.

Bellona: What did you say?– Picus doesn't want me anymore. He adores me, right. worships me stride. I'm the only young wan around this kip who's fit to be on his arm, to be his. We're a couple – not a fuckin' lonely hearts club.

Jaso: That's it girl. You've pushed me too far, ya common brasser.

Silvy: Don't Jas.

Jaso: I will. I've kept her slut carry-on a secret for too long Silvy. *(To Bellona)* … I thought you were my friend. And now ye start insultin' me like a fish-wife. For that, cos no one messes with Jaso McLoughlin, for that, you'll hear my truth—

Silvy: Don't tell her no more.

Bellona: No more what?

Jaso: I lied out of loyalty to ya girl. Didn't want to hurt yer feelings. Jesus, wasn't I the fuckin eejit, I should have pulverized ya with the facts.

Silvy: Jas.

Jaso: *(Explodes)* Right. I'll pulverize ye now. Slap the rasher. You sent me, with your ghrá mo chroí story to Picus. I did yer biddin'. I told you he was OK, I told you he understood. Well, I lied. Bellona. P*ants on fire.* 'Cos Picus told me that he never wants you near him again. That's why he's been avoidin' ya like a leper. He said that you're a sad, vindictive septic strap, and he'll hit ya the next time he lays eyes on ya. *(Pause)* Still waitin' for a phone call? Christ girl ... Ye'll grow a fuckin' beard.

Bellona is devastated.

Silvy: Jas. That's enough.

Jaso: This doesn't involve you, Silvy!

Silvy leaves tactfully.

Jaso: And as for flingin' insults at us, lowlife insults at us – shut it ya flaabag! 'Cos we're happy – very happy. I mightn't be a crolly doll like you, but I have a life Bellona, and Jesus, right now *I am happy* and guess what? I thought you'd be happy for me too. But it seems, you're not. So, you ... just fuck off now and find your own man. Not that you've had any shortage of Mickeys around ya ... ya harlot ... Aeneas McCarthy is laughin' at ya probably, ya loose slapper. You're lucky I didn't tell Picus hah! Picus ... He's probably up the wood, with his Holy Mary. He's been in and out of that wood all week – I've watched them, by Jesus I have. She's wipin' your eye, girl, she's wipin' your eye.

Silvy sprints on re-entry. Music up. He gasps.

Silvy: Jaso c'mon quick! Da's pony escaped. He's tangled in barbed wire. He's bleedin' to death. C'mon.

It rains. Jaso is taken away by Silvy. They look back at Bellona. Bellona is stunned and stuck to the spot with Jaso s unexpected counter-attack. She becomes obsessed. She stares at Jaso. Jaso knows she s said too too much. Silvy is shattered, wants to leave, but can t. Pause.

Bellona: Who? *(No response)* Who Jas? *(Shouts)* Who?

No response. **Jaso** *and* **Silvy** *exit.* **Bellona** *is stunned. Sits. Stands. Bottle in hand.*

A drunker **Rhea**.

Rhea: An image like that never leaves the mind Lil. Poor child, slumped, in a pool of blood. And Circe, stretched on the damp nettles. Neck snapped from a fall. One eye destroyed, gouged out by the hawks.

Rhea *raises her cup silently.* **Bellona** *looks about. Finally, when the actor is ready, she leaps and with purpose, exits.*

Music out. We return to the wood. **Picus** *and* **Circe***, now sitting closer together, near the Scots pine. Silence. More silence. She recovers fully from some grief. We don t see that grief. The pink note is in her hand.*

Circe: I'm grand now.

Pause for ten seconds.

Picus: I'm sorry.

Circe: I knew you'd found it.

Picus: Why didn't ye ask me for it?

Circe: I was too embarrased. I suppose, in a strange way, I didn't want to scare you off. If you'd have known, well, all about me, you might have not come, come back, to talk.

Picus: But I did.

Circe: Yes ... thanks ... question. Why didn't *you say* you'd found it?

Picus: I dunno really. Just the things in the poem. Personal stuff ... about the child, and yer man ... lovin' ya. I didn't want to pry.

Circe: Maybe, in a way ... I wanted it found. A weight lifted.

Picus: Yeah?

Circe: The nuns took me in when I was 11 years old. I vaguely remember living up the country, somewhere else, in

another foster convent … orphanage, whatever. I was
moved, down here … to the nuns of Tinaglasha. I was shy,
troublesome.They fed me, schooled me. Wouldn't let me
outside the door, only the blue moon. Wanted to give me
every chance in life. I know that. But I'd sneak up here, or
down the village, whenever I got a chance. They never
knew. Picture difficult me at 17! I met this man. A strong
man. First man I ever met, as men go. When I got 'into
trouble', with a capital T, they locked me in. They had no
sympathy. Who'd blame them? They had no idea of the
father involved.

Picus: Who was the guy?

Circe: A local fella. Oh Picus, he charmed me, plaumaused
me, fed me lies. And I adored him.

Picus: Did he not, like, stand by ya?

Circe: No, but the nuns did! He was married. I worked
twice as hard, punishment, and guilt, combined. I pleaded to
be allowed out. No. It would have been detrimental for
them, for the good name of the Order. Understandable. I
kept pleading. Finally, after the birth, a deal was struck. I
wasn't fit to be, a mother. My daughter was sent to another
foster home … somewhere. I was never to see her again.
Now if I decided to stay in Tinaglasha, they would allow me
to stay, but only if I dressed as one of them.

Picus: As a nun!

Circe: I'm no nun! They gave me a skin. But no veil. That
would have been pushin' it! Since then, I've worked in the
convent for my keep. Hard work Picus. Those elderly nuns
are tough. Especially the invalids. Changing them, turning
them, spoon by spoon feeding. I suppose, I grew
accustomed to the life … it was all I had … have. Brought
the whole turmoil on myself. The child destroyed me.
*(Silence. She drinks more wine. **Rhea** drinks simultaneously. **Circe**
continues. She looks to the wood)* The trees have memories
Picus. They're as old as the world. Funny, I love the peace,
the solace of their company now, the peace I find here. My
Island Wood.

Picus: Not yours ... the Order's!

Circe: In its dotage. The smell of the place, rotten bark, saplings, flowers at the edge. An everlasting supply for the shrine below. Time ... stock-still. Sometimes I forget my 'disguise' *(Laughs)* and feel like *them.* Julie Andrews how are ya!

Picus: I'm sorry.

Circe: Audrey Hepburn eat yer heart out *(She laughs at herself)*

Picus: Nawthing wrong with Audrey Hepburn. *(Lightening the air)*

Circe: Oh, defending your icon are ya?

Picus: Yeah – so?

Circe: Thought she might be too pure for you.

Picus: Pure – naw. She made a few angelic ones – what about 'Tiffany's'

Circe: 1961.

Picus: George Peppard – fantastic! 'Seen it loads of times.

They both begin to mock the last scene from Breakfast at Tiffany s – fake American accents – laugh

Circe: *(Hepburn)* Hand me my purse will you dahling, a girl can't read that sort of thing without her lipstick. *(Hands him the note)* You read it to me dahling, I don't think I can bear ...

Picus: *(Peppard)* Sure you want me to?

Circe: Mmm *(Nodding yes)*

Picus: *(OK. Reads – taking the paper away and reciting some of this to the air)* 'My dearest little girl. I grieve for all the disgrace of your present circumstances. I have my family to protect, and my name, and I am a coward where these institutions enter. Forget me beautiful child, and may God be with you.'

Circe: Bravo Picus. Off by heart.

Picus: Saw it loads a times.

Circe: Scary, the note at hand and all. *(Laughs)*

Picus: Beautiful night.

Pause.

Circe: Beautiful name. *(Speaks the name with relish)* Picus. Worshipped by the Romans, God of the forest and the field. *(Picus is still. Silence. Circe looks at the paper)* Ye can keep that, but don't expose me to Tinaglasha? *(Smiles)*

Picus: No. Swear. *(Pause, she hands him the note)* Do ye know where your daughter is?

Circe: *(As if changing the subject, looks up)* Listen!

Picus: What's that?

Circe: Shhhhh! Just listen.

They both listen and are still. **Rhea** *speaks.*

Rhea: I wrote to Jaso, Lil. I asked her things. She replied. She told me about Picus, and the lady with no veil. Up in the wood. Smileens, and laughing. Together.

Picus and Circe animate. Circe pointing at a tree.

Circe: There, look …

Picus: What … Where?

Circe: Shhhhh … *(Whispers)* A woodpecker … there …

Picus: Oh yeah, wow! Green. That's rare.

Circe: He's new, new here.

Picus: Great.

Music in. A stillness. **Rhea** *speaks.*

Rhea: A spell Lily, a sick spell … like a calf to milk …

Circe: Picus.

Picus: I knew – a difference, in ya.

Circe: Jet black hair, chocolate eyes. *(Bell rings)* Better go back *(Rises, set to leave – walks)*

Picus: *(Assertive and strong)* How come I never seen you before … like … this summer … I've been workin' beside this wood every summer for the past … well … ever since I was a small kid. How come I never seen ya?

Circe: Just because your eyes are open Picus, doesn't mean you can see.

Picus: Meaning … ?

Circe: Doesn't matter. I've been watching you. *(Smiles beautifully, makes to exit)*

Picus: *(He stops her)* Come here.

Music up. He takes her, kisses her; long, protective, a man equal and older. They devour each other with kisses. **Circe** *leads* **Picus** *into the wood, out of view. The lights fade to black, except for* **Rhea.**

Rhea: Some magic or other. I dunno what colour. Bread, cheese, honey and wine. And the blanket. Vesta's blanket.

Lights up on **Picus** *and* **Circe.** *They return from the wood. She buttons her last button, by her neck.* **Picus** *sits, shirt half undone. They part. She initiates the parting. Music out.*

Circe: Please go.

Picus *is baffled.* **Circe** *clears the blanket of its trappings.*

Picus: What?

He does not move. **Circe** *again …*

Circe: I said, go!

Picus *slowly exits … puzzled and shocked.* **Circe** *looks about. She clears the blanket of its trappings and prepares the space ominously. From behind a tree, slugging from a bottle …*

Bellona: You and yer fuckin' sliotar.

Circe *stops. She is calm, assertive and knowing.*

Circe: Ah Bellona, at last.

Bellona: What are you up to, ya bitch?

Circe: Says the kettle and the pot black.

Bellona: *(Sees the blanket)* Where d'ya get that blanket, that's mine.

Circe: No. It's mine!

Bellona: Ye robbin' whore.

Circe: Perhaps. But I'm not the whore that's aching for my brother.

Bellona: What brother? Jesus.

Circe: Has the penny dropped, Bellona?

Bellona: What?

Circe: *(Mocking her)* 'I gets paniky, guilty and paniky.'

Bellona: What! What are you sayin'?

Circe: Ask your lover!

Bellona: Shut the fuck up! *(Throws the bottle, just misses **Circe**)*

Circe: Ask your brother. Picus.

Bellona: Jesus … Jesus … *(**Bellona** retches and vomits)*

Circe: He'll tell ye all about yer father. Turnus. Turnus Normile. The bastard that he was. The coward he became. The way he treated me, after he planted you in here. *(Indicates her belly)*

Bellona: Ye fuckin' tart … ye cuckoo …

Circe: By Christ he made me suffer! And you did too.

*Bellona recovers somewhat and in rage runs at **Circe**. Mad with rage … they both roar. This echoes loudly. **Bellona** runs into **Circe** and strangely becomes still. She slumps to the wood s floor. **Circe** has a bloodied knife in her hands. **Bellona** gasps for breath, and her last words are …*

Bellona: Jaso.

*Circe freezes. Slowly approaches **Bellona**. She drops the knife.
Circe calm, and still. Music low. **Rhea** rips the plaster from her
arm.*

Rhea: I can't lie to the dead Lil. There was never a sting.
But I needed this. *(Indicates bottle)* Venom in, venom out.

*She drinks, gulping from the bottle. **Circe** drapes **Bellona** s dead
body with the amethyst blanket. **Circe** looks upward at the Scot s
pine. **Rhea** is tired and lost on the bench.*

Rhea: Picus had got that garden knife, from his father Lily.
His father. *(Rhea takes out the note)* Pink paper Lil. 'Love on
the back of a Racin' Docket'. We were packin' to leave for
Mayo. I found it in Picus's room.I knew his father's hand.
Like a spider. He was probably legless drunk when he
penned it to her. In my heart, I had tremblings, our early
years together. I knew he wasn't content. But little did I
think when I was carryin' his son that a witch like her was
carrying his daughter.

*Rhea is ice-cold and bitter. She closes her eyes. They remain closed.
Circe animates …*

Circe: A hawk's egg? No one around here has.

Violin springs to life, a lament. It comes at us in waves of passion.

*Circe, ceremoniously, climbs The Scots pine … She claws upward.
One, two, three metres. All else pales to soot insignificance. The red
image fades. A hawk is heard. Screeching.*

*Front of House music in. The beginning tableau returns. The
grouplets of shock. The figures weep. This time these figures are
visible. All in funeral blacks, **Silvy** comforting **Jaso**, **Picus** standing
alone. **Rhea** finishes …*

Rhea: Lily love, It's me a ghrá. Rhea. Jesus.

*Rhea burns the note. The lights fade to the image of the bloodied
hand, framed in a cube of light. A voice-over dominates, this time
the voice of Turnus Normile.*

Voice Over:
> My love for you is deep and wild
> Don't tell a soul, I beg you please

To keep the secret of our child
Eternally, amongst the trees.

Snap blackout.

The End

There is a wooded strip near my homestead in Cobh, County Cork. It belongs to the Sisters of Mercy, whose convent, of old, is attached to its border. I played there as a small Kinevane – a trespasser. We all did, but in groups of two or three, never a noisy flock. We carved the trees, made first kisses and love, albeit pure. And there was always somebody watching. I never knew who but, mostly, it was someone from above. Angels perhaps, or a host of goblin spies, but I knew this watching was a blessing – in this place of wood, stone and loamy carpet. Above all, there existed a magic. The shadows were frightening and attractive, the nun-worn pathways were ancient and lush. At six, I felt a pagan attachment to its canopy – more than a human child ought to.

At thirty, I learned that the convent was dwindling in numbers. The wood, once alone, was to be surrounded by housing estates and shut in by gutters, fitted kitchens and patio madness. I felt it would all vanish and, in ways, it has. I wanted to verify that this was once a grove of giant soul and heavenly access. A wood that was felled time and time again, hundreds of years back, and its timber exported by the Phoenicians. A forest of unexplained light and shade, a door to God's garden.

I dedicate this play to my deceased father, Denis. A man of steel and heart, a face and body of the sweetest antique oak, with wisdom on tap, like sap for the needy and cold. The trees remember.

Note: *The Nun s Wood* was commissioned by Jim Culleton in 1997 after a rehearsed reading of an idea in skeleton format. With Fishamble's unrelenting support, it finally premiered – full term – in 1998.

Pat Kinevane

The Carnival King

A Play in Two Acts

Ian Kilroy

&

In memory of Bernie Walsh – a man of the theatre

The Carnival King was first produced by Fishamble Theatre Company on 19 July 2001 as part of the Galway Arts Festival in the Bank of Ireland Theatre, NUI Galway. It then toured to the Civic Theatre, Watergate Theatre and Draíocht Studio. The production had the following cast and production team.

Francis Devine John Finegan
Christy Ruane Gerard Byrne
Phyllis Derrane Joan Sheehy
Sergeant Courtney Frank O'Sullivan
Cathal Lynch Eamonn Hunt

Director Jim Culleton
Set Designer Robert Ballagh
Lighting Designer Paul Keogan
Costume Designer Gabby Dowling
Original music Laura Forrest-Hay
Production Manager Trevor Ahearn
Stage Director Shelley Bourke
Stage Manager Marjolijn Venema/Maura Howe
Administrator/PR Cerstin Gundlach
Fight Director Paul Burke
Producer Jo Mangan
Galway Arts Festival Director Rose Parkinson

Acknowledgement is made to thhe Tyrone Gutherie Centre at Annaghmakerrig in Ireland where some of this play was written.

Photo (l-r): Gerard Byrne and Eamonn Hunt as Christy and Cathal
© Colm Hogan.

Dramatis Personae

Christy Ruane, 50s

Phyllis Derrane, 50s

Francis Devine, Teens

Justin Courtney, 40s-50s

Cathal Lynch, 50s

Notes:
The mechanics of the hanging scene, and by necessity the dialogue surrounding it, may vary from production to production. It is best to keep the lines as written, but the order and time of delivery can be worked out in the rehearsal room to best suit the method being used to convey the hanging. Also, the ghost should be cut where it does not have the desired impact; and, of course, kept, if the impact is satisfactory.

ACT ONE

A pub in east County Galway, Ireland. Stairs leading up to living quarters. A few buntings, not yet correctly hung: a ladder stands in place with which to hang them.

Before the lights come up the sound of choral music. The lights slowly rise to a menacing red. A woman walks onstage. She is bloodstained, ghostly, come to a brutal end. She walks upstage and stares intently at the audience, then moves on. The lights come fully up to daylight. **Francis** *Devine is watching a religious programme on daytime television. It is early afternoon.*

The choral music continues. **Francis** *becomes enraptured until he is disturbed by the sounds of primeval shouting and wild African drumming coming from outside. Annoyed,* **Francis** *turns up the volume, but the music from outside stops.* **Francis** *turns the sound down to its previous level. After a few moments, the boss,* **Christy** *Ruane, enters.* **Francis** *quickly fumbles, turns off the TV and makes himself look busy.* **Christy** *Ruane is carrying a large plastic fertiliser bag.*

Francis: Mr Ruane I was just …

Christy: Why haven't you got those buntings up yet? Do you need the whole day or what?

Francis: I was just cleaning the …

Christy: I know what you were doing. Do you think I'm deaf? I heard you zapping away at the TV. A lad your age should be thinking of kissing girls. But no, not our little Saint Francis.

Francis: I'll finish the buntings now so.

Christy: Be sure and hang them right this year.

Francis turns off the TV and goes over to the ladder. He sticks his tongue out at **Christy** *behind his back.*

Christy: Don't think I can't see you. We've mirrors in case you haven't noticed.

Francis climbs the ladder and starts work on the buntings. **Christy**
*takes off his coat and hangs it up. He then places the fertiliser bag
on the counter, goes behind the counter, takes out a large old ledger
and starts doing his accounts.*

Francis: *(Christy is trying to concentrate)* That drumming
would drive you mad. All morning they've been at it,
(Christy looks at his watch) banging away. It's pure savage.
You think they wouldn't be allowed disturb the peace like
that, during the day and all. I don't know why Sergeant
Courtney doesn't do something about it.

Christy: *(Still concentrating)* What harm are they doing?

Francis: Well during business hours ... how are you
supposed to concentrate on your work?

Christy: *(Ironically)* A good question. What's 88.31
multiplied by 10?

Francis: 883 point one.

Christy: Oh yes.

Francis: Were they painted up and all?

Christy: Who?

Francis: Those drummers, the ones making all the racket?

Christy: Yes. Africans.

Francis: Africans?

Christy: Yes. African chieftains with feathers and paint.
The works.

Francis: Feathers and paint?

Christy: Feathers, paint ... that's it.

Francis: Nothing else?

Christy: Nothing else.

Francis: Sure?

Christy: Sure I'm sure. Didn't I catch the sight of a fellow's
slong as proof. All that jigging about and it fell out of his

loin cloth for the world to see. I think Mrs Murphy across the road almost had a stroke she was so excited.

Francis: *(Interested despite himself)* Get away!

Christy: I'm telling you.

Francis: *(Checking his interest)* It's shocking. You think those fellows from the drama society could do something better. What kind of drama is that? Exposing yourself. Couldn't they put on a normal play for a change? Something traditional.

Christy: Isn't African dancing traditional?

Francis: Get away out of that.

Christy: I'm telling you. Our ancestors weren't ones for dressing up all tofty for the theatre. It's more in the line of African dancing they went in for.

Francis: African dancing?

Christy: Of course African dancing. We'd chieftains here as well you know, and as good as any African chieftain. Agh, I don't know what they teach you in school these days. *(**Christy** returns to his calculations)* What's 10 per cent of 750?

Francis: 75.

Christy: Oh yes.

Francis: Well I've enough of that drumming. Are they not done practising for tonight by now?

Christy: *(Getting slightly annoyed as he is trying to concentrate)* How would I know? Go out and ask them.

Francis: No matter. It'll be all over by tomorrow anyhow.

A pause while both continue with their work in silence.

Francis: What's in the bag?

Christy: Mind your own business.

Francis: I was only asking.

Pause.

Christy: Was Phyllis in?

Francis: No. But I saw her cross the street over to Rafferty's.

Christy: Rafferty's Menswear? Yes.

Francis: What would she want over in Rafferty's? She's no fellow to be buying clothes for anymore. It's not your birthday or anything, is it Mr Ruane?

Christy: Is she not allowed to go into a menswear shop if she has a mind to?

Francis: Well I was wondering is all.

Christy: Wondering? Well you must be the only one in town that doesn't know.

Francis: What?

Christy: *(Directing **Francis**. Evasively)* Here. Wrap that around properly now.

Francis: I am. I am. What?

Christy: What what?

Francis: What is it that I'm the only one in town doesn't know?

Christy: Oh yes. Phyllis …

Francis: Yeah?

Christy: She's a transvestite.

Francis: Get away.

Christy: Yes. Always has been.

Francis: You're pulling my leg.

Christy: Well where do you think she goes every Saturday night?

Francis: To the bingo in town.

Christy: That's what you think. It's her transvestite meetings she's at.

Francis: Above in town?

Christy: Yes. Every Saturday night all the transvestites have their meeting in town.

Francis: Lord. And what do they be at?

Christy: Well, dressing up as men for starters … if you're a woman like … and as a woman if you're a man. A regular carnival they have every Saturday.

Francis: Well now I don't think …

Christy: You don't think what?

Francis: Well, it's a bit weird. When it's not just messing. Like other than at carnival time.

Christy: Who asked you for your approval?

Christy leaves his ledger and starts taking the contents out of the bag. He puts each item one by one up on the counter: a long length of hemp rope, nails, a hammer, lipstick, other types of women's make-up, a pair of tights etc. He takes out the receipts for these purchases and starts writing information from them into his ledger.

Francis: And it's only dressing up like?

Christy: Well, for starters.

Francis: What do you mean for starters? What else would they be doing?

Christy: Well, a spot of dancing, and then … well …

Francis: Well what? What then?

Christy: Well then they'd take off all their clothes and sit down to a grand feed of spuds.

Francis: Agh, would you stop pulling my leg. I'm not a fool you know.

Christy: *(Laughing)* I had you going there for a while.

Francis: You had not.

Christy: Well if I hadn't you couldn't tell the difference. Jesus, Francis Devine, sometimes I think you'd swallow your own elbow.

Francis: I would not, and there's no need to be saying Jesus.

Christy: Agh, stop lecturing me and keep an eye on what you're doing. Look. You left a bit hanging down there.

Pause. **Christy** *concentrates on his work.*

Francis: Are you doing the shopping for Phyllis now as well?

Christy: Em … yeah. She's no time these days with the bloodbank work. Jesus, you're a perceptive young fellow Devine.

Francis: Oh yeah, I hear she's collecting blood this week. She never lets up trying to get me to donate. To tell you the truth she kind of gives me the willies. Well, not so much any more …

Christy: It's more giving blood than Phyllis Derrane you're afraid of, I'd say.

Francis: No. I'm telling you, there's something spooky about her. It's because she's an old nurse, not a young one like. Dracula we used call her in school, when she'd come in for the check-ups. Her pale face and dark eyes. Lord save us. One of the lads said he looked in her window one evening, peeking like, and he saw her sleeping in a coffin.

Christy: *(Laughing)* Agh, get away.

Francis: I'm telling you. The amount of stories that used to go round about Drac … about old Mrs. Derrane … well you could hardly count them. We'd always bet she'd show up at the carnival dressed as a vampire one of the years. Never did.

Christy: More's the pity.

The drumming and shouting start up again, but this time more distant.

Francis: Agh, keep it down, can't you.

Christy: I don't know what your problem is Devine. Most young lads your age love the carnival. It's only a bit of crack you know.

The drumming fades away.

Francis: *(Reluctantly)* Ah, I suppose.

Christy: Get into the spirit lad.

Francis: Yes. What are you dressing up as this year Mr Ruane? A woman again is it?

Christy: Well, you'll just have to wait and find out, won't you.

Francis: Agh, go on. Tell me.

Christy: I will not.

Francis: Go on.

Christy: No. A man has his secrets.

Francis: If I tell you what I'm dressing as will you tell me then?

Christy: I can guess what you're dressing as.

Francis: Go on then.

Christy: A priest I suppose.

Francis: A bishop actually.

Christy: Well wouldn't you know it. His Lordship Devine. A girl would need to be careful around you. A chastity belt could be called for.

Christy *grabs at* ***Francis****, who is putting up the buntings.*

Francis: Would you ever lay off! At least I'm a man every year. You won't find me in any women's clothes. Sure if there was a transvestite meeting in town I bet you'd be first in the door every Saturday. All dolled up in your sister's clothes.

Christy: *(Gives **Francis** a sharp look)* What did you say?

Francis: Wup. I'm sorry Mr Ruane. I didn't mean …

Christy: Just you be careful when talking about my sister. Alright?

Francis: I'm sorry Mr Ruane. I didn't mean any disrespect.

Christy: Agh … grand. Just don't speak of her so lightly in your talk.

Christy closes the big ledger and puts it away. He looks at his watch.

Christy: Hurry up with that drape. I've a job for you.

*Francis does as he s told and descends the ladder. **Christy** takes the length of rope off the counter, unravels it and winds it up again by holding one end with his hand and wrapping the rope around his elbow with the other.*

Francis: What's the rope for?

Christy: To hang you with if you're not careful. *(Short pause)* For a clothes line.

Francis: Isn't that a bit thick for a clothes line?

Christy: Do you think I don't know the kind of rope you need for a clothes line?

Francis: I was only saying.

Short pause.

Christy: Look. What I want you to do is take this rope out front and give it a good skipping. Tie something heavy to the end and drag it along. Loosen out the fibres.

Francis: Grand Mr Ruane.

Christy: Good lad. Give it a good thrashing now, do you hear?

Francis: Yes. But what about the decorations?

Christy: Oh, don't worry about them. Leave them to me. When you're finished just leave me in the rope.

Francis: I'm done then?

Christy: Yes. I expect you need to get some dinner, get into costume and all.

Francis: Well fair play to you Mr Ruane.

Christy: You've to be back by eight though, do you hear me now? There'll be a fair crowd in here tonight before the carnival. I'll need a spare pair of hands. *(At this stage **Francis** has the rope and is beginning to exit. **Christy** utters under his breath)* Even if they do belong to a bishop. *(To **Francis** as he exits)* A good thrashing now, do you hear?

Francis: *(Exiting with rope)* No problem Mr Ruane!

*Christy is a little pre-occupied when **Francis** leaves. He begins to absent-mindedly clean up a bit. He looks at the wall where there is a framed pencil sketch of a woman: the walking ghost we saw some minutes before. A card for the same woman is slotted in the frame with the picture. Slipping into a sombre mood he takes it down and examines it. He reads the words on the cover of the card aloud, 'In Loving Memory . He places the card back in its place and continues with minor chores. He looks at his watch. After a few moments he spots the fertiliser bag on the counter. He smiles to himself and goes behind the counter. He looks around. Nobody. He takes a woman s wig from the fertiliser bag and tries it on. He admires himself in the mirror. After a few moments he hears someone coming. He quickly whips off the wig and places it under the counter. He makes himself look busy.*

*Enter **Phyllis** Derrane, **Christy** s friend. As she enters she carries a bag from Rafferty s Menswear. She shouts out to **Francis** as she walks through the door.*

Phyllis: When are you going to give me a pint of that grand young blood of yours, Devine! *(She enters laughing to herself)*

Christy: Jesus Phyllis! You gave me an awful fright.

Phyllis: Bit jumpy today Christy? The nerves acting up on you?

Christy: Aren't they always Phyllis, aren't they always. Raining out?

Phyllis: Not a drop. We always seem to get the weather for the carnival.

Christy: We're blessed that way.

Christy: Here. Leave down that stuff and sit down, take the weight off your feet.

Phyllis leaves down her bags and sits at a stool. However, she keeps looking behind her at the door to see if anyone is listening.

Christy: A drop?

Phyllis: A small one.

Christy pours two small glasses of whiskey.

Christy: Excited about tonight?

Phyllis: Yes. That young lad can't hear us, can he?

Christy: Not at all. He's as curious as an old church cat, but even his ears only reach so far. What is it?

Phyllis: *(Urgently and excitedly, wants to communicate something)* I've something to show you.

Christy: Yes?

Phyllis: *(Fumbles in bag)* Let's just call it, well … the sword of justice.

*Phyllis is interrupted by the entrance of **Francis**. He is carrying a newspaper.*

Francis: Excuse me Mr Ruane, I've your paper.

Christy: Ah. *(Looks at his watch)* That young Mannion is getting later and later delivering it. *(**Francis** is looking at the front page)* Give it here.

*Francis reluctantly hands the paper to **Christy** who begins to look through it hungrily.*

Francis: All set for tonight Mrs Derrane?

Phyllis: Yes Francis.

Francis: What is it this year then?

Phyllis: Well now … you'll just have to wait and see. Let's just say, I've tried my best.

Francis: *(Slightly camp)* Agh, I'm sure your costume's great. And with no clear candidate this year, I wouldn't be surprised if we had a carnival *queen* elected to run proceedings.

Phyllis: Well now to tell you the truth I wouldn't mind being put in charge for the night. *(**Phyllis** looks at the portrait on the wall)* I'd sort a few things out around here.

Francis reads the meaning; he glances at the portrait.

Francis: *(Moving the subject on)* Where did that old tradition come from anyway Mrs Derrane?

Phyllis: *(Broken from her brooding)* What's that?

Francis: The carnival, with a king given power for the night.

Phyllis: *(Drinks)* It's very old around these parts Francis. My grandfather said that it stretched back to pagan times. *(Smiles to herself)* In his day my grandfather was carnival king more times than any man or woman in the town.

Francis: Really?

Phyllis: Did you not hear how he died?

Francis: Well I heard a song about him once.

Phyllis: Agh, it's famous. It was during the carnival once and grandad was awarded the crown for the duration. Now he'd done an ambush a few days before and they were looking for him, they knew well who it was. So instead of running he decided to stay put, right under their noses using his costume as a cover. There he was, being lorded around the town in a wig and mask, the full regalia. And everyone hiding him, knowing well the danger he was in.

Francis: You think he'd have got away so?

Phyllis: One of the Lynches grassed on him. At least we think it was the Lynches. Anyway, even the soldiers didn't interfere with the feast. They waited until sun-up and the carnival's end. Arrested him then, took him away and shot him. Was never seen alive again.

She drinks. Pause.

Francis: Well … now. That's not how I heard it.

Phyllis: What?

Francis: I heard he blew himself up putting down dynamite. Isn't that where Derrane's Hole comes from over by the bridge? From the explosion.

Phyllis: Who told you that rubbish? It's called Derrane's Grave. That's where they buried him. Agh. People round here know nothing. They remember nothing right.

Christy has found what he was looking for in the paper.

Christy: It's here.

Francis: What's that Mr Ruane?

Christy: Kate's anniversary notice. I put it in during the week. *(He reads)* 'Ruane. First anniversary. In loving memory of my sister Kate who was brutally murdered on February thirteenth last. "No rest without justice". From her loving brother Christopher'.

Francis looks in on the paper.

Francis: *(Thinks to himself)* It's funny how a sketch can be closer than a photo.

Christy: What's that?

Francis: Well you know, that doesn't look like your sister at all Mr Ruane.

Christy pulls the paper away and looks closer.

Francis: *(Indicates the portrait on the wall)* That's much more of a likeness.

Christy: *(Anger and disgust)* Agh! They mixed up the photos!

Phyllis: *(Taking the paper)* Give us a look at that. *(She studies the photo)* Yes.

Francis: It's only a small mistake. No one will notice.

Phyllis: *(Leafing through the paper)* I see her 'husband' neglected to put a notice in for her.

Christy: Lynch! Why would he, the bastard. As far as he's concerned the quicker she's forgotten the better. Why would he want reminding everyone. Done his share of acting for the funeral. And all the time thinking on the inheritance. Wouldn't even spend a few quid, not even a few quid of his … murder money! *(Christy is shaking with anger. He pauses to contain himself. He looks at the portrait on the wall)* Poor Katey. *(Emotionally volatile, he is now becoming upset)* Not even a few quid to give her … to give her a notice in the paper.

Phyllis: *(Roughly giving paper to **Francis** so that she can comfort Christy)* Agh now Christy. *(Patting his hand)* Don't upset yourself. *(**Phyllis** gives **Francis** a look as if to say: clear off, can t you see he s upset)* He'll get what's coming to him.

Christy: I hope you're right Phyllis. I hope you're right.

Phyllis: *(Squeezes his hand meaningfully)* I know I'm right Christy.

*Christy picks up that **Phyllis** has something on her mind.*

Francis: I hear they're closing the case.

Phyllis: What?

Francis: No evidence, no case. That's what the Sergeant said. A year with no evidence meant the case would be better forgotten.

Phyllis: When did he say that?

Francis: Met him this morning on the way in.

Short pause.

Christy: *(Impersonal voice)* Somehow I knew it would end like this. He'll come gloating soon. Soon he'll come for the rest. This place. My flat upstairs. It's all Kate's you know, the lot. *(Pause)* He won't get it though. I'll not allow it. *(Drinks. Hand shakes)*

Phyllis: Keep it together now Christy. You don't want a relapse, do you? *(Looks at **Francis**)* Isn't that right Francis? *(**Francis** doesn t answer)* Yes. *(She tries to distract **Christy** from his thoughts)* Anyway, it's no time for brooding. Haven't we our costumes to think about? *(She pours out two whiskeys, gives* *one to* **Christy***)* Here. Get that down you. A bit of training for tonight. Ha?

Christy: (*Taking glass. Lightening up*) Yes. The carnival. Tonight. Yes. The young lad saw you over in Rafferty's earlier.

Francis *is avoiding notice. Hanging around listening.*

Phyllis: (*Indicating bag*) Just getting the finishing touches to my garb.

Christy: You're all set so?

Phyllis: Yes. Just about.

Christy: We'll make a fine pair.

Phyllis: We will indeed. A right respectable pair.

They laugh. Laugh subsides. **Phyllis** *indicates* **Francis** *to* **Christy** *with her eyes.*

Christy: You still here?

Francis: I was thinking you might need me.

Christy: Need you? What would I need you for? Phyllis, what would I need him for? I'd want to be in a bad way. (*Shouts*) Go out and finish that rope!

Francis: You should treat me better. Or I'll—

Christy: You'll what?

Francis *exits. Leaves paper on counter. Leaves door open behind him.*

Christy: It's worse that young fellow is getting. I've heard he's doing the eggs for Lynch now? You'd think he wasn't getting enough here. Ha?

Phyllis: I suppose you can't stop him.

Christy: I could let him go.

Phyllis: Could you really?

Christy: I don't know.

Phyllis: *(Looking after **Francis**)* The youth these days. They'd turn you in for farting.

Christy: You had something on your mind Phyllis?

Phyllis: Yes. It's. Well … this matter of justice. *(Short pause)* It might fall to us to deliver.

Christy: What do you mean?

Phyllis: *(Looks)* Is Francis gone?

Christy: Yes.

Phyllis: You know I was over in Rafferty's earlier. Well, I popped into Murphy's after. Looking for a bulb. Anyway, who walks in the door but Lynch. In he comes, sweating and swaggering, with his dirty old clothes on him … straight from his pigs I'd say.

Christy: What did he want?

Phyllis: Well, he goes up to Murphy saying he's looking for a hammer. He hadn't spotted me in the next aisle. Well Murphy says he's all out of hammers …

Christy: Glad to hear it.

Phyllis: … But maybe there might be one left down in the storeroom. Well Lynch starts scratching his arse waiting. And then he starts wandering around, playing with the merchandise. Anyways, he comes to this brand new kitchen knife and starts messing with it. He picks it up by the handle, his big dirty hands on it, and gives it a good squeeze.

Christy: And he hadn't seen you at all?

Phyllis: No. Well, Murphy comes from the storeroom with a lovely new hammer; a nice wooden handle on it. But Lynch starts complaining how he wanted one with a rubber handle, how the wooden handles always split on him.

Christy: What would he know about hammers?

Phyllis: Well the long and the short of it is that Murphy takes back the hammer and Lynch leaves. I sneak over, take one of Murphy's plastic bags and ease the knife into the bag, careful not to touch it, and *(**Phyllis** pulls the bag containing the knife from her pocket and holds it aloft)* into my bag.

Christy: *(Understanding)* You're a genius woman.

Phyllis: I know.

Christy: *(He excitedly takes the knife)* This is what we've waited for.

Phyllis: *(Christy examines the knife)* Careful now.

Christy: And Murphy didn't see you?

Phyllis: Not at all.

*They laugh. **Christy** pours two more measures.*

Christy: I always knew you were a smart one Phyllis. *(He leaves the knife on the counter)*

Phyllis: I am surely.

Christy: I tell you, this is a blessing. *(Thinks)* But does it amount to evidence?

Phyllis: You've only heard the half of it yet. *(Takes a sip. Looks at the door secretively. All clear)* Not only have we Lynch's prints, but we've Kate's blood on top of it. Nurse Derrane, at your service. Blood. Now that I'd call evidence.

*As **Phyllis** is speaking the last line, enter Sergeant Justin **Courtney**. He is unheard as he enters. He wears very thick eye-glasses and carries a handheld transistor radio very close to his ear on which he is constantly listening to 'The Match .*

Courtney: *(More interested in the match than in his surroundings)* Phyllis. Christy.

Phyllis: *(Surprised; but cooler)* Sergeant Courtney.

***Phyllis** quickly and smoothly takes the knife and puts it back in her pocket.*

Courtney: You're not listening to the match?

Christy: What match?

Courtney holds up his hand for silence as something crucial is happening in the match.

Courtney: *(Disappointed)* Agh! That's the whistle. They'll be lucky to get back with the wind against them in the second half. *(He turns off and puts down the radio)*

Phyllis: They will, Sergeant.

Courtney: *(Gives Phyllis a defensive look; as if to say: are you being ironic?)* Since when are you interested?

Phyllis: To tell you the truth I don't know that much about it Sergeant. *(Winding him up)* But I'll tell you one thing, I'm surprised we have a team at all with all the ecstasy tablets young fellows are taking these days. They're in no fit state to be out training, let alone playing a match.

Courtney: There's none of our team on drugs, and nothing else for that matter. Unless you've *evidence* to the contrary?

Phyllis: *(Warily)* I've no evidence.

Courtney: That's not what you were saying a minute ago. 'Now that I'd call evidence.' Oh I heard you on the way in, in case you think I didn't. Now, what was that about, Mrs Derrane? Is there something you should tell me?

Christy: *(Nervous)* Phyllis was only telling me a story Sergeant.

Courtney: Mrs Derrane?

Phyllis: *(Pause)* What I said was for Christy's ears alone. A private conversation between two citizens. Now, tell me Sergeant. Is it right for the forces of the law to be intruding in on two friends and their private discussion?

Courtney: Private discussion in a public place is not private. And if it's concerning a case of public enquiry, yes: it is right that the forces of the law should be aware of what's going on. Now, what 'evidence' would this be Mrs Derrane? *(Silence)* Out with it.

Phyllis: Well, if you must know, it concerns the serious matter of Paddy Irishman, Paddy Scotsman and Paddy Englishman: three natives of these Celtic Isles.

Courtney: What do you mean the Celtic Isles?

Phyllis: Yes the Celtic Isles, the Welsh included, all but one – the English – are Celtic peoples; and even they have a fair dose of it in the blood. Anyway, the three are sitting in a pub when Paddy Irishman tells the other two lads that he is concerned that his wife is having an affair with a carpenter: having found a hammer and saw under his marriage bed. On hearing this Paddy Scotsman relates how he thinks his wife is having an affair with a farmer, because just the other morning he'd found a wellington and spade under his bed. Well, Paddy Englishman sympathises with the two, and says that he understands their predicament because, as he must confess, he thinks that his own spouse is having an affair with a horse. For that very morning, on looking under his bed, what did he find but a jockey. *(She pauses to take a drink of whiskey)* Now *that* I'd call evidence, Sergeant.

Phyllis looks at *Courtney* dead-pan. *Courtney* feels he's been made a fool of.

Courtney: *(At Christy's snigger)* You seem to find it funny Mr Ruane.

Christy: Well it's better the second time Sergeant.

Courtney polishes his glasses on the end of his pullover as is his habit.

Courtney: Anyway, it's not for reasons of joking that I'm here.

Phyllis: More serious business.

Courtney: Yes. I take it you're aware of developments. We're moving on from the Lynch case. We can't convict the man on suspicion. There's no point in going to court with no evidence. Once the carnival weekend is over that'll be it.

Christy: Just like that?

Courtney: No, not just like that, as you well know. We've searched the place from top to bottom, more than once. Not a thing. We can't keep searching *ad infinitum*. Following tomorrow's search we'll have to let it rest.

Christy: *(Anger rising)* For God's sake!

Courtney: Now I don't like it either Christy. Believe me I'm not easy about leaving a case unsolved, but what can I do? I'm not going arresting the wrong man.

Christy: I'll tell you what you can do. You can go up to Lynch's farm and put handcuffs on him; you can take him down to the station and charge him with murder; you can send him to the judge for trial, the dog, from where, by rights, he'll be taken out and shot! That's what you can do!

Phyllis: Calm down Christy. You'll give yourself a stroke if you're not careful.

Courtney: You'd better listen to Phyllis, Christy. Calm down now before you do yourself harm.

Christy: It will not be myself I'll do harm to.

Courtney: I'll ignore that threat, seeing as you're all worked up like. But be careful now or I'll charge you with threatening an officer of the law, throw you in a cell to cool off.

Christy: Well I'd like to see you try! (**Christy** *slaps the counter and spills* **Phyllis** *drink*) Phyllis, you'll have another?

Phyllis: Grand so Christy.

Christy *pours himself and* **Phyllis** *another whiskey.*

Christy: *(Sarcastically)* I don't suppose you'll be having one yourself, Sergeant.

Courtney: Not while I'm on duty.

Christy: No, I suppose not.

A short tense pause.

Courtney: I'll check the place so.

Christy: Agh. The fire reg-u-la-tions.

*Christy and **Phyllis** drink. **Courtney** takes out a notebook and starts checking that fire regulations have been respected. He checks one thing after another. He ticks off everything he has checked in his notebook.*

Phyllis: *(Breaking pause. To **Courtney**)* You'll be a busy man tonight with the celebrations.

Courtney goes about his work.

Courtney: Same as any other year. *(Sighs)* A weekend of lunacy.

Phyllis: You know Sergeant, when my grandfather was a boy the police cleared out of the place for the carnival. Not a tap done with all the drinking that went on. And no closing time either. *(Drinks)* God be with the days.

Courtney: When your Grandad was a boy? What do you mean? Sure the carnival only started in the Thirties.

Phyllis: Would you get away out of that. Hundreds of years its been going on. An old pagan festival is how it started.

Courtney: *(Dismissive)* Agh. It was the local businessmen who started it to get a few visitors into the town, bring a bit of money into the place. Where do you think the carnival committee comes from? Sure everyone knows that old Peter Lynch set up the first committee in 1935, and started the carnival the year after.

Phyllis: Oh! The official memory of events. I tell you this carnival was here long before you, or any of your kind.

Christy: True for you Phyllis.

Courtney: *(Looking at the buntings; changing the subject)* Are those fireproofed?

Christy: *(Suspicious)* What do you mean?

Courtney: It's regulations that all mobile or suspended decorative embellishments in a public premises be fireproofed.

Christy: Does he mean the buntings?

Courtney: Yes.

Christy: Did them last year.

Courtney: *(Hesitant)* Well …

Courtney ticks off the final thing in his notebook and puts it away.

Phyllis: All in order Sergeant?

Courtney: It seems to be.

Christy: You'll be off so.

Phyllis: Yes. No time for dilly-dallying, what with the search tomorrow and everything, sure you've your hands full.

Christy: Yes.

Courtney: Yes I'd better be off. *(Courtney goes to pick up his radio, as if to go. But he turns at the last moment)* Just one thing.

Christy: Always.

Courtney: By the looks of it you're expecting to have a big party here tonight. Well there'll be no big parties this year. Carnival night or not, you're on your last warning. You'd better close at a respectable hour. I'll be around checking mind? Do you hear me now?

Christy: Check all you want.

Courtney: Don't worry about that.

Phyllis: *(Half to herself)* You'd do as well catching murderers as harassing publicans.

Courtney: What have republicans got to do with anything?

Christy: 'Publicans'. *(To himself)* Deaf as well as blind.

Courtney: You stay out of it Derrane. You've been warned. A respectable hour. If I catch you again I'll close the place. But then again, it isn't *your* place now, is it?

Christy: *(Starts the sentence at a shout, but tapers off the volume throughout)* As you said, you'd better be off.

Courtney stares them out for a second, then goes and picks up his radio. He turns it on and puts it to his ear to listen to the match which has resumed. A goal is scored, he forgets himself and lets out an intense but suppressed utterance of excitement: 'Go on!' He remembers that he is being watched and regains his composure.

Courtney: Phyllis. Christy.

Exit **Courtney**.

Phyllis: *(Looking out the door after* **Courtney***)* That fellow could do with being taken down a peg or two.

Christy: Thinks he's a Lord or something.

Phyllis: Yes … and he has the most common type of blood you know.

Christy goes and closes the door properly after **Courtney***.*

Christy: Would have been promoted years ago but for all his cock-ups.

Phyllis: You know the joke going round is that the only good arrest he made was of young Joe Hennelly, and that was for his own suicide.

Christy and **Phyllis** *laugh.*

Phyllis: God forgive me. I shouldn't be saying that.

Christy pours out two more drinks.

Christy: God rest poor Joe Hennelly.

There is a long pause; the two lost in their thoughts. After a moment **Christy** *looks at Kate s portrait and broods on it.* **Phyllis** *notices.*

Phyllis: I miss her too Christy.

Short pause. Changing subject. Trying to remain upbeat.

Christy: He didn't catch sight of the knife anyhow?

Phyllis: No.

Christy: Good. *(Getting excited)* This is a godsend.

Phyllis: I'm a bit nervous, now I've had time to think on it.

Christy: Phyllis! What are you saying?

Phyllis: Well, planting evidence and all.

Christy: Lynch is guilty.

Phyllis: Yes.

Christy: So what's the problem? If we don't do it he's away with it. Now, would that be right? No. How could Kate rest in peace, with him walking away scot-free? What kind of justice is that? No, we *have* to do it. This has come as a gift. Now you can't spurn a gift, can you? Besides, do you think that mole Courtney will find anything tomorrow? Not a chance. Lynch has the place clean. He's too cute. The way I see it Phyllis, the question isn't, is it right to plant that thing, the question is, could we live with ourselves if we didn't?

Phyllis: I suppose you're right Christy.

Christy: Of course I'm right. *(Drinks)* You'll have to plant it tonight so.

Phyllis: Me?

Christy: Yes you. How could I do it with Sherlock there watching me like a hawk. You saw how he was when he was in here. No. You'll have to do it. New evidence at this stage is suspect enough without me going missing during the carnival to plant it. I'll have to stay in the public eye to be above suspicion.

Phyllis: I don't know now Christy.

Christy: Come on Phyllis.

Phyllis: I've done my part. I'll sort out the blood as well. But fair is fair. You'll have to take it from there.

Christy: But you're the only one can do it. I can't get young Devine to do it, now can I? *(Short pause)* Phyllis?

*Christy gives **Phyllis** a sheepish look.*

Phyllis: Agh! *(Pointing at him; telling him off)* You're my only soft spot Ruane.

Christy: Good, that's settled. *(Christy fills up their glasses)* You'll never pay for a drink here again.

Phyllis: Seems to me I never pay anyhow. *(It strikes Phyllis)* You should put yourself forward.

Christy: Put myself forward?

Phyllis: Yes, for carnival king. There's nowhere more in sight and above suspicion than up on stage. There's no clear candidate this year.

Christy: Do you think I've got a chance?

Phyllis: You're not a bad looking fellow. You'll need … something special though.

Christy: Hold on.

Christy takes the wig out from under the counter and puts it on.

Christy: How's that?

Phyllis: Oh yes! That should do it.

Christy: A ribbon maybe?

Phyllis: *(Simulating rising sexual orgasm)* Yes.

Christy: A little make-up?

Phyllis: Yes.

Christy: Fishnet tights?

Phyllis: Yes! I can almost see the crown on you now.

Christy: You know, I'm feeling a little regal already.

Christy and Phyllis laugh, delighted with themselves.

Christy: A toast! To justice!

Phyllis: To justice! And may Katey rest in peace.

*The two are raising their glasses for the toast when **Francis** re-enters, looking tired and dragging the rope behind him.*

Francis: What's the celebration? Are you two finally getting married?

Christy: *(Whipping off the wig and putting it under the counter)* Whatever gave you that idea? And don't be barging in here so sudden and unannounced like.

Francis: Well I do work here.

Christy: For the moment, yes.

Francis: That's some tough rope you have there Mr Ruane. Well flip it. It nearly killed me.

Phyllis: *(Teasing)* A bit of exercise is good for a young fellow like yourself. Good for the blood.

Francis: There's nothing wrong with my blood Mrs Derrane, except for the fact I've just enough for myself.

Christy: That's Christian altruism for you Phyllis. Here, give that rope here. You can be off.

Francis: *(Throwing the rope up on the counter in front of **Christy**)* You can have it.

Phyllis: *(Finishes her drink)* I'll leave you to it so gentlemen. *(Looks at **Christy**)* I've a few errands to run before the evening's out. What's the plan for later Christy?

Christy: I'll see you back here. The place should be packed around eight. I suppose drinking here first, down to the parade, then on to the marquee for the dance proper.

Phyllis: *(Collecting her things to leave)* Good.

Christy: *(Conspiratorially)* Yes Phyllis. I'll see you later. You're fine about that so?

Phyllis: Yes. I'll get on with it.

Christy: Be sure and call in before eight.

Phyllis: *(As she exits)* Before eight. Yes, I will. Good luck to you now.

Francis: See you Mrs Derrane.

Christy: Right Phyllis.

***Phyllis** exits. **Christy** clears away the glasses. **Francis** looks at **Christy** with curiosity.*

Francis: What's with all the mysterious talk?

Christy: Something between myself and Phyllis.

Francis: *(Face lighting up)* I was right, wasn't I? The two of you are getting married. I always knew you'd get married eventually Mr Ruane. And with Mrs Derrane a widow now, who could be better for you?

Christy: Agh, you don't know your arse from your elbow Devine. Marriage and slavery are one and the same, and they're not for me.

Francis: Now you shouldn't be saying that. Marriage is a sacred—

Christy: Enough talk lad. Who are you working for, eh? Over there now and finish those buntings.

Francis: But you said—

Christy: I don't care what I said. You can run home later. *(Rubbing his hands together)* There's work to be done.

The sound of the African drummers returns in the distance. It gets progressively louder as they approach. The music is retained at its loudest after the blackout.

Christy: There's the drummers on their way back down. They'll be crowding in here soon, tongues hanging out for drink. Ready to laugh and dance and celebrate. Well we'll be ready for them. We won't let them down. *(Christy spreads his arms out, embracing all)* Let them come! Come on, and let the carnival begin!

Blackout and music.

End of Act One.

ACT TWO

A surreal alternative world. Music from end of Act One tapers off into silence. Three in the morning. Set as before; however, decorated and dressed with buntings and a brightly coloured drape. A crowd have come and gone. Evidence of revelry. **Francis** *Devine, in bishop s costume, tidying.*

Francis: For the love of God!

He throws a bra in the bin.

Francis: *(Looks at the clock)* Three in the morning! Three in the morning and still slaving for that clown. Him having the time of his life and me sweating it out. Nothing but a ... 'Your award awaits you in heaven Francis. Keep that in mind now. In mind. Complaining gets you nowhere.' *(Pause)* Agh, the filth of the place!

Francis begins to hear strange noises. He works, doing his best to ignore them, but he is afraid and the atmosphere has become slightly sinister. The silhouette of justice (with her sword and scales) appears behind him. It appears angelic, noble, but crouches down into a demonic form, also in silhouette. **Francis** *has not seen this huge shadow that dominates the stage, when it fades he senses something behind him, he turns quickly, not sure if he has seen the after-image of some spirit. He looks for a moment at the portrait of Kate: could it be her presence? He is now quite afraid and begins to pray out loud for comfort.*

Francis: Our Father who art in heaven, hallowed be thy name. Thy kingdom come, thy will be done on earth ...

A door bangs for no apparent reason: **Francis** *sweeps and prays harder.*

Francis: ... and lead us not into temptation, but deliver us from evil.

Loud singing approaches. Someone starts banging loudly on the door. It is **Phyllis** *and* **Christy.** **Christy** *is dressed half-way between a woman and a king, with a short dress, fishnet tights, a regal*

cloak, a crown on top of his head (held on by a strap) and a crosier.
Phyllis is dressed in a black dress suit, complete with bow-tie and
cane, spats, top-hat, dracula-style cloak, painted moustache and
monocle. She smokes a cigarette on a long cigarette holder. Her
head is totally bald.

Christy: *(From off)* Open up for his royal highness! Open up
I say!

*Francis drops what he s doing and opens the door. **Christy** and*
***Phyllis** stumble in singing, arm in arm. **Phyllis** holds her habitual*
wig in her hand. On entering she throws it away with a flourish.

Christy: Fine girl you are! A bit slow acting on a regal
decree my boy. Look lively I say. Or I'll feed you to the …
to the … animals. *(To the imaginary animals with an imaginary*
whip) Get back! I'll have order here. *(Wags finger at **Francis***
advising) Declaim it, me boy. Declaim it and they respect it.
Authority of voice is authority of lands. Look lively I say!

Phyllis: *(To **Francis**)* Your Lordship. Can I get a
dispensation for Mass tomorrow morning? I don't think I'll
be able to make it. *(She laughs)*

Francis: Look at you. Drunk as sin. And I've to clean up
after you. Can I go now Mr Ruane? I've to serve in the
morning.

Christy: Agh, you're too old to be serving Mass. Listen. Get
myself and the Count here a drink. A good old drop of
whiskey, *(rummages in pocket or bag)* and one for yourself.
(Takes some large fake monopoly money from his pocket/bag, gives
*it to **Francis**)* I'll pay in new money Sir, legal tender of the
realm of Eiropa. A drink. *(Expansive gesture)*

*Phyllis sits at a table; **Christy** attempts to sit at the bar, fails, and*
*joins **Phyllis** at the table. **Francis** does not follow his orders.*

Christy: Well, come on my boy! Look lively!

Francis: I'll finish up in the morning. I really have to be
going home.

Christy: Home my arse. You're mother was as drunk as the
next man. She'll not miss you. Wine I say! Wine!

Francis: You should go to bed the pair of you. You've had enough now. I'll see you in the morning.

Francis moves as if to go. **Christy** *roars with rage. He throws his crosier at* **Francis**, *but misses.*

Christy: You'll go nowhere! *(Pause)* You do work here, don't you? Ha? Well, as long as you do, you do what I say. Do you hear? Now, if you want to keep your job you'll get us whiskey and you'll get it fast.

Francis: *(Shocked and scared by Christy s outburst)* Is it wine or whiskey so?

Christy: No matter. Drink. *(To* **Phyllis***)* Isn't that right, Count?

Phyllis: Yes. No matter. *(Afterthought)* Good lad Francis.

Francis gets two glasses and a bottle of whiskey.

Christy: Now there's a loyal subject. That's what I like to see. Friends shall be rewarded! Rewarded with … with gold! And enemies? What will we do with the enemies, my dear Count?

Phyllis: Drain their blood.

Christy: Yes! Drain their blood. Drain it and ferment it. Pour it now, two fine beakers of the stuff. The finest draught in all the kingdom. Slaking thirst in taverns from Belslow to Ballinafast. *(Francis pours)* Now Count. A verdict from your … your educated palate.

Phyllis: *(With much ceremony, tasting wine, holding up to light)* Cuts a rich colour in the light. *(Swishing around)* Undulates round the perimeter of the glass: a certain syrupy quality. Legs long, yet sturdy. Bouquet? *(Smells)* A hint of oriental spices.

Christy: But the taste, dear Count, the taste?

Phyllis: *(Takes a sip of the whiskey, sloshes it around her mouth, swallows)* O-negative, I would say. 1798.

Christy: A fine vintage! *(To* **Francis***)* Another glass! Another glass for yourself my Lordship.

Francis: I, I don't drink. Can't I just go …

Christy: Another glass I said! *(Tense Pause. Is this a game or is Christy capable of violence?)*

Phyllis: A regal decree me boy.

Christy: Custom is custom. I'm ruler of all these lands. The power to free prisoners. The power to cast judgement. To set a man free or send him to his death. All must obey.

Phyllis: From sundown to sun-up.

Christy: Yes, from sundown to sun-up.

Francis is afraid. He gets a glass for himself. **Christy** *grabs the glass from his hand and pours him a large whiskey. He thrusts the glass back into* **Francis** *s hand.*

Phyllis: Sit down Devine and relax for Christ'sake.

Christy: Yes, sit down. Take a sip now, don't just be holding it.

Francis sits and begins to sip his drink. He is nervous. Pause.

Phyllis: That was some night Christy.

Christy: It certainly was Phyllis. It certainly was. Cheers.

The two click glasses. **Francis** *looks on.*

Phyllis: Some night, and smooth too. Everything smoothly.

Christy: Yes … smooooooth. *(He laughs. To* **Francis***)* You see, myself and the Count here are celebrating tonight Francis. Not that we're celebrating anything in particular, just celebrating … for the sake of it I suppose.

Francis: No harm in that.

Christy: Yes, no harm in that at all. *(Suddenly shouts at* **Francis***)* Pu knird!

Francis: *(To* **Phyllis***)* Is that German?

Christy: Pu knird!

Phyllis: Drink up. It's drink up … backwards.

Phyllis: Just do as he says.

Francis: But I don't really …

Christy: Pu knird!

Phyllis nods, there is no question of escape, they all drink.

Christy: A toast! To justice, for example.

Phyllis: I'll drink to that.

Christy: To justice then.

*Phyllis indicates to **Francis** he should stand up. They all stand.*

Francis: *(Meekly)* To justice.

Christy: Do you know what Count, I think we should make this young lad chaplain. Official chaplain to the king here.

Phyllis: I think so too.

Christy: Kneel down there Devine and I'll appoint you to your new honour. On your knees!

Francis: Agh, I don't want to dirty my gown. I've only got it on loan.

Christy: You're not going to refuse my honour now, are you?

Francis: No, it's just that …

Christy: *(A threat)* Because you know that would really upset me. You wouldn't want to upset me now, would you? On your knees!

Phyllis: Go on there now and do what he says, like a good lad.

Francis: *(Firmly)* I don't have to put up with this.

Christy: *(Roars viciously, instilling fear)* On your knees!

*Francis reluctantly gets on his knees in front of **Christy**.*

Francis: It's not going to hurt, is it?

The game begins to take on a more sinister tone.

Christy: Not unless you want it to. You see, there are two possible rituals for bestowing this honour: ritual A and ritual B. One hurts, but the other is quite painless. Which one is which, however, must remain a secret. Once you have chosen, then all shall be disclosed. Now, choose.

*Christy holds out his two hands, fists closed, knuckles up. Although nothing is in each hand **Francis** must choose one of them.*

Francis: I really have to get home.

Christy: *(Sudden outburst)* Is it home or to Lynch's eggs? Your other little job.

Phyllis: Easy on there Christy.

Francis: Let me go home.

Christy: *(Grabs him by the collar)* If I hear that once more out of you Devine, so help me God!

Phyllis: Easy I said!

Christy: *(Lets go of his collar)* Choose.

Francis chooses one of the hands. Tense pause.

Christy: You have chosen well.

Relief.

Christy: You see your Lordship, even a game like this has something to teach, a moral if you like. If you make the correct choice, then all shall be well. But if you choose unwisely, well ... the consequences can be very great. It's all up to you. Isn't that right my dear Count?

Phyllis: *(Going along with game again)* Certainly right my liege.

Christy: Yes. Now. *(Christy holds aloft an imaginary sword. He places it first on Francis s left shoulder, then moves it to his right.)* By the power invested in me, *(Eyes to heaven)* by the divine Lord himself, may I add, I hereby declare, you, his Lordship Francis Devine, official chaplain to the court of King Christy Ruane. From now ... until kingdom ... come.

(Quickly) In the name of the Father, and of the Son, and of the Holy Ghost, amen.

Phyllis: Amen!

Christy: So, how do you feel me lad? Honoured, doubtless.

Francis: *(Coldly)* I feel little.

Christy: *(Cynical)* And I thought you loved me.

Phyllis: Get into the spirit of it Francis.

Francis gets up.

Christy: Good lad. We'll make a cardinal of you yet. Now. *(To **Phyllis**)* You're always one for the singing Phyllis. How about a song?

Phyllis: I'm not in the mood. Put something on.

Christy: Yes, put something on there, something fitting for the occasion, to lift the spirits. Let's see now.

Christy gets up and goes to the radio/tape recorder behind the bar. He turns it on and starts flicking from channel to channel, from one kind of music to another, until he comes to some wild Cajun dance music, 'Le Chanson de Mardi Gras .

Christy: *(Referring to the different kinds of music, until he gets what he wants)* No. No. Christ, funeral music! *(**Francis** looks a bit sick at this stage)* You're not dead yet Francis, ha? Agh, now. That's the stuff. Something you can dance to. Do you like this kind of music Monsieur Count?

Phyllis: It's grand. Fine and lively.

Christy: Fine and lively indeed.

Phyllis: Great rhythm in it. Fancy a dance sire?

Christy: Well I was going to ask the young lad out, but seeing as you asked first, I'd be more than honoured, Sir.

*Christy and **Phyllis** come together, they bow formally, and begin to dance drunkenly. They fall around the place and spin in wild circles. Eventually they spin into disarray and fall on the floor laughing.*

Suddenly the laughter is interrupted by a loud knock on the door. The mood alters.

Christy: Did you hear that?

Phyllis: The door?

Christy: Turn off the radio Francis.

Francis: *(Loud)* What?

Christy: Shush! I said turn off the radio.

Francis gets up and turns off the radio. It is deadly quiet.

Phyllis: Listen.

Again deadly quiet. Francis makes his way back to his seat. He bangs into something and shatters the silence. He freezes where he is.

Christy: Shush!

Phyllis: It could be Courtney. He said he'd come round and check.

Christy: Not at this hour. He'd be drunk by now. Shush. Everyone quiet now. Not a sound. Ignore him and he'll go away.

After a few moments of tense silence a second loud knock is hammered out.

Lynch: *(from off)* I know you're in there Ruane! Open up!

Christy: Who's that at this hour?

Phyllis: It's not Courtney.

Christy: Someone for late drink I'd say. Well, we'll not deny them. Open up the door Francis. Go on now. We've all had the thirst on us at one time or other.

Francis goes to open the door. After a little fumbling with keys the door opens and Cathal Lynch enters. He is a big fat man in his early fifties. He wears work boots, overalls, a T-shirt and a brown work coat. He has a woollen hat with a bobble on his head, and thick stubble and sideburns on his face. All his clothes are filthy from farmwork, and one gets the impression that he never changes, and may even sleep in his clothes. He carries a brown potato sack in one hand.

Lynch: Close the door Devine. Well, what have we here?

Francis locks the door but leaves the keys in the keyhole.

Christy: *(Sitting on the floor, utter shock)* Lynch!

Lynch: Surprised to see me I take it. You know most decent women around these parts sit on chairs.

Christy: How dare you—

Lynch: Now, now Christy. You'd better be polite. After all, I am your employer now you know, in a kind of a way. Devine, get me a drink.

Christy: *(To Francis)* Stay where you are.

Lynch: A drink.

Francis doesn't know whom to heed.

Lynch: I'd listen to me if I were you Devine. Who do you think owns this place you're working in? A drink.

Francis gets him a glass. Lynch takes it off him and pours his own from the bottle on the table.

Christy: What do you want?

Lynch: Oh, I just thought I'd pay you a little visit, seeing as it's carnival night and all.

Christy: Well you're not welcome here.

Lynch: *(Raising his glass)* Your health, Mrs Derrane.

Phyllis: I hope you choke on it.

Lynch: Now now. You should have a little more respect when taking hospitality in my establishment.

Lynch knocks back his drink. Christy and Phyllis get off the floor. Phyllis sits, Christy remains standing.

Christy: I said, you're not welcome here.

Lynch: What kind of way is that to speak to your own brother-in-law Christy?

Christy: You're no relation of mine. Go now, before I do harm.

Lynch: Harm? I don't think you'll do any harm Christy, not with what I have on you.

Christy: What? What are you talking about?

Lynch: Agh now, let's just leave it at that. Let bygones be bygones. Had a good night Phyllis? *(Pause)* The cat got your tongue Phyllis? Sure come on. Give us a song Derrane. Something about your old grand-daddy. The great republican hero. *(Short pause)* Hello?

Phyllis: I'll not engage in pleasantries with you.

Lynch: No matter. You never were much good at conversation anyway. What was it Katey used say? Oh yes. 'As bright as my black hole'.

Lynch coolly pours himself another drink.

Phyllis: Don't sully her name with your mouth. If the truth's to be known that particular phrase she reserved for you.

Lynch: Always one for answering back Derrane. It's a shame someone didn't beat manners into you years ago.

Christy: *You* have something on me?

Lynch: Well a piece of paper for starters.

Christy: What paper?

Lynch: A little scrap concerning the ownership of a certain property. For starters like. Come here Devine! *(Lynch fills Francis a glass)* Come here and take a drink with your new boss.

Francis comes to Lynch and takes the glass.

Christy: A new boss is it?

Francis: I … I …

Lynch: *(Firmly to Francis)* Drink.

Francis sips.

Lynch: Don't be rude now. All of it.

Francis finishes the drink. After a moment he runs out to the toilet, hand on mouth. We hear him getting sick outside. **Lynch** *laughs.*

Christy: So now you come.

Lynch: You've to clear out within the week.

Christy: You could barely wait the year. Think you're in the clear now and can cause a stir. Is that it?

Lynch: Seven days. We'll say no more on the matter.

Christy: *(Rising anger)* I'll kill you first …

Lynch: Agh, now Ruane. I'm within the law. I'm only taking what's rightfully mine.

Christy: *(Lunging toward **Lynch**)* I'll wring your neck …

*Christy grabs **Lynch** by the throat and tries to choke him … a struggle … **Phyllis** leaps up and intervenes … pulling **Christy** away.*

Phyllis: Hold it! Hold it Christy! Hold on now … have you forgotten the night?

Christy: What?

Phyllis: No use spoiling things now. He'll get what's coming to him.

Christy: *(Remembering)* Yes … Phyllis. You're right. No use in me committing a crime. Yes. No use. I'll leave him to his fate and be done with it. Yes Phyllis.

Phyllis: *(To **Lynch**)* You'll not be around to claim this place anyway Lynch. No. You'll be rotting your days away in a cell. Rotting for the murder of Katey Ruane that everyone knows you committed, that's what you'll be doing. So be off with you. Go home and say your prayers … though they'll do you no good. Hell is the only place you'll be going … so off with you while you can … or so help me God I'll kill you myself.

*Pause. **Lynch** is unmoved, he drinks calmly.*

Lynch: A fine speech Phyllis. A pity you gave up the amateur dramatics when you did … it could have been the national stage for you girl … if it wasn't for the old alopecia. *(Laughs)* But a little less drama and a little more reality is called for. I'm going nowhere.

Phyllis: *(In disgust)* I don't need to stay listening to this.

***Lynch** knocks back another whiskey and throw his glass on the floor.*

Lynch: You'll stay where you are!

Pause.

Lynch: A nice little walk you had for yourself tonight Derrane … got lost did you? You could do better than listen to his highness here. Oh, and by the way, I think you dropped something on your wanderings, a bit of a careless bitch you have working for you Ruane.

***Lynch** takes the blood covered knife from his sack and stabs it into the counter where it sticks upright. **Christy** and **Phyllis** look on in shock.*

Lynch: Exhibit A. *(Drinks from the bottle)* Now, does that look familiar to you Derrane? Ha? I had a knife like that myself for slitting the throats of bitches in heat. No bastard puppies I want on my farm you understand? Yes, it does remind me of a knife I once had, but funny, I don't know what I did with it. Neither myself nor Sergeant Courtney seems able to find it … nor none of the other coppers, how hard they try.

Phyllis: I don't know what you're talking about. Come on Christy. Let's go.

Lynch: Don't know what I'm talking about, is it? I'm no fool, I tell you. You think I don't keep an eye out on carnival night for young pranksters out to let my chickens out or open the gate of a field. Oh yes. But this year who wanders in but Derrane here, thinking no one has seen her and sneaking around. So I thought to myself, well I'll keep quiet, see what she wants. Into the hayshed with her then, in and out real quick, as quiet as a mouse. I let you go, though I should have throttled you there. And what do I find within? *(He slaps the table loudly)* Exhibit A!

Christy: Ring Courtney Phyllis. We've Lynch here, evidence and all … your prints are all over that knife Lynch … and poor Kate's blood too. Who's to know if we planted it? It's your word against ours. Go on ring him Phyllis.

Lynch: I wouldn't get Courtney involved if I were you, Derrane.

Christy: Well, go on!

Phyllis moves.

Lynch: Perverting the course of justice … planting evidence, it's a serious offence you know. You could do time for that Derrane. *(Drinks, finishes bottle and bangs it down on the table)* I think this is a matter for the three of us. Don't you?

Christy: I'll see you rot in a cell yet Lynch. I won't rest till you do.

Lynch: Agh, I don't think so Ruane. You'll be too busy looking for a job. Anyway, I won't put Courtney on the trail of your little night of crime, just move out nice and quiet and all and we'll bury the hatchet. Water under the old bridge. Within the week mind. *(Noticing Phyllis again)* Jesus, Derrane, would you ever put a hat or a scarf or something on you and spare me the sight of you. Almost as ugly as your sister, that one, Ruane. And as loose around the town from what I hear.

Christy can take no more. He goes for Lynch and grabs him by the throat. They fall onto the floor and a struggle begins.

Christy: I'll strangle you!

After initially being on top Christy is overcome by Lynch. Lynch is on top of him and has him by the throat. He begins to choke Christy. Christy is almost finished when Phyllis decides to act. She takes up the empty whiskey bottle and smashes it on **Lynch** *s head, knocking him out.*

Phyllis: Are you all right Christy? Christy, speak to me.

Christy: Ge ... ge ...

Phyllis: Go? Where?

Christy: Get this off me.

Phyllis: Jesus! Sorry. Hold on now.

With great effort **Phyllis** *rolls the unconscious* **Lynch** *off* **Christy.**

Christy: *(Holding his throat)* Is ... is he dead?

Phyllis: No such luck.

There is a loud knock on the door. They freeze.

Phyllis: Lynch didn't have a twin? Did he?

Christy: Shussh!

They listen. Another knock comes and a drunk **Courtney** *speaks from off.*

Courtney: Open up there Ruane! I can hear you moving within!

Phyllis: Courtney!

Christy: *(Panicking)* Jesus Phyllis, what'll we do?

Phyllis: Hold on now, just keep calm ... we'll ... we'd better let him in ...

Christy: But ... what about Lynch?

Phyllis: He knows we're in here, give me a hand, we'll ...

Christy: *(Referring to* **Lynch***)* He'll do us for attempted murder ... any excuse to get me ... I'm telling you.

Courtney: Ruane! *(Knocking)*

Phyllis: Wait ...

Phyllis *rips the hanging off the wall and covers* **Lynch** *with it, after first laying him flat.*

Phyllis: Now …

Christy: But …

Phyllis: You've nothing to worry about … he can't prosecute you … it's only the pair of us … two old friends having a chat … go on now.

Reluctantly **Christy** *opens the door,* **Phyllis** *sits down and looks calm. Enter Sergeant* **Courtney** *lighting a cigarette; although drunk he is pretending to be sober. He has a slight cut on his head. He carries his radio which is now smashed and broken.*

Christy: Agh, Sergeant … how are you?

Courtney: I hope you're not selling drink at this hour, Ruane.

Christy: Not at all Sergeant … it's only myself and Phyllis having a chat.

Courtney: *(Suspicious)* Yes … *(Seeing her without her wig)* Mrs. Derrane?

Phyllis: What brings you out so late, Sergeant? *(Noticing the cut on* **Courtney** *s head)* Are you all right?

Courtney: *(Embarrassed)* Oh … yes. Phyllis … how are you. Em … *(Explaining the cut)* there was a fight over at the nightclub … young Hannan again … I got called out to break it up. Thought I'd check in on you on the way home.

Courtney *is eyeing the whiskey. He leaves down his broken radio.*

Christy: No one hurt I hope?

Courtney: Not seriously anyway.

Phyllis: Well, as you can see it's just the pair of us … so … I expect you'll want to get back to bed with your early start tomorrow.

Courtney: My early start?

Christy: Yes … down at Lynch's place.

Phyllis *notices that they have forgotten the knife, and positions herself in front of it.*

Courtney: What?

Christy: Lynch's. The search?

Courtney: Oh yes … yes. I'll leave you to it so … you'd do well getting to bed.

Christy: Yes, we're just going now.

Phyllis: I was on my way out the door Sergeant.

Courtney: Grand so. I'll be off. Be sure and lock up now … I don't want people coming seeing the light on and knocking … do you hear me Ruane?

Christy: No problem Sergeant Courtney … Good night now.

Courtney turns to go, but turns back, wanting an ashtray to extinguish his cigarette. He walks over to the counter on which is placed an ashtray … beside the knife that both Christy and Phyllis had forgotten. Courtney puts out his cigarette and notices the knife.

Courtney: *(Pulling the knife out of the counter and holding it up with a chuckle, Christy and Phyllis freeze)* Ha! I see Rafferty did his usual trick as a butcher. Jesus, will he ever change his costume and give us all a bit of a surprise.

Courtney puts the knife down and takes the opportunity to rob a whiskey bottle on the counter. He goes to exit.

Courtney: Good night so … and lock up lively now Ruane … do you hear me?

Christy: Yes. Right away Sergeant.

Courtney: Christy. Phyllis.

Courtney exits and Christy and Phyllis relax.

Christy: Good night.

Phyllis: Night Sergeant.

Pause.

Christy: My nerves are shot.

Phyllis: Tell me about it.

The two sit.

Phyllis: Well, that puts paid to that.

Christy: What?

Phyllis: The evidence … it's spoiled now … Courtney's prints all over it.

Christy: Yes. The blind fart.

Phyllis: A good plan well banjaxed.

Christy: That's putting it mildly. We could still kill him.

Phyllis: Well I'll have no part in it.

Christy: *(Considers murdering Lynch)* It's a high price for justice.

Phyllis: Too high a price.

Christy *has not stopped considering killing **Lynch**. Pause. They drink.*

Phyllis: Unless …

Christy: Unless what?

Phyllis: We could get a confession out of him.

Christy: Agh … he'll never confess.

Phyllis: He might if he was scared enough.

Christy: Nothing would scare that bastard.

Phyllis: If we killed him it would.

Christy: *(Hopeful)* You're for it so?

Phyllis: No, but he doesn't know that.

*A groan comes out of **Lynch**.*

Christy: Shush. He's coming round. What are you suggesting?

Phyllis: I think we can get our evidence yet. Well, if we convince him we're going to cut his throat or something we can get him to say anything … all we have to do is get it on tape.

Christy: *(Pause. Thinks)* But will it stand up in court?

Phyllis: Evidence is evidence.

Christy: True enough.

Phyllis: Right then, that's settled.

Christy: Wait. I've a better idea.

Christy runs behind the bar and gets the rope from earlier. Possibly using the counter as a mask, he puts a noose on it. He will mount the ladder to fix the rope for a hanging.

Christy: You do the tape recorder … there should be a tape in it.

Phyllis goes to the tape recorder and sets it up. Phyllis, finished setting up, comes to take the drape off Lynch. At this moment Francis re-emerges from the toilet, looking pale and a little unsteady on his feet. He slumps in a chair near Christy.

Francis: I don't feel well.

Christy: *(Seeing Francis)* Ah, the dead arose and appeared to many.

Phyllis: I'll spancel this pig.

Phyllis ties Lynch s hands, maybe with some bunting

Christy: Give us a hand, get that ladder and set it up there next to the stairs. Hurry!

Francis: What happened him?

Christy: Never mind, just do as you're told.

Francis: What are you doing to him?

Christy: Never mind. Get a move on. Hold that ladder. Phyllis, get a stool, Lynch, get up!

Christy is probably up the ladder at this stage. Phyllis will use the knife to threaten and restrain Lynch, direct him where she wants him to go.

(Lynch groans.)

Phyllis: *(Referring to Lynch)* Seems like Lazarus here's awake.

Lynch: *(Groans)* My head.

Christy: Bit of a headache there Lynch? Well, well, well. Hold that ladder Francis.

Lynch: Where am I?

Christy: Remember now, you've the right to remain silent. *(Laughs).*

Lynch: Where am I? *(Remembers, becoming more aware of his surroundings)* Agh!

Christy: You, for your information, are in the just and regal court of Christopher Ruane. Get up you big heap.

Phyllis: Get up or I'll slit your throat.

Francis: What's going on?

Christy: Get up on the stool now.

Lynch, before he knows what has been happening, has a knife held to his throat and is forced to mount the hangman s stool.

Lynch: Agh, give over with the show Ruane, you wouldn't know how to hang up your coat.

Christy: Shut up.

Phyllis: Now there is a pretty picture.

Lynch: What are you saying? Untie me. Untie me Ruane or I'll kick your fucking head in.

Christy: That's no way to address royalty. Mind your tongue when you have an audience with the king. *(To Francis)* A throne your Lordship. *(Indicating a throne-like chair in the bar)* Francis, get that chair. Let's have a throne worthy of a trial.

Phyllis: A great idea, a throne.

Francis: Are you hurting him?

Christy: Up on the counter with it your lordship.

Francis puts the 'throne on the bar counter.

Lynch: Stop play-acting Ruane.

Christy: The drape. Put the drape over it.

Francis puts the drape over the throne. It has the effect of making the chair look like an actual royal throne. Christy climbs into his throne and holds one end of the rope, with Lynch s neck in a noose at the other end.

Lynch: Stop pulling for Christ'sake. Untie me Francis.

Christy: *(Pulling on the rope, inflicting pain)* Shut up!

Lynch: Untie me I said!

Francis considers.

Christy: *(Strikes Francis)* Stay where you are Devine, or you'll join him on the gallows!

Christy pulls on the rope, inflicts pain and has Lynch submissive and silent for a time.

Christy: Another word and I'll tear your head off! *(Pause. Gathers himself)* Phyllis, tie him up!

Phyllis: With pleasure.

Phyllis ties the hanging rope off behind the counter.

Christy: Now, my loyal subjects. We are gathered here today for the trial of one Cathal Lynch. The rotund heap you see before you. He stands accused of the most heinous murder of the gentle Kate Ruane, whom he had the gall to call wife. My crosier Francis, bring me my crosier.

Lynch: Stay where you are Devine.

Christy: My crosier! *(Francis obeys)* I tell you this, and swear upon it, by this, *(Christy now has the crosier)* this staff, that dead, will never again put forth fruit and branches, now the brazen knife has stripped its flesh. By this I swear to see right done. We pass it through the generations upholding the time-honoured customs of the people. This staff will be the force behind my judgement. *(Christy uses the crosier to pound three times)* The court is now in session!

Lynch: All you Ruanes were nothing but peasants …

Phyllis: *(Wielding knife)* You will bleed.

Christy: The judge presiding is the Sovereign of the realm itself, the Moon-king and dispenser of rare justice, his highness Christopher Ruane. Note taker and assembled moral majority, the esteemed Count Derrane, sits on your side sinister, the left. And as court clerk, we have a man of the cloth, no less. A lad of honest years but of wavering loyalty. A youth who must prove his allegiance this very night.

Lynch: Peasants and dirt-farmers …

Phyllis: Kill the fucker! Off with his head!

Christy: Order in the court! You will have your head, but in the fullness of time. The niceties of civilisation demand some theatrics first: due process, wigs and gowns.

Lynch: Cut your shite!

Christy: Ah, the blubber blurts. Count. *(Phyllis silences Lynch with the knife)* Let us begin. Will the court clerk please fetch a tome appropriate to the fiscal faith of the man in the dock, so he may take his oath. A man so representative of his nation. The house ledger! Fetch it Devine!

Francis: I don't like this.

Christy: As I say!

Francis goes and gets the ledger.

Lynch: You're going too far Ruane.

Christy: Not as far as you went when you murdered my sister.

*Francis comes with the ledger. He brings it to **Lynch** who is standing up on the chair.*

Francis: What do you want me to do?

Christy: Now. I seem to be at a loss. What comes first? The sentence or the evidence? Recalling some of my training in *juris prudence*—

Francis: Do you want this?

Christy: Shut up! You're too late for the oath. It is the sentence first, which of course is death, followed by the evidence. Proceed with your interrogation dear Count. *(Lynch is fidgeting with his ropes)*

Francis: Mr Ruane, I really think—

Christy: Shut up I said!

Francis: I'll have no further part in this. You've gone too far.

Christy: *(Strikes Francis again)* Shut!

Francis does as he is told.

Phyllis: Thank you me law. [*My Lord*]

Phyllis gets up and walks around, arms behind back, a barrister-at-law.

Phyllis: Mr Lynch. You stand here accused of murder. A most serious and grave accusation, especially against a man such as yourself, a man prominent in the local farming community.

Lynch: I'll get you for this Derrane!

Phyllis: *(Holds knife to Lynch s testicles)* As you have heard the sentence is death. But before the administration of the sentence I have one serious question to put to you, and this, may I impress upon you *(She places the knife between Lynch s legs, threatening castration)* is your opportunity to contest your innocence before the court. Now Mr Lynch, the question. What, Mr Lynch, what is your favourite colour?

Lynch: You damned bitch!

Christy: Funny. I thought it was an apt question, considering the circumstances. I myself, however, would have enquired after the preferred funerary rite. *(To Lynch)*

Would you prefer to be interred in the ground or cremated? I think a pyre would become you ... but for the stench of burning fat.

Lynch: I'll kill you Ruane.

Christy: A better burial than my sister got.

Lynch: I'll kill you, you hear me?

Christy: This is no joke.

Lynch: You'll follow your fucking sister if I've anything to do with it.

Christy pulls on the rope hard, and simultaneously stands up and shouts ...

Christy: Contempt!

Francis: Easy.

Christy: Contempt *in facie curiae. (He belts* **Lynch** *with his crosier)* Before I hang you I want to hear it from you ... you killed Katey, didn't you?

Lynch: Take this thing off me.

Christy: You killed her, didn't you?

Christy begins to pull the rope, forcing **Lynch** *to stand on his toes.*

Lynch: You're choking me!

Francis: Mrs Derrane ...

Christy: How did you do it? How did you kill Katey? How did you kill her Lynch?

Francis: Mrs Derrane ...

Lynch: Let me down Ruane! Or so help me God—

Christy: How?

Lynch: I stabbed her in her bed! Just what the bitch deserved!

Christy: You murdering bastard!

Francis: *(Shocked)* You stabbed her?

Phyllis: Christy … the tape recorder. *(Christy is too far gone to hear her)*

Lynch: The same bed she whored in!

Christy: Lies! Lies!

Lynch: The truth! Katey Ruane was nothing but a whore!

Christy: You lying bastard!

Lynch: She got only what was coming to her!

Christy: *(Pulling harder on the rope)* Lying bastard!

Phyllis: I think I have the thing working!

Lynch: I spit on you Ruane! And all the Ruanes!

Lynch spits at Christy. Christy in a rage pulls away the stool supporting Lynch. Lynch gives a blood-curdling roar, chokes, and is silent. He is left hanging.

Christy: I think I've killed him.

A final image of Lynch hanging, then lights down.

End of Act Two.

Interval.

ACT THREE

*The next morning. There is no sign of **Lynch** or the noose.*
Remnants of night in the air. The walking ghost of the dead woman
*enters. She goes to **Francis**, who is lying asleep, and stares at him*
*intently. She moves on and exits. **Francis** stirs in his sleep. He is*
wrapped in the drape, which gives him a mummy-like appearance.
As a distant bell sounds mid-day, he slowly sits up. There are vomit
stains on his clothes. He goes to the door and opens it, takes a breath
of fresh air but quickly returns to refresh himself with some water.
*As **Francis** is busy refreshing himself, **Christy** enters, coming down*
the stairs; he has slept in his costume.

Christy: *(Holding his head)* Jesus!

***Christy** slumps into a chair.*

Christy: Francis? Is that you Francis?

Francis: Um.

Christy: Bring me a pint of water.

Francis: No.

Christy: Agh, come on. Good lad.

Francis: Get your own water.

Christy: Do what you're told.

Francis: I don't have to listen to you. You're not the
carnival king today you know … get your own water. I'm
sick.

Christy: What has you sick?

***Francis** doesn t answer. Pause.*

Christy: What time is it?

Francis: Look at the clock.

***Christy** looks at the clock, it is almost mid-day.*

Christy: 12, Jesus. *(Pause).* What are you doing here anyway?

Francis: I must have fallen asleep.

Christy: Where?

Francis: Counter.

Christy: Christ. I can't remember a thing. *(Pause)* I thought you didn't drink.

Francis: I don't.

Christy: *(Small laugh … but it hurts to laugh)* Neither do I.

A clock in the pub sounds mid-day.

Christy: Christ, my head. That clock is always different to the one at the church.

Francis: Well, it is *your* clock.

Pause.

Christy: Shouldn't you be getting to Mass?

Francis: *(Realisation)* Oh golly! *(Panic)* I'm supposed to serve.

Christy: 'Golly'. Is that the best you can come up with?

Francis: *(Starts to brush the vomit stains with his hand)* I can still make it if I—

Christy: 'Damn' or something at least would be more appropriate. So genteel. Forget it. You can't go in that state, not until you clean yourself up. Besides, you're too late already.

Francis: *(Feeling nauseous again, goes to sink and spits)* I'll say I was sick.

Christy: What are you saying? That's how most bishops look after a good night out.

Francis: *(Viciously)* Go to hell.

Christy: That's more like it.

Pause.

Christy: Look, Francis. I don't know what I said last night, I can't rightly remember anything. But I know when I'm drinking I can be a bit, well … difficult. So if I said anything out-of-order, well, it meant nothing. Do you hear?

Francis: I hear.

Christy: Well?

Francis: *(Pause)* The whole thing's a bit of a haze.

Phyllis comes down the stairs. She is dressed as in Act Two, her clothes in disarray like Christy s, however, she is now wearing her wig.

Phyllis: Noon? *(She looks at Christy in the chair)* You'd swear your chariot had turned into a pumpkin, Ruane. You look like shite.

She sits in a chair.

Phyllis: Get us a pint of water like a good lad.

No answer.

Christy: I was wondering who it was snoring in the bed beside me … all I could see was the dress suit.

Francis: She slept in the bed beside you?

Christy: Agh no … the spare bed—

Francis: You said—

Christy: I don't know what I'm saying … I'm a little rattled today.

Phyllis: Doesn't know his arse from his elbow.

Christy: Yes, don't know my arse from my elbow. Go on Francis, a pint of water.

Francis: I'm not working today.

Christy: You are.

Francis: I'm not.

Christy: Well I certainly didn't give you the day off.

Francis: I'm taking it off. Sick leave.

Christy: You can't do that.

Francis: I can … I've to get home. I have to catch Mass on the radio. I don't like working Sundays anyhow.

Christy: I've never heard him complain about getting paid double time for working a Sunday before. Aren't you supporting your mother on it? And saving for the seminary?

Phyllis: Sunday. The Sabbath. What's that about?

Christy: Sounds a bit superstitious. Is it some kind of superstition, Francis? You're not a member of any cult I hope?

Phyllis: Yes, cults. Virgins and blood galore.

Christy: No, that's the church, my dear.

Francis: From sundown to sun-up. You're familiar with that ritual, your highness? Well, the Sabbath's the sacred version. Something you'd know nothing about.

Christy: A tad touchy today.

Phyllis: A bit bitchy indeed.

Christy: Sacred how?

Francis: Spiritual. Things of the spirit.

Christy: Ah. The spirit. Well if you don't mind I'll stick to the body. There's both eating and drinking in it! *(Laughs)*

Phyllis: Yes, and hangovers.

Christy: Well you can't have everything, now can you? But the carnal. When it comes down to it that's the side I'll take. Sweet and solid. Like an apple. None of this positing a better world out there. All that's a bit chancy for me. We're here and we're here now. Enough. Isn't that enough? It strikes me as disdainful to be wanting more. When there's a pageant on you'd prefer to go home and dream. Turn your back on creation. Not I. I know a good thing when I see it.

Phyllis: You're in top form Christy, for a man that can barely stand.

Christy: I must still be drunk.

Francis: You must and the rot you're talking. That kind of philosophy ends in the grave. Sweet and solid. What about decay? Have you ever thought of that? The dance stops there I tell you. It's the eternal that's worth real attention. All your hankering after justice. What else is that but positing a better world. If you're so happy with this one, then what's all this blab about seeing right done? Personally I'd like to think that there's something beyond the grave.

Christy grows quiet.

Christy: Now there's the educated lad.

Phyllis: *(Pause)* Get us a pint of water, there's the boy.

Christy: Forget the water. The only thing that will cure that head of yours is whiskey.

Phyllis: I don't know Christy.

Christy: Keep the party going!

Phyllis: That's not a good idea.

Christy: Ah, come on now Phyllis, of course it's a good idea.

Francis: You'd do better listening to Mrs Derrane.

Christy: *(Turning on Francis)* I didn't ask for your opinion, now did I! No. Keep it to yourself. Can a man not have a drink, when he wants to have a drink?

*Squints his eyes and squeezes his two temples with the thumb and index finger of one hand, holding back some pain 'Jesus'! Shudders. He makes the same gesture again, controlling his thoughts. **Francis** gets a bottle of whiskey and gives it to **Christy**.*

Christy: Now. Now. That whiskey. Just today again. Continue on into today. *(He drinks)* That's more like it Phyllis. Who says we can't dance from midnight to midday and beyond. Right into the heart of it. Romping our way rightly. The unending carnival! Imagine. Borders collapse. Each man king and subject. And justice, like the air itself.

Francis: I hope it does you some good, though I doubt it.

Christy: Ease on there lad. We got drunk together, I'll never forget that, at least I wouldn't if I could remember. But you're not so bad. Phyllis. A number to raise the spirits.

Phyllis: I'm not up to you.

Christy: Agh, come on now. Something festive. 'Fi ... Fi ... Finnegan's Wake'.

Francis: Sleep might be more in order.

Christy: Just a bit of it.

Phyllis: You're definitely still drunk. But seeing as you're so handsome. Alright.

Phyllis clears her throat.

Phyllis: How's it start?

Christy: Tim Finnegan.

Phyllis: Yes. I'd rather not.

Christy: For me Phyllis. Come on.

Phyllis: Grand so. But if I start I'll only finish when your ears start bleeding. *(Clears throat again, then sings first verse, losing it towards the end)* Tim Finnegan lived on Walking Street. A gentleman Irish mighty odd. He had a tongue both rich and sweet. And to rise in the world he carried a hod. Now. *(Thinks)* Now, Tim had a sort of tip-plin' way. With the love of the liquor he was born. *(Thinks. Gives up)* I can't remember the words.

Christy: Agh now!

Phyllis: How's it go again?

Francis: *(Getting ready to go)* I'll leave you.

Christy: You know. He slips or something. Drunk. Kills himself.

Phyllis: No. He was murdered. Wasn't he? Hit on the head.

Christy: It doesn't matter. Make it up. Slips, shot, hung. Who cares?

Francis: I'll drop in tomorrow?

Phyllis: *(Slowly realising and remembering)* He wasn't hung anyhow.

Christy: Well, just finish him off whatever way you see fit.

Phyllis: He wasn't hung. Was he Christy?

Christy: He … *(Realising)* Well … maybe he was.

Phyllis: Oh my God …

Christy: I think he was.

Phyllis: Christy.

Christy: Definitely was, Phyllis.

*Both **Phyllis** and **Christy** look at where **Lynch** was hanging, then at each other.*

Francis: *(Exiting)* Bye!

Phyllis: I think I have the tune now.

Christy: Yes … Francis! Francis!

Francis: *(Re-enters)* What?

Christy: You slept here last night, didn't you?

Francis: Yes. On that bloody counter.

Phyllis: You slept on the counter you say Francis?

Francis: Yes.

Christy: And before that you were here last night, weren't you?

Francis: Yeah, cleaning up your mess till near four in the morning … enough is enough …

Christy: Oh, no problem lad … take the day off … and Monday … but you slept here?

Francis: Yes.

Christy: Drunk ?

Francis: Of course drunk … what with you and Lynch forcing drink down my throat. I'd expect that of you, but I really think that Mr Lynch, I really think that Mr Lynch … that …

Phyllis: I've a feeling I know what you think.

Francis: I think that Mr Lynch …

Christy: Don't panic now.

Francis: Was here last night. And …

Phyllis: Calm yourself.

Francis: Jesus, murder.

Christy: Well, I wouldn't put it that way.

Francis: Oh my God.

Phyllis: Murder is such an ugly word.

Francis: You murdered him. Hu … hung him.

Christy: Easy on there.

Francis: I'll … I'll have to tell the Sergeant.

Phyllis: Don't be hasty now, Francis.

Francis: I'll have to tell him right away.

Christy: I don't think that's such a good idea.

Francis: *(Angry)* I don't care what you think. I've had enough of you and what you think. I've had enough, do you hear?

Christy: Well, with your involvement, that's all. I'd leave the Sergeant out of it.

Francis: My involvement? What the hell are you talking about? I had nothing to do with it. I'm off. Don't try and stop me.

Christy: Grand so. *(As **Francis** goes)* But it's a shame to see a young lad with such prospects … well, throw it all away.

Phyllis: Jail can be a hard place Francis.

Francis: *(Stopping)* Don't try it. You'll be the ones going to jail.

Phyllis: You're very sure Francis.

Christy: It's quick you forget.

Francis: Forget. Forget what?

Phyllis: The court clerk me boy. Tying up a man …

Francis: I never …

Phyllis: … and taking part in his illegal trial and execution. How's your memory now, Mr Court Clerk? If I remember rightly, you were pretty central in the whole affair. You know, a court of law would see you as part of 'the gang'.

Christy: *(Arms open wide)* Welcome to the gang, Francis.

Francis: You made me … ordered me.

Phyllis: No matter.

Francis: It was against my will.

Christy: Will?

Francis: I was forced. Afraid.

Phyllis: Fear is of little consequence. The motivation is incidental. It is the action that is all. And what do your actions speak of?

Christy: Aiding and abetting. An accomplice to murder, pure and simple.

Francis: Christ!

Phyllis: Don't take it too hard Francis. The bastard had it coming.

Francis: To have killed a man …

Phyllis: The man was a murderer. Now we didn't set out to kill him, that just kind of happened. But now it's done. At least there is some kind of justice to it all.

Christy: Don't be too hard on yourself young fellow. A life in the priesthood will more than pay for this one misdemeanour. Besides, if you got done they'd never let you into the fold. Because of one mistake? You know rightly. Saul, Paul ... whatever. Didn't he kill countless Christians and go on to be a father of the church? Now, what's one man compared to that. Kill a few more and they might make you a saint. No. Better keep this our little secret.

Francis is silent, contemplating his actions.

Phyllis: Agh, he'll be alright.

Christy: He'll be fine?

Pause

Phyllis: You did well.

Christy: I did well how?

Phyllis: *(Drinking)* Agh ... up, early like. Where'd you put him?

Christy: What ?

Phyllis: Lynch. Where'd you put him?

Christy: I didn't put him anywhere.

Phyllis: I'm in no mood.

Christy: I'm telling you! I didn't put him anywhere.

Phyllis: You must have hid the body somewhere ?

Christy: Last thing I remember was Lynch hanging from that rafter there ... after that my head went all kind of funny ...

Phyllis: A blackout.

Christy: Next thing I know I'm woken up by your snoring.

Phyllis: I don't snore ... you can't remember a thing?

Christy: I was hoping you'd taken him down.

Phyllis: No, you must have cut him down. As far as I remember I left you drinking a night-cap to Lynch's soul in hell ... you must have cut him down.

Christy: If I did I can't remember. Jesus, maybe I did?

Phyllis: Well if you did you couldn't have dragged him far ... not with the weight of him ... he must be around here some place.

Christy: I suppose I would have put him somewhere near, somewhere out of sight.

Phyllis: You'd never have got him up those steps.

Christy: I could barely get myself up.

Phyllis: He must be around some place ... we'll check. Francis, give us a hand. Stop moping and make yourself useful.

Christy and Phyllis check in different places. Francis very reluctantly does the same. After a moment Phyllis comes in from the garden.

Phyllis: Christ, I think I have him!

Christy and Francis re-enter.

Christy: Where?

Phyllis: The garden. There's something looks like a grave. I was afraid to look. Come on.

Christy: Wait. Wait now. That's only the dog was knocked down. I tried burying him, but the ground was too stony. That's not Lynch.

Phyllis: Back to it then. Come on Francis!

They all exit, looking in different places. After a moment Francis comes back in.

Francis: (*Shouting to others offstage*) I have him! I have him!

Christy and Phyllis re-enter.

Christy: Where?

Francis: There's a corpse in the yard. Burnt to a cinder. Smell of petrol off it. Jesus the smell!

Christy: Agh! That's only the dog again.

Francis: The dog?

Christy: When I couldn't bury him I decided a pyre was the best option. Didn't really work though. Just kind of roasted him.

Francis: The poor dog.

Christy: Back to it. He has to be around here somewhere.

They all exit again to various locations. After a few moments **Christy** *comes in bearing a bloody cleaver, his arms full with bloody raw meat–big chucks of it, hacked up crudely.*

Christy: Heh! Heh!

Phyllis *and* **Francis** *re-enter.* **Christy** *dumps the meat–in its plastic wrapping–on the bar counter.*

Francis: Oh my God!

Phyllis: Jesus, Christy.

Christy: I can't rightly remember, but it just struck me to check the freezer. I'm always hacking up sheep for the stew we do. Well, that's as good a place as any for a Christian like Lynch, I thought. I must have done the job quickly. It's a bit messy.

Phyllis: Christ. That's not all of it?

Christy: Well, there's more of him back in the freezer.

Francis: Much more?

Christy: Well, he was a fair old size.

Phyllis is inspecting the meat.

Phyllis: A fair old size is right.

Christy: Fat, to be precise.

Francis: Couldn't it do with last rites, or something?

Phyllis: Fat, yes. So you filleted him and all?

Christy: What?

Phyllis: Well, there's very little fat on this meat. I'd call that lean, wouldn't you Francis?

Francis: *(Inspecting the meat)* Well, yes. That's lean all right.

Phyllis: A good job too. Almost as good as Gillane's Butchers, I'd say. And you did that and the state you were in? God you're some man Christy. I'd call that talent.

Christy: That's not Lynch?

Phyllis: Of course it's not him. That meat's lean. If it was Lynch you'd have to boil it for a week before you'd boil off the lard.

Christy: I suppose you're right. Well then, I've no idea what I did with him. He was so mean he might have rotted already.

Francis: I'm off. This is your problem. I'll have nothing more to do with it. As far as I'm concerned this never happened. I wasn't even here. God forgive me.

Christy: *(Getting angry)* Go on then. Clear off. You're useless anyway. Go on home and say your rosary.

Phyllis: Is it safe to let him go?

Christy: Either that or we kill him.

Christy is considering killing Francis, wielding cleaver.

Phyllis: You understand lad that you're an accomplice, as guilty in the eyes of the law as Christy there. One word and you're gone. One word, in your whole life, understand? No seminary, and what of your mother? Who'd look after her now? You see the seriousness of it? Jail is what I'm talking about. Say nothing ... if for no other reason than to save your own skin.

Francis: *(Agrees with Phyllis)* Damn you.

Phyllis: Christy, he wasn't here.

Christy: Phyllis, he wasn't here.

Phyllis: *(To Francis)* Go on.

Francis exits.

Christy: *(Shouting after Francis as he exits)* Tonight, nine sharp, and don't be late!

Pause. Christy sits and sips some of his whiskey. Phyllis clears away the meat and cleaver, then sits and takes her drink, thinking.

Phyllis: You wouldn't have taken him outside … in the car maybe?

Christy: I was in no fit state to drive … I would have killed someone.

Phyllis: Well somewhere else, out in the small shed?

Christy: *(Thinks)* No. The place was locked up, and Francis had the keys. I'm very strict about that, Francis knows never to leave the place open.

Phyllis: Well he couldn't have just disappeared.

Christy: Well where is he?

Phyllis: You're the one who should know that. You were that drunk?

Christy: You know yourself Phyllis.

Phyllis: There's nothing for it but to get you drunk again … you might remember if you're in the same state … *(She fills his glass)* … here, start getting that down you.

Christy: Well … if you think it will do some good. *(Christy drinks)*. Agh … I don't know if I'll be able to keep it down.

Phyllis: *(Pouring him another)* Come on now … keep going.

Christy: *(Burps)* Jesus ! That's hard tack. *(Christy drinks)*.

Phyllis: *(Pouring yet another)* Are you beginning to feel anything?

Christy: Well … no.

Phyllis: *(Fills his glass again, and hers also)* Another so … and I'll give you some help.

Christy: If you say so.

They drink.

Phyllis: Well ? Anything coming to you ?

Christy: Wait. *(He pours another drink for himself and knocks it back).* I think I'm beginning to get something. *(He takes a slug out of the bottle)* It's getting closer.

He takes another drink from the bottle.

Christy: Yes. I think I almost have it now.

The proceedings are interrupted by a loud knock on the door.

Courtney: *(From off)* You in there Ruane?

Christy: Jesus, Courtney. *(Panic)* What's he want?

Phyllis: Jesus!

Christy jumps back from the door in fright. Enter Sergeant Courtney, holding a plastic bag, and Lynch. Lynch has the purple and black ring of a bruise around his neck.

Lynch: There he is Sergeant, the murdering bastard!

Courtney: Quiet now Mr Lynch, I'll do the talking.

Lynch: Thought maybe you'd seen the last of me, ha?

Courtney: I said quiet, Cathal. Mr Ruane please take a seat. I'd like to ask you a few questions. Mrs Derrane, you sit down as well.

Courtney: Cathal, you sit too.

Christy: I thought you were …

Phyllis: Shhh!

Lynch sits, a distance away from the others … but facing them.

Courtney: Now. This should not take too long. As you know the county team are playing, kick off in a few minutes, and I intend to catch the most of it. We should have won that draw yesterday. But we've a good chance in the replay today. So listen now and don't waste my time. *(Looks at his watch)* I think I should tell you from the outset Mr Ruane that Cathal, Mr Lynch here, is making certain accusations against you. As I was saying. There are particular accusations being made concerning certain events, occurrences of a criminal nature that may have come to pass in the vicinity in the recent past. Occurrences that may have involved particular individuals, possibly in a criminal capacity ... but that is yet to be determined. The accusation is being made against one particular well-known member of the community by another, also well-known to many in the area. However, it is not for me to decide whether this crime has been perpetrated by this particular individual, it is rather my duty to secure the general welfare of the ordinary citizen ... in general. As such, it is my responsibility to determine if a breach of the law has occurred, in this case a most serious and heinous breach of the law. If this is indeed the case ... as it currently appears ... then it falls on me to investigate what evidence there may be to support this particular accusation made by this certain individual. In the event that I happen to discover what I consider to be satisfactory evidence on which to base an arrest of this particular person, then so be it. Yet, in order to remind and caution all concerned, let me just point out that—

Phyllis: Excuse me Sergeant.

Courtney: What?

Phyllis: I was wondering if you could just be a little more specific?

Courtney: I would appreciate it if I was not interrupted.

Phyllis: I'm sorry Sergeant, it's just that it appears that there is an accusation being made against Mr Ruane here ... and I'm sure he'd like to know just what it is ... if you would come to the point.

Lynch: I'll tell you what it is ... that bastard tried to murder me, that's what!

Christy: I'm not the murderer around here.

*Both **Christy** and **Lynch** have risen from their seats. **Courtney** blows his whistle to restore order.*

Courtney: Hold it! Hold it the pair of you! *(Silence).* Now, let me just get one thing clear … I'm running this show, right? So you speak when I ask you to speak, and when I ask you to shut up you shut up, clear? *(Pause. They sit again. Looks at his watch)* You may have no interest in the game on today, but I do. Now I don't want to end up listening to this match on the radio, is that clear? If we win this we've a clear run at the championship, it's life and death out there today, and the lads are fitter than ever. I don't know if you appreciate the historic chance on offer. It's been three generations since we beat these bastards, and we've a passionate squad this year. So time is of the essence. Leave the talking to me and we'll have this cleared up in quick time. Right? Grand then.

Phyllis: Em … Sergeant?

Courtney: What?

Phyllis: The accusation?

Courtney: Well, in short … as you are all aware I had business to conduct up at Cathal's place this morning … business concerning the supposed murder by him of the late Mrs Lynch.

Christy: Ruane was her name.

Lynch: I'll not argue with that.

Courtney: Gentlemen please! If you would let me continue.

Lynch: Sorry Justin … ah, Sergeant.

Courtney: Well, as you know I was making a final search for any incriminating evidence against … Mr Lynch here. I, accompanied by two fellow officers, therefore called to Mr Lynch's farm at about ten o'clock this morning. As you may imagine I wanted to notify Mr Lynch of my presence, as we had pre-arranged that I would on my arrival. Nevertheless, I was surprised to find him absent. Regardless of this I, with the aid of my colleagues, decided to set about the search as planned. Beginning with the hay shed, we systematically worked our way through the hen-house, out-house, slurry pit, and tool shed–in that order. As arranged, we were joined by the Garda sub-aqua team at approximately eleven o'clock.

Phyllis: Garda sub-aqua team?

Courtney: *(To Christy)* Garda O'Connell have sub-aqua experience—

Phyllis: Oh yes, he almost drowned as a young lad.

Courtney: Derrane!

Phyllis: Sorry Sergeant.

Courtney: As I was saying ... with the aid of Garda O'Connell we set about a search of the small flooded area of the Lynch property. Our search yielding nothing, and failing to gain admittance to the Lynch house itself, due to the absence of the occupant, we duly decided to end the search and formally close the case.

Christy: Didn't even search the house !

Lynch: *(Taking the house keys out of his pocket and holding them up)* Search the house ... there's the keys for you ... go on.

Christy: Yes, search the house.

Lynch: I've nothing to hide Ruane ... go on Sergeant, take the keys and search the house from top to bottom ... you'll find nothing.

Courtney: That won't be necessary.

Lynch: *(Putting the keys back in his pocket)* You heard the man. That won't be necessary. Case closed. Isn't that right Sergeant?

Courtney: As I said, case closed.

Lynch: Case closed.

Courtney: That case is closed, but quite another one is just opening.

Phyllis: I don't know what you're talking about.

Courtney: Well, what I'm talking about is who do I meet staggering up by that old dynamite pit, Derrane's Hole, this morning?

Phyllis: That's no hole. I won't hear my grandfather's grave talked of like that.

Lynch: Agh, give over Derrane. He blew himself up with his own bomb, sure everyone knows that. Go on Justin.

Christy: He was shot by the likes of you and dumped there.

Lynch: Go on Sergeant.

Courtney: I'll tell you who we met as we were leaving Lynch's place, the absent Cathal Lynch himself. The poor man almost dead as it happens, a noose around his neck, and barely able to speak. You'd hardly see the likes of it in theatrics. Had to sit him down, free him and let him get his breath for a few minutes before he could utter a word. But when he could speak … well what an interesting story he had to tell. Isn't that right Cathal?

Lynch: That's right Sergeant. Lucky I had wind left to speak at all.

Courtney: Yes. Lucky he had wind left at all and the state he was in.

Phyllis: Seems like all he's full of is wind.

Courtney: I wouldn't be so smart if I were you Derrane, and the position you're in.

Phyllis: I think you'll find I'm in no position, but go on with Lynch's little scéal … *(to Lynch)* and I thought the flights of your fancy only rose to the heights of a sheep's back passage … you're surprising me Lynch.

Lynch: *(To Courtney)* What's she implying?

Courtney: *(Ignores Lynch and Phyllis)* As I was saying. I'm sure both of you will be interested where this story is going. *(Looks at his watch)* Anyways …

Courtney is aiming at dramatic effect. He takes out a cigarette and lights it with a flourish.

Courtney: As I was saying.

Phyllis: And so eloquently Sergeant.

Courtney: *(Ignoring her)* What does Mr Lynch tell me but of how he paid you a little social visit after the carnival the night previously ... a visit concerning matters of business.

Christy: Business.

Lynch: Yes, business.

Courtney: And of how an argument arose out of these matters of business ...

Christy: Out of matters of business! And he murdering my sister!

Lynch: That matter's closed Ruane.

Courtney: And arising out of other matters admittedly. And of how this argument got out of hand, so out of hand that you first assault the man with a bottle. Concealed, as I have found out, this crime from an officer of the law on his rounds, myself, in case you think I've forgotten. And of how you then conducted a trial in a bogus and illegitimate court of law, then attempted to murder the man, Mr Lynch here, in a drunken rage by the method of hanging him by the neck ... and all during after-hours drinking, may I add.

Phyllis: Hanging him by the neck ... how else would you hang a man? By the arm? Such rubbish.

Christy: Yes, pure rubbish.

Courtney: Well if it's such rubbish could you please tell me how the offended party came by such a grisly wound? Mr Lynch, please.

Lynch stands up, pulls down his collar and displays his wound for all to see.

Phyllis: Could be through some kind of weird sexual practice ... I've heard stories.

Lynch: What stories?

Christy: Got his neck caught somewhere it shouldn't have been if you ask me.

Courtney: A trained eye will recognise these markings as consistent with friction burn caused by the unnatural tightening of natural fibres around the subject's neck, natural fibres such as those found in the common rope … thank you Mr Lynch. In short he was hung by the neck.

Courtney: You seem to know a lot about it Sergeant, have you hung many men in your time?

Courtney: Unfortunately that penalty has been repealed for serious offences.

Phyllis: Well even if we can accept that Lynch was in fact hung, who's to say that either myself or Mr Ruane here had a part in it. For all we know it could have been an attempted suicide on Lynch's part … an attempted suicide motivated by … guilt perhaps.

Christy: Yes, he could have tried to hang himself.

Lynch: Rot! Pure rot as you well know.

Courtney: I think that can be ruled out.

Christy: And why can you tell me is that?

Courtney: Well in the first place there is no sign of guilt in the offended subject.

Christy: Well that's for certain.

Courtney: And secondly, if Mr Lynch's story holds out, young Francis Devine should be a witness to his presence here this last night gone, his presence and the hostility showed to him by Mr Ruane here. Mr Lynch contends that the lad, being led astray, played a central part in the unlawful proceedings—coaxed on as he was by the consumption of intoxicating liquor. Serving alcohol to minors, that's another offence for the record.

Christy: That proves nothing.

Phyllis: And he went home early.

Christy: Yes, the lad went home early, was barely here half the night. Ask him yourselves. He'll put you straight.

Lynch: Where is he? Let the lad speak for himself. He'll speak, I assure you.

Courtney: And thirdly. Not only can young Devine vouch for Lynch's presence here last night, and the reason for that presence ...

Lynch: The matters of business.

Courtney: The matters of business. Does that wireless work?

Christy: Yes.

Courtney: If you don't mind, I'll just see who won the toss. They should be starting about now.

Christy: Fire ahead.

Courtney spots the frayed end of the hanging rope still attached to the bar where it had been tied off by Phyllis.

Courtney: The matters of business. But also, if Mr Lynch's story holds, there should be a piece of actual physical evidence remaining as testament to the crime that was committed here this very night past. The remains of a rope owned by you Mr Ruane, purchased only yesterday as I myself can testify, with the intention and premeditated purpose of murdering Mr Lynch for reasons of greed and misguided revenge, the likes of which I have thankfully never encountered before in all my years in the force, and I dearly hope I will never again have the misfortune to come across.

Courtney takes the noose-end of the rope out of his plastic bag and holds its frayed end next to the frayed end of the piece of rope still attached to the bar.

Courtney: Seems like we have a match.

Christy: For your information, Sergeant, that's my missing clothes line.

Lynch: Clothes line? Sure that's too thick for a clothes line.

Courtney: Clothes line or not, I think we have sufficient evidence on which to base an arrest. Finger printing and forensics will see to the rest. Christopher Ruane, I hereby charge you with the attempted murder of Cathal Lynch. You're coming with me to the station. As for you Phyllis Derrane, you're charged with being his accomplice. Now come on the pair of you, I've more serious things to attend to.

Phyllis: *(Breaking her silence)* I wouldn't be so hasty if I were you, Sergeant.

Courtney: What are you talking about?

Phyllis: Well as I see it you don't have any evidence at all. A man in your position, and with your *experience* would want to be awful careful about who he arrests … about arresting the wrong man, for example.

Lynch: Wrong man!

Courtney: I have clear evidence Derrane. Lynch's story checks out all the way. I've got the right man alright. It's plain as day that Ruane had a go at murdering Lynch. The rope matching and the wound all stand up as clear evidence. Oh I think I've nothing to worry about Derrane.

Phyllis: I wouldn't be so sure. And if I were you I would be sure … Superintendent … ah, sorry, Sergeant Courtney.

Lynch: Don't listen to her. Come on and we go.

Courtney: What's there to doubt? Get your things now and come on.

Phyllis: Well did it ever cross your mind that maybe Lynch wanted you to think Christy had a go at murdering him … to get him out of the way and have a clear run at the property and all.

Lynch: I've a legal right to the place.

Christy: Be quiet.

Phyllis: Yes, but it would make things a lot smoother to get rid of Christy, paint him as a murderer in the eyes of the town. People might suspect he even murdered his own sister, and then set to murdering you, the last large obstacle to his clear ownership of the business. Oh I can hear the talk already.

Lynch: Yes, maybe that's what happened.

Phyllis: *(Putting her arm out to restrain the agitated **Christy**)* Or maybe that's what you want people to think happened.

Courtney: We'll talk about this later at the station. I've the evidence I need.

Phyllis: Evidence left for you to find. Lynch was here last night alright. And yes, there was an argument ... an argument about Lynch taking over the place. But that was that. Lynch came in here full of drink and roaring like a bull.

Lynch: Crap!

Phyllis: A fight broke out and that's when Lynch was knocked cold. That's all Christy is guilty of. Assault. As far as we were concerned we'd leave Lynch to sleep it off, maybe he wouldn't even remember in the morning. He must have come to and either tried to hang himself or set up this little drama for your benefit, who knows ... I was upstairs asleep with Christy. I'm the only witness you need. And as Francis Devine will tell you, the only one you've got.

Lynch: Such a load of crap. Come on Sergeant, take them away.

Courtney: You were in bed with Christy Ruane?

Phyllis: And I'm not ashamed of it. I'm a widow as you know, and Christy here is a single man. There's nothing wrong with that. Anyway, do you seriously think Sergeant if Mr Ruane hung Lynch there that he'd still be walking around annoying people. No, he'd be down in hell where he belongs, roasting for his sins and the murder of Katey Ruane. That's where he'd be.

Christy: Exactly!

Phyllis: So if I were you Sergeant I'd have a little review of your so-called evidence, before you go making any hasty decisions.

Lynch: Don't listen to her Justin. There's more than enough proof here to stand up in court ... I'm telling you, a conviction like this and you're Superintendent in no time ... come on now.

Phyllis: You call this proof! With Devine home early you've no witness, a bit of old rope and no corpse. Listen to reason, Sergeant ... it's his word against ours ... the word of one suspected murderer against that of two decent local people that were never in any trouble in their lives.

Christy: She's right you know, Sergeant.

Courtney: Wait now and I'll have a think for myself.

Lynch: There's nothing to think about!

Courtney: Quiet, just give me a minute.

Courtney: *(Considers)* What about that bruise on his neck? Now you can't account for that.

Phyllis: Self-inflicted. Gave himself an old tug with the noose.

Lynch: Arragh, bollocks!

Courtney: Self-inflicted?

Phyllis: It's common enough you know, Sergeant. This little fiasco is of Lynch's making. Get rid of Christy to take over the property, and at the same time clear his name in the eyes of the town. I'm only surprised he had the brains to think of it. I'm sorry Sergeant, but I think you're as much the victim here as ourselves. You've been taken in by a hoax.

Lynch: A hoax my arse!

Courtney: A hoax you say?

Phyllis: As plain as day a hoax. Look, the man is alive. As for that rope–that's merely circumstantial evidence. It's all a bit too flimsy to risk wrongly arresting a man. Well, let's just say, it wouldn't be too good for your prospects, not again, if you'll pardon me saying so. Drink, Sergeant?

*(At this point **Phyllis** might hold up a bottle of whiskey similar to the one **Courtney** robbed in Act II. **Courtney** does not respond to her)*

Lynch: You're not going to listen to that bitch, are you?

Christy: Hey, mind your language.

Courtney: *(His confidence undermined)* We're in no rush.

Lynch: What?

Courtney: Well, I've been thinking, Cathal. Maybe the case isn't as clear as we thought it was. I mean, it seems there's been no real harm done.

Lynch: No harm done?

Courtney: Well, on closer examination of the case, it seems there is some evidence lacking on which to base an arrest.

Lynch: Have you lost it or something?

Courtney: Calm down Cathal.

Lynch: Calm down!

Courtney: Look … the place is yours anyway, and you seem to be fine and all … maybe there's no need to …

Lynch: What?

Courtney: … To pursue this further. I thought it was a clear case. You have to understand my position. I can't go arresting someone whenever I like, you know. There are rules and regulations binding me. No. On closer inspection, this case doesn't fulfil the criteria on which to base an arrest.

Lynch: It's an open and shut case!

Courtney: I've my reputation to think of, and professional standards to uphold.

Phyllis: That's right Sergeant.

Lynch: Damn your standards … arrest these bastards!

Courtney: *(Getting up)* There's not enough in it, Cathal, come on, we're leaving.

Lynch: Leaving!

Courtney: Leaving. I'm sorry for the inconvenience Mrs Derrane, Mr Ruane. I'm sure you'll understand that a mistake has been made, and you'll accept my apologies for it.

Phyllis: Well, it was an inconvenience. But seeing as we're all human. Well, we'll just say no more about it. Isn't that right Christy?

Christy: That's right Phyllis. Not another word on the matter.

Lynch: What is this? The bastard tried to kill me. *(Grabbing a bottle with which to attack* **Christy***)* I swear I'll …!

*Courtney restrains **Lynch**.*

Courtney: Calm down Cathal. Calm down or I'll be forced to—

Lynch: Forced to what? Forced to arrest me! *(Throws bottle on ground)* Agh! For God's sake! You haven't heard the last of this, do you hear! To hell with the lot of you!

Lynch storms out, slamming the door behind him.

Courtney: You'll forgive Mr Lynch. As you can see, he's a little upset.

Christy: Murderers get like that.

Courtney: Well … I suppose I'll be off. Once again, sorry for the … for the trouble, Mrs Derrane.

Phyllis: Think nothing of it. *(Short pause)* You'll miss the match at this stage.

Courtney: Yes. I'll see the highlights on the television tonight. *(Gets an idea)* But, if you wouldn't mind … *(Indicating the radio)* … I might just … for the score?

Christy: Be my guest.

Courtney goes to the radio, glasses on the end of his nose; he is unsure how to work it, fiddles with it. Lynch re-enters.

Lynch: I still want you out within the week, Ruane ... do you hear me now?

Christy: Well, we'll see about that.

Lynch: *(Disgust)* Agh ! *(To Courtney)* Are you coming or what!

Courtney: One minute.

Francis enters. He is still dressed in bishop s costume.

Francis: *(Seeing Lynch)* Jesus! Lynch! In the name of God!

Courtney hits the play button on the machine, playing the tape from the night before.

Taped voices and sound effects from earlier.

Christy: You lying bastard!

Phyllis: I think I have the thing working!

Lynch: I spit on you Ruane! And all the Ruanes!

Phyllis: Jesus Christy! Cut the rope! I ...

Christy: I think I've killed him.

Recording cuts out.

Everyone freezes where they are, there is total silence. There is a look of utter shock on the faces of Christy and Phyllis. After a moment Lynch starts to laugh a dirty laugh of victory. Courtney, realising what he has heard, again assumes a position of authority.

Courtney: Well, well, well. What have we here?

Lynch: I think I'd call that evidence Sergeant.

Courtney: I think you're right Mr Lynch ... wherever it came from, I think you're right. If you don't mind, Mr Ruane *(Takes tape)*, I think I'll take this little recording into my possession. Evidence you understand. *(To Phyllis)* Clear evidence worth more than the word of any criminal, I should think. I suppose you've an explanation for this as well, Derrane.

Phyllis: I … I …

Courtney: You can save your words for official questioning. All I want to know is … why in the name of God were you taping an attempted hanging?

Christy: That's not what it seems now Sergeant.

Phyllis: That's enough Christy.

Christy: But it's only a—

Phyllis: Shut up! *(Pause).* We were trying to scare Lynch … get a confession out of him … we didn't mean to hang him. And the bastard did confess !

Lynch: And where is the confession?

Courtney: Yes … where is that confession?

Phyllis: I couldn't get the damned machine working … I taped the wrong part.

Lynch: Ha! Confession my arse. There was no confession Sergeant … on my word there was none … I'm an innocent man. Wronged. I loved my wife, wouldn't do a thing to harm her. I haven't been right since her death … I never stop thinking about her … her face—

Phyllis: The only face you remember is a face in the agony of death. I hope it haunts you till the grave Lynch, and afterwards. For if in this life there's no justice , I dearly hope there is another. Only then would the likes of you get dealt out fair punishment.

Courtney: That's enough out of you Derrane. You've done enough talking for one day. As for that confession of yours … I see no evidence of it … and with no evidence there is no confession. Besides, that no longer concerns me.

Lynch: Yes … that's no longer of any concern.

Christy: Francis, tell him!

Courtney: Agh, young Devine. What gives us the honour of your presence?

Francis: The ... the ... the rosary beads. I forgot them.

Courtney: Father Neaghtain will be wanting them back. Well he'll have to wait. You've some business with me first.

Francis: Business, what business?

Courtney: The minor matter of playing a part in an attempted murder.

Phyllis: Francis. Tell them about the confession. Tell them what Lynch said.

Christy: Go on Francis. You're an honest lad. People will believe you.

Phyllis: If you're afraid of trouble ... well, we forced you. We made you take part against your will.

Christy: Poured drink down you.

Phyllis: Yes. Yes. That's it.

Courtney: Well, young Devine. What's this about a confession? Did you hear a confession?

*There is a pause. All the focus is on **Francis**. His dilemma is unbearable. As he is about to speak, **Lynch** jumps in.*

Lynch: The lad wasn't here.

Christy: What?

Courtney: What?

Lynch: You heard the tape. There was three voices on there–mine, Ruane's and Derrane's. The young lad wasn't here. He let me in alright, but that's it. He left after. He'd no part in the proceedings.

Courtney: In your earlier statement you said ...

Lynch: I'd been half-hung, how could I know what I was saying? No. The young lad had gone home long before. I misremembered earlier.

Courtney: Is this right Francis?

Christy: Francis, I know what we said. But you have to tell the truth. You were here weren't you? You heard the confession.

Francis: I ... I ...

Lynch: Murder Francis. Attempted murder. You'd no part in that, did you? No. It's not in your nature. You were never here. Heard no confession. Isn't that right lad?

Courtney: Is that right Francis?

Christy: Francis?

Short Pause.

Francis: That's right. I was never here.

Lynch: Good lad. *(Laughing)* Good lad.

Christy: *(Hurt)* Francis. Please. You can't let this happen. You can't let him win. I know we've had our differences. I'm sorry. Listen to your conscience boy.

Phyllis: Leave him Christy. He was going that way from the start.

Courtney: Ruane, you're under arrest for attempted murder.

Christy: *(Pause as the cuffs are put on)* Fools prosper and the unjust lauded. First the crucifixion, then the dice divides what's left. It rolls with no reason, falls where it's weighted. The judge, with his wig and his bag of tricks, plays the script ... and is paid. Katey ...

Christy is led out by Courtney

Lynch: You're not the carnival king today, Ruane!

Courtney: *(From off)* O'Connell, put him in the car!

There is a lull after Christy s departure. A weird calm in the air. Pause. Courtney re-enters.

Courtney: As for you Derrane. I'll have you for assisting in the whole business, withholding information, attempting to pervert the course of justice—

Phyllis: Not afraid of me anymore Sergeant?

Courtney: The way I see it Phyllis, the way things have turned out I've nothing to fear from the likes of you. You're on the wrong end of justice. It's more likely I'll get a promotion for putting you away.

Phyllis: Question.

Courtney: What?

Phyllis: *(To Lynch)* How did you survive?

Lynch: Wouldn't you like to know? I blacked out alright. But when I came round on the floor there was no sign of anyone. It's a wonder I wasn't killed.

Phyllis: More's the pity. Sergeant, take me somewhere where I don't have to look at this.

Courtney takes Phyllis tightly by the arm and escorts her out the door. Pause.

Lynch: *(Goes to Francis and puts his arm around him)* That's my boy Francis. Make sure now that you always pick the winner and you won't go wrong. Sure what did Ruane ever do for you, ha? A waste of space.

Courtney re-enters.

Courtney: Well, Cathal. I think I should say that I'm sorry for … for doubting you.

Lynch: Agh, don't mention it Justin. A man in your position has to be careful … has to set an example to others … or else the whole shop would go awry.

Courtney: Now that's the truth Cathal. The thin blue line between order and chaos … that's what a police force is you know. Without us it'd be pure anarchy all over the place, and then where would we be?

Lynch: Where would we be indeed.

Courtney: *(Macho buddy laugh with Lynch)* It'd be carnival all the time, ha?

Lynch: *(Joining in)* Right. Transvestites running the shop.

The two men have a laugh, which subsides into an air of warm affection.

Courtney: Well I suppose I'd better get those two down to HQ.

Lynch: Agh sure, what's the rush? Won't you have a drink with me first. To celebrate?

Courtney: Well … I'd better not Cathal. I'd better not.

Lynch: *(Hint of begging)* Agh … just the one!

Courtney: I've really to be off.

Lynch: I'll pour them sure …

Courtney: *(Firmly)* Sorry Cathal. I really have to go.

Lynch: *(Disappointed)* I suppose you'll want to catch the end of the match.

Courtney: Yes. Francie. Do you want a lift?

Francis: Thanks. Em … That'll be great.

Courtney: There's clouds on the horizon. I'll say we'll get a downpour. Come on so. Cathal.

Lynch: Sergeant.

***Courtney** and **Francis** exit. **Lynch** is left alone, drinking. Ghost appears behind him. Slow to dark.*

The End.

As the delicate processes of the production and reception of the theatre event are beyond a writer's power, allow me here to comment only on the script, on the kind of things that coloured it and the concerns that occupied me in writing it.

Memory, of course, was central. The childhood memory of an inebriated man climbing the central supporting pole of a carnival marquee, while a crowd danced to music below. The memory of camp clowns in the spectacle of a circus. The memory of the pounding drums of a fiery parade through the festive streets of the town where I grew up. These sprees that are termed 'the second life' of the people: life as it is lived at times of celebration. Then there was the influence of the more conventional stage.

What interested me about Synge's *The Playboy of the Western World* or Gogol's *The Government Inspector* was the anarchic festivity at the drama's heart. The incredulous reaction of admiration for the man that murdered his father, or the unlikely event of mistaken identity in a provincial Russian town, and its consequences. There was something comic and beyond everyday 'reality' at work, and yet essential truths were conveyed when the laughter subsided.

In *The Carnival King*, there is not the attempt to recreate life or a direct reflection of it, but rather an interest in the archetypes and energies that lie beneath life. Just as in 'the second life' of the people at carnival time, in the play everyday reality falls away, hierarchies reverse, normal law and order is suspended and an alternative order emerges, where habitually denied justice is sought, by means that are often darkly insurgent.

In the individual, carnival overthrows everyday logic and reason. Transgressive behaviour is explored, violent energies are unleashed and the world is perceived as changed and reality as heightened. For society, carnival brings with it similar upheavals. The revolutionary spirit is set loose, with all its power to liberate, as well as its power to commit the most violent acts in the name of that liberation.

That idea of pre-Lenten carnival may be commonplace in other counties, but in Ireland it has long been repressed. There is no specific festival of abandon at Mardi Gras, and yet the energy and subversion of carnival persists in the Puck Fair, certain communal celebrations and the traditional wake.

It is not the facts of any actual festival then that shaped *The Carnival King*, but rather the energy behind the festive itself. The midnight court of Brian Merriman, carnival celebrations experienced in east Galway as a child, and a certain spate of murders in County Galway came together in my imagination. They coalesced into something. Then my grandmother put flesh on the bones of a murder story I'd read in the newspapers, of how a man killed his wife and there was not the evidence to convict him. I had a play.

My own concern with justice, and of its impossibility under established hierarchies, resonated with my grandmother's tale and the carnivals of my youth. The buried ghosts of the 'illegitimate' courts of the War of Independence, divisions of the Civil War and the submerged, half-remembered and contested histories of that period and the subsequent Troubles sent the whole thing echoing, bringing back sub-texts.

When Fishamble Theatre Company – Jim Culleton and Maureen Kennelly at the time – generously commissioned a play, solely on the strength of my long poem *Brood* and the subsequent film that was made of it, what I would write and its structure was immediately clear to me. It would be a journey into 'the liminal zone'– just like that excursion into the forest in *A Midsummer Night s Dream*. In short, a traditional three-act structure: law in place, law suspended and law reinstated. I wanted to use that structure, which usually presents the reinstatement of an enlightened order, to show the reinstatement of inequitable rule. The writings of Umberto Eco on carnival and how it ultimately reinforces the status quo were a big influence on me at the time of writing. The people are allowed party at carnival time, allowed let off steam, but ultimately they have to go back to work for the same master and the same wages.

Beyond that, I simply wanted to have a laugh. The comic potential of death and resurrection myths, of missing bodies and men dressed in women's clothing, old-fashioned inept policemen and anti-clerical jibes – these are what fuelled the writing. This is the stuff of popular entertainment and comedy, as much as the stock and trade of the dramatist.

So here it stands alone on the page. Separate now from the various visions of those that made up the delicate chain of the theatre event in its first and maybe only production. Now it is only the score, awaiting with hope another performance that may or may never come. Bare on the page – with its strengths and its faults for the world to see – it is released.

Ian Kilroy

The Editor

Jim Culleton is the Artistic Director of Fishamble. He has also directed for 7:84 (Scotland), the Passion Machine, Tinderbox, Project Arts Centre, Amharclann de hIde, the Ark, Second Age, TNL Canada, Scotland's Ensemble @ Dundee Rep and Draíocht. For Fishamble/Pigsback, Jim has directed plays by Michael West, Deirdre Hines, Gavin Kostick, Marina Carr, Colin Teevan, Joseph O'Connor, Mark O'Rowe, Pat Kinevane, Dermot Bolger, Maeve Binchy and Ian Kilroy. He has contributed to books for Carysfort Press and Ubu, and previously co-edited *Contemporary Irish Mono-logues* also for New Island Books.

The Playwrights

Deirdre Hines graduated from TCD in 1989 with an honours degree in Drama and English. *Howling Moons, Silent Sons* won the Stewart Parker Trust Award for Best New Play in 1992. Deirdre went on to write *Ghost Acreage at Vixen Time* for the Passion Machine's 'Songs of the Reaper Festival' in 1994. Other plays include *A Moving Destiny* (1996) produced by Yew Theatre Company and *Dreamframe* (2000) produced for Fishamble's 'Y2K Festival'. Plays for children include *Golden Moon* (1997) and *Borrowed Days* (1999) produced and performed by the children of Kilmacrennan National School, Co Donegal. She received two Arts Council grants in 1994 and 1998 respectively. She works full time as a Community Development worker for Travellers in Longford.

Ian Kilroy was born in 1969. He grew up in Galway where he completed a BA in English and Philosophy at University College Galway. After graduation, he stayed on at UCG as a tutor in Philosophy and English, obtaining an MA for his thesis on The Centrally Located National Theatre. He also worked with Druid Theatre Company, then moved to Paris. His poem *'Brood* was made into a film and broadcast on Network 2 in 1998. He returned from France to complete an

MA in Journalism at Dublin City University. Awarded a first-class honour and the first Veronica Guerin Scholarship for investigative journalism at Dublin City University, he now lives in Dublin. Former Arts Correspondent at *Magill* magazine, he currently writes for the *Irish Times*, *Magill* and the *Sunday Tribune*.

Pat Kinevane was born in Cobh, Co Cork. He moved to Dublin in 1989 and began working as an actor with the Abbey Theatre. Since then, Pat has worked with almost every theatre company in Ireland including The Gate, Druid, the Gaiety, Fishamble and the Passion Machine. Pat began writing for Fishamble in 1997 and completed *The Nun s Wood* which won the BBC/Stewart Parker Trust Award in 1999. Fishamble also produced his next play *The Plains of Enna* in the 2000 Dublin Theatre Festival. Pat is now writing a third play for the company. Other works by Pat include *La Feria*, *The Forgotten* and *The Death of Herod*. Pat has many credits in radio drama, television and film (including the *Beckett on Film* project and work with directors such as Martin Scorsese, John Boorman and Ron Howard). He has toured with productions to Australia, USA, Italy, Scotland and London.

Gavin Kostick has had a number of plays produced in Ireland, the UK and the USA over the last eight years. For Pigsback, he wrote *The Ash Fire, Jack Ketch s Gallows Jig* and *The Flesh Addict*, all directed by Jim Culleton. For the Gaiety School of Acting, he wrote *The Drowning Room, Fox and Crow* and *The Man Who Couldn t Cross Roads*, all directed by Patrick Sutton. He adapted *The Picture of Dorian Gray* for the Gate, directed by Alan Stanford, *Lazarus, The Buffetting* and *The Harrowing of Hell* for Michael Scott's 'Mysteries 2000', wrote *The Asylum Ball* for Calypso, directed by Bairbre NiChaoimh, and wrote and directed *Forked* for Bedrock's 'Theatre of Cruelty' season and *Doom Raider* for Fishamble's 'Y2K Festival.' He is Fishamble's Literary Officer.

Joseph O'Connor was born in Dublin. He has written ten Irish number one bestsellers, including the acclaimed novels

Cowboys and Indians (shortlisted for the Whitbread Prize), *Desperadoes, The Salesman, Inishowen* and *Star of the Sea* (November 2002) and the non-fiction collections *The Secret World of the Irish Male, The Irish Male at Home and Abroad* and *The Last of the Irish Males*. His work has been translated into eighteen languages and has won many prizes, including the Hennessy New Irish Writer of the Year Award, the Macaulay Fellowship of the Irish Arts Council, the Miramax Screenwriting Award and the London 'Time Out' Travel Writing Prize. *Red Roses and Petrol* was shortlisted for the Stewart Parker Awards and named 'Play of the Year' by 'In Dublin' magazine, also winning 'Best Director' for Jim Culleton, and 'Best Actress' for Anne Kent.

Mark O'Rowe began writing in 1994. *The Aspidistra Code* received a rehearsed reading at the Peacock Theatre, Dublin. *From Both Hips* was produced by Fishamble and won the Stewart Parker BBC radio drama award. *Howie the Rookie*, was produced by the Bush Theatre, London, transferring to Dublin and Edin-burgh. It won the 1999 George Devine Award and the 1999 Rooney Prize for Irish Literature. *Made in China* was produced by the Peacock Theatre. He lives in Dublin.

Acknowledgements

The editor wishes to thank the following for their help with this book: Fishamble Theatre Company, Jo Mangan, Gavin Kostick, Cerstin Gundlach, Eoin Kennelly, Maureen Kennelly, Siobhan Maguire, Ken Monaghan, Andrew Parkes, Christine Poulter, Clodagh O'Donoghue, Daniel Culleton, Liam & Dolores Culleton, Pat Kinevane, Joe O'Connor, Deirdre Hines, Mark O'Rowe, Ian Kilroy, Ciara Considine, Edwin Higel and all at New Island Books, Enid Reid-Whyte, Dermot McLaughlin, Mary Hickey and all at the Arts Council, Jack Gilligan and all at Dublin City Council Arts Office, Julia Tyrrell, Hamilton Asper Management, Sean & Doreen O'Donoghue, Hilda Doyle, Phelim Donlon, Jennifer Johnston, Frank McGuinness, Declan Kiberd, Ronit Lentin, Fintan O'Toole, Dennis Kennedy, Siobhan Bourke, Maeve Binchy, Cathy Leeney, Sebastian Barry, Brendan Kennelly, Gerard Stembridge, Dermot Bolger, Colm Tóibín, Clíodhna Ní Anluain

A special thank you to all the actors, writers, directors, designers, composers, production crew, stage management and administrative personnel that have worked with Fishamble and to all Fishamble's sponsors and audiences.

Performance Rights

All professional and amateur rights in these plays are strictly reserved and applications for permission to perform them must be made before rehearsals begin. For *The Ash Fire* and *From Both Hips* please apply to Nick Marston at Curtis Brown, Haymarket House, 28/29 Haymarket, London SW14 4SP. For *Red Roses and Petrol* please apply to Conrad Williams at Blake Friedmann, 122, Arlington Road, London NW1 7HP. For *Howling Moons Silent Sons, The Nun s Wood* and *The Carnival King* please apply to Fishamble Theatre Company, Shamrock Chambers, 1-2 Eustace Street, Dublin 2.